The History of
The Standard
Oil Company
In Two Volumes

Vol. I

IDA M. TARBELL
INTRODUCTION BY DANNY SCHECHTER

COSIMOCLASSICS

NEW YORK

The History of The Standard Oil Company, Vol. I (in two volumes)
Cover Copyright © 2009 by Cosimo, Inc.
Introduction copyright © 2009 by Danny Schechter

The History of The Standard Oil Company, Vol. I (in two volumes) was originally
published in 1904.

For information, address:
P.O. Box 416, Old Chelsea Station
New York, NY 10011

or visit our website at:
www.cosimobooks.com

Ordering Information:
Cosimo publications are available at online bookstores. They may
also be purchased for educational, business or promotional use:
- *Bulk orders:* special discounts are available on bulk orders for reading
groups, organizations, businesses, and others. For details contact
Cosimo Special Sales at the address above or at info@cosimobooks.com.
- *Custom-label orders:* we can prepare selected books with your cover or
logo of choice. For more information, please contact Cosimo at
info@cosimobooks.com.

Cover Design by www.popshopstudio.com

ISBN: 978-1-60520-761-2

From the time the Central Association announced itself, independent refiners and the producers as a body watched developments with suspicion. They had little to go on. They had no means of proving what was actually the fact that the Central Association was the Standard Oil Company working secretly to bring its competitors under control or drive them out of business. They had no way of knowing what was actually the fact that the Standard had contracts with the Central, Erie and the Pennsylvania which gave them rebates on the lowest tariff which others paid. That this must be the case, however, they were convinced, and they determined early in 1876 to call on Congress for another investigation. A hearing was practically insured, for Congress since 1872 had given serious attention to the transportation troubles.

—from Chapter Six: "Strengthening the Foundations"

The History of The Standard Oil Company

What Ida Tarbell and this Classic History Has to Teach Us

In this era of financial crisis compounded, and even perhaps enabled, by a dearth of investigative reporting, it is valuable to go back in time to learn from the work of great journalists with the courage to have taken on avaricious corporations and irresponsible business practices.

Perhaps no book demands our attention and respect as much as the one now in your hands. The unabridged edition, long out of print, of Ida Tarbell's study/expose of the history of the Standard Oil Company is an American classic, a model of careful research, detailed analysis, clear expository writing, and social mission. It has been hailed as one of the top ten of journalism's greatest hits.

There is so much about this book that commends it to our attention. It goes after and demystifies one of the icons and sacred cows in our history, John D. Rockefeller, whose name lives on in charitable giving and in Rockefeller Center in Midtown Manhattan. It takes on a corporation that helped build America at a terrible and for years largely unreported cost.

This book shows how one investigator, in many ways a self-taught and totally committed writer, unmasked a large and complex entity and wrote about it in a popular fashion, first in a well-known mainstream magazine and then in an engrossing two-volume book.

It shows how a study published in 1904 still has relevance for a country that a century later has, if anything, come totally under the sway of its greedy financiers, banks, and industrial corporations, who deserve a similar dispassionate examination.

Author Ida Tarbell spent years on the project, motivated in part by her own life experience growing up in the oil county of Pennsylvania exploited by the

Rockefeller interests. Her own father was devastated by corporate shenanigans, as she would later write: "[S]uddenly [our] gay, prosperous town received a blow between the eyes." The 1872 South Improvement scheme, a hidden agreement between the railroads and refiners led by Rockefeller, hit the Pennsylvania Oil Region like a tidal wave. It hit the Tarbells too, leaving behind painful memories that would be rekindled thirty years later. "Out of the alarm and bitterness and confusion, I gathered from my father's talk a conviction to which I still hold— that what had been undertaken was wrong."

Tarbell was a pioneer in tackling this and other multilayered stories, and is honored in media studies and women's studies. The United States Post Office even issued a stamp in salute of her achievements.

Even though she has a personal reason for elucidating the oil story, she did not rush into it. She joined small newspapers and magazines, refining her writing skills. She moved to Paris to continue her education, fascinated by the life of Madame Roland, the leader of an influential salon during the French Revolution. She wrote her biography, and was recruited to write for McClure's magazine, a popular title. A series she wrote on Abraham Lincoln doubled the magazine's circulation. She followed that up with a series on Napoleon. She was becoming well known for her skills in writing about history and for her passion for her characters.

At the same time, like others of her times, she could not remain aloof from events such as the rise of the big trusts that were throwing their weight around, corrupting politicians and virtually controlling government. (Sound familiar?) Tarbell started to write about the rapidly changing economic landscape and the rise of monopolistic trusts that were "disturbing and confusing people."

At that time a new president, Theodore Roosevelt, was exposing corruption in business. He supported what was then called "muckraking" by reporters to educate the public. Tarbell then decided to tell the story of Standard Oil to make these issues more vivid. She convinced her publisher to run a three-part series on the oil trust. That series was the basis for the far more detailed books she wrote and published years later. Her work was so well documented that it led to the breakup of Standard Oil under the 1911 Sherman Anti-Trust Act.

She went after Rockefeller frontally but always backed up her convictions with evidence, some of which was obtained from a Standard Oil insider who must have believed she would be complimentary and gave her the inside skinny. She knew how to get sources to cooperate.

Of Rockefeller, she wrote:

"Rockefeller and his associates did not build the Standard Oil Co. in the board rooms of Wall Street banks. They fought their way to control by rebate and drawback, bribe and blackmail, espionage and price cutting, by ruthless... efficiency of organization."

Tarbell herself retained a professional cool. She actually rejected the term muckraker and focused more on establishing the facts than agitating for change.

She was critical of those who, perhaps like myself, believe in a legitimate fusion of journalism and activism, writing:

"All the radical element, and I numbered many friends among them, were begging me to join their movements. I soon found that most of them wanted attacks. They had little interest in balanced findings. Now I was convinced that in the long run the public they were trying to stir would weary of vituperation, that if you were to secure permanent results the mind must be convinced."

And convince she did. She followed her own drummer.

She wrote two books on women but never joined the suffrage movement and asked for no special favors. She found some women accepting a lesser role. "I had been disturbed for some time by what seemed to me the calculated belittling of the past achievements of women by many active in the campaign for suffrage. They agreed with their opponents that women had shown little or no creative power. That, they argued, was because man had purposely and jealously excluded her from his field of action. The argument was intended, of course, to arouse women's indignation, stir them to action. It seemed to me rather to throw doubt on [their] creative capacity." In contrast, she always believed women had lots of creative capacity. In fact, for a writer dealing with political and social issues, she most admired inspiration, writing:

"Imagination is the only key to the future. Without it none exists—with it all things are possible."

Tarbell was versatile, hardworking, and could not be easily labeled or refuted because of the care she took in her work.

As you read this history, and remember the times she wrote about and think of today, and the way magnates and marketers have enriched themselves at the expense of our society. And then think of the journalists who have embedded themselves in our corporate culture and who need to learn from the work and example of Ida Minerva Tarbell.

Danny Schechter
investigative journalist and author
New York, 2009

JOHN DAVISON ROCKEFELLER IN 1904

Born July 8, 1839

CONTENTS

CHAPTER ONE

THE BIRTH OF AN INDUSTRY

CHAPTER TWO

THE RISE OF THE STANDARD OIL COMPANY

CONTENTS

CHAPTER THREE

THE OIL WAR OF 1872

CHAPTER FOUR

"AN UNHOLY ALLIANCE"

CONTENTS

CHAPTER FIVE

LAYING THE FOUNDATIONS OF A TRUST

CHAPTER SIX

STRENGTHENING THE FOUNDATIONS

CONTENTS

CHAPTER SEVEN

THE CRISIS OF 1878

A RISE IN OIL—A BLOCKADE IN EXPORTS—PRODUCERS DO NOT GET THEIR SHARE OF THE PROFITS—THEY SECRETLY ORGANISE THE PETROLEUM PRODUCERS' UNION AND PROMISE TO SUPPORT PROPOSED INDEPENDENT PIPE-LINES—ANOTHER INTERSTATE COMMERCE BILL DEFEATED AT WASHINGTON —"IMMEDIATE SHIPMENT"—INDEPENDENTS HAVE TROUBLE GETTING CARS—RIOTS THREATENED—APPEAL TO GOVERNOR HARTRANFT—SUITS BROUGHT AGAINST UNITED PIPE-LINES, PENNSYLVANIA RAILROAD AND OTHERS—INVESTIGATIONS PRECIPITATED IN OTHER STATES—THE HEP-BURN COMMISSION AND THE OHIO INVESTIGATION—EVIDENCE THAT THE STANDARD IS A CONTINUATION OF THE SOUTH IMPROVEMENT COMPANY— PRODUCERS FINALLY DECIDE TO PROCEED AGAINST STANDARD OFFICIALS— ROCKEFELLER AND EIGHT OF HIS ASSOCIATES INDICTED FOR CONSPIRACY.

CHAPTER EIGHT

THE COMPROMISE OF 1880

THE PRODUCERS' SUIT AGAINST ROCKEFELLER AND HIS ASSOCIATES USED BY THE STANDARD TO PROTECT ITSELF—SUITS AGAINST THE TRANSPOR-TATION COMPANIES ARE DELAYED—TRIAL OF ROCKEFELLER AND HIS ASSOCIATES FOR CONSPIRACY POSTPONED—ALL OF THE SUITS WITH-DRAWN IN RETURN FOR AGREEMENTS OF THE STANDARD AND THE PENNSYLVANIA TO CEASE THEIR PRACTICES AGAINST THE PRODUCERS— WITH THIS COMPROMISE THE SECOND PETROLEUM PRODUCERS' UNION COMES TO AN END—PRODUCERS THEMSELVES TO BLAME FOR NOT STAND-ING BEHIND THEIR LEADERS—STANDARD AGAIN ENFORCES ORDERS OBJEC-TIONABLE TO PRODUCERS—MORE OUTBREAKS IN THE OIL REGIONS— ROCKEFELLER HAVING SILENCED ORGANISED OPPOSITION PROCEEDS TO SILENCE INDIVIDUAL COMPLAINT . . . . .

"An Institution is the lengthened shadow of one man."
EMERSON, IN ESSAY ON "SELF-RELIANCE."

"The American Beauty Rose can be produced in its splendor and fragrance only by sacrificing the early buds which grow up around it."
J. D. ROCKEFELLER, JR., IN AN ADDRESS ON TRUSTS, TO THE STUDENTS OF BROWN UNIVERSITY.

PREFACE

THIS work is the outgrowth of an effort on the part of the editors of McClure's Magazine to deal concretely in their pages with the trust question. In order that their readers might have a clear and succinct notion of the processes by which a particular industry passes from the control of the many to that of the few, they decided a few years ago to publish a detailed narrative of the history of the growth of a particular trust. The Standard Oil Trust was chosen for obvious reasons. It was the first in the field, and it has furnished the methods, the charter, and the traditions for its followers. It is the most perfectly developed trust in existence; that is, it satisfies most nearly the trust ideal of entire control of the commodity in which it deals. Its vast profits have led its officers into various allied interests, such as railroads, shipping, gas, copper, iron, steel, as well as into banks and trust companies, and to the acquiring and solidifying of these interests it has applied the methods used in building up the Oil Trust. It has led in the struggle against legislation directed against combinations. Its power in state and Federal government, in the press, in the college, in the pulpit, is generally recognised. The perfection of the organisation of the Standard, the ability and daring with which it has carried out its projects, make it the pre-eminent trust of the world—the one whose story is best fitted to illuminate the subject of combinations of capital.

Another important consideration with the editors in deciding that the Standard Oil Trust was the best adapted to illustrate their meaning, was the fact that it is one of the very few business organisations of the country whose growth could be traced in trustworthy documents. There is in existence just such documentary material for a history of the Standard Oil Company as there is for a history of the Civil War or the French Revolution, or any other national episode which has divided men's minds. This has come about largely from the fact that almost constantly since its organisation in 1870 the Standard Oil Company has been under investigation by the Congress of the United States and by the Legislatures of various states in which it has operated, on the suspicion that it was receiving rebates from the railroads and was practising methods in restraint of free trade. In 1872 and again in 1876 it was before Congressional committees, in 1879 it was before examiners of the Commonwealth of Pennsylvania and before committees appointed by the Legislatures of New York and of Ohio for investigating railroads. Its operations figured constantly in the debate which led up to the creation of the Interstate Commerce Commission in 1887, and again and again since that time the Commission has been called upon to examine directly or indirectly into its relation with the railroads.

In 1888, in the Investigation of Trusts conducted by Congress and by the state of New York, the Standard Oil Company was the chief subject for examination. In the state of Ohio, between 1882 and 1892, a constant warfare was waged against the Standard in the courts and Legislature, resulting in several volumes of testimony. The Legislatures of many other states concerned themselves with it. This hostile legislation compelled the trust to separate into its component parts in 1892, but investigation did not cease; indeed, in the last great industrial inquiry, conducted by the Commission appointed by President McKinley, the Standard Oil Company was constantly under discussion, and hundreds of pages of testimony on it appear in the nineteen volumes of reports which the Commission has submitted.

This mass of testimony, all of it submitted under oath it should be remembered, contains the different charters and agreements under which the Standard Oil Trust has operated, many contracts and agreements with railroads, with refineries, with pipe-lines, and it contains the experiences in business from 1872 up to 1900 of multitudes of individuals. These experiences have exactly the quality of the personal reminiscences of actors in great events, with the additional value that they were given on the witness stand, and it is fair, therefore, to suppose that they are more cautious and exact in statements than many writers of memoirs are. These investigations, covering as they do all of the important steps in the development of the trust, include full accounts of the point of view of its officers in regard to that development, as well as their explanations of many of the operations over which controversy has arisen. Hundreds of pages of sworn testimony are found in these volumes from John D. Rockefeller, William Rockefeller, Henry M. Flagler, H. H. Rogers, John D. Archbold, Daniel O'Day and other members of the concern.

Aside from the great mass of sworn testimony accessible to the student there is a large pamphlet literature dealing with different phases of the subject, and there are files of the numerous daily newspapers and monthly reviews, supported by the Oil Regions, in the columns of which are to be found not only statistics but full reports of all controversies between oil men. No complete collection of this voluminous printed material has ever been made, but several small collections exist, and in one or another of these I have been able to find practically all of the important documents relating to the subject. Mrs. Roger Sherman of Titusville, Pennsylvania, owns the largest of these collections, and in it are to be found copies of the rarest pamphlets. Lewis Emery, Jr., of

Bradford, the late E. G. Patterson of Titusville, the late Henry D. Lloyd, author of "Wealth *vs.* Commonwealth," William Hasson of Oil City, and P. C. Boyle, the editor of the Oil City Derrick, have collections of value, and they have all been most generous in giving me access to their books.

But the documentary sources of this work are by no means all printed. The Standard Oil Trust and its constituent companies have figured in many civil suits, the testimony of which is still in manuscript in the files of the courts where the suits were tried. These manuscripts have been examined on the ground, and in numerous instances full copies of affidavits and of important testimony have been made for permanent reference and study. I have also had access to many files of private correspondence and papers, the most important being that of the officers and counsel of the Petroleum Producers' Union from 1878 to 1880, that covering the organisation from 1887 to 1895 of the various independent companies which resulted in the Pure Oil Company, and that containing the material prepared by Roger Sherman for the suit brought in 1897 by the United States Pipe Line against certain of the Standard companies under the Sherman anti-trust law.

As many of the persons who have been active in the development of the oil industry are still living, their help has been freely sought. Scores of persons in each of the great oil centres have been interviewed, and the comprehension and interpretation of the documents on which the work is based have been materially aided by the explanations which the actors in the events under consideration were able to give.

When the work was first announced in the fall of 1901, the Standard Oil Company, or perhaps I should say officers of the company, courteously offered to give me all the assistance in their power, an offer of which I have freely taken advantage. In accepting assistance from Standard men as from independents I distinctly stated that I wanted facts, and that I reserved the right to use them according to my own judgment of their meaning, that my object was to learn more perfectly what was actually done—not to learn what my informants thought of what had been done. It is perhaps not too much to say that there is not a single important episode in the history of the Standard Oil Company, so far as I know it, or a notable step in its growth, which I have not discussed more or less fully with officers of the company.

It is needless to add that the conclusions expressed in this work are my own.

I. M. T.

LIST OF ILLUSTRATIONS

LIST OF ILLUSTRATIONS

LIST OF ILLUSTRATIONS

THE HISTORY OF
THE STANDARD OIL COMPANY

CHAPTER ONE

THE BIRTH OF AN INDUSTRY

PETROLEUM FIRST A CURIOSITY AND THEN A MEDICINE—DISCOVERY OF
ITS REAL VALUE—THE STORY OF HOW IT CAME TO BE PRODUCED IN
LARGE QUANTITIES—GREAT FLOW OF OIL—SWARM OF PROBLEMS TO
SOLVE—STORAGE AND TRANSPORTATION—REFINING AND MARKETING—
RAPID EXTENSION OF THE FIELD OF OPERATION—WORKERS IN GREAT
NUMBERS WITH PLENTY OF CAPITAL—COSTLY BLUNDERS FREQUENTLY
MADE—BUT EVERY DIFFICULTY BEING MET AND OVERCOME—THE NORMAL
UNFOLDING OF A NEW AND WONDERFUL OPPORTUNITY FOR INDIVIDUAL
ENDEAVOUR.

ONE of the busiest corners of the globe at the opening of the year 1872 was a strip of Northwestern
Pennsylvania, not over fifty miles long, known the
world over as the Oil Regions. Twelve years before
this strip of land had been but little better than a wilderness;
its chief inhabitants the lumbermen, who every season cut
great swaths of primeval pine and hemlock from its hills,
and in the spring floated them down the Allegheny River
to Pittsburg. The great tides of Western emigration had
shunned the spot for years as too rugged and unfriendly for
settlement, and yet in twelve years this region avoided by
men had been transformed into a bustling trade centre, where
towns elbowed each other for place, into which three great
trunk railroads had built branches, and every foot of whose
soil was fought for by capitalists. It was the discovery and
development of a new raw product, petroleum, which had
made this change from wilderness to market-place. This
product in twelve years had not only peopled a waste place
of the earth, it had revolutionised the world's methods of

illumination and added millions upon millions of dollars to the wealth of the United States.

Petroleum as a curiosity, and indeed in a small way as an article of commerce, was no new thing when its discovery in quantities called the attention of the world to this corner of Northwestern Pennsylvania. The journals of many an early explorer of the valleys of the Allegheny and its tributaries tell of springs and streams the surfaces of which were found covered with a thick oily substance which burned fiercely when ignited and which the Indians believed to have curative properties. As the country was opened, more and more was heard of these oil springs. Certain streams came to be named from the quantities of the substance found on the surface of the water, as "Oil Creek" in Northwestern Pennsylvania, "Old Greasy" or Kanawha in West Virginia. The belief in the substance as a cure-all increased as time went on and in various parts of the country it was regularly skimmed from the surface of the water as cream from a pan, or soaked up by woollen blankets, bottled, and peddled as a medicine for man and beast.

Up to the beginning of the 19th century no oil seems to have been obtained except from the surfaces of springs and streams. That it was to be found far below the surface of the earth was discovered independently at various points in Kentucky, West Virginia, Ohio and Pennsylvania by persons drilling for salt-water to be used in manufacturing salt. Not infrequently the water they found was mixed with a dark-green, evil-smelling substance which was recognised as identical with the well-known "rock-oil." It was necessary to rid the water of this before it could be used for salt, and in many places cisterns were devised in which the brine was allowed to stand until the oil had risen to the surface. It was then run into the streams or on the ground. This practice was soon discovered to be dangerous, so easily did the oil ignite.

In several places, particularly in Kentucky, so much oil was obtained with the salt-water that the wells had to be abandoned. Certain of these deserted salt wells were opened years after, when it was found that the troublesome substance which had made them useless was far more valuable than the brine the original drillers sought.

Naturally the first use made of the oil obtained in quantities from the salt wells was medicinal. By the middle of the century it was without doubt the great American medicine. "Seneca Oil" seems to have been the earliest name under which petroleum appeared in the East. It was followed by a large output of Kentucky petroleum sold under the name "American Medicinal Oil." Several hundred thousand bottles of this oil are said to have been put up in Burkesville, Kentucky, and to have been shipped to the East and to Europe. The point at which the business of bottling petroleum for medicine was carried on most systematically and extensively was Pittsburg. Near that town, at Tarentum in Alleghany County, were located salt wells owned and operated in the forties by Samuel M. Kier. The oil which came up with the salt-water was sufficient to be a nuisance, and Mr. Kier sought a way to use it. Believing it had curative qualities he began to bottle it. By 1850 he had worked up this business until "Kier's Petroleum, or Rock-Oil" was sold all over the United States. The crude petroleum was put up in eight-ounce bottles wrapped in a circular setting forth in good patent-medicine style its virtues as a cure-all, and giving directions about its use. While it was admitted to be chiefly a liniment it was recommended for cholera morbus, liver complaint, bronchitis and consumption, and the dose prescribed was three teaspoonfuls three times a day! Mr. Kier's circulars are crowded with testimonials of the efficacy of rock-oil, dated anywhere between 1848 and 1853. Although his trade in this oil was so extensive he was not

[5]

satisfied that petroleum was useful only as a medicine. He was interested in it as a lubricator and a luminant. That petroleum had the qualities of both had been discovered at more than one point before 1850. More than one mill-owner in the districts where petroleum had been found was using it in a crude way for oiling his machines or lighting his works, but though the qualities of both lubricator and luminant were present, the impurities of the natural oil were too great to make its use general. Mr. Kier seems to have been the first man to have attempted to secure an expert opinion as to the possibility of refining it. In 1849 he sent a bottle of oil to a chemist in Philadelphia, who advised him to try distilling it and burning it in a lamp. Mr. Kier followed the advice, and a five-barrel still which he used in the fifties for refining petroleum is still to be seen in Pittsburg. His trade in the oil he produced at his little refinery was not entirely local, for in 1858 we find him agreeing to sell to Joseph Coffin of New York at 62½ cents a gallon 100 barrels of "carbon oil that will burn in the ordinary coal-oil lamp."

Although Mr. Kier seems to have done a good business in rock-oil, neither he nor any one else up to this point had thought it worth while to seek petroleum for its own sake. They had all simply sought to utilise what rose before their eyes on springs and streams or came to them mixed with the salt-water for which they drilled. In 1854, however, a man was found who took rock-oil more seriously. This man was George H. Bissell, a graduate of Dartmouth College, who, worn out by an experience of ten years in the South as a journalist and teacher, had come North for a change. At his old college the latest curiosity of the laboratory was shown him—the bottle of rock-oil—and the professor contended that it was as good, or better, than coal for making illuminating oil. Bissell inquired into its origin, and was told that it came from oil springs located in Northwestern Pennsylvania on the farm of a lumber firm, Brewer, Watson and Company. These springs had long yielded a supply of oil which was regularly collected and sold for medicine, and was used locally by mill-owners for lighting and lubricating purposes.

Bissell seems to have been impressed with the commercial possibilities of the oil, for he at once organised a company, the Pennsylvania Rock-Oil Company, the first in the United States, and leased the lands on which these oil springs were located. He then sent a quantity of the oil to Professor Silliman of Yale College, and paid him for analysing it. The professor's report was published and received general attention. From the rock-oil might be made as good an illuminant as any the world knew. It also yielded gas, paraffine, lubricating oil. "In short," declared Professor Silliman, "your company have in their possession a raw material from which, by simple and not expensive process, they may manufacture very valuable products. It is worthy of note that my experiments prove that nearly the whole of the raw product may be manufactured without waste, and this solely by a well-directed process which is in practice in one of the most simple of all chemical processes." *

The oil was valuable, but could it be obtained in quantities great enough to make the development of so remote a locality worth while? The only method of obtaining it known to Mr. Bissell and his associates in the new company was from the surface of oil springs. Could it be obtained in any other way? There has long been a story current in the Oil Regions that the Pennsylvania Rock-Oil Company received its first notion of drilling for oil from one of those trivial incidents which so often turn the course of human affairs. As the story goes, Mr. Bissell was one day walking down Broadway when he halted to rest in the shade of an

* See Appendix, Number 1. Professor Silliman's report on petroleum.

[7]

awning before a drug store. In the window he saw on a bottle a curious label, "Kier's Petroleum, or Rock-Oil," it read, "Celebrated for its wonderful curative powers. A natural Remedy; Produced from a well in Allegheny Co., Pa., four hundred feet below the earth's surface," etc. On the label was the picture of an artesian well. It was from this well that Mr. Kier got his "Natural Remedy." Hundreds of men had seen the label before, for it went out on every one of Mr. Kier's circulars, but this was the first to look at it with a "seeing eye." As quickly as the bottle of rock-oil in the Dartmouth laboratory had awakened in Mr. Bissell's mind the determination to find out the real value of the strange substance, the label gave him the solution of the problem of getting oil in quantities—it was to bore down into the earth where it was stored, and pump it up.

Professor Silliman made his report to the Pennsylvania Rock-Oil Company in 1855, but it was not until the spring of 1858 that a representative of the organisation, which by this time had changed hands and was known as the Seneca Oil Company, was on the ground with orders to find oil. The man sent out was a small stockholder in the company, Edwin L. Drake, "Colonel" Drake as he was called. Drake had had no experience to fit him for his task. A man forty years of age, he had spent his life as a clerk, an express agent, and a railway conductor. His only qualifications were a dash of pioneer blood and a great persistency in undertakings which interested him. Whether Drake came to Titusville ordered to put down an artesian well or not is a mooted point. His latter-day admirers claim that the idea was entirely his own. It seems hardly credible that men as intelligent as Professor Silliman, Mr. Bissell, and others interested in the Pennsylvania Rock-Oil Company, should not have taken means of finding out how the familiar "Kier's Rock-Oil" was obtained. Professor Silliman at least must have known

[8]

E. L. DRAKE

In 1859 Drake drilled near Titusville, Pennsylvania, the first artesian well put down for petroleum. He is popularly said to have " discovered oil."

of the quantities of oil which had been obtained in different states in drilling salt wells; indeed, in his report (see Appendix, Number 1) he speaks of "wells sunk for the purpose of accumulating the product." In the "American Journal of Science" for 1840—of which he was one of the editors—is an account of a famous oil well struck near Burkesville, Kentucky, about 1830, when drilling for salt. It seems probable that the idea of seeking oil on the lands leased by the Petroleum Rock-Oil Company by drilling artesian wells had been long discussed by the gentlemen interested in the venture, and that Drake came to Titusville with instructions to put down a well. It is certain, at all events, that he was soon explaining to his superiors at home the difficulty of getting a driller, an engine-house and tools, and that he was employing the interval in trying to open new oil springs and make the old ones more profitable.

The task before Drake was no light one. The spot to which he had been sent was Titusville, a lumberman's hamlet on Oil Creek, fourteen miles from where that stream joins the Allegheny River. Its chief connection with the outside world was by a stage to Erie, forty miles away. This remoteness from civilisation and Drake's own ignorance of artesian wells, added to the general scepticism of the community concerning the enterprise, caused great difficulty and long delays. It was months before Drake succeeded in getting together the tools, engine and rigging necessary to bore his well, and before he could get a driller who knew how to manipulate them, winter had come, and he had to suspend operations. People called him crazy for sticking to the enterprise, but that had no effect on him. As soon as spring opened he borrowed a horse and wagon and drove over a hundred miles to Tarentum, where Mr. Kier was still pumping his salt wells, and was either bottling or refining the oil which came up with the brine. Here Drake hoped to find a driller.

He brought back a man, and after a few months more of experiments and accidents the drill was started. One day late in August, 1859, Titusville was electrified by the news that Drake's Folly, as many of the onlookers had come to consider it, had justified itself. The well was full of oil. The next day a pump was started, and twenty-five barrels of oil were gathered.

There was no doubt of the meaning of the Drake well in the minds of the people of the vicinity. They had long ago accepted all Professor Silliman had said of the possibilities of petroleum, and now that they knew how it could be obtained in quantity, the whole country-side rushed out to obtain leases. The second well in the immediate region was drilled by a Titusville tanner, William Barnsdall—an Englishman who at his majority had come to America to make his fortune. He had fought his way westward, watching always for his chance. The day the Drake well was struck he knew it had come. Quickly forming a company he began to drill a well. He did not wait for an engine, but worked his drill through the rock by a spring pole.* It took three months, and cost $3,000 to do it, but he had his reward. On February 1, 1860, he struck oil—twenty-five barrels a day—and oil was

* An elastic pole of ash or hickory, twelve to twenty feet long, was fastened at one end to work over a fulcrum. To the other end stirrups were attached, or a tilting platform was secured, by which two or three men produced a jerking motion that drew down the pole, its elasticity pulling it back with sufficient force, when the men slackened their hold, to raise the tools a few inches. The principle resembled that of the treadle-board of a sewing machine, operating which moves the needle up and down. The tools were swung in the driving pipe, or the "conductor"—a wooden tube eight or ten inches square, placed endwise in a hole dug to the rock—and fixed by a rope to the spring pole, two or three feet from the workmen. The strokes were rapid, and a sand pump—a spout three inches in diameter, with a hinged bottom opening inward and a valve working on a sliding rod, somewhat in the manner of a syringe—removed the borings mainly by sucking them into the spout as it was drawn out quickly. *McLaurin's " History of Petroleum."*

selling at eighteen dollars a barrel. In five months the English tanner had sold over $16,000 worth of oil.

A lumberman and merchant of the village, who long had had faith in petroleum if it could be had in quantity, Jonathan Watson, one of the firm of Brewer, Watson and Company, whose land the Pennsylvania Rock-Oil Company had leased, mounted his horse as soon as he heard of the Drake well, and, riding down the valley of Oil Creek, spent the day in leasing farms. He soon had the third well of the region going down, this too by a spring pole. This well started off in March at sixty gallons a minute, and oil was selling at sixty cents a gallon. In two years the farm where this third well was struck had produced 165,000 barrels of oil.

Working an unfriendly piece of land a few miles below the Drake well lived a man of thirty-five. Setting out for himself at twenty-two, he had won his farm by the most dogged efforts, working in saw-mills, saving his earnings, buying a team, working it for others until he could take up a piece of land, hoarding his savings here. For what? How could he know? He knew well enough when Drake struck oil, and hastened out to buy a share in a two-acre farm. He sold it at a profit, and with the money put down a well, from which he realised $70,000. A few years later the farm he had slaved to win came into the field. In 1871 he refused a million dollars for it, and at one time he had stored there 200,000 barrels of oil.

A young doctor who had buried himself in the wilderness saw his chance. For a song he bought thirty-eight acres on the creek, six miles below the Drake well, and sold half of it for the price he had paid to a country storekeeper and lumberman of the vicinity, one Charles Hyde. Out of this thirty-eight acres millions of dollars came; one well alone— the Mapleshade—cleared one and one-half millions.

On every rocky farm, in every poor settlement of the

region, was some man whose ear was attuned to Fortune's call, and who had the daring and the energy to risk everything he possessed in an oil lease. It was well that he acted at once; for, as the news of the discovery of oil reached the open, the farms and towns of Ohio, New York, and Pennsylvania poured out a stream of ambitious and vigorous youths, eager to seize what might be there for them, while from the East came men with money and business experience, who formed great stock companies, took up lands in parcels of thousands of acres, and put down wells along every rocky run and creek, as well as over the steep hills. In answer to their drill, oil poured forth in floods. In many places pumping was out of the question; the wells flowed 2,000, 3,000, 4,000 barrels a day—such quantities of it that at the close of 1861 oil which in January of 1860 was twenty dollars a barrel had fallen to ten cents.

Here was the oil, and in unheard-of quantities, and with it came all the swarm of problems which a discovery brings. The methods Drake had used were crude and must be improved. The processes of refining were those of the laboratory and must be developed. Communication with the outside world must be secured. Markets must be built up. Indeed, a whole new commercial machine had to be created to meet the discovery. These problems were not realised before the region teemed with men to wrestle with them—men "alive to the instant need of things." They had to begin with so simple and elementary a matter as devising something to hold the oil. There were not barrels enough to be bought in America, although turpentine barrels, molasses barrels, whiskey barrels—every sort of barrel and cask—were added to new ones made especially for oil. Reservoirs excavated in the earth and faced with logs and cement, and box-like structures of planks or logs were tried at first but were not satisfactory. A young Iowa school teacher and farmer, visiting at his home in Erie County, went to the region. Immediately he saw his chance. It was to invent a receptacle which would hold oil in quantities. Certain large producers listened to his scheme and furnished money to make a trial tank. It was a success, and before many months the school-teacher was buying thousands of feet of lumber, employing scores of men, and working them and himself—day and night. For nearly ten years he built these wooden tanks. Then seeing that iron tanks—huge receptacles holding thousands of barrels where his held hundreds—were bound to supersede him, he turned, with the ready adaptability which characterised the men of the region, to producing oil for others to tank.

After the storing problem came that of transportation. There was one waterway leading out—Oil Creek, as it had been called for more than a hundred years,—an uncertain stream running the length of the narrow valley in which the oil was found, and uniting with the Allegheny River at what is now known as Oil City. From this junction it was 132 miles to Pittsburg and a railroad. Besides this waterway were rough country roads leading to the railroads at Union City, Corry, Erie and Meadville. There was but one way to get the oil to the bank of Oil Creek or to the railroads, and that was by putting it into barrels and hauling it. Teamsters equipped for this service seemed to fall from the sky. The farms for a hundred miles around gave up their boys and horses and wagons to supply the need. It paid. There were times when three and even four dollars a barrel were paid for hauling five or ten miles. It was not too much for the work. The best roads over which they travelled were narrow, rough, unmade highways, mere openings to the outer world, while the roads to the wells they themselves had to break across fields and through forests. These roads were made almost impassable by the great number of heavily freighted wagons travelling over them. From the big wells a constant procession of teams ran, and it was no uncommon thing for a visitor to the Oil Regions to meet oil caravans of a hundred or more wagons. Often these caravans were held up for hours by a dangerous mud-hole into which a wheel had sunk or a horse fallen. If there was a possible way to be made around the obstruction it was taken, even if it led through a farmer's field. Indeed, a sort of guerilla warfare went on constantly between the farmers and the teamsters. Often the roads became impassable, so that new ones had to be broken, and not even a shot-gun could keep the driver from going where the passage was least difficult. The teamster, in fact, carried a weapon which few farmers cared to face, his terrible "black snake," as his long, heavy black whip was called. The man who had once felt the cruel lash of a "black snake" around his legs did not often oppose the owner.

With the wages paid him the teamster could easily become a kind of plutocrat. One old producer tells of having a teamster in his employ who for nine weeks drew only enough of his earnings to feed himself and horses. He slept in his wagon and tethered the team. At the end of the time he "thought he'd go home for a clean shirt" and asked for a settlement. It was found that he had $1,900 to his credit. The story is a fair illustration both of the habits and the earnings of the Oil Creek teamsters. Indispensable to the business they became the tyrants of the region—working and brawling as suited them, a genius not unlike the flatboat-men who once gave colour to life on the Mississippi, or the cowboys who make the plains picturesque to-day. Bad as their reputation was, many a man found in their ranks the start which led later to wealth and influence in the oil business. One of the shrewdest, kindest, oddest men the Oil Regions ever knew, Wesley Chambers, came to the top from the teamster class. He had found his way to the creek after eight years of unsuccessful gold-hunting in California. "There's my chance," he said, when he saw the lack of teams and boats, and he set about organising a service for transporting oil to Pittsburg. In a short time he was buying horses of his own and building boats. Wide-awake to actualities, he saw a few years later that the teamster and the boat were to be replaced by the pipeline and the railroad, and forestalled the change by becoming a producer.

In this problem of transportation the most important element after the team was Oil Creek and the flatboat. A more uncertain stream never ran in a bed. In the summer it was low, in the winter frozen; now it was gorged with ice, now running mad over the flats. The best service was gotten out of it in time of low water through artificial freshets. Milldams, controlled by private parties, were frequent along the creek and its tributaries. By arrangement these dams were cut on a certain day or days of the week, usually Friday, and on the flood or freshet the flatboats loaded with barrels of oil were floated down stream. The freshet was always exciting and perilous and frequently disastrous. From the points where they were tied up the boatmen watched the coming flood and cut themselves loose the moment after its head had passed them. As one fleet after another swung into the roaring flood the danger of collision and jams increased. Rare indeed was the freshet when a few wrecks did not lie somewhere along the creek, and often scores lay piled high on the bank—a hopeless jam of broken boats and barrels, the whole soaked in petroleum and reeking with gas and profanity. If the boats rode safely through to the river, there was little further danger.

The Allegheny River traffic grew to great proportions— fully 1,000 boats and some thirty steamers were in the fleet, and at least 4,000 men. This traffic was developed by men who saw here their opportunity of fortune, as others had seen it in drilling or teaming. The foremost of these men was an Ohio River captain, driven northward by the war, one J. J. Vandergrift. Captain Vandergrift had run the full gamut of river experiences from cabin-boy to owner and commander of his own steamers. The war stopped his Mississippi River trade. Fitting up one of his steamers as a gun-boat, he turned it over to Commodore Foote and looked for a new stream to navigate. From the Oil Region at that moment the loudest cry was for barrels. He towed 4,000 empty casks up the river, saw at once the need of some kind of bulk transportation, took his hint from a bulk-boat which an ingenious experimenter was trying, ordered a dozen of them built, towed his fleet to the creek, bought oil to fill them, and then returned to Pittsburg to sell his cargo. On one alone he made $70,000.

But the railroad soon pressed the river hard. At the time of the discovery of oil three lines, the Philadelphia and Erie, the Buffalo and Erie (now the Lake Shore), connecting with the Central, and the Atlantic and Great Western, connecting with the Erie, were within teaming distance of the region. The points at which the Philadelphia and Erie road could be reached were Erie, forty miles from Titusville, Union City, twenty-two miles, and Corry, sixteen miles. The Buffalo and Erie was reached at Erie. The Atlantic and Great Western was reached at Meadville, Union City and Corry, and the distances were twenty-eight, twenty-two and sixteen miles, respectively. Erie was the favourite shipping point at first, as the wagon road in that direction was the best. The amount of freight the railroads carried the first year of the business was enormous. Of course connecting lines were built as rapidly as men could work. By the beginning of 1863 the Oil Creek road, as it was known, had reached Titusville from Corry. This gave an eastern connection by both the Philadelphia and Erie and the Atlantic and Great Western, but as the latter was constructing a branch from Meadville to

Franklin, the Oil Creek road became the feeder of the former principally. Both of these roads were completed to Oil City by 1865.

The railroads built, the vexatious, time-taking, and costly problem of getting the oil from the well to the shipping point still remained. The teamster was still the tyrant of the business. His day was almost over. He was to fall before the pipe-line. The feasibility of carrying oil in pipes was discussed almost from the beginning of the oil business. Very soon after the Drake well was struck oil men began to say that the natural way to get this oil from the wells to the railroads was through pipes. In many places gravity would carry it; where it could not, pumps would force it. The belief that this could be done was so strong that as early as February, 1862, a company was incorporated in Pennsylvania for carrying oil in pipes or tubes from any point on Oil Creek to its mouth or to any station on the Philadelphia and Erie Railroad. This company seems never to have done more than get a charter. In 1863 at least three short pipe-lines were put into operation. The first of these was a two-inch pipe, through which distillate was pumped a distance of three miles from the Warren refinery at Plumer to Warren's Landing on the Allegheny River. The one which attracted the most attention was a line two and one-half miles in length carrying crude oil from the Tarr farm to the Humboldt refinery at Plumer. Various other experiments were made, both gravity and pumps being trusted for propelling the oil, but there was always something wrong; the pipes leaked or burst, the pumps were too weak; shifting oil centres interrupted experiments which might have been successful. Then suddenly the man for the need appeared, Samuel Van Syckel. He came to the creek in 1864 with some money, hoping to make more. He handled quantities of oil produced at Pithole, several miles from a shipping point, and saw his profits eaten up by teamsters. Their tyranny aroused his ire and his wits and he determined to build a pipe-line from the wells to the railroad. He was greeted with jeers, but he went doggedly ahead, laid a two-inch pipe, put in three relay pumps, and turned in his oil. From the start the line was a success, carrying eighty barrels of oil an hour. The day that the Van Syckel pipe-line began to run oil a revolution began in the business. After the Drake well it is the most important event in the history of the Oil Regions.

The teamsters saw its meaning first and turned out in fury, dragging the pipe, which was for the most part buried, to the surface, and cutting it so that the oil would be lost. It was only by stationing an armed guard that they were held in check. A second line of importance, that of Abbott and Harley, suffered even more than that of Van Syckel. The teamsters did more than cut the pipe; they burned the tanks in which oil was stored, laid in wait for employees, threatened with destruction the wells which furnished the oil, and so generally terrorised the country that the governor of the state was called upon in April, 1866, to protect the property and men of the lines. The day of the teamster was over, however, and the more philosophical of them accepted the situation; scores disappeared from the region, and scores more took to drilling. They died hard, and the cutting and plugging of pipe-lines was for years a pastime of the remnant of their race.

If the uses to which oil might be put and the methods for manufacturing it had not been well understood when the Drake well was struck, there would have been no such imperious demand as came for the immediate opening of new territory and developing methods of handling and carrying it on a large scale. But men knew already what the oil was good for, and, in a crude way, how to distil it. The process of distillation also was free to all. The essential apparatus was very simple—a cast-iron still, usually surrounded by brick-work, a copper worm, and two tin- or zinc-lined tanks. The still was filled with crude oil, which was subjected to a high enough heat to vapourise it. The vapour passed through a cast-iron goose-neck fitted to the top of the still into the copper worm, which was immersed in water. Here the vapour was condensed and passed into the zinc-lined tank. This product, called a distillate, was treated with chemicals, washed with water, and run off into the tin-lined tank, where it was allowed to settle. Anybody who could get the apparatus could "make oil," and many men did—badly, of course, to begin with, and with an alarming proportion of waste and explosions and fires, but with experience they learned, and some of the great refineries of the country grew out of these rude beginnings.

Luckily not all the men who undertook the manufacturing of petroleum in these first days were inexperienced. The chemists to whom are due chiefly the processes now used—Atwood, Gessner, and Merrill—had for years been busy making oils from coal. They knew something of petroleum, and when it came in quantities began at once to adapt their processes to it. Merrill at the time was connected with Samuel Downer, of Boston, in manufacturing oil from Trinidad pitch and from coal bought in Newfoundland. The year oil was discovered Mr. Downer distilled 7,500 tons of this coal, clearing on it at least $100,000. As soon as petroleum appeared he and Mr. Merrill saw that here was a product which was bound to displace their coal, and with courage and promptness they prepared to adapt their works. In order to be near the supply they came to Corry, fourteen miles from the Drake well, and in 1862 put up a refinery which cost $250,000. Here were refined thousands of barrels of oil, most of which was sent to New York for export. To the Boston works the firm sent crude, which was manufactured for the home trade and for shipping to California and Australia. The processes used in the Downer works at this early day were in all essentials the same as are used to-day.

In 1865 William Wright, after a careful study of "Petrolia," as the Oil Regions were then often called, published with Harper and Brothers an interesting volume in which he devotes a chapter to "Oil Refining and Refiners." Mr. Wright describes there not only the Downer works at Corry, but a factory which if much less important in the development of the Oil Regions held a much larger place in its imagination. This was the Humboldt works at Plumer. In 1862 two Germans, brothers, the Messrs. Ludovici, came to the oil country and, choosing a spot distant from oil wells, main roads, or water courses, erected an oil refinery which was reported to have cost a half million dollars. The works were built in a way unheard of then and uncommon now. The foundations were all of cut stone. The boiler and engines were of the most expensive character. A house erected in connection with the refinery was said to have been finished in hard wood with marble mantels, and furnished with rich carpets, mirrors, and elaborate furniture. The lavishness of the Humboldt refinery and the formality with which its business was conducted were long a tradition in the Oil Regions. Of more practical moment are the features of the refinery which Mr. Wright mentions: one is that the works had been so planned as to take advantage of the natural descent of the ground so that the oil would pass from one set of vessels to another without using artificial power, and the other that the supply of crude oil was obtained from the Tarr farm three miles away, being forced by pumps, through pipes, over the hills.

Mr. Wright found some twenty refineries between Titusville and Oil City the year of his visit, 1865. In several factories that he visited they were making naphtha, gasoline, and benzine for export. Three grades of illuminating oils—"prime white," "standard white," and "straw colour"—were made everywhere; paraffine, refined to a pure white article like that of to-day, was manufactured in quantities by the Downer works; and lubricating oils were beginning to be made.

As men and means were found to put down wells, to devise and build tanks and boats and pipes and railroads for handling the oil, to adapt and improve processes for manufacturing, so men were found from the beginning of the oil business to wrestle with every problem raised. They came in shoals, young, vigorous, resourceful, indifferent to difficulties, greedy for a chance, and with each year they forced more light and wealth from the new product. By the opening of 1872 they had produced nearly 40,000,000 barrels of oil, and had raised their product to the fourth place among the exports of the United States, over 152,000,000 gallons going abroad in 1871, a percentage of the production which compares well with what goes to-day.* As for the market, they had developed it until it included almost every country of the earth—China, the East and West Indies, South America and Africa. Over forty different European ports received refined oil from the United States in 1871. Nearly a million gallons were sent to Syria, about a half million to Egypt, about as much to the British West Indies, and a quarter of a million to the Dutch East Indies. Not only were illuminating oils being exported. In 1871 nearly seven million gallons of naphtha, benzine, and gasoline were sent abroad, and it became evident now for the first time that a valuable trade in lubricants made from petroleum was possible. A discovery by Joshua Merrill of the Downer works opened this new source of wealth to the industry. Until 1869 the impossibility of deodorising petroleum had prevented its use largely as a lubricant, but in that year

* In 1871 the petroleum exports were 152,195,167 gallons. The production was 5,795,000 barrels, or 243,390,000 gallons.

Mr. Merrill discovered a process by which a deodorised lubricating oil could be made. He had both the apparatus for producing the oil and the oil itself patented. The oil was so favourably received that the market sale by the Downer works was several hundred per cent. greater in a single year than the firm had ever sold before.

The oil field had been extended from the valley of Oil Creek and its tributaries down the Allegheny River for fifty miles and probably covered 2,000 square miles. The early theory that oil followed the streams had been exploded, and wells were now drilled on the hills. It was known, too, that if oil was found in the first sand struck in the drilling, it might be found still lower in a second or third sand. The Drake well had struck oil at 69½ feet, but wells were now drilled as deep as 1,600 feet. The extension of the field, the discovery that oil was under the hills as well as under streams, and to be found in various sands, had cost enormously. It had been done by "wild-catting," as putting down experimental wells was called, by following superstitions in locating wells, such as the witch-hazel stick, or the spiritualistic medium, quite as much as by studying the position of wells in existence and calculating how oil belts probably ran. As the cost of a well was from $3,000 to $8,000,* according to its location, and as 4,374 of the 5,560 wells drilled in the first ten years of the business (1859 to 1869) were "dry-holes," or were abandoned as unprofitable, something of the daring it took to operate on small means, as most producers did in the beginning, is evident. But they loved the game, and every man of them would stake his last dollar on the chance of striking oil.

With the extension of the field rapid strides had been made in tools, in rigs, in all of the various essentials of drilling a well. They had learned to use torpedoes to open up hard rocks,

* Estimate of J. T. Henry in his "Early and Later History of Petroleum," 1873. The "Petroleum Monthly" in 1873 estimated the cost to be from $2,725 to $4,416.

naphtha to cut the paraffine which coated the sand and stopped the flow of oil, seed bags to stop the inrush of a stream of water. They lost their tools less often, and knew better how to fish for them when they did. In short, they had learned how to put down and care for oil wells.

Equal advances had been made in other departments, fewer cars were loaded with barrels, tank cars for carrying in bulk had been invented. The wooden tank holding 200 to 1,200 barrels had been rapidly replaced by the great iron tank holding 20,000 or 30,000 barrels. The pipe-lines had begun to go directly to the wells instead of pumping from a general receiving station, or "dump," as it was called, thus saving the tedious and expensive operation of hauling. From beginning to end the business had been developed, systematised, simplified.

Most important was the simplification of the transportation problem by the development of pipe-lines. By 1872 they were the one oil gatherer. Several companies were carrying on the pipe-line business, and two of them had acquired great power in the Oil Regions because of their connection with trunk lines. These were the Empire Transportation Company and the Pennsylvania Transportation Company. The former, which had been the first business organisation to go into the pipe-line business on a large scale, was a concern which had appeared in the Oil Regions not over six months before Van Syckel began to pump oil. The Empire Transportation Company had been organised in 1865 to build up an east and west freight traffic *via* the Philadelphia and Erie Railroad, a new line which had just been leased by the Pennsylvania. Some ten railroads connected in one way or another with the Philadelphia and Erie, forming direct routes east and west. In spite of their evident community of interest these various roads were kept apart by their jealous fears of one another. Each insisted on its own time-table, its own rates, its own way of doing things. The shipper *via* this route must make a separate bargain with each road and often submit to having his freight changed at terminals from one car to another because of the difference of gauge. The Empire Transportation Company undertook to act as a mediator between the roads and the shipper, to make the route cheap, fast, and reliable. It proposed to solicit freight, furnish its own cars and terminal facilities, and collect money due. It did not make rates, however; it only harmonised those made by the various branches in the system. It was to receive a commission on the business secured, and a rental for the cars and other facilities it furnished.

It was a difficult task the new company undertook, but it had at its head a remarkable man to cope with difficulties. This man, Joseph D. Potts, was in 1865 thirty-six years old. He had come of a long and honourable line of iron-masters of the Schuylkill region of Pennsylvania, but had left the great forge towns with which his ancestors had been associated—Pottstown, Glasgow Forge, Valley Forge—to become a civil engineer. His profession had led him to the service of the Pennsylvania Railroad, where he had held important positions in connection with which he now undertook the organisation of the Empire Transportation Company. Colonel Potts—the title came from his service in the Civil War—possessed a clear and vigorous mind; he was far-seeing, forceful in execution, fair in his dealings. To marked ability and integrity he joined a gentle and courteous nature.

The first freight which the Empire Transportation Company attacked after its organisation was oil. The year was a great one for the Oil Regions, the year of Pithole. In January there had suddenly been struck on Pithole Creek in a wilderness six miles from the Allegheny River a well, located with a witch-hazel twig, which produced 250 barrels a day—and oil was selling at eight dollars a barrel! Wells followed in rapid succession. In less than ten months the field was doing over 10,000 barrels a day. This sudden flood of oil caused a tremendous excitement. Crowds of speculators and investors rushed to Pithole from all over the country. The Civil War had just closed, soldiers were disbanding, and hundreds of them found their way to the new oil field. In six weeks after the first well was struck Pithole was a town of 6,000 inhabitants. In less than a year it had fifty hotels and boarding-houses; five of these hotels cost $50,000 or more each. In six months after the first well the post-office of Pithole was receiving upwards of 10,000 letters per day and was counted third in size in the state—Philadelphia, Pittsburg, and Pithole being the order of rank. It had a daily paper, churches, all the appliances of a town.

The handling of the great output of oil from the Pithole field was a serious question. There seemed not enough cars in the country to carry it and shippers resorted to every imaginable trick to get accommodations. When the agent of the Empire Transportation Company opened his office in June, 1865, and demonstrated his ability to furnish cars regularly and in large numbers, trade rapidly flowed to him. Now the Empire agency had hardly been established when the Van Syckel pipe-line began to carry oil from Pithole to the railroad. Lines began to multiply. The railroads saw at once that they were destined speedily to do all the gathering and hastened to secure control of them. Colonel Potts's first pipe-line purchase was a line running from Pithole to Titusville, which as yet had not been wet.

When the Empire Transportation Company took over this line nothing had been demonstrated but that oil could be driven, by relay pumps, five miles through a two-inch pipe. The Empire's first effort was to get a longer run by fewer pumps. The agent in charge, C. P. Hatch, believed that oil could be brought the entire ten and one-half miles from Pithole to Titusville by one pump. He met with ridicule, but he insisted on trying it in the new line his company had acquired. The experiment was entirely successful. Improvements followed as rapidly as hands could carry out the suggestions of ingenuity and energy. One of the most important made the first year of the business was connecting wells by pipe directly with the tanks at the pumping stations, thus doing away with the expensive hauling in barrels to the "dump." A new device for accounting to the producer for his oil was made necessary by this change, and the practice of taking the gauge or measure of the oil in the producer's tank before and after the run and issuing duplicate "run tickets" was devised by Mr. Hatch. The producers, however, were not all "square"; it sometimes happened that they sold oil by a transfer order on the pipe-line, which they did not have in the line! To prevent these the Empire Transportation Company in 1868 began to issue certificates for credit balances of oil; these soon became the general mediums of trade in oil, and remain so to-day.

One of the cleverest of the pipe-line devices of the Empire Company was its assessment for waste and fire. In running oil through pipes there is more or less lost by leaking and evaporation. In September, 1868, Mr. Hatch announced that thereafter he would deduct two per cent. from oil runs for wastage. The assessment raised almost a riot in the region, meetings were held, the Empire Transportation Company was denounced as a highway robber, and threats of violence were made if the order was enforced. While this excitement was in progress there came a big fire on the line. Now the company's officials had been studying the question of fire insurance from the start. Fires in the Oil Regions were as regular a feature of the business as explosions used to be on the Mississippi steamboats, and no regular fire insurance company would take the risk. It had been decided that at the first fire there should be announced what was called a "general average assessment," that is, a fire tax, and to be ready, blanks had been prepared. Now in the thick of the resistance to the wastage assessment came a fire and the line announced that the producers having oil in the line must pay the insurance. The controversy at once waxed hotter than ever, but was finally compromised by the withdrawal in this case of the fire insurance if the producers would consent to the tax for waste. They did consent, and later when fires occurred the general average assessment was applied without serious opposition. Both of these practices prevail to-day. By the end of 1871 the Empire Transportation Company was one of the most efficient and respected business organisations in the oil country.

Its chief rival was the Pennsylvania Transportation Company, an organisation which had its origin in the second pipe-line laid in the Oil Regions. This line was built by Henry Harley, a man who for fully ten years was one of the most brilliant figures in the oil country. Harley was a civil engineer by profession, a graduate of the Troy Polytechnic Institute, and had held a responsible position for some time as an assistant of General Herman Haupt in the Hoosac Tunnel. He became interested in the oil business in 1862, first as a buyer of petroleum, then as an operator in West Virginia. In 1865 he laid a pipe-line from one of the rich oil farms of the creek to the railroad. It was a success, and from this venture Harley and his partner, W. H. Abbott, one of the wealthiest and most active men in the country, developed an important transportation system. In 1868 Jay Gould, who as president of the Erie road was eager to increase his oil freight, bought a controlling interest in the Abbott and Harley lines, and made Harley "General Oil Agent" of the Erie system. Harley now became closely associated with Fisk and Gould, and the three carried on a series of bold and piratical speculations in oil which greatly enraged the oil country. They built a refinery near Jersey City, extended their pipe-line system, and in 1871, when they reorganised under the name of the Pennsylvania Transportation Company, they controlled probably the greatest number of miles of pipe of any company in the region, and then were fighting the Empire bitterly for freight.

There is no part of this rapid development of the business more interesting than the commercial machine the oil men had devised by 1872 for marketing oil. A man with a thousand-barrel well on his hands in 1862 was in a plight. He had got to sell his oil at once for lack of storage room or let it run on the ground, and there was no exchange, no market, no telegraph, not even a post-office within his reach where he could arrange a sale. He had to depend on buyers who came to him. These buyers were the agents of the refineries in different cities, or of the exporters of crude in New York. They went from well to well on horseback, if the roads were not too bad, on foot if they were, and at each place made a special bargain varying with the quantity bought and the difficulty in getting it away, for the buyer was the transporter, and, as a rule, furnished the barrels or boats in which he carried off his oil. It was not long before the speculative character of the oil trade due to the great fluctuations in quantity added a crowd of brokers to the regular buyers who tramped up and down the creek. When the railroads came in the trains became the headquarters for both buyers and sellers. This was the more easily managed as the trains on the creek stopped at almost every oil farm. These trains became, in fact, a sort of travelling oil exchange, and on them a large percentage of all the bargaining of the business was done.

The brokers and buyers first organised and established headquarters in Oil City in 1869, but there was an oil exchange in New York City as early as 1866. Titusville did not have an exchange until 1871. By this time the pipe-lines had begun to issue certificates for the oil they received, and the trading was done to a degree in these. The method was simple, and much more convenient than the old one. The producer ran his oil into a pipe-line, and for it received a certificate showing that the line held so much to his credit; this certificate was transferred when the sale was made and presented when the oil was wanted.

One achievement of which the oil men were particularly proud was increasing the refining capacity of the region. At the start the difficulty of getting the apparatus for a refinery to the creek had been so enormous that the bulk of the crude had been driven to the nearest manufacturing cities—Erie, Pittsburg, Cleveland. Much had gone to the seaboard, too, and Boston, New York, Philadelphia and Baltimore were all doing considerable refining. There was always a strong feeling in the Oil Regions that the refining should be done at home. Before the railroads came the most heroic efforts were made again and again to get in the necessary machinery. Brought from Pittsburg by water, as a rule, the apparatus had to be hauled from Oil City, where it had been dumped on the muddy bank of the river—there were no wharfs—over the indescribable roads to the site chosen. It took weeks— months sometimes—to get in the apparatus. The chemicals used in the making of the oil, the barrels in which to store it—all had to be brought from outside. The wonder is that under these conditions anybody tried to refine on the creek. But refineries persisted in coming, and after the railroads came, increased; by 1872 the daily capacity had grown to nearly 10,000 barrels, and there were no more complete or profitable plants in existence than two or three of those on the creek. The only points having larger daily capacity were Cleveland and New York City. Several of the refineries had added barrel works. Acids were made on the ground. Iron works at Oil City and Titusville promised soon to supply the needs of both drillers and refiners. The exultation was great, and the press and people boasted that the day would soon come when they would refine for the world. There in their own narrow valleys should be made everything which petroleum would yield. Cleveland, Pittsburg—the seaboard —must give up refining. The business belonged to the Oil Regions, and the oil men meant to take it.

A significant development in the region was the tendency among many of the oil men to combine different branches of the business. Several large producers conducted shipping agencies for handling their own and other people's oil. The firm of Pierce and Neyhart was a prominent one carrying on this double business in the sixties and early seventies. J. J. Vandergrift, who has been mentioned already as one of the first men to take hold of the transportation problem, early became interested in production. As soon as the pipe-line was demonstrated to be a success he began building lines. He also added to his interests a large refinery, the Imperial of Oil City. Captain Vandergrift by 1870 produced, transported and refined his own oil as well as transported and refined much of other people's. It was a common practice for a refinery in the Oil Regions to pipe oil directly to its works by its own line, and in 1872 one refinery in Titusville, the Octave, carried its refined oil a mile or more by pipe to the railroad. Although most of the refineries at this period sold their products to dealers and exporters, the building up of markets by direct contact with new territory was beginning to be a consideration with all large manufacturers. The Octave of Titusville, for instance, chartered a ship in 1872 to load with oil and send in charge of its own agent into South American ports.

The odds against the oil men in developing the business had not been merely physical ones. There had been more than the wilderness to conquer, more than the possibilities of a new product to learn. Over all the early years of their struggle and hardships hovered the dark cloud of the Civil

War. They were so cut off from men that they did not hear of the fall of Sumter for four days after it happened, and the news for the time blotted out interest even in flowing wells. Twice at least when Lee invaded Pennsylvania the whole business came to a stand-still, men abandoning the drill, the pump, the refinery to make ready to repel the invader. They were taxed for the war—taxes rising to ten dollars per barrel in 1865—one dollar on crude and twenty cents a gallon on refined (the oil barrel is usually estimated at forty-two gallons). They gave up their quota of men again and again at the call for recruits, and when the end came and a million men were cast on the country, this little corner of Pennsylvania absorbed a larger portion of men probably than any other spot in the United States. The soldier was given the first chance everywhere at work, he was welcomed into oil companies, stock being given him for the value of his war record. There were lieutenants and captains and majors—even generals—scattered all over the field, and the field felt itself honoured, and bragged, as it did of all things, of the number of privates and officers who immediately on disbandment had turned to it for employment.

It was not only the Civil War from which the Oil Regions had suffered; in 1870 the Franco-Prussian War broke the foreign market to pieces and caused great loss to the whole industry. And there had been other troubles. From the first, oil men had to contend with wild fluctuations in the price of oil. In 1859 it was twenty dollars a barrel, and in 1861 it had averaged fifty-two cents. Two years later, in 1863, it averaged $8.15, and in 1867 but $2.40. In all these first twelve years nothing like a steady price could be depended on, for just as the supply seemed to have approached a fixed amount, a "wildcat" well would come in and "knock the bottom out of the market." Such fluctuations were the natural element of the speculator, and he came early, buying in quantities and holding in storage tanks for higher prices. If enough oil was held, or if the production fell off, up went the price, only to be knocked down by the throwing of great quantities of stocks on the market. The producers themselves often held their oil, though not always to their own profit. A historic case of obstinate holding occurred in 1871 on the "McCray farm," the most productive field in the region at that time. Prices were hovering around three dollars, and McCray swore he would not sell under five dollars. He bought, hired and built iron tankage until he had upward of 200,000 barrels. There was great loss from leakage and from evaporation and there were taxes, but McCray held on, refusing four dollars, $4.50, and even five dollars. Evil times came in the Oil Regions soon after and with them "dollar oil." McCray finally was obliged to sell his stocks at about $1.20 per barrel. To develop a business in face of such fluctuations and speculation in the raw product took not only courage—it took a dash of the gambler. It never could have been done, of course, had it not been for the streams of money which flowed unceasingly and apparently from choice into the regions. In 1865 Mr. Wright calculated that the oil country was using a capital of $100,000,000. In 1872 the oil men claimed the capital in operation was $200,000,000. It has been estimated that in the first decade of the industry nearly $350,000,000 was put into it.

Speculation in oil stock companies was another great evil. It reached its height in 1864 and 1865—the "flush times" of the business. Stocks in companies whose holdings were hardly worth the stamps on the certificates were sold all over the land. In March, 1865, the aggregate capital of the oil companies whose charters were on file in Albany, New York, was $350,-000,000, and in Philadelphia alone in 1864 and 1865 1,000 oil companies, mostly bogus, are said to have been formed. These swindles were dignified by the names of officers of distinction in the United States army, for the war was coming to an end and the name of a general was the most popular and persuasive argument in the country. Of course there came a collapse. The "oil bubble" burst in 1866, and it was nothing but the irrepressible energy of the region which kept the business going in the panic which followed.

Then there was the disturbing effect of foreign competition. What would become of them if oil was found in quantities in other countries? A decided depression of the market occurred in 1866 when the government sent out reports of developments of foreign oil fields. If there was oil in Japan, China, Burmah, Persia, Russia, Bavaria, in the quantities the government reports said, why, there was trouble in store for Pennsylvania, the oil men argued, and for a day the market fell—it was only for a day. Men forgot easily in the Oil Regions in the sixties.

An evil in their business which they were only beginning to grasp fully in 1871 was the unholy system of freight discrimination which the railroads were practising. Three trunk lines competed for the business by 1872—the Pennsylvania, which had leased the Philadelphia and Erie, the Erie and the Central. (The latter road reached the Oil Regions by a branch from Ashtabula on the Lake Shore and Michigan Southern division to Oil City; this branch was completed in 1868.) The Pennsylvania claimed the oil traffic as a natural right; for the Oil Regions were in Pennsylvania, and did not Tom Scott own that state? The Erie road for about five years had been in the hands of those splendid pirates, Jay Gould and "Jim" Fisk. Naturally they took all they could get of the oil traffic and took it by freebooting methods. "Corners" and "rings" were their favourite devices for securing trade, and more than once their aid had carried through daring and unscrupulous speculations in oil. The Central in this period was waging its famous desperate war on the Erie, Commodore Vanderbilt having marked that highway for his own along with most other things in New York State. All three of the roads began as early as 1868 to use secret rebates on the published freight rates in oil as a means of securing traffic. This practice had gone on until in 1871 any big producer, refiner, or buyer could bully a freight agent into a special rate. Those "on the inside," those who had "pulls," also secured special rates. The result was that the open rate was enforced only on the innocent and the weak.

Serious as all these problems were, there was no discouragement or shrinking from them. The oil men had rid themselves of bunco men and burst the "oil bubbles." They had harnessed the brokers in exchanges and made strict rules to govern them. They had learned not to fear the foreigners, and to take with equal *sang froid* the "dry-hole" which made them poor, or the "gusher" which made them rich. For every evil they had a remedy. They were not afraid even of the railroads, and loudly declared that if the discriminations were not stopped they would build a railroad of their own. Indeed, the evils in the oil business in 1871, far from being a discouragement, rather added to the interest. They had never known anything but struggle—with conquest—and twelve years of it was far from cooling their ardour for a fair fight.

More had been done in the Oil Regions in the first dozen years than the development of a new industry. From the first there had gone with the oil men's ambition to make oil to light the whole earth a desire to bring civilisation to the wilderness from which they were drawing wealth, to create an orderly society from the mass of humanity which poured pell-mell into the region. A hatred of indecency first drew together the better element of each of the rough communities which sprang up. Whiskey-sellers and women flocked to the region at the breaking out of the excitement. Their first shelters were shanties built on flatboats which were towed from place to place. They came to Rouseville—a collection of pine shanties and oil derricks, built on a muddy flat—as for-

THE DRAKE WELL IN 1859—THE FIRST OIL WELL

FAC-SIMILE OF A LABEL USED BY S. M. KIER IN ADVERTISING ROCK-OIL OBTAINED IN
DRILLING SALT WELLS NEAR TARENTUM, PENNSYLVANIA

FAGUNDUS—A TYPICAL OIL TOWN

lorn and disreputable a town in appearance as the earth ever saw. They tied up for trade, and the next morning woke up from their brawl to find themselves twenty miles away, floating down the Allegheny River. Rouseville meant to be decent. She had cut them loose, and by such summary vigilance she kept herself decent. Other towns adopted the same policy. By common consent vice was corralled largely in one town. Here a whole street was given up to dance-houses and saloons, and those who must have a "spree" were expected to go to Petroleum Centre to take it.

Decency and schools! Vice cut adrift, they looked for a school teacher. Children were sadly out of place, but there they were, and these men, fighting for a chance, saw to it that a shanty, with a school teacher in it, was in every settlement. It was not long, too, before there was a church, a union church. To worship God was their primal instinct; to defend a creed a later development. In the beginning every social contrivance was wanting. There were no policemen, and each individual looked after evil-doers. There were no firemen, and every man turned out with a bucket at a fire. There were no bankers, and each man had to put his wealth away as best he could until a peripatetic banker from Pittsburg relieved him. At one time Dr. Egbert, a rich operator, is said to have had $1,800,000 in currency in his house. There were no hospitals, and in 1861, when the horrible possibilities of the oil fire were first demonstrated by the burning of the Rouse well, a fire at which nineteen persons lost their lives, the many injured found welcome and care for long weeks in the little shanties of women already overburdened by the difficulties of caring for families in the rough community.

Out of this poverty and disorder they had developed in ten years a social organisation as good as their commercial. Titusville, the hamlet on whose outskirts Drake had drilled his well, was now a city of 10,000 inhabitants. It had an opera

house, where in 1871 Clara Louise Kellogg and Christine
Nilsson sang, Joe Jefferson and Janauschek played, and Wen-
dell Phillips and Bishop Simpson spoke. It had two prosperous and fearless newspapers. Its schools prepared for college.
Oil City was not behind, and between them was a string of
lively towns. Many of the oil farms had a decent community
life. The Columbia farm kept up a library and reading-room
for its employees; there was a good schoolhouse used on Sunday for services, and there was a Columbia farm band of no
mean reputation in the Oil Regions.

Indeed, by the opening of 1872, life in the Oil Regions had
ceased to be a mere make-shift. Comforts and orderliness and
decency, even opportunities for education and for social life,
were within reach. It was a conquest to be proud of, quite as
proud of as they were of the fact that their business had been
developed until it had never before, on the whole, been in so
satisfactory a condition.

Nobody realised more fully what had been accomplished
in the Oil Regions than the oil men themselves. Nobody
rehearsed their achievements so loudly. "In ten years," they
were fond of saying, "we have built this business up from
nothing to a net product of six millions of barrels per annum.
We have invented and devised all the apparatus, the appliances, the forms needed for a new industry. We use a capital
of $200,000,000, and support a population of 60,000 people.
To keep up our supply we drill 100 new wells per month,
at an average cost of $6,000 each. We are fourth in the exports
of the United States. We have developed a foreign market,
including every civilised country on the globe."

But what had been done was, in their judgment, only a
beginning. Life ran swift and ruddy and joyous in these men.
They were still young, most of them under forty, and they
looked forward with all the eagerness of the young who have
just learned their powers, to years of struggle and develop-

[36]

ment. They would solve all these perplexing problems of over-production, of railroad discrimination, of speculation. They would meet their own needs. They would bring the oil refining to the region where it belonged. They would make their towns the most beautiful in the world. There was nothing too good for them, nothing they did not hope and dare. But suddenly, at the very heyday of this confidence, a big hand reached out from nobody knew where, to steal their conquest and throttle their future. The suddenness and the blackness of the assault on their business stirred to the bottom their manhood and their sense of fair play, and the whole region arose in a revolt which is scarcely paralleled in the commercial history of the United States.

CHAPTER TWO

THE RISE OF THE STANDARD OIL COMPANY

JOHN D. ROCKEFELLER'S FIRST CONNECTION WITH THE OIL BUSINESS—
STORIES OF HIS EARLY LIFE IN CLEVELAND—HIS FIRST PARTNERS—
ORGANISATION OF THE STANDARD OIL COMPANY IN JUNE, 1870—ROCKE-
FELLER'S ABLE ASSOCIATES—FIRST EVIDENCE OF RAILWAY DISCRIMINA-
TIONS IN THE OIL BUSINESS—REBATES FOUND TO BE GENERALLY GIVEN
TO LARGE SHIPPERS—FIRST PLAN FOR A SECRET COMBINATION—THE
SOUTH IMPROVEMENT COMPANY—SECRET CONTRACTS MADE WITH THE
RAILROADS PROVIDING REBATES AND DRAWBACKS—ROCKEFELLER AND
ASSOCIATES FORCE CLEVELAND REFINERS TO JOIN THE NEW COMBINA-
TION OR SELL—RUMOUR OF THE PLAN REACHES THE OIL REGIONS.

THE chief refining competitor of Oil Creek in 1872 was Cleveland, Ohio. Since 1869 that city had done annually more refining than any other place in the country. Strung along the banks of Walworth and Kingsbury Runs, the creeks to which the city frequently banishes her heavy and evil-smelling burdens, there had been since the early sixties from twenty to thirty oil refineries. Why they were there, more than 200 miles from the spot where the oil was taken from the earth, a glance at a map of the railroads of the time will show: By rail and water Cleveland commanded the entire Western market. It had two trunk lines running to New York, both eager for oil traffic, and by Lake Erie and the canal it had for a large part of the year a splendid cheap waterway. Thus, at the opening of the oil business, Cleveland was destined by geographical position to be a refining center.

Men saw it, and hastened to take advantage of the opportunity. There was grave risk. The oil supply might not hold

[38]

out. As yet there was no certain market for refined oil. But a sure result was not what drew people into the oil business in the early sixties. Fortune was running fleet-footed across the country, and at her garment men clutched. They loved the chase almost as they did success, and so many a man in Cleveland tried his luck in an oil refinery, as hundreds on Oil Creek were trying it in an oil lease. By 1865 there were thirty refineries in the town, with a capital of about a million and a half dollars and a daily capacity of some 2,000 barrels. The works multiplied rapidly. The report of the Cleveland Board of Trade for 1866 gives the number of plants at the end of that year as fifty, and it dilates eloquently on the advantages of Cleveland as a refining point over even Pittsburg, to that time supposed to be the natural centre for the business. If the railroad and lake transportation men would but adopt as liberal a policy toward the oil freights of Cleveland as the Pennsylvania Railroad was adopting toward that of Pittsburg, aided by her natural advantages the town was bound to become the greatest oil refining centre in the United States. By 1868 the Board of Trade reported joyfully that Cleveland was receiving within 300,000 barrels as much oil as Pittsburg. In 1869 she surpassed all competitors. "Cleveland now claims the leading position among the manufacturers of petroleum with a very reasonable prospect of holding that rank for some time to come," commented the Board of Trade report. "Each year has seen greater consolidation of capital, greater energy and success in prosecuting the business, and, notwithstanding some disastrous fires, a stronger determination to establish an immovable reputation for the quantity and quality of this most important product. The total capital invested in this business is not less than four millions of dollars and the total product of the year would not fall short of fifteen millions."

Among the many young men of Cleveland who, from the

start, had an eye on the oil-refining business and had begun to take an active part in its development as soon as it was demonstrated that there was a reasonable hope of its being permanent, was a young firm of produce commission merchants. Both members of this firm were keen business men, and one of them had remarkable commercial vision—a genius for seeing the possibilities in material things. This man's name was Rockefeller—John D. Rockefeller. He was but twenty-three years old when he first went into the oil business, but he had already got his feet firmly on the business ladder, and had got them there by his own efforts. The habit of driving good bargains and of saving money had started him. He himself once told how he learned these lessons so useful in money-making, in one of his frequent Sunday-school talks to young men on success in business. The value of a good bargain he learned in buying cord-wood for his father: "I knew what a cord of good solid beech and maple wood was. My father told me to select only the solid wood and the straight wood and not to put any limbs in it or any punky wood. That was a good training for me. I did not need any father to tell me or anybody else how many feet it took to make a cord of wood."

And here is how he learned the value of investing money:

"Among the early experiences that were helpful to me that I recollect with pleasure was one in working a few days for a neighbour in digging potatoes—a very enterprising, thrifty farmer, who could dig a great many potatoes. I was a boy of perhaps thirteen or fourteen years of age, and it kept me very busy from morning until night. It was a ten-hour day. And as I was saving these little sums I soon learned that I could get as much interest for fifty dollars loaned at seven per cent. —the legal rate in the state of New York at that time for a year—as I could earn by digging potatoes for 100 days. The impression was gaining ground with me that it was a

JOHN D. ROCKEFELLER IN 1872

good thing to let the money be my slave and not make myself a slave to money." Here we have the foundation principles of a great financial career.

When young Rockefeller was thirteen years old, his father moved from the farm in Central New York, where the boy had been born (July 8, 1839), to a farm near Cleveland, Ohio. He went to school in Cleveland for three years. In 1855 it became necessary for him to earn his own living. It was a hard year in the West and the boy walked the streets for days looking for work. He was about to give it up and go to the country when, to quote the story as Mr. Rockefeller once told it to his Cleveland Sunday-school, "As good fortune would have it I went down to the dock and made one more application, and I was told that if I would come in after dinner—our noon-day meal was dinner in those days—they would see if I could come to work for them. I went down after dinner and I got the position, and I was permitted to remain in the city." The position, that of a clerk and bookkeeper, was not lucrative. According to a small ledger which has figured frequently in Mr. Rockefeller's religious instructions, he earned from September 26, 1855, to January, 1856, fifty dollars. "Out of that," Mr. Rockefeller told the young men of his Sunday-school class, "I paid my washerwoman and the lady I boarded with, and I saved a little money to put away."

He proved an admirable accountant—one of the early-and-late sort, who saw everything, forgot nothing and never talked. In 1856 his salary was raised to twenty-five dollars a month, and he went on always "saving a little money to put away." In 1858 came a chance to invest his savings. Among his acquaintances was a young Englishman, M. B. Clark. Older by twelve years than Rockefeller he had left a hard life in England when he was twenty to seek fortune in America. He had landed in Boston in 1847, without a penny or a friend, and it had taken three months for him to earn money to get to Ohio. Here he had taken the first job at hand, as man-of-all-work, wood-chopper, teamster. He had found his way to Cleveland, had become a valuable man in the houses where he was employed, had gone to school at nights, had saved money. They were two of a kind, Clark and Rockefeller, and in 1858 they pooled their earnings and started a produce com-

Roby Frank, cabinet maker, bds 17 Johnson
ROBY E. W. & CO. (Edward W. Roby and William H.
    Keith), wood and coal, C. & P. R. R. Coal Pier, and
    Merwin n Columbus St. Bridge
Rochert Conrad, h 175 St Clair.
Rock John, bar keeper. bds 11 Public Square
ROCKAFELLOW JOHN J., coal, C. & P. R. R. Coal Pier,
    h 183 Prospect
Rockefeller John D., book-keeper, h 35 Cedar
Rockefeller William, physician, h 35 Cedar av
Rockett Morris, rectifier, h 182 St Clair
Rockwell Edward, Sec. C. & P. R. R., bds Weddell House

Fragment of a page in the city directory of Cleveland, Ohio, for 1857. This is the first year in which the name John D. Rockefeller appears in the directory. The same entry is made in 1858. The next year, 1859, Mr. Rockefeller is entered as a member of the firm of Clark and Rockefeller.

mission business on the Cleveland docks. The venture succeeded. Local historians credit Clark and Rockefeller with doing a business of $450,000 the first year. The war came on, and as neither partner went to the front, they had full chance to take advantage of the opportunity for produce business a great army gives. A greater chance than furnishing army supplies, lucrative as most people found that, was in the oil business (so Clark and Rockefeller began to think), and in 1862, when an Englishman of ability and energy, one Samuel Andrews, asked them to back him in starting a refinery, they put in $4,000 and promised to give more if necessary. Now Andrews was a mechanical genius. He devised new processes, made a better and better quality of oil, got larger and larger percentages of refined from his crude. The little refinery grew big, and Clark and Rockefeller soon had $100,000 or more in it. In the meantime Cleveland was growing as a refining centre. The business which in 1860 had been a gamble was by 1865 one of the most promising industries of the town. It was but the beginning—so Mr. Rockefeller thought—and in that year he sold out his share of the commission business and put his money into the oil firm of Rockefeller and Andrews.

In the new firm Andrews attended to the manufacturing. The pushing of the business, the buying and the selling, fell to Rockefeller. From the start his effect was tremendous. He had the frugal man's hatred of waste and disorder, of middlemen and unnecessary manipulation, and he began a vigorous elimination of these from his business. The residuum that other refineries let run into the ground, he sold. Old iron found its way to the junk shop. He bought his oil directly from the wells. He made his own barrels. He watched and saved and contrived. The ability with which he made the smallest bargain furnishes topics to Cleveland story-tellers to-day. Low-voiced, soft-footed, humble, knowing every point in every man's business, he never tired until he got his wares at the lowest possible figure. "John always got the best of the bargain," old men tell you in Cleveland to-day, and they wince though they laugh in telling it. "Smooth," "a *savy* fellow," is their description of him. To drive a good bargain was the joy of his life. "The only time I ever saw John Rockefeller enthusiastic," a man told the writer once, "was when a report came in from the creek that his buyer had secured a cargo of oil at a figure much below the market price. He bounded from his chair with a shout of joy, danced up and down, hugged me, threw up his hat, acted so like a madman that I have never forgotten it."

He could borrow as well as bargain. The firm's capital was limited; growing as they were, they often needed money, and had none. Borrow they must. Rarely if ever did Mr. Rockefeller fail. There is a story handed down in Cleveland from

[43]

the days of Clark and Rockefeller, produce merchants, which is illustrative of his methods. One day a well-known and rich business man stepped into the office and asked for Mr. Rockefeller. He was out, and Clark met the visitor. "Mr. Clark," he said, "you may tell Mr. Rockefeller, when he comes in, that I think I can use the $10,000 he wants to invest with me for your firm. I have thought it all over."

"Good God!" cried Clark, "we don't want to invest $10,000. John is out right now trying to borrow $5,000 for us."

It turned out that to prepare him for a proposition to borrow $5,000 Mr. Rockefeller had told the gentleman that he and Clark wanted to invest $10,000!

"And the joke of it is," said Clark, who used to tell the story, "John got the $5,000 even after I had let the cat out of the bag. Oh, he was the greatest borrower you ever saw!"

These qualities told. The firm grew as rapidly as the oil business of the town, and started a second refinery—William A. Rockefeller and Company. They took in a partner, H. M. Flagler, and opened a house in New York for selling oil. Of all these concerns John D. Rockefeller was the head. Finally, in June, 1870, five years after he became an active partner in the refining business, Mr. Rockefeller combined all his companies into one—the Standard Oil Company. The capital of the new concern was $1,000,000. The parties interested in it were John D. Rockefeller, Henry M. Flagler, Samuel Andrews, Stephen V. Harkness, and William Rockefeller.*

The strides the firm of Rockefeller and Andrews made after the former went into it were attributed for three or four years mainly to his extraordinary capacity for bargaining and borrowing. Then its chief competitors began to suspect something. John Rockefeller might get his oil cheaper now and

* See Appendix, Number 2. First act of incorporation of the Standard Oil Company.

then, they said, but he could not do it often. He might make close contracts for which they had neither the patience nor the stomach. He might have an unusual mechanical and practical genius in his partner. But these things could not

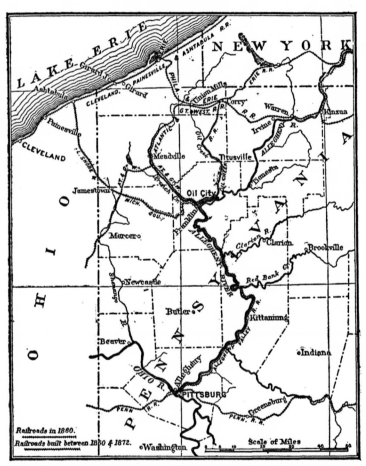

Map of Northwestern Pennsylvania, showing the relation of the Oil Regions to the railroads in 1859, when oil was "discovered."

explain all. They believed they bought, on the whole, almost as cheaply as he, and they knew they made as good oil and with as great, or nearly as great, economy. He could sell at no better price than they. Where was his advantage? There was but one place where it could be, and that was in transportation. He must be getting better rates from the railroads than they were. In 1868 or 1869 a member of a rival firm long in the business, which had been prosperous from the start, and which prided itself on its methods, its economy and its energy, Alexander, Scofield and Company, went to the Atlantic and Great Western road, then under the Erie management, and complained. "You are giving others better rates than you are us," said Mr. Alexander, the representative of the firm. "We cannot compete if you do that." The railroad agent did not attempt to deny it—he simply agreed to give Mr. Alexander a rebate also. The arrangement was interesting. Mr. Alexander was to pay the open, or regular, rate on oil from the Oil Regions to Cleveland, which was then forty cents a barrel. At the end of each month he was to send to the railroad vouchers for the amount of oil shipped and paid for at forty cents, and was to get back from the railroad, in money, fifteen cents on each barrel. This concession applied only to oil brought from the wells. He was never able to get a rebate on oil shipped eastward.* According to Mr. Alexander, the Atlantic and Great Western gave the rebates on oil from the Oil Regions to Cleveland up to 1871 and the system was then discontinued. Late in 1871, however, the firm for the first time got a rebate on the Lake Shore road on oil brought from the field.

Another Cleveland man, W. H. Doane, engaged in shipping crude oil, began to suspect about the same time as Mr. Alexander that the Standard was receiving rebates. Now Mr. Doane had always been opposed to the "drawback business," but it was impossible for him to supply his customers with crude oil at as low a rate as the Standard paid if it received a

---

* Testimony of Mr. Alexander before the Committee of Commerce of the United States House of Representatives, April, 1872.

rebate and he did not, and when it was first generally rumoured in Cleveland that the railroads were favouring Mr. Rockefeller he went to see the agent of the road. "I told him I did not want any drawback, unless others were getting it; I wanted it if they were getting it, and he gave me at that time ten cents drawback." This arrangement Mr. Doane said had lasted but a short time. At the date he was speaking—the spring of 1872—he had had no drawback for two years.

A still more important bit of testimony as to the time when rebates first began to be given to the Cleveland refiners and as to who first got them and why, is contained in an affidavit made in 1880 by the very man who made the discrimination.* This man was General J. H. Devereux, who in 1868 succeeded Amasa Stone as vice-president of the Lake Shore Railroad. General Devereux said that his experience with the oil traffic had begun with his connection with the Lake Shore; that the only written memoranda concerning oil which he found in his office on entering his new position was a book in which it was stated that the representatives of the twenty-five oil-refining firms in Cleveland had agreed to pay a cent a gallon on crude oil removed from the Oil Regions. General Devereux says that he soon found there was a deal of trouble in store for him over oil freight. The competition between the twenty-five firms was close, the Pennsylvania was "claiming a patent right" on the transportation of oil and was putting forth every effort to make Pittsburg and Philadelphia the chief refining centres. Oil Creek was boasting that it was going to be the future refining point for the world. All of this looked bad for what General Devereux speaks of as the "then very limited refining capacity of Cleveland." This remark shows how new he was to the business, for, as we have

* See Appendix, Number 3. Affidavit of James H. Devereux. At the time General Devereux made this affidavit, 1880, he was president of the New York, Pennsylvania and Ohio Railroad.

already seen, Cleveland in 1868 had anything but a limited refining capacity. Between three and four million dollars were invested in oil refineries, and the town was receiving within 35,000 barrels of as much oil as New York City, and within 300,000 as much as Pittsburg, and it was boasting that the next year it would outstrip these competitors, which, as a matter of fact, it did.

The natural point for General Devereux to consider, of course, was whether he could meet the rates the Pennsylvania were giving and increase the oil freight for the Lake Shore. The road had a branch running to Franklin, Pennsylvania, within a few miles of Oil City. This he completed, and then, as he says in his affidavit, "a sharper contest than ever was produced growing out of the opposition of the Pennsylvania Railroad in competition. Such rates and arrangements were made by the Pennsylvania Railroad that it was publicly proclaimed in the public print in Oil City, Titusville and other places that Cleveland was to be wiped out as a refining centre as with a sponge." General Devereux goes on to say that all the refiners of the town, without exception, came to him in alarm, and expressed their fears that they would have either to abandon their business there or move to Titusville or other points in the Oil Regions; that the only exception to this decision was that offered by Rockefeller, Andrews and Flagler, who, on his assurance that the Lake Shore Railroad could and would handle oil as cheaply as the Pennsylvania Company, proposed to stand their ground at Cleveland and fight it out on that line. And so General Devereux gave the Standard the rebate on the rate which Amasa Stone had made with all the refiners. Why he should not have quieted the fears of the twenty-four or twenty-five other refiners by lowering their rate, too, does not appear in the affidavit. At all events the rebate had come, and, as we have seen, it soon was suspected and others went after it, and in some cases got it. But the rebate seems to have been granted generally only on oil brought from the Oil Regions. Mr. Alexander claims he was never able to get his rate lowered on his Eastern shipments. The railroad took the position with him that if he could ship as much oil as the Standard he could have as low a rate, but not otherwise. Now in 1870 the Standard Oil Company had a daily capacity of about 1,500 barrels of crude. The refinery was the largest in the town, though it had some close competitors. Nevertheless on the strength of its large capacity it received the special favour. It was a plausible way to get around the theory generally held then, as now, though not so definitely crystallised into law, that the railroad being a common carrier had no right to discriminate between its patrons. It remained to be seen whether the practice would be accepted by Mr. Rockefeller's competitors without a contest, or, if contested, would be supported by the law.

What the Standard's rebate on Eastern shipments was in 1870 it is impossible to say. Mr. Alexander says he was never able to get a rate lower than $1.33 a barrel by rail, and that it was commonly believed in Cleveland that the Standard had a rate of ninety cents. Mr. Flagler, however, the only member of the firm who has been examined under oath on that point, showed, by presenting the contract of the Standard Oil Company with the Lake Shore road in 1870, that the rates varied during the year from $1.40 to $1.20 and $1.60, according to the season. When Mr. Flagler was asked if there was no drawback or rebate on this rate he answered, "None whatever."

It would seem from the above as if the one man in the Cleveland oil trade in 1870 who ought to have been satisfied was Mr. Rockefeller. His was the largest firm in the largest refining centre of the country; that is, of the 10,000 to 12,000 daily capacity divided among the twenty-five or twenty-six refiners of Cleveland he controlled 1,500 barrels. Not only was

Cleveland the largest refining centre in the country, it was gaining rapidly, for where in 1868 it shipped 776,356 barrels of refined oil, in 1869 it shipped 923,933, in 1870 1,459,500, and in 1871 1,640,499.* Not only did Mr. Rockefeller control the largest firm in this most prosperous centre of a prosperous business, he controlled one of amazing efficiency. The combination, in 1870, of the various companies with which he was connected had brought together a group of remarkable men. Samuel Andrews, by all accounts, was the ablest mechanical superintendent in Cleveland. William Rockefeller, the brother of John D. Rockefeller, was not only an energetic and intelligent business man, he was a man whom people liked. He was open-hearted, jolly, a good story-teller, a man who knew and liked a good horse—not too pious, as some of John's business associates thought him, not a man to suspect or fear, as many a man did John. Old oil men will tell you on the creek to-day how much they liked him in the days when he used to come to Oil City buying oil for the Cleveland firm. The personal quality of William Rockefeller was, and always has been, a strong asset of the Standard Oil Company. Probably the strongest man in the firm after John D. Rockefeller was Henry M. Flagler. He was, like the others, a young man, and one who, like the head of the firm, had the passion for money, and in a hard self-supporting experience, begun when but a boy, had learned, as well as his chief, some of the principles of making it. He was untiring in his efforts to increase the business, quick to see an advantage, as quick to take it. He had no scruples to make him hesitate over the ethical quality of a contract which was advantageous. Success, that is, making money, was its own justification. He was not a secretive man, like John D. Rockefeller, not a dreamer, but he could keep his mouth shut when necessary and he knew the worth of a financial dream when

* Report for 1871 of the Cleveland Board of Trade.

it was laid before him. It must have been evident to every business man who came in contact with the young Standard Oil Company that it would go far. The firm itself must have known it would go far. Indeed nothing could have stopped the Standard Oil Company in 1870—the oil business being what it was—but an entire change in the nature of the members of the firm, and they were not the kind of material which changes.

With such a set of associates, with his organisation complete from his buyers on the creek to his exporting agent in New York, with the transportation advantages which none of his competitors had had the daring or the persuasive power to get, certainly Mr. Rockefeller should have been satisfied in 1870. But Mr. Rockefeller was far from satisfied. He was a brooding, cautious, secretive man, seeing all the possible dangers as well as all the possible opportunities in things, and he studied, as a player at chess, all the possible combinations which might imperil his supremacy. These twenty-five Cleveland rivals of his—how could he at once and forever put them out of the game? He and his partners had somehow conceived a great idea—the advantages of combination. What might they not do if they could buy out and absorb the big refineries now competing with them in Cleveland? The possibilities of the idea grew as they discussed it. Finally they began tentatively to sound some of their rivals. But there were other rivals than these at home. There were the creek refiners! They were there at the mouth of the wells. What might not this geographical advantage do in time? Refining was going on there on an increasing scale; the capacity of the Oil Regions had indeed risen to nearly 10,000 barrels a day— equal to that of New York, exceeding that of Pittsburg by nearly 4,000 barrels, and almost equalling that of Cleveland. The men of the oil country loudly declared that they meant to refine for the world. They boasted of an oil kingdom which

[51]

eventually should handle the entire business and compel Cleveland and Pittsburg either to abandon their works or bring them to the oil country. In this boastful ambition they were encouraged particularly by the Pennsylvania Railroad, which naturally handled the largest percentage of the oil. How long could the Standard Oil Company stand against this competition?

There was another interest as deeply concerned as Mr. Rockefeller in preserving Cleveland's supremacy as a refining centre, and this was the Lake Shore and New York Central Railroads. Let the bulk of refining be done in the Oil Regions and these roads were in danger of losing a profitable branch of business. This situation in regard to the oil traffic was really more serious now than in 1868 when General Devereux had first given the Standard a rebate. Then it was that the Pennsylvania, through its lusty ally the Empire Transportation Company, was making the chief fight to secure a "patent right on oil transportation." The Erie was now becoming as aggressive a competitor. Gould and Fisk had gone into the fight with the vigour and the utter unscrupulousness which characterised all their dealings. They were allying themselves with the Pennsylvania Transportation Company, the only large rival pipe-line system which the Empire had. They were putting up a refinery near Jersey City, and they were taking advantage shrewdly of all the speculative features of the new business.

As competition grew between the roads, they grew more reckless in granting rebates, the refiners more insistent in demanding them. By 1871 things had come to such a pass in the business that every refiner suspected his neighbour to be getting better rates than he. The result was that the freight agents were constantly beset for rebates, and that the large shippers were generally getting them on the ground of the quantity of oil they controlled. Indeed it was evident that the

W. G. WARDEN

Secretary of the South Improvement Company.

PETER H. WATSON

President of the South Improvement Company.

CHARLES LOCKHART

A member of the South Improvement Company, and later of the Standard Oil Company. At his death in 1904 the oldest living oil operator.

HENRY M. FLAGLER IN 1882

Active partner of John D. Rockefeller in the oil business since 1867. Officer of the Standard Oil Company since its organization in 1870.

rebate being admitted, the only way in which it could be adjusted with a show of fairness was to grade it according to the size of the shipment.

Under these conditions of competition it was certain that the New York Central system must work if it was to keep its great oil freight, and the general freight agent of the Lake Shore road began to give the question special attention. This man was Peter H. Watson. Mr. Watson was an able patent lawyer who served under the strenuous Stanton as an Assistant-Secretary of War, and served well. After the war he had been made general freight agent of the Lake Shore and Michigan Southern Railroad, and later president of the branch of that road which ran into the Oil Regions. He had oil interests principally at Franklin, Pennsylvania, and was well known to all oil men. He was a business intimate of Mr. Rockefeller and a warm friend of Horace F. Clark, the son-in-law of W. H. Vanderbilt, at that time president of the Lake Shore and Michigan Southern Railroad. As the Standard Oil Company was the largest shipper in Cleveland and had already received the special favour from the Lake Shore which General Devereux describes, it was natural that Mr. Watson should consult frequently with Mr. Rockefeller on the question of holding and increasing his oil freight. It was equally natural, too, that Mr. Rockefeller should use his influence with Mr. Watson to strengthen the theory so important to his rapid growth—the theory that the biggest shipper should have the best rate.

Two other towns shared Cleveland's fear of the rise of the Oil Regions as a refining centre, and they were Pittsburg and Philadelphia, and Mr. Rockefeller and Mr. Watson found in certain refiners of these places a strong sympathy with any plan which looked to holding the region in check. But while the menace in their geographical positions was the first ground of sympathy between these gentlemen, something more than local troubles occupied them. This was the condition of the refining business as a whole. It was unsatisfactory in many particulars. First, it was overdone. The great profits on refined oil and the growing demand for it had naturally caused a great number to rush into its manufacture. There was at this time a refining capacity of three barrels to every one produced. To be sure, few if any of these plants expected to run the year around. Then, as to-day, there were nearly always some stills in even the most prosperous works shut down. But after making a fair allowance for this fact there was still a much larger amount of refining actually done than the market demanded. The result was that the price of refined oil was steadily falling. Where Mr. Rockefeller had received on an average 58¾ cents a gallon for the oil he exported in 1865, the year he went into business, in 1870 he received but 26⅜ cents. In 1865 he had a margin of forty-three cents, out of which to pay for transportation, manufacturing, barrelling and marketing and to make his profits. In 1870 he had but 17⅛ cents with which to do all this. To be sure his expenses had fallen enormously between 1865 and 1870, but so had his profits. The multiplication of refiners with the intense competition threatened to cut them down still lower. Naturally Mr. Rockefeller and his friends looked with dismay on this lowering of profits through gaining competition.

Another anxiety of the American refiners was the condition of the export trade. Oil had risen to fourth place in the exports of the United States in the twelve years since its discovery, and every year larger quantities were consumed abroad, but it was crude oil, not refined, which the foreigners were beginning to demand; that is, they had found they could import crude, refine it at home, and sell it cheaper than they could buy American refined. France, to encourage her home refineries, had even put a tax on American refined.

In the fall of 1871, while Mr. Rockefeller and his friends

were occupied with all these questions, certain Pennsylvania refiners, it is not too certain who, brought to them a remarkable scheme, the gist of which was to bring together secretly a large enough body of refiners and shippers to persuade all the railroads handling oil to give to the company formed special rebates on its oil, and drawbacks on that of other people. If they could get such rates it was evident that those outside of their combination could not compete with them long and that they would become eventually the only refiners. They could then limit their output to actual demand, and so keep up prices. This done, they could easily persuade the railroads to transport no crude for exportation, so that the foreigners would be forced to buy American refined. They believed that the price of oil thus exported could easily be advanced fifty per cent. The control of the refining interests would also enable them to fix their own price on crude. As they would be the only buyers and sellers, the speculative character of the business would be done away with. In short, the scheme they worked out put the entire oil business in their hands. It looked as simple to put into operation as it was dazzling in its results. Mr. Flagler has sworn that neither he nor Mr. Rockefeller believed in this scheme.* But when they found that their friend Peter H. Watson, and various Philadelphia and Pittsburg parties who felt as they did about the oil business, believed in it, they went in and began at once to work up a company—secretly. It was evident that a scheme which aimed at concentrating in the hands of one company the business now operated by scores, and which proposed to effect this consolidation through a practice of the railroads which was contrary to the spirit of their charters, although freely indulged in, must be worked with fine discretion if it ever were to be effective.

* See Appendix, Number 4. Testimony of Henry M. Flagler on the South Improvement Company.

The first thing was to get a charter—quietly. At a meeting held in Philadelphia late in the fall of 1871 a friend of one of the gentlemen interested mentioned to him that a certain estate then in liquidation had a charter for sale which gave its owners the right to carry on any kind of business in any country and in any way; that it could be bought for what it would cost to get a charter under the general laws of the state, and that it would be a favour to the heirs to buy it. The opportunity was promptly taken. The name of the charter bought was the "Southern (usually written South) Improvement Company." For a beginning it was as good a name as another, since it said nothing.

With this charter in hand Mr. Rockefeller and Mr. Watson and their associates began to seek converts. In order that their great scheme might not be injured by premature public discussion they asked of each person whom they approached a pledge of secrecy. Two forms of the pledges required before anything was revealed were published later. The first of these, which appeared in the New York Tribune, read as follows:

I, A. B., do faithfully promise upon my honour and faith as a gentleman that I will keep secret all transactions which I may have with the corporation known as the South Improvement Company; that, should I fail to complete any bargains with the said company, all the preliminary conversations shall be kept strictly private; and, finally, that I will not disclose the price for which I dispose of my product, or any other facts which may in any way bring to light the internal workings or organisation of the company. All this I do freely promise.

Signed.......................

Witnessed by......................

A second, published in a history of the "Southern Improvement Company," ran:

The undersigned pledge their solemn words of honour that they will not communicate to any one without permission of Z (name of director of Southern Improvement Company) any information that he may convey to them, or any of them, in relation to the Southern Improvement Company.

....

Witness........................

That the promoters met with encouragement is evident from the fact that, when the corporators came together on January 2, 1872, in Philadelphia, for the first time under their charter, and transferred the company to the stockholders, they claimed to represent in one way or another a large part of the refining interest of the country. At this meeting 1,100 shares of the stock of the company, which was divided into 2,000 $100 shares, were subscribed for, and twenty per cent. of their value was paid in. Just who took stock at this meeting the writer has not been able to discover. At the same time a discussion came up as to what refiners were to be allowed to go into the new company. Each of the men represented had friends whom he wanted taken care of, and after considerable discussion it was decided to take in every refinery they could get hold of. This decision was largely due to the railroad men. Mr. Watson had seen them as soon as the plans for the company were formed, and they had all agreed that if they gave the rebates and drawbacks all refineries then existing must be taken in upon the same level. That is, while the incorporators had intended to kill off all but themselves and their friends, the railroads refused to go into a scheme which was going to put anybody out of business—the plan if they went into it must cover the refining trade as it stood. It was enough that it could prevent any one in the future going into the business.

Very soon after this meeting of January 2 the rest of the stock of the South Improvement Company was taken. The complete list of stockholders, with their holdings, was as follows:

William Frew, Philadelphia............................... 10 shares
W. P. Logan, Philadelphia............................... 10 "
John P. Logan, Philadelphia............................. 10 "
Charles Lockhart, Pittsburg............................. 10 "
Richard S. Waring, Pittsburg............................ 10 "

W. G. Warden, Philadelphia	475	shares
O. F. Waring, Pittsburg	475	"
P. H. Watson, Ashtabula, Ohio	100	"
H. M. Flagler, Cleveland	180	"
O. H. Payne, Cleveland	180	"
William Rockefeller, Cleveland	180	"
J. A. Bostwick, New York	180	"
John D. Rockefeller, Cleveland*	180	"

2,000 shares

Mr. Watson was elected president and W. G. Warden of Philadelphia secretary of the new association. It will be noticed that the largest individual holdings in the company were those of W. G. Warden and O. F. Waring, each of whom had 475 shares. The company most heavily interested in the South Improvement Company was the Standard Oil of Cleveland, J. D. Rockefeller, William Rockefeller and H. M. Flagler, all stockholders of that company, each having 180 shares—540 in the company. O. H. Payne and J. A. Bostwick, who soon after became stockholders in the Standard Oil Company, also had each 180 shares, giving Mr. Rockefeller and his associates 900 shares in all.

It has frequently been stated that the South Improvement Company represented the bulk of the oil-refining interests in the country. The incorporators of the company in approaching the railroads assured them that this was so. As a matter of fact, however, the thirteen gentlemen above named, who were the only ones ever holding stock in the concern, did not control over one-tenth of the refining business of the United States in 1872. That business in the aggregate amounted to a daily capacity of about 45,000 barrels—from 45,000 to 50,000, Mr. Warden put it—and the stockholders of the South Im-

* List of stockholders given by W. G. Warden, secretary of the South Improvement Company, to a Congressional Investigating Committee which examined Mr. Warden and Mr. Watson in March and April, 1872.

provement Company owned a combined capacity of not over 4,600 barrels. In assuring the railroads that they controlled the business, they were dealing with their hopes rather than with facts.

The organisation complete, there remained contracts to be made with the railroads. Three systems were to be interested: The Central, which, by its connection with the Lake Shore and Michigan Southern, ran directly into the Oil Regions; the Erie, allied with the Atlantic and Great Western, with a short line likewise tapping the heart of the region; and the Pennsylvania, with the connections known as the Allegheny Valley and Oil Creek Railroad. The persons to be won over were: W. H. Vanderbilt, of the Central; H. F. Clark, president of the Lake Shore and Michigan Southern; Jay Gould, of the Erie; General G. B. McClellan, president of the Atlantic and Great Western; and Tom Scott, of the Pennsylvania. There seems to have been little difficulty in persuading any of these persons to go into the scheme after they had been assured by the leaders that all of the refiners were to be taken in. This was a verbal condition, however, not found in the contracts they signed. This important fact Mr. Warden himself made clear when three months later he was on the witness stand before a committee of Congress appointed to look into the great scheme. "We had considerable discussion with the railroads," Mr. Warden said, "in regard to the matter of rebate on their charges for freight; they did not want to give us a rebate unless it was with the understanding that all the refineries should be brought into the arrangement and placed upon the same level."

Q. You say you made propositions to railroad companies, which they agreed to accept upon the condition that you could include all the refineries?

A. No, sir; I did not say that; I said that was the understanding when we discussed this matter with them; it was no proposition on our part; they discussed it, not in the form of a proposition that the refineries should be all taken in, but it was the intention and resolution of the company from the first that that should be the result; we never had any other purpose in the matter.

Q. In case you could take the refineries all in, the railroads proposed to give you a rebate upon their freight charges?

A. No, sir; it was not put in that form; we were to put the refineries all in upon the same terms; it was the understanding with the railroad companies that we were to have a rebate; there was no rebate given in consideration of our putting the companies all in, but we told them we would do it; the contract with the railroad companies was with us.

Q. But if you did form a company composed of the proprietors of all these refineries, you were to have a rebate upon your freight charges?

A. No; we were to have a rebate anyhow, but were to give all the refineries the privilege of coming in.

Q. You were to have the rebate whether they came in or not?

A. Yes, sir.

*   *   *

"What effect were these arrangements to have upon those who did not come into the combination . . . ?" asked the chairman.

"I do not think we ever took that question up," answered Mr. Warden.

A second objection to making a contract with the company came from Mr. Scott of the Pennsylvania road and Mr. Potts of the Empire Transportation Company. The substance of this objection was that the plan took no account of the oil producer—the man to whom the world owed the business. Mr. Scott was strong in his assertion that they could never succeed unless they took care of the producers. Mr. Warden objected strongly to forming a combination with them. "The interests of the producers were in one sense antagonistic to ours: one as the seller and the other as the buyer. We held in argument that the producers were abundantly able to take care of their own branch of the business if they took care of the quantity produced." So strongly did Mr. Scott argue, however, that finally the members of the South Improvement Company yielded, and a draft of an agreement, to be proposed to the producers, was drawn up in lead-pencil; it was

THOMAS A. SCOTT

The contract of the South Improvement Company with the Pennsylvania Railroad was signed by Mr. Scott, then vice-president of the road.

WILLIAM H. VANDERBILT

The contract of the South Improvement Company with the New York Central was signed by Mr. Vanderbilt, then vice-president of the road.

JAY GOULD

President of the Erie Railroad in 1872. Signer of the contract with the South Improvement Company.

COMMODORE CORNELIUS VANDERBILT

President of the New York Central Railroad when the contract with the South Improvement Company was signed.

never presented. It seems to have been used principally to
quiet Mr. Scott.

The work of persuasion went on swiftly. By the 18th of
January the president of the Pennsylvania road, J. Edgar
Thompson, had put his signature to the contract, and soon
after Mr. Vanderbilt and Mr. Clark signed for the Central
system, and Jay Gould and General McClellan for the Erie.
The contracts to which these gentlemen put their names fixed
gross rates of freight from all *common points,* as the leading
shipping points within the Oil Regions were called, to all
the great refining and shipping centres—New York, Philadelphia, Baltimore, Pittsburg and Cleveland. For example,
the open rate on crude to New York was put at $2.56. On
this price the South Improvement Company was allowed a
rebate of $1.06 for its shipments; but it got not only this
rebate, it was given in cash a like amount on each barrel of
crude shipped by parties outside the combination.

The open rate from Cleveland to New York was two dollars,
and fifty cents of this was turned over to the South Improvement Company, which at the same time received a rebate
enabling it to ship for $1.50. Again, an independent refiner
in Cleveland paid eighty cents a barrel to get his crude from
the Oil Regions to his works, and the railroad sent forty cents
of this money to the South Improvement Company. At the
same time it cost the Cleveland refiner in the combination but
forty cents to get his crude oil. Like drawbacks and rebates
were given for all points—Pittsburg, Philadelphia, Boston
and Baltimore.

An interesting provision in the contracts was that full way-
bills of all petroleum shipped over the roads should each day
be sent to the South Improvement Company. This, of course,
gave them knowledge of just who was doing business outside
of their company—of how much business he was doing, and
with whom he was doing it. Not only were they to have full

knowledge of the business of all shippers—they were to have access to all books of the railroads.

The parties to the contracts agreed that if anybody appeared in the business offering an equal amount of transportation, and having equal facilities for doing business with the South Improvement Company, the railroads might give them equal advantages in drawbacks and rebates, but to make such a miscarriage of the scheme doubly improbable each railroad was bound to co-operate as "far as it legally might to maintain the business of the South Improvement Company against injury by competition, and lower or raise the gross rates of transportation for such times and to such extent as might be necessary to overcome the competition. The rebates and drawbacks to be varied *pari passu* with the gross rates." *

The reason given by the railroads in the contract for granting these extraordinary privileges was that the "magnitude and extent of the business and operations" purposed to be carried on by the South Improvement Company would greatly promote the interest of the railroads and make it desirable for them to encourage their undertaking. The evident advantages received by the railroad were a regular amount of freight,— the Pennsylvania was to have forty-five per cent. of the East-bound shipments, the Erie and Central each 27½ per cent., while West-bound freight was to be divided equally between them—fixed rates, and freedom from the system of cutting which they had all found so harassing and disastrous. That is, the South Improvement Company, which was to include the entire refining capacity of the company, was to act as the evener of the oil business.†

It was on the second of January, 1872, that the organisation

* Article Fourth: Contract between the South Improvement Company and the Pennsylvania Railroad Company, January 18, 1872.

† See Appendix, Number 5. Contract between the South Improvement Company and the Pennsylvania Railroad Company. Dated January 18, 1872.

of the South Improvement Company was completed. The day before the Standard Oil Company of Cleveland increased its capital from $1,000,000 to $2,500,000, "all the stockholders of the company being present and voting therefor." * These stockholders were greater by five than in 1870, the names of O. B. Jennings, Benjamin Brewster, Truman P. Handy, Amasa Stone, and Stillman Witt having been added. The last three were officers and stockholders in one or more of the railroads centring in Cleveland. Three weeks after this increase of capital Mr. Rockefeller had the charter and contracts of the South Improvement Company in hand, and was ready to see what they would do in helping him carry out his idea of wholesale combination in Cleveland. There were at that time some twenty-six refineries in the town—some of them very large plants. All of them were feeling more or less the discouraging effects of the last three or four years of railroad discriminations in favour of the Standard Oil Company. To the owners of these refineries Mr. Rockefeller now went one by one, and explained the South Improvement Company. "You see," he told them, "this scheme is bound to work. It means an absolute control by us of the oil business. There is no chance for anyone outside. But we are going to give everybody a chance to come in. You are to turn over your refinery to my appraisers, and I will give you Standard Oil Company stock or cash, as you prefer, for the value we put upon it. I advise you to take the stock. It will be for your good." Certain refiners objected. They did not want to sell. They did want to keep and manage their business. Mr. Rockefeller was regretful, but firm. It was useless to resist, he told the hesitating; they would certainly be crushed if they did not accept his offer, and he pointed out in detail, and with gentleness, how beneficent the scheme really was—preventing the creek

* See Appendix, Number 6. Standard Oil Company's application for increase of capital stock to $2,500,000 in 1872.

refiners from destroying Cleveland, ending competition, keeping up the price of refined oil, and eliminating speculation. Really a wonderful contrivance for the good of the oil business.

That such was Mr. Rockefeller's argument is proved by abundant testimony from different individuals who succumbed to the pressure. Mr. Rockefeller's own brother, Frank Rockefeller, gave most definite evidence on this point in 1876 when he and others were trying to interest Congress in a law regulating interstate commerce.

"We had in Cleveland at one time about thirty establishments, but the South Improvement Company was formed, and the Cleveland companies were told that if they didn't sell their property to them it would be valueless, that there was a combination of railroad and oil men, that they would buy all they could, and that all they didn't buy would be totally valueless, because they would be unable to compete with the South Improvement Company, and the result was that out of thirty there were only four or five that didn't sell."

"From whom was that information received?" asked the examiner.

"From the officers of the Standard Oil Company. They made no bones about it at all. They said: 'If you don't sell your property to us it will be valueless, because we have got advantages with the railroads.'"

"Have you heard those gentlemen say what you have stated?" Frank Rockefeller was asked.

"I have heard Rockefeller and Flagler say so," he answered.

W. H. Doane, whose evidence on the first rebates granted to the Cleveland trade we have already quoted, told the Congressional committee which a few months after Mr. Rockefeller's great coup tried to find out what had happened in

Cleveland: "The refineries are all bought up by the Standard Oil works; they were forced to sell; the railroads had put up the rates and it scared them. Men came to me and told me they could not continue their business; they became frightened and disposed of their property." Mr. Doane's own business, that of a crude oil shipper, was entirely ruined, all of his customers but one having sold.

To this same committee Mr. Alexander, of Alexander, Scofield and Company, gave his reason for selling:

"There was a pressure brought to bear upon my mind, and upon almost all citizens of Cleveland engaged in the oil business, to the effect that unless we went into the South Improvement Company we were virtually killed as refiners; that if we did not sell out we should be crushed out. My partner, Mr. Hewitt, had some negotiations with parties connected with the South Improvement Company, and they gave us to understand, at least my partner so represented to me, that we should be crushed out if we did not go into that arrangement. He wanted me to see the parties myself; but I said to him that I would not have any dealings with certain parties who were in that company for any purpose, and I never did. We sold at a sacrifice, and we were obliged to. There was only one buyer in the market, and we had to sell on their terms or be crushed out, as it was represented to us. It was stated that they had a contract with railroads by which they could run us into the ground if they pleased. After learning what the arrangements were I felt as if, rather than fight such a monopoly, I would withdraw from the business, even at a sacrifice. I think we received about forty or forty-five cents on the dollar on the valuation which we placed upon our refinery. We had spent over $50,000 on our works during the past year, which was nearly all that we received. We had paid out $60,000 or $70,000 before that; we considered our works at their cash value worth seventy-five per cent. of their cost. According to our valuation our establishment was worth $150,000, and we sold it for about $65,000, which was about forty or forty-five per cent. of its value. We sold. to one of the members, as I suppose, of the South Improvement Company, Mr. Rockefeller; he is a director in that company; it was sold in name to the Standard Oil Company, of Cleveland, but the arrangements were, as I understand it, that they were to put it into the South Improvement Company. I am stating what my partner told me; he did all the business; his statement was that all these works were to be merged into the South Improvement Company. I never talked with any members of the South Improvement Company myself on the subject; I declined to have anything to do with them."

Mr. Hewitt, the partner who Mr. Alexander says carried on the negotiations for the sale of the business, appeared before an investigating committee of the New York State Senate in 1879 and gave his recollections of what happened. According to his story the entire oil trade in Cleveland became paralysed when it became known that the South Improvement Company had "grappled the entire transportation of oil from the West to the seaboard." Mr. Hewitt went to see the freight agents of the various roads; he called on W. H. Vanderbilt, but from no one did he get any encouragement. Then he saw Peter H. Watson of the Lake Shore Railroad, the president of the company which was frightening the trade. "Watson was non-committal," said Mr. Hewitt. "I got no satisfaction except, 'You better sell—you better get clear—better sell out—no help for it.'" After a little time Mr. Hewitt concluded with his partners that there was indeed "no help for it," and he went to see Mr. Rockefeller, who offered him fifty cents on the dollar on the constructive account. The offer was accepted. There was nothing else to do, the firm seems to have concluded. When they came to transfer the property Mr. Rockefeller urged Mr. Hewitt to take stock in the new concern. "He told me," said Mr. Hewitt, "that it would be sufficient to take care of my family for all time, what I represented there, and asking for a reason, he made this expression, I remember: '*I have ways of making money that you know nothing of.*'"

A few of the refiners contested before surrendering. Among these was Robert Hanna, an uncle of Mark Hanna, of the firm of Hanna, Baslington and Company. Mr. Hanna had been refining since July, 1869. According to his own sworn statement he had made money, fully sixty per cent. on his investment the first year, and after that thirty per cent. Some time in February, 1872, the Standard Oil Company asked an interview with him and his associates. They wanted to buy his works, they said. "But we don't want to sell," objected Mr. Hanna. "You can never make any more money, in my judgment," said Mr. Rockefeller. "You can't compete with the Standard. We have all the large refineries now. If you refuse to sell, it will end in your being crushed." Hanna and Baslington were not satisfied. They went to see Mr. Watson, president of the South Improvement Company and an officer of the Lake Shore, and General Devereux, manager of the Lake Shore road. They were told that the Standard had special rates; that it was useless to try to compete with them. General Devereux explained to the gentlemen that the privileges granted the Standard were the legitimate and necessary advantage of the larger shipper over the•smaller, and that if Hanna, Baslington and Company could give the road as large a quantity of oil as the Standard did, with the same regularity, they could have the same rate. General Devereux says they "recognised the propriety" of his excuse. They certainly recognised its authority. They say that they were satisfied they could no longer get rates to and from Cleveland which would enable them to live, and "reluctantly" sold out. It must have been reluctantly, for they had paid $75,000 for their works, and had made thirty per cent. a year on an average on their investment, and the Standard appraiser allowed them $45,000. "Truly and really less than one-half of what they were absolutely worth, with a fair and honest competition in the lines of transportation," said Mr. Hanna, eight years later, in an affidavit.*

Under the combined threat and persuasion of the Standard, armed with the South Improvement Company scheme, almost the entire independent oil interest of Cleveland collapsed in three months' time. Of the twenty-six refineries, at least twenty-one sold out. From a capacity of probably not over 1,500 barrels of crude a day, the Standard Oil Company rose

* See Appendix, Number 7. Affidavits of George O. Baslington.

[67]

in three months' time to one of 10,000 barrels. By this manœuvre it became master of over one-fifth of the refining capacity of the United States.* Its next individual competitor was Sone and Fleming, of New York, whose capacity was 1,700 barrels. The Standard had a greater capacity than the entire Oil Creek Regions, greater than the combined New York refiners. The transaction by which it acquired this power was so stealthy that not even the best informed newspaper men of Cleveland knew what went on. It had all been accomplished in accordance with one of Mr. Rockefeller's chief business principles—"Silence is golden."

While Mr. Rockefeller was working out the "good of the oil business" in Cleveland, his associates were busy at other points. Charles Lockhart in Pittsburg and W. G. Warden in Philadelphia were particularly active, though neither of them accomplished any such sweeping benefaction as Mr. Rockefeller had. It was now evident what the stockholders of the South Improvement Company meant when they assured the railroads that all the refiners were to go into the scheme, that, as Mr. Warden said, they "never had any other purpose in the matter!" A little more time and the great scheme would be an accomplished fact. And then there fell in its path two of

---

*In 1872 the refining capacity of the United States was as follows, according to Henry's "Early and Later History of Petroleum":

	Barrels
Oil Regions	9,231
New York	9,790
Cleveland	12,732
Pittsburg	6,090
Philadelphia	2,061
Baltimore	1,098
Boston	3,500
Erie	1,168
Other Points	901
Total	46,571

those never-to-be-foreseen human elements which so often block great manœuvres. The first was born of a man's anger. The man had learned of the scheme. He wanted to go into it, but the directors were suspicious of him. He had been concerned in speculative enterprises and in dealings with the Erie road which had injured these directors in other ways. They didn't want him to have any of the advantages of their great enterprise. When convinced that he could not share in the deal, he took his revenge by telling people in the Oil Regions what was going on. At first the Oil Regions refused to believe, but in a few days another slip born of human weakness came in to prove the rumour true. The schedule of rates agreed upon by the South Improvement Company and the railroads had been sent to the freight agent of the Lake Shore Railroad, but no order had been given to put them in force. The freight agent had a son on his death-bed. Distracted by his sorrow, he left his office in charge of subordinates, but neglected to tell them that the new schedules on his desk were a secret compact, whose effectiveness depended upon their being held until all was complete. On February 26, the subordinates, ignorant of the nature of the rates, put them into effect. The independent oil men heard with amazement that freight rates had been put up nearly 100 per cent. They needed no other proof of the truth of the rumours of conspiracy which were circulating. It now remained to be seen whether the Oil Regions would submit to the South Improvement Company as Cleveland had to the Standard Oil Company.

CHAPTER THREE

THE OIL WAR OF 1872

IT was not until after the middle of February, 1872, that the people of the Oil Regions heard anything of the plan which was being worked out for their "good." Then an uneasy rumour began running up and down the creek. Freight rates were going up. Now an advance in a man's freight bill may ruin his business; more, it may mean the ruin of a region. Rumour said that the new rate meant just this; that is, that it more than covered the margin of profit in any branch of the oil business. The railroads were not going to apply the proposed tariffs to everybody. They had agreed to give to a company unheard of until now—the South Improvement Company—a special rate considerably lower than the new open rate. It was only a rumour and many people discredited it. *Why* should the railroads ruin the Oil Regions to build up a company of outsiders?

But facts began to be reported. Mr. Doane, the Cleveland

shipper already quoted, told how suddenly on the 22d of February, without notice, his rate from the Oil Regions to Cleveland was put up from thirty-five cents a barrel to sixty-five cents, an advance of twenty-four dollars on a carload.* Mr. Josiah Lombard of the New York refining firm of Ayres, Lombard and Company was buying oil for his company at Oil City. Their refinery was running about 12,000 barrels a month. On the 19th of February the rate from Oil City to Buffalo, which had been forty cents a barrel, was raised to sixty-five cents, and a few days later the rate from Warren to New York was raised from eighty-seven cents to $2.14. Mr. Lombard was not aware of this change until his house in New York reported to him that the bills for freight were so heavy that they could not afford to ship and wanted to know what was the matter.†

On the morning of February 26, 1872, the oil men read in their morning papers that the rise which had been threatening had come; moreover, that all members of the South Improvement Company were exempt from the advance. At the news all oildom rushed into the streets. Nobody waited to find out his neighbour's opinion. On every lip there was but one word, and that was "conspiracy." In the vernacular of the region, it was evident that "a torpedo was filling for that scheme."

In twenty-four hours after the announcement of the increase in freight rates a mass-meeting of 3,000 excited, gesticulating oil men was gathered in the opera house at Titusville. Producers, brokers, refiners, drillers, pumpers were in the crowd. Their temper was shown by the mottoes on the banners which they carried: "Down with the conspirators"— "No compromise"—"Don't give up the ship!" Three days

*A History of the Rise and Fall of the South Improvement Company. Testimony of W. H. Doane, page 45.

†A History of the Rise and Fall of the South Improvement Company. Testimony of Josiah Lombard, page 57.

later as large a meeting was held at Oil City, its temper more warlike if possible; and so it went. They organised a Petroleum Producers' Union,* pledged themselves to reduce their production by starting no new wells for sixty days and by shutting down on Sundays, to sell no oil to any person known to be in the South Improvement Company, but to support the creek refiners and those elsewhere who had refused to go into the combination, to boycott the offending railroads, and to build lines which they would own and control themselves. They sent a committee to the Legislature asking that the charter of the South Improvement Company be repealed, and another to Congress demanding an investigation of the whole business on the ground that it was an interference with trade. They ordered that a history of the conspiracy, giving the names of the conspirators and the designs of the company, should be prepared, and 30,000 copies sent to "judges of all courts, senators of the United States, members of Congress and of State Legislatures, and to all railroad men and prominent business men of the country, *to the end that enemies of the freedom of trade may be known and shunned by all honest men.*"

They prepared a petition ninety-three feet long praying for a free pipe-line bill, something which they had long wanted, but which, so far, the Pennsylvania Railroad had prevented their getting, and sent it by a committee to the Legislature; and for days they kept 1,000 men ready to march on Harrisburg at a moment's notice if the Legislature showed signs of refusing their demands. In short, for weeks the whole body of oil men abandoned regular business and surged from town to town intent on destroying the "Monster," the "Forty Thieves," the "Great Anaconda," as they called the mysterious South Improvement Company. Curiously enough, it

* See Appendix, Number 8. Organisation of the Petroleum Producers' Union of 1872.

was chiefly against the combination which had secured the discrimination from the railroads—not the railroads which had granted it—that their fury was directed. They expected nothing but robbery from the railroads, they said. They were used to that; but they would not endure it from men in their own business.

When they began the fight the mass of the oil men knew nothing more of the South Improvement Company than its name and the fact that it had secured from the railroads advantages in rates which were bound to ruin all independent refiners of oil and to put all producers at its mercy. Their tempers were not improved by the discovery that it was a secret organisation, and that it had been at work under their very eyes for some weeks without their knowing it. At the first public meeting this fact came out, leading refiners of the region relating their experience with the "Anaconda." According to one of these gentlemen, J. D. Archbold— the same who afterward became vice-president of the Standard Oil Company, which office he now holds—he and his partners had heard of the scheme some months before. Alarmed by the rumour, a committee of independent refiners had attempted to investigate, but could learn nothing until they had given a promise not to reveal what was told them. When convinced that a company had been formed actually strong enough to force or persuade the railroads to give it special rates and refuse them to all persons outside, Mr. Archbold said that he and his colleagues had gone to the railway kings to remonstrate, but all to no effect. The South Improvement Company by some means had convinced the railroads that they owned the Oil Regions, producers and refiners both, and that hereafter no oil of any account would be shipped except as they shipped it. Mr. Archbold and his partners had been asked to join the company, but had refused, declaring that the whole business was iniquitous,

[73]

that they would fight it to the end, and that in their fight they would have the backing of the oil men as a whole. They excused their silence up to this time by citing the pledge * exacted from them before they were informed of the extent and nature of the South Improvement Company.

Naturally the burning question throughout the Oil Regions, convinced as it was of the iniquity of the scheme, was, Who are the conspirators? Whether the gentlemen concerned regarded themselves in the light of "conspirators" or not, they seem from the first to have realised that it would be discreet not to be identified publicly with the scheme, and to have allowed one name alone to appear in all signed negotiations. This was the name of the president, Peter H. Watson. However anxious the members of the South Improvement Company were that Mr. Watson should combine the honours of president with the trials of scapegoat, it was impossible to keep their names concealed. The Oil City Derrick, at that time one of the most vigorous, witty, and daring newspapers in the country, began a black list at the head of its editorial columns the day after the raise in freight was announced, and it kept it there until it was believed complete. It stood finally as it appears on the opposite page.

This list was not exact, but it was enough to go on, and the oil blockade, to which the Petroleum Producers' Union had pledged itself, was now enforced against the firms listed, and as far as possible against the railroads. All of these refineries had their buyers on the creek, and although several of them were young men generally liked for their personal and business qualities, no mercy was shown them. They were refused oil by everybody, though they offered from seventy-five cents to a dollar more than the market price. They were ordered at one meeting "to desist from their nefarious business or leave the Oil Region," and when they

* See page 56.

JOHN D. ARCHBOLD IN 1872

Now vice-president of the Standard Oil Company. Mr. Archbold, whose home, in 1872, was in Titusville, Pennsylvania, although one of the youngest refiners of the Creek, was one of the most active and efficient in breaking up the South Improvement Company.

declined they were invited to resign from the oil exchanges of which they were members. So strictly, indeed, was the blockade enforced that in Cleveland the refineries were closed and meetings for the relief of the workmen were held. In spite of the excitement there was little vandalism, the

THE BLACK LIST.

P. H. WATSON, PRES. S. I. CO.

Charles Lockhart,

W. P. Logan,

R. S. Waring,

A. W. Bostwick,

W. G. Warden,

John Rockefeller,

Amasa Stone.

These seven are given as the Directors of the Southern Improvement Company. They are refiners or merchants of petroleum

Atlantic & Gt. Western Railway.

L. S. & M. S. Railway.

Philadelphia & Erie Railway.

Pennsylvania Central Railway

New York Central Railway.

Erie Railway.

Behold "The Anaconda" in all his hideous deformity!

only violence at the opening of the war being at Franklin, where a quantity of the oil belonging to Mr. Watson was run on the ground.

The sudden uprising of the Oil Regions against the South Improvement Company did not alarm its members at first. The excitement would die out, they told one another. All that they needed to do was to keep quiet and stay out of the oil country. But the excitement did not die out. Indeed, with every day it became more intense and more wide-spread. When Mr. Watson's tanks were tapped he began to protest in letters to a friend, F. W. Mitchell, a prominent banker and oil man of Franklin. The company was misunderstood, he complained. "Have a committee of leading producers appointed," he wrote, "and we will show that the contracts with the railroads are as favourable to the producing as to other interests; that the much-denounced rebate will enhance the price of oil at the wells, and that our entire plan in operation and effect will promote every legitimate American interest in the oil trade." Mr. Mitchell urged Mr. Watson to come openly to the Oil Regions and meet the producers as a body. A mass-meeting was never a "deliberative body," Mr. Watson replied, but if a few of the leading oil men would go to Albany or New York, or any place favourable to calm investigation and deliberation, and therefore outside of the atmosphere of excitement which enveloped the oil country, he would see them. These letters were read to the producers, and a motion to appoint a committee was made. It was received with protests and jeers. Mr. Watson was afraid to come to the Oil Regions, they said. The letters were not addressed to the association, they were private—an insult to the body. "We are lowering our dignity to treat with this man Watson," declared one man. "He is free to come to these meetings if he wants to." "What is there to negotiate about?" asked another. "To open a negotiation is to concede that we are wrong. Can we go halves with these middlemen in their swindle?" "He has set a trap for us," declared another. "We cannot treat with him without guilt," and the motion was voted down.

The stopping of the oil supply finally forced the South Improvement Company to recognise the Producers' Union officially by asking that a committee of the body be appointed to confer with them on a compromise. The producers sent back a pertinent answer. They believed the South Improvement Company meant to monopolise the oil business. If that was so they could not consider a compromise with it. If they were wrong, they would be glad to be enlightened, and they asked for information. First: the charter under which the South Improvement Company was organised. Second: the articles of association. Third: the officers' names. Fourth: the contracts with the railroads which signed them. Fifth: the general plan of management. Until we know these things, the oil men declared, we can no more negotiate with you than we could sit down to negotiate with a burglar as to his privileges in our house.

The Producers' Union did not get the information they asked from the company at that time, but it was not long before they had it, and much more. The committee which they had appointed to write a history of the South Improvement Company reported on March 20, and in April the Congressional Committee appointed at the insistence of the oil men made its investigation. The former report was published broadcast, and is readily accessible to-day. The Congressional Investigation was not published officially, and no trace of its work can now be found in Washington, but while it was going on reports were made in the newspapers of the Oil Regions, and at its close the Producers' Union published in Lancaster, Pennsylvania, a pamphlet called "A History of the Rise and Fall of the South Improvement Company," which contains the full testimony taken by the committee. This pamphlet is rare, the writer never having been able to find a copy save in three or four private collections. The most important part of it is the testimony of Peter H. Watson, the president, and W. G. Warden, the secretary of the South Improvement Company. It was in these documents that the oil men found full justification for the war they were carrying on and for the losses they had caused themselves and others. Nothing, indeed, could have been more damaging to a corporation than the publication of the charter of the South Improvement Company. As its president told the Congressional Investigating Committee, when he was under examination, "this charter was a sort of clothes-horse to hang a scheme upon." As a matter of fact it was a clothes-horse big enough to hang the earth upon. It granted powers practically unlimited. There really was no exaggeration in the summary of its powers made and scattered broadcast by the irate oil men in their "History of the Rise and Fall of the South Improvement Company": *

The South Improvement Company can own, contract, or operate any work, business, or traffic (save only banking); may hold and transfer any kind of property, real or personal; hold and operate on any leased property (oil territory, for instance); make any kind of contract; deal in stock, securities, and funds; loan its credit, guarantee any one's paper; manipulate any industry; may seize upon the lands of other parties for railroading or *any other purpose;* may absorb the improvements, property or franchises of any other company, *ad infinitum;* may fix the fares, tolls, or freights to be charged on lines of transit operated by it, or on any business it gives to *any other company* or line, without limit.

Its capital stock can be expanded or "watered" at liberty; it can change its name and location at pleasure; can go anywhere and do almost anything. It is not a Pennsylvania corporation only; it can, so far as these enactments are valid, or are confirmed by other Legislatures, operate in any state or territory; its directors must be only citizens of the United States—not necessarily of Pennsylvania. It is responsible to no one; its stockholders are only liable to the amount of their stock in it; its directors, when wielding all the princely powers of the corporation, are also responsible only to the amount of their stock in it; it may control the business of the continent and hold and transfer millions of property, and yet be rotten to the core. It is responsible to no one; makes no reports of its acts or financial condition; its records and deliberations are secret; its capital illimitable; its object unknown. It can be here to-day, to-morrow away. Its domain is the whole country; its business everything. Now it is petroleum it grasps and monopolises; next year it may be iron, coal, cotton, or breadstuffs. They are landsmen granted perpetual letters of marque to prey upon all commerce everywhere.

When the course of this charter through the Pennsylvania Legislature came to be traced, it was found to be devious

* See Appendix, Number 9. Charter of the South Improvement Company.

and uncertain. The company had been incorporated in 1870, and vested with all the "powers, privileges, duties and obligations" of two earlier companies—the Continental Improvement Company and the Pennsylvania Company, both of which were children of that interesting body known as the "Tom Scott Legislature." The act incorporating the company was never published, the name of the member introducing it was never known, and no votes on it are recorded. The origin of the South Improvement Company has always remained in darkness. It was one of thirteen "improvement" companies chartered in Pennsylvania at about the same time, and enjoying the same commercial *carte blanche*.

Bad as the charter was in appearance, the oil men found that the contracts which the new company had made with the railroads were worse. These contracts advanced the rates of freight from the Oil Regions over 100 per cent.—an advance which more than covered the margin of profit on their business—but it was not the railroad that got the greater part of this advance; it was the South Improvement Company. Not only did it ship its own oil at fully a dollar a barrel cheaper on an average than anybody else could, but it received fully a dollar a barrel "rake-off" on every barrel its competitors shipped. It was computed and admitted by the members of the company who appeared before the investigating committee of Congress that this discrimination would have turned over to them fully $6,000,000 annually on the carrying trade. The railroads expected to receive about one and a half millions more than from the existing rates. That is, an additional cost of about $1.25 a barrel was added to crude oil, and it was computed that this would enable the refiners to advance their wholesale price at least four cents a gallon. It is hardly to be wondered at that when the oil men had before them the full text of these contracts they refused absolutely to accept the repeated assertions of the members of the South Improvement Company that their scheme was intended only for "the good of the oil business." The committee of Congress could not be persuaded to believe it either. "Your success meant the destruction of every refiner who refused for any reason to join your company, or whom you did not care to have in, and it put the producers entirely in your power. It would make a monopoly such as no set of men are fit to handle," the chairman of the committee declared. Of course Mr. Warden, the secretary of the company, protested again and again that they meant to take in all the refiners, but when he had to admit that the contracts with the railroads were not made on this condition, his protestations met with little credence. Besides, there was the damning fact that no refiners had come in except those in Cleveland, and that they with one accord testified that they had yielded to force. Not a single factory in either New York or the Oil Regions was in the combination. The fact that the producers had never been approached in any way looked very bad for the company, too. Mr. Watson affirmed and reaffirmed before the committee that it was the intention of the company to take care of the producers. "It was an essential part of this contract that the producers should join it," he declared. But no such condition was embodied in the contract. It was verbal only, and, besides, it had never been submitted to the producers themselves in any form until after the trouble in the Oil Regions began. The committee, like the oil men, insisted that under the circumstances no such verbal understanding was to be trusted.*

No part of the testimony before the committee made a worse impression than that showing that the chief object of the combination was to put up the price of refined oil to

* See Appendix, Number 10. Draft of contract between the South Improvement Company and producers of petroleum in the valley of the Allegheny and its tributaries. Dated January, 1872.

the consumer, though nobody had denied from the first that this was the purpose. In a circular, intended for private circulation, which appeared in the newspapers about this time explaining the objects of the South Improvement Company, this was made clear:

"The object of this combination of interests," ran the circular, "is understood to be twofold: firstly, to do away, at least in a great measure, with the excessive and undue competition now existing between the refining interest, by reason of there being a far greater refining capacity than is called for or justified by the existing petroleum-consuming requirements of the world; secondly, to avoid the heretofore undue competition between the various railroad companies transporting oil to the seaboard, by fixing a uniform rate of freight, which it is thought can be adhered to by some such arrangement as guaranteeing to each road some such percentages of the profit of the aggregate amount of oil transported, whether the particular line carries it or not. It is also asserted that a prominent feature of the combination will be to limit the production of refined petroleum to such amounts as may serve, in a great measure, to do away with the serious periodical depressions in the article. Is it also to be expected that, desiring to curtail the production of refined petroleum in this country, the railroads will not offer any additional facilities for exportation of the crude article."

A writer in the Oil City Derrick, quoted in the Cleveland Herald, March 2, 1872, said: "The ring pretend that they will make their margin out of the consumers. That is, that they will put refined up to a figure that will enable them to pay well for crude. . . . The consumers are the avowed victims, since they must pay a price which will warrant the ring in going on with their operations. And the producers' security for the price is a mere matter of discretion."

Wherever the members of the company discussed the subject they put forward this object as one sufficient to justify the combination. If refined oil was put up everybody in the trade would make more money. To this end the public ought to be willing to pay more.

When Mr. Warden was under examination by the committee the chairman said to him: "Under your arrangement, the public would have been put to an additional expense of $7,500,000 a year." "What public?" said Mr. Warden. "They would have had to pay it in Europe." "But to keep up the price abroad you would have to keep up the price at home," said the chairman. Mr. Warden conceded the point: "You could not get a better price for that exported without having a better price here," he said.*

Mr. Watson contended that the price could be put up with benefit to the consumer. And when he was asked how, he replied: "By steadying the trade. You will notice what all those familiar with this trade know, that there are very rapid and excessive fluctuations in the oil market; that when these fluctuations take place the retail dealers are always quick to note a rise in price, but very slow to note a fall. Even if two dollars a barrel had been added to the price of oil under a steady trade, I think the price of the retail purchaser would not have been increased. That increased price would only amount to one cent a quart (four cents a gallon), and I think the price would not have been increased to the retail dealer because the fluctuations would have been avoided. That was one object to be accomplished." †

The committee were not convinced, however, that a scheme which began by adding four cents to the price of a gallon of oil could be to the good of the consumer. Nor did anything appear in the contracts which showed how the fluctuations in the price of oil were to be avoided. These fluctuations

* See Appendix, Number 11. Extracts from the testimony of W. G. Warden.
† See Appendix, Number 12. Extracts from the testimony of Peter H. Watson.

were due to the rise and fall in the crude market, and that depended on the amount of crude coming from the ground. The South Improvement Company might assert that they meant to bring the producers into their scheme and persuade them to keep down the amount of production in the same way they meant to keep down refined, so that the price could be kept steadily high, but they had nothing to prove that they were sincere in the intention, nothing to prove that they had thought of the producer seriously until the trouble in the Oil Regions began. It looked very much to the committee as if the real intention of the company was to keep up the price of refined to a certain figure by limiting the output, and that there was nothing to show that it would not go up with crude though it might not go down with it! Under these circumstances it seemed as if a fluctuating market which gave a moderate average was better for the consumer than the steady high price which Mr. Watson thought so good for the public. Thirty-two cents a gallon was the ideal price they had in view, though refined had not sold for that since 1869, the average price in 1870 being 26⅜ and in 1871 24¼. The refiner who in 1871 sold his oil at 24¼ cents a gallon cleared easily fifty-two cents a barrel—a large profit on his investment, —but the refiners in the early stages of this new industry had made much larger profits. It was to perpetuate these early profits that they had gone into the South Improvement Company.

It did not take the full exposition of the objects of the South Improvement Company, brought out by the Congressional Investigating Committee, with the publication of charters and contracts, to convince the country at large that the Oil Regions were right in their opposition. From the first the sympathy of the press and the people were with the oil men. It was evident to everybody that if the railroads had made the contracts as charged (and it daily became more evident they had done so), nothing but an absolute monopoly of the whole oil business by this combination could result. It was robbery, cried the newspapers all over the land. "Under the thin guise of assisting in the development of oil-refining in Pittsburg and Cleveland," said the New York Tribune, "this corporation has simply laid its hand upon the throat of the oil traffic with a demand to 'stand and deliver.'" And if this could be done in the oil business, what was to prevent its being done in any other industry? Why should not a company be formed to control wheat or beef or iron or steel, as well as oil? If the railroads would do this for one company, why not for another? The South Improvement Company, men agreed, was a menace to the free trade of the country. If the oil men yielded now, all industries must suffer from their weakness. The railroads must be taught a lesson as well as would-be monopolists.

The oil men had no thought of yielding. With every day of the war their backbone grew stiffer. The men were calmer, too, for their resistance had found a ground which seemed impregnable to them, and arguments against the South Improvement Company now took the place of denunciations. On all sides men said, This is a transportation question, and now is the time to put an end once and forever to the rebates. The sentiment against discrimination on account of amount of freight or for any other reason had been strong in the country since its beginning, and it now crystallised immediately. The country so buzzed with discussion on the duties of the railroads that reporters sent from the Eastern newspapers commented on it. Nothing was commoner, indeed, on the trains which ran the length of the region and were its real forums, than to hear a man explaining that the railways derived their existence and power from the people, that their charters were contracts with the people, that a fundamental provision of these contracts was that there should be no discriminating in favour of one person or one town, that such a discrimination was a violation of charter, that therefore the South Improvement Company was founded on fraud, and the courts must dissolve it if the railways did not abandon it. The Petroleum Producers' Union which had been formed to grapple with the "Monster" actually demanded interstate regulation, for in a circular sent out to newspapers and boards of trade asking their aid against the conspiracy they included this paragraph: "We urge you to exert all your influence with your representatives in Congress to support such measures offered there as will prohibit for all future time any monopoly of railroads or other transportation companies from laying embargoes upon the trade between states by a system of excessive freights or unjust discrimination against buyers or shippers in any trade by the allowance of rebates or drawbacks to any persons whatever. This is a matter of national importance, and only the most decided action can protect you and us from the scheming strength of these monopolies."

How the whole question appeared to an intelligent oil man, one, too, who had had the courage to resist in the attack on the trade in Cleveland, and who still was master of his own refinery, is shown by the following letter to the Cleveland Herald:

EDS. HERALD: As I understand, the financial success of this South Improvement Company is based upon contracts made with the officers (either individually or otherwise) of all the railroads leading out of the Oil Region, by which they (the South Improvement Company) receive as a draw-back certain excess of freights, not only on every barrel of oil shipped out of the Oil Regions by or to themselves, but also on every barrel of oil shipped out of the Oil Regions by or to other refiners, or dealers, or consumers.

The first advance in freights to Cleveland has already been made, viz.: on crude oil, from forty cents to sixty-five cents per barrel. This seemingly slight advance has already caused one party that I know of to pay an excess of over $2,000. Other firms have paid larger or smaller sums, according to the quantity of oil they were compelled to have. This excess, we suppose, goes directly to swell the profits of the South Improvement Company.

This is only the beginning. The whole extent of the evil that may be done to producers, refiners, dealers and consumers, and to the public generally, if this corporation—or rather combination of corporations—is successful, is so deep and varied and far reaching, that it cannot be fully comprehended and I will not attempt it in detail, but only suggest a few inquiries.

Where will be their limits?

How high will they advance freights?

How low will they force the price of crude?

How high refined?

Will they adopt a liberal policy for producers, or will they destroy their interests and *crush out* the oil production entirely? Will they be liberal with dealers and consumers and adopt uniform rules with steady prices, or will they take advantage of times and circumstances and force ruinous corners upon the trade?

These and many other questions are pertinent, for clearly if they can control the shipment they can control the price of oil, and if they can control the price to the extent of twenty-five cents per barrel, they can control it entirely. If they can control it entirely, where will be their limit? Who will dictate a line of policy to them? And may not one of the greatest and most important industries of this country be destroyed and hundreds of thousands of business men be made bankrupt if this combination is successful and has the disposition to work ruin? I do not say that I think they will work ruin. They undoubtedly will attempt to make all the money they can and will pursue such a policy as in their judgment will bring them the utmost amount of profits, regardless of consequences, but what that policy will be, of course, we can not judge.

It is understood that the parties to this combination excuse themselves and their action before the public by reciting the undoubted facts in the case. They are these: that the refining of oil as a business has been of late and is now overdone; that the capacity for refining petroleum in this country exceeds the production in the ratio of three barrels to one; that the railroads have reduced freights to the lowest extreme, and were even losing money; that refiners, in spite of all their efforts, could not earn their running expenses; that the *special interests of Cleveland* as a refining point were in danger of being lost; and that this great business might go to other points, and the millions of dollars in refining property here be sacrificed, and thousands of men thrown out of employment; that real estate would depreciate, and that many other collateral troubles connected with the loss of this business would follow; and that *now*, by the consummation of the plans of this monopoly, all these evils will be avoided.

In answer to this—assuming that the refining interest of Cleveland is a *unit* in this corporation, that of Pittsburg another, that of New York another, and that of Philadelphia another—it follows that it is immaterial to the stockholders of the "South Improvement Company" whether the oil produced at the Oil Regions is refined by them at their works in Cleveland, or at Pittsburg, or in New York, or in Philadelphia. It would not affect their dividends at all, provided they refined the oil at the cheapest point for them to do so. That place might be Cleveland; it might be Pittsburg, or it might *not* be either of them; but it might be New York or Philadelphia. Therefore, so long as it is for the pecuniary advantage of this combination to refine at Cleveland they may do so, but no longer, and should it be for the interest of the combination to discontinue their works at Cleveland, what would become of the oil-refining interest at this point ? That question everyone can answer. Therefore I see little weight to the argument used that this monopoly is for the benefit of Cleveland. Hence, I do not consider the *special danger* to Cleveland by any means as averted.

But without discussing this position, its advantages or disadvantages, as an oil-refining center—for it has both in a marked degree—on general principles I will assert that the laws of business and manufacturing interests, like the laws of supply and demand, are unchangeable, and that a prosperity such as this monopoly would bring us is a forced prosperity, consequently not permanent, but temporary and fictitious in character, and damaging in its ultimate results; and more than all this, if the refining prosperity of Cleveland could be re-established permanently by means of the success of this monopoly, we could not afford to accept it at the cost proposed, viz., that of enriching ourselves at the expense of those who are weaker, but are in power.

We have just refused to build an opera-house because we should, by using the only means we could command to do so, compromise our morality. How much more emphatically should we refuse to accept any benefits to our city which have their origin in unmitigated fraud! In the opera-house instance just cited the managers use no compulsion, no unwilling man was to be forced by them to buy a ticket and take his chances; but the South Improvement Company force every producer to take a less price for his oil without rendering him an equivalent.

They force every refiner who is in their way to prosecute his business against them as competitors at fearful odds, and perhaps at the expense of a royalty on every barrel; or to sell his works and abandon his business to the South Improvement Company at any paltry price they may dictate.

They also force every consumer of oil on this broad continent, after paying all the legitimate cost of producing, refining, and transportation on oil, to pay them also an additional tribute—for what ? Absolutely nothing.

The railroad companies derive their existence and power to act under charters granted them by the citizens (through their Legislatures) of the several states in which they exist. This charter is a contract made by and between the citizens of the one part and the railroad company on the other, and both parties bind themselves alike to the faithful performance of the conditions of the contract. One of the fundamental provisions of this contract is that there shall be no discrimination shown to any individuals, or body of individuals, as to facilities or privileges of doing business with such railroad company; on the contrary, the railroad company is expressly required in all cases to charge uniform rates for the transportation of freight and passengers.

They must, if desired, carry the freight for A that they do for B, AND ALWAYS AT THE SAME PRICE. Any deviation from this stipulated condition is a wilful and fraudulent violation of their contract. If it is by means of such violations of contracts on the part of the several railroad companies connected with them that the South Improvement Company expects success, then the whole gigantic STRUCTURE IS ESTABLISHED UPON FRAUD AS A BASIS, AND IT OUGHT TO COME DOWN. Very respectfully,

CLEVELAND, OHIO, March 5, 1872. F. M. BACKUS.

The oil men now met the very plausible reasons given by the members of the company for their combination more intelligently than at first. There were grave abuses in the business, they admitted; there was too great refining capacity; but this they argued was a natural development in a new business whose growth had been extraordinary and whose limits were by no means defined. Time and experience would regulate it. Give the refiners open and regular freights, with no favours to any one, and the stronger and better equipped would live, the others die—but give all a chance. In fact, time and energy would regulate all the evils of which they complained if there were fair play.

The oil men were not only encouraged by public opinion and by getting their minds clear on the merits of their case; they were upheld by repeated proofs of aid from all sides; even the women of the region were asking what they could do, and were offering to wear their "black velvet bonnets" all summer if necessary. Solid support came from the independent refiners and shippers in other parts of the country who were offering to stand in with them in their contest. New York was already one of the chief refining centres of

HENRY H. ROGERS IN 1872

Now President of the National Transit Company and a director of the Standard Oil Company. The opposition to the South Improvement Company among the New York refiners was led by Mr. Rogers.

the country, and the South Improvement Company had left it entirely out of its combination. As incensed as the creek itself, the New York interests formed an association, and about the middle of March sent a committee of three, with H. H. Rogers, of Charles Pratt and Company, at its head, to Oil City, to consult with the Producers' Union. Their arrival in the Oil Regions was a matter of great satisfaction. What made the oil men most exultant, however, was their growing belief that the railroads—the crux of the whole scheme—were weakening.

However fair the great scheme may have appeared to the railroad kings in the privacy of the council chamber, it began to look dark as soon as it was dragged into the open, and signs of a scuttle soon appeared. General G. B. McClellan, president of the Atlantic and Great Western, sent to the very first mass-meeting this telegram:

NEW YORK, February 27, 1872.

Neither the Atlantic and Great Western, nor any of its officers, are interested in the South Improvement Company. Of course the policy of the road is to accommodate the petroleum interest.

G. B. McCLELLAN.

A great applause was started, only to be stopped by the hisses of a group whose spokesman read the following:

Contract with South Improvement Company signed by George B. McClellan, president for the Atlantic and Great Western Railroad. I only signed it after it was signed by all the other parties.

JAY GOULD.

The railroads tried in various ways to appease the oil men. They did not enforce the new rates. They had signed the contracts, they declared, only after the South Improvement Company had assured them that all the refineries and producers were to be taken in. Indeed, they seem to have realised within a fortnight that the scheme was doomed, and to have been quite ready to meet cordially a committee of oil men which

[89]

went East to demand that the railroads revoke their contracts with the South Improvement Company. This committee, which was composed of twelve persons, three of them being the New York representatives already mentioned, began its work by an interview with Colonel Scott at the Colonial Hotel in Philadelphia. With evident pride the committee wrote back to the Producers' Union: "Mr. Scott, differing in this respect from the railroad representatives whom we afterwards met, notified us that he would call upon us at our hotel." An interesting account of their interview was given to the Hepburn Committee in 1879 by W. T. Scheide, one of the number:

We saw Mr. Scott on the 18th of March, 1872, in Philadelphia, and he said to us that he was very much surprised to hear of this agitation in the Oil Regions; that the object of the railroads in making this contract with the South Improvement Company was to obtain an evener to pool the freight—pool the oil freights among the different roads; that they had been cutting each other on oil freights for a number of years, and had not made any money out of it, although it was a freight they should have made money from; that they had endeavoured to make an arrangement among themselves, but had always failed; he said that they supposed that the gentlemen representing the South Improvement Company represented the petroleum trade, but as he was now convinced they did not, he would be very glad to make an arrangement with this committee, who undoubtedly did represent the petroleum trade; the committee told him that they could not make any such contract; that they had no legal authority to do so; he said that could be easily fixed, because the Legislature was then in session, and by going to Harrisburg a charter could be obtained in a very few days; the committee still said that they would not agree to any such arrangement, that they did not think the South Improvement Company's contract was a good one, and they were instructed to have it broken, and so they did not feel that they could accept a similar one, even if they had the power.

Leaving Colonel Scott the committee went on to New York, where they stayed for about a week, closely watched by the newspapers, all of which treated the "Oil War" as a national affair. Their first interview of importance in New

York was with Commodore Vanderbilt, who said to them very frankly at the beginning of their talk: "I told Billy (W. H. Vanderbilt) not to have anything to do with that scheme." The committee in its report said that the Commodore fully agreed with them upon the justice of their claims, and frequently asserted his objections to any combination seeking a monopoly of other men's property and interests. He told them that if what they asked was that the railroads should fix a tariff which, while giving them a paying rate, would secure the oil men against drawbacks, rebates, or variations in the tariff, he would willingly co-operate. The Commodore ended his amiable concessions by reading the committee a letter just received from the South Improvement Company offering to co-operate with the producers and refiners or to compromise existing differences. The oil men told the Commodore emphatically that they would not treat with the South Improvement Company or with anyone interested in it nor would they recognise its existence. And this stand they kept throughout their negotiations though repeated efforts were made by the railroad men, particularly those of the Central system, to persuade them to a compromise.

At the meeting with the officials of the Erie and the Atlantic and Great Western the committee was incensed by being offered a contract similar to that of the South Improvement Company—on consideration that the original be allowed to stand. It seemed impossible to the railroad men that the oil men really meant what they said and would make no terms save on the basis of no discriminations of any kind to anybody. They evidently believed that if the committee had a chance to sign a contract as profitable as that of the South Improvement Company, all their fair talk of "fair play"—"the duty of the common carrier"—"equal chance to all in transportation"—would at once evaporate. They failed utterly at first to comprehend that the Oil War of 1872 was an uprising against an injustice, and that the moral wrong of the thing had taken so deep a hold of the oil country that the people as a whole had combined to restore right. General McClellan of the Atlantic and Great Western and Mr. Diven, one of the Erie's directors, were the only ones who gave the committee any support in their position.

The final all-important conference with the railroad men was held on March 25, at the Erie offices. Horace Clark, president of the Lake Shore and Michigan Southern Railroad, was chairman of this meeting, and, according to H. H. Rogers' testimony before the Hepburn Committee, in 1879, there were present, besides the oil men, Colonel Scott, General McClellan, Director Diven, William H. Vanderbilt, Mr. Stebbins, and George Hall. The meeting had not been long in session before Mr. Watson, president of the South Improvement Company, and John D. Rockefeller presented themselves for admission. Up to this time Mr. Rockefeller had kept well out of sight in the affair. He had given no interviews, offered no explanations. He had allowed the president of the company to wrestle with the excitement in his own way, but things were now in such critical shape that he came forward in a last attempt to save the organisation by which he had been able to concentrate in his own hands the refining interests of Cleveland. With Mr. Watson he knocked for admission to the council going on in the Erie offices. The oil men flatly refused to let them in. A dramatic scene followed, Mr. Clark, the chairman, protesting in agitated tones against shutting out his "life-long friend, Watson." The oil men were obdurate. They would have nothing to do with anybody concerned with the South Improvement Company. So determined were they that although Mr. Watson came in he was obliged at once to withdraw. A Times reporter who witnessed the little scene between the two supporters of the tottering company after its president was turned out of the meeting

[92]

remarked sympathetically that Mr. Rockefeller soon went away, "looking pretty blue."

The acquiescence of the "railroad kings" in the refusal of the oil men to recognise representatives of the South Improvement Company was followed by an unwilling promise to break the contracts with the company. Another strong effort was made to persuade the independents to make the same contracts on condition that they shipped as much oil, but they would not hear of it. They demanded open rates, with no rebates to anyone. Horace Clark and W. H. Vanderbilt particularly stuck for this arrangement. Their opposition to the oil men's position was so strong that the latter in reporting it to the Union said: "We feel it proper to say that we are in no wise indebted to these gentlemen for any courtesy or consideration received at their hands." So well did the committee fight its battle and so strongly were they supported by the New York refiners that the railroads were finally obliged to consent to revoke the contracts and to make a new one embodying the views of the Oil Regions. The contract finally signed at this meeting by H. F. Clark for the Lake Shore road, O. H. P. Archer for the Erie, W. H. Vanderbilt for the Central, George B. McClellan for the Atlantic and Great Western, and Thomas A. Scott for the Pennsylvania, agreed that all shipping of oil should be made on "a basis of perfect equality to all shippers, producers, and refiners, and that no rebates, drawbacks, or other arrangements of any character shall be made or allowed that will give any party the slightest difference in rates or discriminations of any character whatever." * It was also agreed that the rates should not be liable to change either for increase or decrease without first giving William Hasson, president of the Producers' Union, at least ninety days' notice.

The same rate was put on refined oil from Cleveland, Pitts-

* See Appendix, Number 13. Contract of March 25, 1872.

burg and the creek, to Eastern shipping points; that is, Mr. Rockefeller could send his oil from Cleveland to New York at $1.50 per barrel; so could his associates in Pittsburg; and this was what it cost the refiner on the creek; but the latter had this advantage: he was at the wells. Mr. Rockefeller and his Pittsburg allies were miles away, and it cost them, by the new contract, fifty cents to get a barrel of crude to their works. The Oil Regions meant that geographical position should count, that the advantages Mr. Rockefeller had by his command of the Western market and by his access to a cheap Eastward waterway should be considered as well as their own position beside the raw product.

This contract was the first effective thrust into the great bubble. Others followed in quick succession. On the 28th the railroads officially annulled their contracts with the company. About the same time the Pennsylvania Legislature repealed the charter. On March 30 the committee of oil men sent to Washington to be present during the Congressional Investigation, now about to begin, spent an hour with President Grant. They wired home that on their departure he said: "Gentlemen, I have noticed the progress of monopolies, and have long been convinced that the national ·government would have to interfere and protect the people against them." The President and the members of Congress of both parties continued to show interest in the investigation, and there was little or no dissent from the final judgment of the committee, given early in May, that the South Improvement Company was the "most gigantic and daring conspiracy" a free country had ever seen. This decision finished the work. The "Monster" was slain, the Oil Regions proclaimed exultantly.

And now came the question, What should they do about the blockade established against the members of the South Improvement Company? The railroads they had forgiven; should they forgive the members of the South Improvement

Company? This question came up immediately on the repeal of the charter. The first severe test to which their temper was put was early in April, when the Fisher Brothers, a firm of Oil City brokers, sold some 20,000 barrels of oil to the Standard Oil Company. The moment the sale was noised a perfect uproar burst forth. Indignant telegrams came from every direction condemning the brokers. "Betrayal," "infamy," "mercenary achievement," "the most unkindest cut of all," was the gist of them. From New York, Porter and Archbold telegraphed annulling all their contracts with the guilty brokers. The Oil Exchange passed votes of censure, and the Producers' Union turned them out. A few days later it was learned that a dealer on the creek was preparing to ship 5,000 barrels to the same firm. A mob gathered about the cars and refused to let them leave. It was only by stationing a strong guard that the destruction of the oil was prevented.

But something had to be done. The cooler heads argued that the blockade, which had lasted now forty days, and from which the region had of course suffered enormous loss, should be entirely lifted. The objects for which it had been established had been accomplished—that is, the South Improvement Company had been destroyed—now let free trade be established. If anybody wanted to sell to "conspirators," it was his lookout. A long and excited meeting of men from the entire oil country was held at Oil City to discuss the question.

The president of the Petroleum Producers' Union, Captain William Hasson, in anticipation of the meeting, had sent to the officers of all the railroads which had been parties to the South Improvement Company, the following telegram:

OFFICE PETROLEUM PRODUCERS' UNION,
OIL CITY, PENNSYLVANIA, April 4, 1872.

We are informed by parties known as members of the South Improvement Company, now representing the Standard Oil Company, who are in the market overbidding other shippers, that all contracts between the railroad companies and South

Improvement and Standard Companies are cancelled. Will you please give us official notice whether such contracts are cancelled or not? The people in mass-meeting assembled have instructed the executive committee not to sell or ship any oil to these parties until we receive such notice. Please answer at once, as we fear violence and destruction of property.

Signed   WILLIAM HASSON, President.

General McClellan, Horace F. Clark, Thomas A. Scott, and W. H. Vanderbilt all sent emphatic telegrams in reply, asserting that the South Improvement contracts had been cancelled and that their roads had no understanding of any nature in regard to freights with the Standard Oil Company. "The only existing arrangement is with you," telegraphed General McClellan. W. H. Vanderbilt reminded Mr. Hasson that the agreement of March 25, between the railroad companies and the joint committee of producers and refiners, was on a basis of perfect equality for all, and the inference was, how could Mr. Vanderbilt possibly make a special arrangement with the Standard? From the Standard Oil Company the following was received:

CLEVELAND, OHIO, April 8, 1872.

To CAPTAIN WILLIAM HASSON: In answer to your telegram, this company holds no contract with the railroad companies or any of them, or with the South Improvement Company. The contracts between the South Improvement Company and the railroads have been cancelled, and I am informed you have been so advised by telegram. I state unqualifiedly that reports circulated in the Oil Region and elsewhere, that this company, or any member of it, threatened to depress oil, are false.

JOHN D. ROCKEFELLER, President.

After reading all the telegrams the committee submitted its report. The gist of it was that since they had official assurance that the hated contracts were cancelled, and that since they had secured from all the trunk lines a "fair rate of freight, equal to all shippers and producers, great or small, with an abolition of the system of rebates and drawbacks," the time had arrived "to open the channels of trade to all parties desiring to purchase or deal in oil on terms of equality." The

[96]

report was received with "approbation and delight" and put an official end to the "Oil War."

But no number of resolutions could wipe out the memory of the forty days of terrible excitement and loss which the region had suffered. No triumph could stifle the suspicion and the bitterness which had been sown broadcast through the region. Every particle of independent manhood in these men whose very life was independent action had been outraged. Their sense of fair play, the saving force of the region in the days before law and order had been established, had been violated. These were things which could not be forgotten. There henceforth could be no trust in those who had devised a scheme which, the producers believed, was intended to rob them of their property.

It was inevitable that under the pressure of their indignation and resentment some person or persons should be fixed upon as responsible, and should be hated accordingly. Before the lifting of the embargo this responsibility had been fixed. It was the Standard Oil Company of Cleveland, so the Oil Regions decided, which was at the bottom of the business, and the "Mephistopheles of the Cleveland company," as they put it, was John D. Rockefeller. Even the Cleveland Herald acknowledged this popular judgment. "Whether justly or unjustly," the editor wrote, "Cleveland has the odium of having originated the scheme." This opinion gained ground as the days passed. The activity of the president of the Standard in New York, in trying to save the contracts with the railroads, and his constant appearance with Mr. Watson, and the fact brought out by the Congressional Investigation that a larger block of the South Improvement Company's stock was owned in the Standard than in any other firm, strengthened the belief. But what did more than anything else to fix the conviction was what they had learned of the career of the Standard Oil Company in Cleveland. Before the Oil War the company had been known simply as one of several successful firms in that city. It drove close bargains, but it paid promptly, and was considered a desirable customer. Now the Oil Regions learned for the first time of the sudden and phenomenal expansion of the company. Where there had been at the beginning of 1872 twenty-six refining firms in Cleveland, there were but six left. In three months before and during the Oil War the Standard had absorbed twenty plants. It was generally charged by the Cleveland refiners that Mr. Rockefeller had used the South Improvement scheme to persuade or compel his rivals to sell to him. "Why," cried the oil men, "the Standard Oil Company has done already in Cleveland what the South Improvement Company set out to do for the whole country, and it has done it by the same means."

By the time the blockade was raised, another unhappy conviction was fixed on the Oil Regions—the Standard Oil Company meant to carry out the plans of the exploded South Improvement Company. The promoters of the scheme were partly responsible for the report. Under the smart of their defeat they talked rather more freely than their policy of silence justified, and their remarks were quoted widely. Mr. Rockefeller was reported in the Derrick to have said to a prominent oil man of Oil City that the South Improvement Company could work under the charter of the Standard Oil Company, and to have predicted that in less than two months the gentlemen would be glad to join him. The newspapers made much of the following similar story reported by a New York correspondent:

A prominent Cleveland member of what was the South Improvement Company had said within two days: "The business *now* will be done by the Standard Oil Company. We have a rate of freight by water from Cleveland to New York at seventy cents. No man in the trade shall make a dollar this year. We purpose to manipulating the market as to run the price of crude on the creek as low as two and a half. We mean to show the world that the South Improvement Company was organised for business and means business in spite of opposition. The same thing has been said in substance by the leading Philadelphia member."

"The trade here regards the Standard Oil Company as simply taking the place of the South Improvement Company and as being ready at any moment to make the same attempt to control the trade as its progenitors did," said the New York Bulletin about the middle of April. And the Cleveland Herald discussed the situation under the heading, "South Improvement Company *alias* Standard Oil Company." The effect of these reports in the Oil Regions was most disastrous. Their open war became a kind of guerilla opposition. Those who sold oil to the Standard were ostracised, and its president was openly scorned.

If Mr. Rockefeller had been an ordinary man the outburst of popular contempt and suspicion which suddenly poured on his head would have thwarted and crushed him. But he was no ordinary man. He had the powerful imagination to see what might be done with the oil business if it could be centered in his hands—the intelligence to analyse the problem into its elements and to find the key to control. He had the essential element of all great achievement, a steadfastness to a purpose once conceived which nothing can crush. The Oil Regions might rage, call him a conspirator, and all those who sold him oil, traitors; the railroads might withdraw their contracts and the Legislature annul his charter; undisturbed and unresting he kept at his great purpose. Even if his nature had not been such as to forbid him to abandon an enterprise in which he saw promise of vast profits, even if he had not had a mind which, stopped by a wall, burrows under or creeps around, he would nevertheless have been forced to desperate efforts to keep up his business. He had increased his refining capacity in Cleveland to 10,000 barrels on the strength of the South Improvement Company contracts. These contracts were annulled, and in their place was one signed by officials of all the oil-shipping roads refusing rebates to everybody. His geographical position was such that it cost him under these new contracts fifty cents more to get oil from the wells to New York than it did his rivals on the creek. True, he had many counterbalancing advantages—a growing Western market almost entirely in his hands, lake traffic, close proximity to all sorts of accessories to his manufacturing, but this contract put him on a level with his rivals. By his size he should have better terms than they. What did he do?

He got a rebate. Seven years later Mr. Rockefeller's partner, H. M. Flagler, was called before a commission of the Ohio State Legislature appointed to investigate railroads. He was asked for the former contracts between his company and the railroads, and among others he presented one showing that from "the first of April until the middle of November, 1872," their East-bound rate was $1.25, twenty-five cents less than that set by the agreement of March 25th, between the oil men and the railroads.* The discrepancy between the date Mr. Flagler gives for this contract and that of Mr. Vanderbilt's telegram to Mr. Hasson stating that his road had no contract with the Standard Oil Company, April 6, and of Mr. Rockefeller's own telegram stating he had no contracts with the railroads, April 8, the writer is unable to explain. How had Mr. Rockefeller been able to get this rebate? Simply as he had always done—by virtue of the quantity he shipped. He was able to say to Mr. Vanderbilt, I can make a contract to ship sixty car-loads of oil a day over your road—nearly 4,800 barrels; I cannot give this to you regularly unless you will make me a concession; and Mr. Vanderbilt made the concession while he was signing the contract with the oil men. Of course the rate was secret, and Mr. Rockefeller probably understood now, as he had not two months before, how essen-

* See Appendix, Number 14. Testimony of Henry M. Flagler.

tial it was that he keep it secret. His task was more difficult now, for he had an enemy active, clamorous, contemptuous, whose suspicions had reached that acute point where they could believe nothing but evil of him—the producers and independent refiners of the Oil Regions. It was utterly impossible that he should ever silence this enemy, for their points of view were diametrically opposed.

They believed in independent effort—every man for himself and fair play for all. They wanted competition, loved open fight. They considered that all business should be done openly; that the railways were bound as public carriers to give equal rates; that any combination which favoured one firm or one locality at the expense of another was unjust and illegal. This belief long held by many of the oil men had been crystallised by the uprising into a common sentiment. It had become the moral code of the region.

Mr. Rockefeller's point of view was different. He believed that the "good of all" was in a combination which would control the business as the South Improvement Company proposed to control it. Such a combination would end at once all the abuses the business suffered. As rebates and special rates were essential to this control, he favoured them. Of course Mr. Rockefeller must have known that the railroad was a common carrier, and that the common law forbade discrimination. But he knew that the railroads had not obeyed the laws governing them, that they had regularly granted special rates and rebates to those who had large amounts of freight. That is, you were able to bargain with the railroads as you did with a man carrying on a strictly private business depending in no way on a public franchise. Moreover, Mr. Rockefeller probably believed that, in spite of the agreements, if he did not get rebates somebody else would; that they were for the wariest, the shrewdest, the most persistent. If somebody was to get rebates, why not he? This point of view was no uncommon one. Many men held it and felt a sort of scorn, as practical men always do for theorists, when it was contended that the shipper was as wrong in taking rates as the railroads in granting them.

Thus, on one hand there was an exaggerated sense of personal independence, on the other a firm belief in combination; on one hand a determination to root out the vicious system of rebates practised by the railway, on the other a determination to keep it alive and profit by it. Those theories which the body of oil men held as vital and fundamental Mr. Rockefeller and his associates either did not comprehend or were deaf to. This lack of comprehension by many men of what seems to other men to be the most obvious principles of justice is not rare. Many men who are widely known as good, share it. Mr. Rockefeller was "good." There was no more faithful Baptist in Cleveland than he. Every enterprise of that church he had supported liberally from his youth. He gave to its poor. He visited its sick. He wept with its suffering. Moreover, he gave unostentatiously to many outside charities of whose worthiness he was satisfied. He was simple and frugal in his habits. He never went to the theatre, never drank wine. He gave much time to the training of his children, seeking to develop in them his own habits of economy and of charity. Yet he was willing to strain every nerve to obtain for himself special and unjust privileges from the railroads which were bound to ruin every man in the oil business not sharing them with him. He was willing to array himself against the combined better sentiment of a whole industry, to oppose a popular movement aimed at righting an injustice, so revolting to one's sense of fair play as that of railroad discriminations. Religious emotion and sentiments of charity, propriety and self-denial seem to have taken the place in him of notions of justice and regard for the rights of others.

Unhampered, then, by any ethical consideration, undismayed by the clamour of the Oil Regions, believing firmly as ever that relief for the disorders in the oil business lay in combining and controlling the entire refining interest, this man of vast patience and foresight took up his work. That work now was to carry out some kind of a scheme which would limit the output of refined oil. He had put his competitors in Cleveland out of the way. He had secured special privileges in transportation, but there were still too many refineries at work to make it possible to put up the price of oil four cents a gallon. It was certain, too, that no scheme could be worked to do that unless the Oil Regions could be mollified. That now was Mr. Rockefeller's most important business. Just how he began is not known. It is only certain that the day after the newspapers of the Oil Regions printed the report of the Congressional Committee on Commerce denouncing the South Improvement Company as "one of the most gigantic and dangerous conspiracies ever attempted," and declaring that if it had not been checked in time it "would have resulted in the absorption and arbitrary control of trade in all the great interests of the country." * Mr. Rockefeller and several other members of the South Improvement Company appeared in the Oil Regions. They had come, they explained, to present a new plan of co-operation, and to show the oil men that it was to their interest to go into it. Whether they would be able to obtain by persuasion what they had failed to obtain by assault was now an interesting uncertainty.

* The report of the committee of Congress which investigated the South Improvement Company was not made until May 7, over a month after the organisation was destroyed by the cancelling of the contracts with the railroads.

CHAPTER FOUR

"AN UNHOLY ALLIANCE"

ROCKEFELLER AND HIS PARTY NOW PROPOSE AN OPEN INSTEAD OF A SECRET COMBINATION—"THE PITTSBURG PLAN"—THE SCHEME IS NOT APPROVED BY THE OIL REGIONS BECAUSE ITS CHIEF STRENGTH IS THE REBATE—ROCKEFELLER NOT DISCOURAGED—THREE MONTHS LATER BECOMES PRESIDENT OF NATIONAL REFINERS' ASSOCIATION—FOUR-FIFTHS OF REFINING INTEREST OF UNITED STATES WITH HIM—OIL REGIONS AROUSED—PRODUCERS' UNION ORDER DRILLING STOPPED AND A THIRTY DAY SHUT-DOWN TO COUNTERACT FALLING PRICE OF CRUDE—PETROLEUM PRODUCERS' AGENCY FORMED TO ENABLE PRODUCERS TO CONTROL THEIR OWN OIL—ROCKEFELLER OUTGENERALS HIS OPPONENTS AND FORCES A COMBINATION OF REFINERS AND PRODUCERS—PRODUCERS' ASSOCIATION AND PRODUCERS' AGENCY SNUFFED OUT—NATIONAL REFINERS' ASSOCIATION DISBANDS—ROCKEFELLER STEADILY GAINING GROUND.

THE feeling of outrage and resentment against the Standard Oil Company, general in the Oil Regions at the close of the Oil War because of the belief that it intended to carry on the South Improvement Company in some new way, was intensified in the weeks immediately following the outbreak by the knowledge that Mr. Rockefeller had been so enormously benefited by the short-lived concern. Here he was shipping Eastward over one road between 4,000 and 5,000 barrels of refined oil a day—oil wrung from his neighbours by an outrageous conspiracy, men said bitterly. This feeling was still keen when Mr. Rockefeller and several of his colleagues in the South Improvement scheme suddenly, in May, 1873, appeared on the streets of Titusville. The men who had fought him so desperately now stared in amazement at the smiling,

unruffled countenance with which he greeted them. Did
not the man know when he was beaten? Did he not realise
the opinion the Oil Regions held of him? His placid de-
meanour in the very teeth of their violence was discon-
certing.

Not less of a shock was given the country by the knowledge
that Mr. Rockefeller, Mr. Flagler, Mr. Waring and the
other gentlemen in their party were pressing a new alliance,
and that they claimed that their new scheme had none of the
obnoxious features of the defunct South Improvement Company, though it was equally well adapted to work out the
"good of the oil business."

For several days the visiting gentlemen slipped around,
bland and smiling, from street corner to street corner, from
office to office, explaining, expostulating, mollifying. "You
misunderstand our intention," they told the refiners. "It is to
save the business, not to destroy it, that we are come. You
see the disorders competition has wrought in the oil industry.
Let us see what combination will do. Let us make an experiment—that is all. If it does not work, then we can go back to
the old method."

Although Mr. Rockefeller was everywhere, and heard
everything in these days, he rarely talked. "I remember well
how little he said," one of the most aggressively independent
of the Titusville refiners told the writer. "One day several of
us met at the office of one of the refiners, who, I felt pretty
sure, was being persuaded to go into the scheme which they
were talking up. Everybody talked except Mr. Rockefeller.
He sat in a rocking-chair, softly swinging back and forth, his
hands over his face. I got pretty excited when I saw how
those South Improvement men were pulling the wool over
our men's eyes, and making them believe we were all going
to the dogs if there wasn't an immediate combination to put
up the price of refined and prevent new people coming into

the business, and I made a speech which, I guess, was pretty
warlike. Well, right in the middle of it John Rockefeller
stopped rocking and took down his hands and looked at
me. You never saw such eyes. He took me all in, saw just how
much fight he could expect from me, and I knew it, and then
up went his hands and back and forth went his chair."

For fully a week this quiet circulation among the oil men
went on, and then, on May 15 and 16, public meetings
were held in Titusville, at which the new scheme which
they had been advocating was presented publicly. This new
plan, called the "Pittsburg Plan"* from the place of its birth,
had been worked out by the visiting gentlemen before they
came to the Oil Regions. It was a most intelligent and compre-
hensive proposition.

As in the case of the South Improvement scheme, a company
was to be formed to run the refining business of the whole
country, but this company was to be an open instead of a
secret organisation, and all refiners were to be allowed to
become stockholders in it. The owners of the refineries who
went into the combination were then to run them in certain
particulars according to the direction of the board of the
parent company; that is, they were to refine only such an
amount of oil as the board allowed, and they were to keep
up the price for their output as the board indicated. The
buying of crude oil and the arrangements for transportation
were also to remain with the directors. Each stockholder was
to receive dividends whether his plant operated or not. The
"Pittsburg Plan" was presented tentatively. If anything better
could be suggested they would gladly accept it, its advocates
said. "All we want is a practical combination. We are wed
to no particular form."

The first revelation of the public meetings at which the
"Pittsburg Plan" was presented was that in the days Mr.

* See Appendix, Number 15. The Pittsburg Plan.

Rockefeller and his friends had been so diligently shaking hands with the oil men from Titusville to Oil City they had made converts—that they had not entered these open meetings until they had secured the assurance of co-operation in any plan of consolidation which might be effected from some of the ablest refiners and business men of the creek, notably from J. J. Vandergrift of Oil City, and from certain firms of Titusville with which John D. Archbold was connected. All of these persons had fought the South Improvement Company, and they all now declared that if the proposed organisation copied that piratical scheme they would have nothing to do with it, that their allegiance to the plan was based on their conviction that it was fair to all—who went in!—and that it was made necessary by over-refining, underselling, and by the certainty that the railroads could not be trusted to keep their contracts. It was evident that the possible profits and power to be gained by a successful combination had wiped out their resentment against the leaders of the South Improvement Company, and that if they had the assurance, as they must have had, that rebates were a part of the game, they justified themselves by the reflection that somebody was sure to get them, and that it might as well be they as anybody.

The knowledge that a considerable body of the creek refiners had gone over to Mr. Rockefeller awakened a general bitterness among those who remained independent. "Deserters," "ringsters," "monopolists," were the terms applied to them, and the temper of the public meetings, as is evident from the full reports the newspapers of the Oil Region published, became at once uncertain. There were long pauses in the proceedings, everybody fearing to speak. Mr. Rockefeller is not reported as having spoken at all, the brunt of defense and explanation having fallen on Mr. Flagler, Mr. Frew and Mr. Waring. Two or three times the convention wrangled to the point of explosion, and one important refiner,

[107]

M. N. Allen, who was also the editor of the Titusville Courier, one of the best papers in the region, took his hat and left. Before the end of the convention the supporters of combination ought to have felt, if they did not, that they had been a little too eager in pressing an alliance on the Oil Regions so soon after outraging its moral sentiment.

The press and people were making it plain enough, indeed, that they did not trust the persuasive advocates of reform. On every street corner and on every railroad train men reckoned the percentage of interest the stockholders of the South Improvement Company would have in the new combination. It was too great. But what stirred the Oil Region most deeply was its conviction that the rebate system was regarded as the keystone of the new plan. "What are you going to do with the men who prefer to run their own business?" asked a representative of the Oil City Derrick of one of the advocates of the plan. "Go through them," was reported to be his laconic reply. "But how?" "By the co-operation of transportation"—that is, by rebates. Now the Oil Region had been too recently convicted of the sin of the rebate, and had taken too firm a determination to uproot the iniquitous practice to be willing to ally itself with any combination which it suspected of accepting privileges which its neighbours could not get or would not take.

At the very time the association of refiners was under consideration an attempt was made to win over the producers by offering, through their union, to buy all their oil at five dollars a barrel for five years. Oil was four dollars at the time. The producers refused. Such an agreement could only be kept, they said, by an association which was an absolute monopoly, fixing prices of refined to satisfy its own greed. All they wanted of the producer was to be a party to their conspiracy. When they had destroyed his moral force and completed their monopoly they would pay him what they pleased for oil, and the price would not be five dollars! What could he do then? He would be their slave, there would be no other buyer—could be none, since they would control the entire transportation system.

The upshot of the negotiations was that again the advocates of combination had to retire from the Oil Regions defeated. *"Sic semper tyrannis, sic transit gloria* South Improvement Company," sneered the Oil City Derrick, which was given to sprinkling Latin phrases into its forceful and picturesque English. But the Derrick underrated both the man and the principle at which it sneered. A great idea was at work in the commercial world. It had come to them saddled with crime. They now saw nothing in it but the crime. The man who had brought it to them was not only endowed with far vision, he was endowed with an indomitable purpose. He meant to control the oil business. By one manœuvre, and that a discredited one, he had obtained control of one-fifth of the entire refining output of the United States. He meant to secure the other four-fifths. He might retire now, but the Oil Region would hear of him again. It did. Three months later, in August, 1872, it was learned that the scheme of consolidation which had been presented in vain at Titusville in May had been quietly carried out, that four-fifths of the refining interest of the United States, including many of the creek refiners, had gone into a National Refiners' Association, of which Mr. Rockefeller was president, and one of their own men, J. J. Vandergrift, was vice-president. The news aroused much resentment in the Oil Regions. The region was no longer solid in its free-trade sentiment, no longer undividedly true to its vow that the rebate system as applied to the oil trade must end. There was an enemy at home. The hard words which for months men had heaped on the distant heads of Cleveland and Pittsburg refiners, they began to pour out, more discreetly to be sure, on the heads of their neighbours. It boded ill for the interior peace of the Oil Regions.

The news that the refiners had actually consolidated aroused something more than resentment. The producers generally were alarmed. If the aggregation succeeded they would have one buyer only for their product, and there was not a man of them who believed that this buyer would ever pay them a cent more than necessary for their oil. Their alarm aroused them to energy. The association which had scattered the South Improvement Company was revived, and began at once to consider what it could do to prevent the consolidated refiners getting the upper hand in the business.

The association which now prepared to contest the mastery of the oil business with Mr. Rockefeller and those who had joined him was a curious and a remarkable body. Its membership, drawn from the length and breadth of the Oil Regions, included men whose production was thousands of barrels a day and men who were pumping scarcely ten barrels; it included college-bred men who had come from the East with comfortable sums to invest, and men who signed their names with an effort, had never read a book in their lives, and whose first wells they had themselves "kicked down." There were producers in it who had made and lost a half-dozen fortunes, and who were, apparently, just as buoyant and hopeful as when they began. There were those who had never put down a dry well, and were still unsatisfied. However diverse their fortunes, their breeding, and their luck, there was no difference in the spirit which animated them now.

The president of the association was Captain William Hasson, a young man both by his knowledge of the Oil Regions and the oil business well fitted for the position. Captain Hasson was one of the few men in the association who had been in the country before the discovery of oil. His father had bought, in the fifties, part of the grant of land at the mouth of Oil Creek, made in 1796 to the Indian chief Cornplanter, and had moved on it with his family. Four years after the

M. N. ALLEN

Independent refiner of Titusville. Editor of the *Courier*, an able opponent of the South Improvement Company.

JOHN FERTIG

Prominent oil operator. Until 1893 active in Producers' and Refiners' Company (independent).

CAPT. WILLIAM HASSON

President of the Petroleum Producers' Association of 1872.

JOHN L. MC KINNEY

Prominent oil operator. Until 1889 an independent. Now member of the Standard Oil Company.

discovery of oil he and his partner disposed of 300 acres of the tract they owned for $750,000. Young Hasson had seen Cornplanter, as the site of his father's farm was called, become Oil City; he had seen the mill, blacksmith shop and country tavern give way to a thriving town of several thousand inhabitants. All of his interests and his pride were wrapped up in the industry which had grown up about him. Independent in spirit, vigorous in speech, generous and just in character, William Hasson had been thoroughly aroused by the assault of the South Improvement Company, and under his presidency the producers had conducted their successful campaign. The knowledge that the same man who had been active in that scheme had now organised a national association had convinced Captain Hasson of the necessity of a counter move, and he threw himself energetically into an effort to persuade the·oil producers to devise an intelligent and practical plan for controlling their end of the business, and then stand by what they decided on.

Captain Hasson and those who were working with him would have had a much more difficult task in arousing the producers to action if it had not been for the general dissatisfaction over the price of oil. The average price of crude in the month of August, 1872, was $3.47½. The year before it had been $4.42½, and that was considered a poverty price. It was pretty certain that prices would fall still lower, that "three-dollar oil" was near at hand. Everybody declared three dollars was not a "living price" for oil, that it cost more than that to produce it. The average yield of the wells in the Oil Region in 1872 was five barrels a day. Now a well cost at that time from $2,500 to $8,000, exclusive of the price of the lease. It cost eight to ten dollars a day to pump a well, exclusive of the royalty interest—that is, the proportion of the production turned over to the land-owner, usually one-fourth.* If

* Estimate given in the Oil City Derrick for September 10, 1872.

[111]

a man had big wells, and many of them, he made big profits on "three-dollar oil," but there were comparatively few "big producers." The majority of those in the business had but few wells, and these yielded only small amounts.

If he had been contented to economise and to accept small gains, even the small producer could live on a much lower price than three dollars; but nobody in the Oil Regions in 1872 looked with favour on economy, and everybody despised small things. The oil men as a class had been brought up to enormous profits, and held an entirely false standard of values. As the Derrick told them once in a sensible editorial, "their business was born in a balloon going up, and spent all its early years in the sky." They had seen nothing but the extreme of fortune. One hundred per cent. per annum on an investment was in their judgment only a fair profit. If their oil property had not paid for itself entirely in six months, and begun to yield a good percentage, they were inclined to think it a failure. Now nothing but five-dollar oil would do this, so great were the risks in business; and so it was for five-dollar oil, regardless of the laws of supply and demand, that they struggled. They were notoriously extravagant in the management of their business. Rarely did an oil man write a letter if he could help it. He used the telegraph instead. Whole sets of drilling tools were sometimes sent by express. It was no uncommon thing to see near a derrick broken tools which could easily have been mended, but which the owner had replaced by new ones. It was anything to save bother with him. Frequently wells were abandoned which might have been pumped on a small but sure profit. In those days there were men who looked on a ten-barrel (net) well as hardly worth taking care of. And yet even at fifty cents a barrel such a well would have paid the owner $1,800 a year. The simple fact was that the profits which men in trades all over the country were glad enough to get, the oil producer despised. The one great thing which the Oil Regions did not understand in 1872 was economy. As a matter of fact the oil-producing business was going through a stage in its natural development similar to oil refining. Both, under the stimulus of the enormous profits in the years immediately following the discovery of oil, had been pushed until they had outstripped consumption. The competition resulting from the inrush of producers and refiners and the economies which had been worked out were bringing down profits. The combinations attempted by both refiners and producers in these years were really efforts to keep up prices to the extravagant point of the early speculative years.

Now the drop in the price of oil everybody recognised to be due to a natural cause. Where a year before the production had been 12,000 barrels a day, it was now 16,000. The demand for refined had not increased in proportion to this production of crude, and oil stocks had accumulated until the tanks of the region were threatening to overflow. And there was no sign of falling off. Under these circumstances it needed little argument to convince the oil men that if they were to get a better price they must produce no more than the world would use. There was but one way to effect this—to put down no new wells until the stocks on hand were reduced and the daily production was brought down to a marketable amount.

Under the direction of the Producers' Association an agitation at once began in favour of stopping the drill for six months. It was a drastic measure. There was hardly an oil operator in the entire region who had not on hand some piece of territory on which he was planning to drill, or on which he had not wells under way. Stopping the drill meant that all of the aggressive work of his business should cease for six months. It meant that his production, unreplenished, would gradually fall off, until at the end of the period he would have probably not over half of what he had now; that then he must begin over again to build up. It meant, too, that he was at the mercy of neighbours who might refuse to join the movement, and who by continuing to drill would drain his territory. It seemed to him the only way of obtaining a manageable output of crude, however, and accordingly, when late in the month of August the following pledge to stop the drill was circulated, the great majority of the producers signed it:

Whereas, The extreme low price of oil requires of producers that operations therefor shall cease for the present: Now we, the producers, land-owners and others, residents of the Pennsylvania Oil Region, do hereby bind ourselves to each other not to commence the drilling of any more wells for the period of six months from the first day of September next, not to lease any lands owned or controlled by us for the purpose of operations during the same period, and we also agree to use all honourable means to prevent others from boring. This we agree to, and bind ourselves to each other under a forfeiture of $2,000 for each well commenced by either of us within the period above limited—the same to be collected as any other debt. It is, however, understood by the undersigned that this forfeiture is not to apply to any wells where the erection of rigs is completed or under way, or that may be commenced before the first day of September aforesaid.

The chief objection to this pledge came from land-owners in Clarion County. They were the "original settlers," plodding Dutch farmers, whose lives had always been poor and hard and shut-in. The finding of oil had made them rich and greedy. They were so ignorant that it was difficult to transact business of any nature with them. It was not unusual for a Clarion County farmer, if offered an eighth royalty, to refuse it on the ground that it was too little, and to ask a tenth. A story used to be current in the Oil Regions of a producer who, returning from an unsuccessful land hunt in Clarion County was asked why he had not secured a certain lease. "Well," he said, "farmers wanted seven-eighths of the oil as a royalty, wanted me to furnish barrels and to paint *both* heads. I agreed to everything but the last. I could afford to paint but one head, and so he wouldn't sign the lease." When the proposition to stop the drill for six months was brought to these men, who at the time owned the richest territory in the oil field, no amount of explanation could make them understand it. They regarded it simply as a scheme to rob them, and would not sign. Outside of this district, however, the drill stopped over nearly all the field on the first of September.

There was nothing but public opinion to hold the producers to their pledge. But public opinion in those days in the Oil Regions was fearless and active and asserted itself in the daily newspapers and in every meeting of the association. The whole body of oil men became a vigilance committee intent on keeping one another loyal to the pledge. Men who appeared at church on Sunday in silk hats, carrying gold-headed canes—there were such in the Oil Region in 1872—now stole out at night to remote localities to hunt down rumours of drilling wells. If they found them true, their dignity did not prevent their cutting the tools loose or carrying off a band wheel.

Stopping the drill afforded no immediate relief to the producers. It was for the future. And as soon as the Petroleum Producers' Association had the movement well under way, it proposed another drastic measure—a thirty days' shut-down —by which it was meant that all wells should cease pumping for a month. Nothing shows better the compact organisation and the determination of the oil producers at this time than the immediate response they gave to this suggestion. In ten days scarcely a barrel of oil was being pumped from end to end of the Oil Regions. "That a business producing three million dollars a month, employing 10,000 labouring men and fifty million dollars of capital, should be entirely suspended, dried up, stopped still as death by a mutual voluntary agreement, made and perfected by all parties interested, within a space of ten days—this is a statement that staggers belief—a spectacle that takes one's breath away," cried the Derrick, which was using all its wits to persuade the producers to limit their production. It was certainly a spectacle which saddened the heart, however much one might applaud the grim resolution of the men who were carrying it out. The crowded oil farms where creaking walking-beams sawed the air from morning until night, where engines puffed, whistles screamed, great gas jets flared, teams came and went, and men hurried to and fro, became suddenly silent and desolate, and this desolation had an ugliness all its own—something unparalleled in any other industry of this country. The awkward derricks, staring cheap shanties, big tanks with miles and miles of pipe running hither and thither, the oil-soaked ground, blackened and ruined trees, terrible roads—all of the common features of the oil farm to which activity gave meaning and dignity—now became hideous in inactivity. Oil seemed a curse to many a man in those days as he stood by his silent wells and wondered what was to become of his business, of his family, in this clash of interests.

While the producers were inaugurating these movements, Captain Hasson and a committee were busy making out the plan of the permanent association which was to control the business of oil-producing and prevent its becoming the slave of the refining interest. The knowledge that such an organisation was being worked out kept the oil country in a ferment. In every district suggestions, practical and impractical, wise and foolish, occupied every producers' meeting and kept the idle oil men discussing from morning until night. At one mass-meeting the following resolution was actually passed by a body of revengeful producers:

Resolved, that to give a wider market throughout the world to petroleum, to enhance its price and to protect producers from unjust combinations of home refiners, a committee be appointed to ask the representatives of foreign governments at Washington to request their respective governments to put a proper tariff on refined oil and to admit crude oil free into the ports of their respective governments.

Toward the end of October Captain Hasson presented the

scheme which he and the committee had prepared. It proposed that there should be established what was called a Petroleum Producers' Agency.* This agency was really an incorporated company with a capital of one million dollars, the stock of which was to be subscribed to only by the producers or their friends. This agency was to purchase all the oil of the members of the association at at least five dollars a barrel. If stocks could be kept down so that the market took all of the oil at once, the full price was to be paid at once in cash; if not, the agency was to store the oil in tanks it was to build, and a portion of the price was to be paid in tank certificates. By thus controlling all the oil, the agency expected to protect the weakest as well as the strongest producer, to equalise the interest of different localities, to prevent refiners and exporters from accumulating stocks, and to prevent gambling in oil. The agency was to take active means to collect reliable information about the oil business—the number of wells drilling, the actual production, the stocks on hand—things which had never been done to anybody's satisfaction. Indeed, one of the standing causes for quarrels between the various newspapers of the region was their conflicting statistics about production and stocks. It was to make a study of the market and see what could be done to increase consumption. It was to oppose monopolies and encourage competition, and, if necessary, it was to provide co-operative refineries which the producers should own and control.

The spirit of the agency, as explained by Captain Hasson, was most liberal, considering the interests of even the drillers and pumpers. "Advise every employee to take at least one share of stock for himself," he said in his address, "and one for his wife and each of his children, and encourage him to pay for it out of his saved earnings or out of his monthly pay. If he is not able to keep up his instalments, assure him

*See Appendix, Number 16. "The Agency."

that you will help him, and then take care to do it. You will thus do him a double kindness, and benefit his family by encouraging habits of thrift and economy. You owe this much to him who so nobly seconded your efforts to gain control of the market by stopping work. You had all to gain, and he had nothing to hope for but your benefit. Now show your appreciation of his acts by this evidence of your regard for his welfare."

The plan was received with general enthusiasm, and when it came up for adoption it went through with a veritable whoop. Indeed, within a few moments after its official acceptance, which took place in Oil City on October 24, $200,000 worth of stock was taken, and less than two weeks later it was announced that more than the desired million dollars had been subscribed, that the trustees and officers had been elected, and that the agency was ready for work. For the first time in the history of the oil business the producers were united in an organisation, which, if carried out, would regulate the production of oil to something like the demand for it, would prevent stocks from falling into the hands of speculators, and would provide a strong front to any combination with monopolistic tendencies. Only one thing was necessary now to make the producer a fitting opponent to his natural enemy, the refiner. That thing was loyalty to the agency he had established. The future of the producer at that moment was in his own hand. Would he stick? By every sign he would. He thought so himself. He had acted so resolutely and intelligently up to this point that even Mr. Rockefeller seems to have thought so.

During the entire three months that the producers had been organising, the refiners had been making divers overtures to them. In August several of the refiners sought certain of the big producers and privately proposed a two-headed combination which should handle the whole business, from drilling to exportation. The proposition they made was most alluring to men suffering from low prices. "Carry out your plans to limit your production and guarantee to sell only to us," said Mr. Rockefeller's representative, "and we will give you four dollars a barrel for your oil. We will also establish a sliding scale, and for every cent a gallon that refined oil advances we will give you twenty-five cents more on your barrel of crude. The market price of crude oil, when this offer was made, was hovering around three dollars. "How," asked the producer, "can you do this?" "We expect, by means of our combination, to get a rebate of seventy-five cents a barrel," was the answer. "But the railroads have signed an agreement to give no rebates," objected the producers.

"As if the railroads ever kept an agreement," answered the worldly-wise refiners. "Somebody will get the rebates. It is the way the railroads do business. If it is to be anybody, we propose it shall be our combination." Now it was clear enough to the men approached that the great body of their association would never go into any scheme based on rebates, and they said so. The refiners saw no disadvantage in that fact. "We don't want *all* the producers. We only want the big ones. The small producer under our arrangement must die, as the small refiner must." The proposition never got beyond the conference chamber. It was too cynical. Several conferences of the same nature took place later between representatives of the two interests, but nothing came of them. The two associations were kept apart by the natural antagonism of their ideals and their policy. Captain Hasson and his followers were working on an organisation which aimed to protect the weakest as well as the strongest; which welcomed everybody who cared to come into the business; which encouraged competition and discountenanced any sort of special privilege. Mr. Rockefeller and his associates proposed to save the strong and eliminate the weak, to limit the membership to those who came in now, to prevent competition by securing exclusive privileges. Their program was cold-blooded, but it must be confessed that it showed a much firmer grasp on the commercial practices of the day, and a much deeper knowledge of human nature as it operates in business, than that of the producers.

The formation of the Producers' Agency brought the refiners back to the Oil Regions in greater earnest than ever. The success of that organisation gave them an active antagonist, one which, as it held the raw material, could at any time actually shut up their refineries by withholding oil. The vigour, the ability, the determination the new organisation had displayed made it a serious threat to the domination Mr. Rockefeller and his associates had dreamed. It must be placated. On November 8, immediately after it was announced that the entire million dollars' worth of stock was taken, an agent of the Standard Oil Company in Oil City was ordered to buy oil from the agency—6,000 barrels of oil at $4.75 a barrel —and the order was followed by this telegram from Mr. Rockefeller:

"It has been represented to us that if we would buy of the producers' agent at Oil City and pay $4.75 per barrel, they would maintain the price. We are willing to go farther and buy only of the producers' agent, hence the order we have given you. See Hasson and others and let there be a fair understanding on this point. We will do all in our power to maintain prices, and continue to buy, provided our position is fully understood. We do this to convince producers of our sincerity, and to assist in establishing the market."

A more adroit move could not have been made at this moment. This purchase was a demonstration that the Refiners' Association could and would pay the price the producers asked; that they asked nothing better, in fact, than to ally themselves with the agency. The events of the next three weeks, on the contrary, showed the agency that it would be some time before anybody else would pay them any such price as that Mr. Rockefeller promised. The reason was evident enough. In spite of the stopping of the drill, in spite of the thirty days' shut-down, production was increasing. Indeed, the runs * for November were greater than they had ever been in any single month since the beginning of the oil business. A large number of wells under way when the drill was stopped had "come in big." New territory had been opened up by unexpected wildcats. The shut-down had done less than was expected to decrease stocks. It was evident that the Producers' Association had a long and severe task before it to bring the crude output down to anything like the demand. Could the great body of producers be depended upon to take still further measures to lesson their production, and at the same time would they hold their oil until the agency had the mastery of the situation? Their tanks were overflowing. Many of them were in debt and depending on their sales to meet their obligations—even to meet their daily personal expenses. It was little wonder that they grew restive as they began to realise that the agency in which they had seen immediate salvation from all their ills could only be made effective by months more of self-sacrifice, of agitation, of persistent effort from every man of them. With every day they became more impatient of the bonds the agency had set for them, and the leaders soon realised that some immediate tangible results must be given the mass of oil men, or there was danger of a stampede.

A strong feature of the genius of John D. Rockefeller has always been his recognition of the critical moment for action in complicated situations. He saw it now, and his representatives again came to the creek seeking an alliance. Their arguments, as they found their way from the private meetings into

* The amount of production was computed from the oil run through the pipe-lines, all of which had their gaugers and were supposed to report their runs at regular intervals.

the press and the street, ran something like this: "Our combination is the only big buyer. We are in the thing to stay, and shall remain the only big buyer. You might erect refineries and oppose us, but it would take months, and while you are waiting how are you going to hold the producers? You cannot do it. We can easily get all the oil we want to-day at our own price from the men who sell from necessity, and yet your agency is in the first flush of enthusiasm. Sell only to us and we will buy 15,000 barrels a day from you. Refuse an alliance with us and you will fail."

Overwhelmed by the length and severity of the struggle before them if they insisted on independence, fearful lest the scattered and restless producers could not be held much longer, convinced by their confident arguments that the refiners could keep their promise, the council finally agreed to a plan of union which the Derrick dubbed the "Treaty of Titusville." A terrible hubbub followed the announcement that a treaty was proposed and would probably be adopted by the association. The same old arguments which had greeted each overture from the refiners were gone over again. It would be a monopoly. The price they offered for crude depended upon their getting an unnaturally high price for refined. The markets of the world would refuse to pay this price when it was discovered that it was kept up by an agreement which was contrary to the laws of supply and demand. And, besides, the parties could not trust each other. *Timeo Danaos et dona ferentes.* Liberal translation—Mind your eye when the Cleveland refiners get generous," cautioned the Derrick. As always, the ghost of the South Improvement Company was between them. On the other hand, it was argued that it was Hobson's choice, "combine or bust," there is no other market. We cannot wait for one. We have a million barrels of oil on hand—the refiners will take 15,000 barrels a day for "spot cash." And after all, concluded the

JAMES S. TARR

Owner of the "Tarr Farm," one of the richest oil
territories on Oil Creek.

WILLIAM BARNSDALL

The second oil well on Oil Creek was put down by
Mr. Barnsdall.

JAMES S. MCCRAY

Owner of the McCray Farm near Petroleum Centre.

WILLIAM A. ABBOTT

One of the most prominent of the early oil producers,
refiners and pipe-line operators

"philosophical," if you can't do as well as you want to, do the best you can.

On December 12 the proposed treaty was laid before the producers at Oil City. It aroused a debate so acrimonious that even the Derrick suppressed it. Captain Hasson led the opposition. In his judgment there was but one course for the producers—to keep themselves free from all entanglements and give themselves time to build up solidly the structure they had planned. If they had followed his advice the whole history of the Oil Regions would have been different. But they did not follow it. The treaty was ratified by a vote of twenty-seven to seven. The excitement and the personalities the association indulged in at their meeting augured ill for its future, but when a week later a committee sent to see the refiners came back from New York with a contract signed by Mr. Rockefeller,* the president, and bearing with them an order for 200,000 barrels of oil at $3.25, there was a general feeling that, after all, an alliance might not be so bad a thing. 200,000 barrels was a big order and would do much to relieve their distress. Their formal sense was quieted, too, by the assurance that the producers before signing the contract had insisted that the Refiners' Combination enter into an agreement to take no rebates as long as the alliance lasted. The main points of the agreement decided upon were that the Refiners' Association should admit all *existing* refiners to its society, and the Producers' Association *all* producers present and to come—that the former company should buy only of the latter, the latter sell only to the former, and that the agency should bind all producers enjoying its privileges to handle their oil through it. The refiners were to buy such daily quantities as the markets of the world would take and at a price governed by the price of refined, five dollars per bar-

* See Appendix, Number 17. Contract between Petroleum Producers' Association and Petroleum Refiners' Association.

rel when refined was selling at twenty-six cents a gallon. Either association could discontinue the agreement on ten days' notice. The producers, before signing the contract, insisted that the Refiners' Combination sign an agreement to take no rebates as long as the alliance lasted. This agreement in regard to rebates read as follows:

"*Whereas*, it is deemed desirable to execute a contract of even date herewith between the Petroleum Producers' Association and the Petroleum Refiners' Association for the purpose of securing a co-operation for mutual protection, it is agreed by the Refiners' Association that sections one and three of a contract made the 25th of March, 1872, between certain trunk lines of railroads and a committee of producers and refiners shall be and remain in full force.

"Petroleum Refiners' Association,
"JOHN D. ROCKEFELLER, *President.*"

The sections of the contract of the 25th of March referred to agreed that no rebates or contracts or other arrangements should be made which would give any party the slightest difference in rates, and that the rates should not be changed either for increase or decrease without first giving Mr. Hasson, the president of the Producers' Union, at least ninety days' notice in writing. As we now know, Mr. Rockefeller himself was receiving rebates when he signed this agreement.

And now, at last, after five months of incessant work, the agency was ready to begin disposing of oil. They set to work diligently at once to apportion the 200,000 barrels the refiners had bought among the different districts. It was a slow and irritating task, for a method of apportionment and of gathering had to be devised, and, as was to be expected, it aroused more or less dissatisfaction and many charges of favouritism. The agency had the work well under way, however, and had shipped about 50,000 barrels when, on January 14, it was suddenly announced that the refiners had *refused to take any more of the contract oil!*

There was a hurried call of the Producers' Council and a

demand for an explanation. A plausible one was ready from Mr. Rockefeller. "You have not kept your part of the contract—you have not limited the supply of oil*—there is more being pumped to-day than ever before in the history of the region. We can buy all we want at $2.50, and oil has sold within the week at two dollars. If you will not, or cannot, stop overproduction, can you expect us to pay your price? We keep down the output of refined, and so keep up the price. If you will not do the same, you must not expect high prices."

What could the producers reply? In spite of their heroic measures, they had not been able to curtail their output. It seemed as if Nature, outraged that her generosity should be so manipulated as to benefit only the few, had opened her veins to flood the earth with oil, so that all men might know that here was a light cheap enough for the poorest of them. Her lavish outpouring now swept away all of the artificial restraints the producers and refiners had been trying to build. The Producers' Association seemed suddenly to comprehend their folly in supposing that when 5,000 barrels more of oil was produced each day than the market demanded any combination could long keep the contract the refiners had made with them; and their unhappy session, made more unhappy by the reading of bitter and accusing letters from all over the discontented region, ended in a complete stampede from the refiners, the vote for dissolving the alliance having but one dissenting voice.

There were few tears shed in the Oil Regions over the rupture of the contract. The greater part of the oil men had called it from the beginning an "unholy alliance," and rejoiced that it was a fiasco. If the alliance had been all that came to an end, the case would not have been so serious, but it

* The agency was pledged by its constitution to limit the supply of crude, but this stipulation did not appear in the contract signed by the two associations. It was a verbal understanding.

[125]

was not. The breaking of the alliance proved the death of the agency and the association. The leaders who had disapproved of the treaty withdrew from active work; the supporters of the alliance, demoralised by its failure, were glad to keep quiet. A few spasmodic efforts to stop the drill, to inaugurate another shut-down, were made, but failed. Most of the producers felt that, as oil was so low, their only safety was in getting as large a production as they could, and a perfect fever of development followed. The Producers' Association, after ten months of as exciting and strenuous effort as an organisation has ever put in, was snuffed out almost in a day. It was to be five years before the oil men recovered sufficiently from the shock of this collapse to make another united effort. If Mr. Rockefeller felt in the fall of 1872 that the "good of the oil business" required the dissolution of the Producers' Agency, he could not have acted with more acumen than he did in leading them into an alliance, and at the psychological moment throwing up his contract.

Humiliated as the producers were by their failure, they soon found consolation in the knowledge that the Refiners' Association was in trouble. A serious thing, in fact, had happened. When the official report of the year's exports and imports came out, it was shown that the exports of refined oil had fallen off for the first time in the history of the business. In 1871, 132,178,843 gallons had been exported. In 1872, only 118,259,832 were exported. Just as alarming was the proof that the shale and coal oil refineries of Europe had taken a fresh start—that they were selling their products more cheaply than kerosene could be imported and sold. There was a general outcry from all over the country that Mr. Rockefeller and his associates were running the oil business by keeping up the price of refined oil beyond what the price of crude justified. The producers, eager for a scape-goat, argued that the low price of crude was due to decreased consumption as well as over-production, and their ill-will against Mr. Rocke-feller flared up anew. In the meantime the Refiners' Associ-ation was having troubles of its own. The members were not limiting their output as they had agreed—that is, it was dis-covered every now and then that a refinery was making more oil than Mr. Rockefeller had directed. Again, what was more fatal to the success of the association, members sometimes sold at a lower price than that set by Mr. Rockefeller. These restrictions were fundamental to the success of the combina-tion, and the members were called together at Saratoga in June, 1873, and after a long session the association was dissolved.

There was loud exultation in the unthinking part of the Oil Regions over the dissolution of the refiners. The "Junior Anaconda" was dead. The wiser part of the region did not exult. They knew that though the combination might dis-solve, the Standard Oil Company of Cleveland still controlled its one-fifth of the capacity of the country; that not only had Mr. Rockefeller been able to hold the twenty refineries he had bolted so summarily at the opening of 1872, but he had assimilated them so thoroughly that he was making enormous profits. Mr. Rockefeller's contracts with the Central Rail-road alone in 1873 and 1874 obliged him for seven months of the year to ship at least 100,000 barrels of refined oil a month to the seaboard. As a matter of fact he never shipped less than 108,000 barrels, and in one month of the period it rose to 180,000.* Now in 1873 he made, at the very lowest figure, three cents a gallon on his oil. Estimating his ship-ments simply at 700,000 barrels a year—and they were much more—his profits for that year were $1,050,000, and this ac-counts for no profits on about thirty-five per cent. of the Stand-ard output, which was sold locally or shipped Westward.

*Testimony of H. M. Flagler before the Ohio State Commission for investigating railroad freight discrimination, March, 1879. See Appendix, Number 14.

Little wonder that the Cleveland refiners who had been snuffed out the year before, and who saw their plants run at such advantage, grew bitter, or that gossip said the daily mail of the president of the Standard Oil Company was enlivened by so many threats of revenge that he took extraordinary precautions about appearing unguarded in public.

It is worth noticing that these great profits were not being used for private purposes. In 1872 the Standard Oil Company paid a dividend of thirty-seven per cent., but in 1873 they cut it to fifteen per cent. The profits were going almost solidly into the extension and solidification of the business. Mr. Rockefeller was building great barrel factories, thus cutting down to the minimum one of a refiner's heaviest expenses. He was buying tank cars that he might be independent of the vagaries of the railroads in allotting cars. He was gaining control of terminal facilities in New York. He was putting his plants into the most perfect condition, introducing every improved process which would cheapen his manufacturing by the smallest fraction of a cent. He was diligently hunting methods to get a larger percentage of profit from crude oil. There was, perhaps, ten per cent. of waste at that period in crude oil. It hurt him to see it unused, and no man had a heartier welcome from the president of the Standard Oil Company than he who would show him how to utilise any proportion of his residuum. In short, Mr. Rockefeller was strengthening his line at every point, and to no part of it was he giving closer attention than to transportation.

CHAPTER FIVE

LAYING THE FOUNDATIONS OF A TRUST

VIDENCE OF REAPPEARANCE OF REBATES SOON AFTER AGREEMENT OF
MARCH 25 IS SIGNED — PRINCIPLE THOROUGHLY ESTABLISHED THAT
LARGE SHIPPERS SHALL HAVE ADVANTAGES OVER SMALL SHIPPERS
IN SPITE OF RAILROADS' DUTY AS COMMON CARRIERS—AGREEMENT
WORKED OUT BY WHICH THREE ROADS ARE TO HAVE FIXED PERCENT-
AGE OF EASTERN SHIPMENTS—OIL REGIONS ROBBED OF THEIR GEO-
GRAPHICAL ADVANTAGE—THE RUTTER CIRCULAR—ROCKEFELLER NOW
SECRETLY PLANS REALISATION OF HIS DREAM OF PERSONAL CONTROL
OF THE REFINING OF OIL — ORGANISATION OF THE CENTRAL ASSO-
CIATION—H. H. ROGERS' DEFENCE OF THE PLAN—ROCKEFELLER'S QUIET
AND SUCCESSFUL CANVASS FOR ALLIANCES WITH REFINERS—THE REBATE
HIS WEAPON—CONSOLIDATION BY PERSUASION OR FORCE—MORE TALK
OF A UNITED EFFORT TO COUNTERACT THE MOVEMENT.

THROUGHOUT 1872, while the producers and
refiners were working out associations and alliances
to regulate the output of crude and refined oil,
the freight rates over the three great oil-carrying
roads were publicly supposed to be those settled by the
agreement of March 25. Except by the sophisticated it was
believed that the railroads were keeping their contracts.
The Lake Shore and Michigan Southern and the New York
Central had never kept them, as we have seen. Mr. Flagler's
statement that the Standard received a rebate of twenty-five
cents a barrel from April 1 to November 15, 1872, would
seem to show that while with one hand Mr. Clark and Mr.
Vanderbilt signed the agreement with the oil men that henceforth freights should be "on a basis of perfect equality to all

shippers, producers and refiners, and that no rebates, drawbacks, or other arrangements of any character should be made or allowed that would give any party the slightest difference in rates or discriminations of any character whatever," with the other they had signed an arrangement to give a twenty-five-cent rebate to Mr. Rockefeller! They certainly had a strong incentive for ignoring their pledge. Consider what Mr. Rockefeller could offer the road—sixty car-loads of oil a day, over 4,000 barrels. General Devereux points out in the affidavit already mentioned * what this meant. It permitted them to make up a solid oil train and run it out every day. By running nothing else they reduced the average time of a freight car from Cleveland to New York and return from thirty days to ten days. The investment for cars to handle their freight was reduced by this arrangement to about one-third what it would have been if several different persons were shipping the same amount every day. Promptness was insured in forwarding and returning (a drawback of from fifty dollars to $150 a day accrued if it was late, so that the Standard was bound to ship promptly); and all the inconvenience of dealing with many shippers each with his peculiar whim or demand was avoided. It was certainly worth a rebate to the Central, and the Central not having any prejudices in favour of keeping agreements because they were agreements naturally conceded what Mr. Rockefeller wanted. There was another point. If the Central did not concede to Mr. Rockefeller's terms it undoubtedly would lose the freight. There was the lake and the canal and there was the Erie!

Now it is not supposable that such an arrangement would go on long without leaking out in the upper oil circles. We have evidence that it did not. Indeed, there was among certain intelligent oil men a conviction when the agreement was signed that the New York roads would not regard it—that

* See Appendix, Number 3.

if they did it would ruin the refining business of Cleveland. W. T. Scheide, a member of the oil men's committee making this contract, the agent of one of the largest oil shippers in the country, Adnah Neyhart, in some frank and suggestive testimony given to the Hepburn Committee in 1879, said that at the time the arrangement was made he did not think anybody connected with the business expected it would last. "My reason for that was that it was an impossible agreement," said Mr. Scheide. "The immediate effect of it would have been to have utterly destroyed fifty-five per cent. of the refining interest of the country; that is to say, Cleveland and Pittsburg, which during the previous four years had shipped fifty-five per cent. of all the oil out of the Oil Regions—they, in addition to paying the rates of freights which all other refiners would have had to pay, were required to pay fifty cents a barrel on their crude oil to their works." The refiners in Cleveland and Pittsburg had of course always paid to get crude oil to their works, even the South Improvement Company tariffs provided for that, and under that arrangement Cleveland had come to be in 1871 the chief refining centre of the country. The chairman of the committee examining Mr. Scheide suggested it was a "temporary impossibility which would have adjusted itself," which Mr. Scheide admitted. "Yes, sir, naturally, it would have adjusted itself I suppose, but the effect was very marked at the time."

So strong was Mr. Scheide's conviction that the New York roads would not stand the new rates that on the 10th of April he went to the Pennsylvania railroad and asked for a rebate on Mr. Neyhart's crude shipments—and got it. What the rebate was he does not state, but Mr. Flagler tells us in his testimony * that in December he discovered that the Pennsylvania was shipping for as low as $1.05 a barrel. And for

* See Appendix, Number 14.

one month he got from Mr. Vanderbilt a rate of $1.05 on his 4,000 barrels a day.

Mr. Scheide was also shipping refined oil over the Erie. George R. Blanchard, who in October, 1872, became the general freight agent of the Erie, told the Hepburn Committee in 1879 that he found on entering his position that $7,000 in rebates had been paid Mr. Scheide for Mr. Neyhart in the month of September, 1872, on this refined. He does not say how long this had been going on. Mr. Blanchard found at the same time the March 25 agreement. He asked why it was not observed, and the reply convinced him that it had not been kept more than two weeks by the Pennsylvania and Central systems. "The representations made to me," says Mr. Blanchard, "also convinced the Atlantic and Great Western as to what our rivals were doing, and that railway company and our own decided to continue to pay the twenty-four cents per barrel drawback then being paid on the rate of $1.35, provided by their producers' agreement of March 25, 1872."

But Mr. Blanchard was shipping only Mr. Neyhart's refined, and naturally he looked for more business and was willing to give a rebate to get it. He soon had some from another of the oil men who had signed the agreement of March 25. This was Mr. Bennett, of Titusville, who with J. D. Archbold and his other partners entered into a contract with Mr. Blanchard to ship their entire product for a year at a rate considerably below the one agreed upon on March 25.* The contract was a short-lived one, for in November Mr. Bennett and his partners turned their shipments over to the Pennsylvania. The Erie had some compensation, however, in the fact that in July, 1873, Mr. Neyhart's crude shipments had all come to them. Mr. Scheide, Mr. Neyhart's agent, explained

* See Appendix, Number 18. Testimony of George R. Blanchard on rebates granted by the Erie Railroad.

to the Hepburn Commission that he left the Pennsylvania because of what he considered "very bad treatment—a discrimination against us in furnishing us cars." The Pennsylvania had indeed undertaken to carry out the clause in the agreement of March 25 which stipulated that there should be no discrimination in furnishing cars. Mr. Scheide, considering himself "their shipper," that is, shipping larger quantities more regularly than anybody else, and as a consequence having better rates, thought it unfair that the cars should be pro rated,* and left the road, giving his business to the Erie, where presumably he got assurances that cars would be furnished to shippers according to the quantity and regularity of shipments. Mr. Scheide's excellent testimony is good evidence of how deep a hold the principle that the large shippers are to have all the advantages had taken hold of some of the best men in the oil country, although the oil country as a whole utterly repudiated the "rebate business." These details, all drawn from sworn testimony, show how, before a year had passed after the end of the Oil War, all the roads were practising discrimination, how a few shippers were again engaged in a scramble for advantages, and how the big shippers were bent on re-establishing the principle supposed to have been overthrown by the Oil War that one shipper is more convenient and profitable for a road than many, and this being so, the matter of a road's duty as a common carrier has nothing to do with the question.†

This was the situation when in June, 1873, General Devereux, whom we have met on the Lake Shore road, became president of the Atlantic and Great Western. Now at this time Peter H. Watson, the president of the South Improve-

* See Appendix, Number 19. Testimony of W. T. Scheide.

† See Appendix, Number 20. Statements of amounts paid for overcharges and rebates on oil during the year 1873 by the New York, Lake Erie and Western Railroad.

ment Company, was president of the Erie. The two at once looked into the condition of their joint oil traffic. They found the rebate system abolished a year before again well intrenched. Nevertheless the Erie was not doing much business. The entire shipments of oil over the Erie for 1873 were but 762,000 barrels out of a total of 4,963,000. Naturally they went to work to build up a trade, and their relations being what they had been with the Standard, the company controlling a third of the country's refining capacity, they went to them to see if they could not get a percentage of their seaboard shipments from Cleveland. Mr. Rockefeller was willing to give them shipments if they would make the rates as low as were given to any of his competitors on any of the roads, and if they would deliver his oil at Hunter's Point, Brooklyn, where he had oil yards, and where the Central delivered, or if they would not do that if they would lease their own oil yards to him. There was an excellent business reason for making that latter demand, which Mr. Blanchard explained to the Hepburn Commission:

"The Standard," said Mr. Blanchard, "had a force of men, real estate, houses, tanks and other facilities at Hunter's Point for receiving and coopering the oil; and they had their cooperage materials delivered over there. The arrangement prior to that time was that the Erie Company performed this service for its outside refiners at Weehawken, for which the Erie Company made specific charges and added them to their rates for freight. The Standard Company said to us: 'We do the business at low cost at Hunter's Point because we are expert oil men and know how to handle it; we pay nobody a profit, and cannot and ought not to pay you a profit for a service that is not transportation any more than inspecting flour or cotton; and the New York Central delivers our oil at that point. Now if you will deliver our oil at Hunter's Point and permit us to do this business, you may do so; we want to do that business, and we cannot pay to the Erie Railway Company at Wee-hawken a profit on all of those staves, heads, cooperage, fill-ing, refilling and inspection, for we have our own forces of men and our own yards necessary for this work in another part of the harbour of New York; and it is not a part of your business as a carrier, anyway.'

"In lieu thereof and for the profits that we could have made from the aggregate of these charges, we said to them: 'If you will pay us a fixed profit upon each one of these barrels of oil arriving here, you may take the yards and run them subject to certain limitations as to what you shall do for other people who continue to ship oil to the same yards.' They were only able to make this arrangement with us because of their controlling such a large percentage of shipment, and because of permanent facilities in Brooklyn; if the larger percentage of shipments had belonged to outside parties, and they had had no yards of their own, we would probably have retained the yards ourselves."

A contract was signed on April 17, 1874. By it the Standard agreed to ship fifty per cent. of the products of its refineries by the Erie at rates "no higher than is paid by the competitors of the Standard Oil Company from competing Western refin-eries to New York by all rail lines," and to give all oil patrons of the Erie system a uniform price and fair and equal facili-ties at the Weehawken yards.* It was a very wise business deal for both parties. It made Mr. Rockefeller the favoured shipper of a second trunk line (the Central system was already his) and it gave him the control of that road's oil terminal so that he could know exactly what other oil patrons of the road were doing—one of the advantages the South Improvement contract looked out for, it will be remembered. As for the Erie, it tied up to them an important trade and again put them into a

* See Appendix, Number 21. Agreement of 1874 between the Erie Railroad system and the Standard Oil Company.

position to have something to say about the division of the oil traffic, the bulk of which outside of the Standard Oil Company the Pennsylvania was handling. In connection with the Central the Erie now said to the Pennsylvania that henceforth they proposed to maintain their position as oil shippers.

The natural result of the determination of the Central and Erie to get from the Pennsylvania a percentage of its freight was, of course, increased cutting, and it looked as if a rate war was inevitable. At this juncture Colonel Potts of the Empire Transportation Company, handling all of the Pennsylvania freight, suggested to his rivals that it would be a favourable time for the three trunk lines to pool their seaboard oil freight. In the discussions of this proposition, which, of course, involved a new schedule of rates, there being now practically none, it was suggested that henceforth freights be so adjusted that they would be equal to all refiners, on crude and refined from all points. Such an equalisation seems at first glance an unsolvable puzzle. The agents found it intricate enough. Throughout the summer of 1874 they worked on it, holding meetings at Long Branch and Saratoga and calling into their counsels a few of the leading refiners, pipe-line men and producers whom they could trust to keep quiet about the project.

By the first of September they had an agreement worked out by which each of the three roads was to have a fixed percentage of Eastern shipments. The rates to the seaboard were to amount to the same for all refiners wherever located. That is, to use one of the illustrations employed by Mr. Blanchard in explaining the scheme to the Hepburn Commission: "Suppose 100 barrels of refined oil to have been sent from Cleveland to New York by rail; the consignee was required to first pay freight therefor at New York upon delivery $1.90; to make this quantity of refined oil at that time, he had already paid freight on say 133½ barrels of crude oil from the pipes to

FLEET OF OIL BOATS AT OIL CITY IN 1864

Cleveland at thirty-five cents per barrel or say $46.67; he had therefore paid out from the pipes to the refinery and thence to New York by transportation only, on 100 barrels refined and the quantity of crude oil required to make it, $236.67 or $2.37 per barrel; therefore, at the end of the month we refunded the $46.67 already paid on the crude oil. So that the rate paid net was $1.90 to him and all other refiners."

In case of the refineries situated at the seaboard the cost of carrying from the Oil Regions the 133½ barrels of crude oil required to make 100 barrels of refined was made exactly the same as carrying the 100 barrels of refined made in the West and transported East. This really amounted to charging nothing for getting the crude oil to a refinery wherever it was situated, as the following clause in the agreement shows: "The roads transporting the refined oil shall refund to the refiners as a drawback the charges paid by them upon the crude oil reaching their refineries by rail." This paragraph provided for this crude rebate contained a second clause, which read: "And the roads transporting through crude oil to the Eastern seaboard shall refund to the shippers twenty-two cents per barrel; both of said drawbacks to be paid only on oil reaching the initial points of rail shipment, through pipes, the owners of which maintain agreed rates of pipage." The paragraph announced two new and startling intentions on the part of the oil-carrying roads: first, that they intended to strip the Oil Regions of the advantage of geographical position at the wells by sending oil free to Cleveland and Pittsburg, New York and Philadelphia, at the same time leaving these cities the advantages accruing from their position as manufacturing centres and close to domestic markets; second, that they had entered into a combination with certain pipe-lines to drive certain others out of existence.

Mr. Blanchard gave the reasons of these two revolutionary

moves to the Hepburn Committee. It was "urgently represented to the trunk lines," he said, "by some refiners at the
West as well as by others at the seaboard, and also by crude
shippers and receivers and by owners of pipe-lines, that it
was in every way desirable that the refiners of Cleveland and
Pittsburg, and those at the seaboard be put upon a basis of
equalisation in the gross rates of transportation to and from
the refineries." Now to do this the element of distance had
to be disregarded. Cleveland was 150 miles west of the Oil
Regions, but she must be treated as if she were at the same
distance from the seaboard. As soon as the proposition was
made, certain of the refiners and producers objected unless the
railroads went further and equalised rates on coal, acids,
cooperage, etc. This, however, the roads declined to do.

As for the second clause—the rebate on all oil coming from
pipes which kept up a fixed pipage—it came about in this
way. While the railroad men were in conference at Long
Branch, Henry Harley, the president of the Pennsylvania
Transportation Company, came to them and said that he
believed the scheme of equalisation could not be carried out
unless some kind of an alliance was made with the pipe-lines.
There had been a large increase in the number of pipes in
the four or five years preceding, and a situation had arisen
not unlike that in every other branch of the oil business. There
was perhaps twice the pipe capacity needed for gathering all
the oil produced, and as the pipes were under at least a dozen
different managements, each fighting for business, the result
was, of course, just what it had been on the railroads and
in the markets—severe cutting of prices, rebates, special secret arrangements, confusion and loss. It had been only nine
years since the first pipe-line had been a success, and considering the phenomenal growth of the business and the important
part the pipe played in it, it was of course a situation natural
enough. Like the overgrowth of refining and of production, it

was something only time and solidification of business could remedy.

Mr. Harley laid the situation before the railroad men and said to them: "We want you to help us keep up an even and equal pipage rate. Here we are representatives of the nine most important lines in the Oil Regions. We want to put a stop to cutting and keep up a rate of thirty cents. Can't you help us?" Now up to this time the railroad had had nothing to do with pipe-line charges. It was, and still is, the custom for the buyer of the oil to pay the pipage, that is, the oil producer on running the oil into the pipe-line received a credit certificate for the oil. If he held it in the line long he paid a storage charge. When he sold the oil, the line ran it, and the buyer paid the charge for running. Now the United Pipe Lines proposed to the railroads a through rate from the wells to the seaboard as low as they currently made from the receiving points on the railway, the pipes to get twenty per cent. of this through rate. The railroads were to agree not to receive oil from buyers except at as high a rate as the pipes charged; and to allow no pipe-line outside of the alliance a through rate from the wells. The memorandum said squarely that the intent and purpose of this was to make the United Pipes the sole feeders of the railroads. It was a plan not unlike the South Improvement Company in design—to put everybody but yourself out of business, and it had the merit of stating its intent and purpose with perfect candour.*

The railroad men seem not to have objected to the purpose, only to the terms of the proposed arrangement. Mr. Blanchard told the pipe committee that he regarded it as the most violent attempt on the part of the tail to wag the dog that he had ever seen, and the representatives of the other roads agreed.

* See Appendix, Number 22. Agreement of 1874 between the railroads and pipe-lines.

They saw at once, however, how much more solid their own position would be if they could be sure that no pipe-line delivering to them would cut its rate, if there could be in effect a through rate from the wells, and after some discussion they proposed to the pipe-lines to add twenty-two cents a barrel to the rail charges; that is, if the rate to the seaboard was $1.25, to collect from the shipper $1.47, and in case he could show that he had taken his oil from one of the United Pipes to give him a rebate of twenty-two cents. Mr. Blanchard said that they proposed to do this until proof was had that the associated pipe-lines were acting in good faith. Of course this arrangement did not change the pipe-lines' methods of collecting in the least. It simply forced a uniform charge, and this charge was to be, it should be noticed, regardless of distance. The charge for collecting and delivering oil was to be thirty cents a barrel whether it was carried one or ten miles—a practice which prevails to-day.

While these negotiations were going on, the Oil Regions as a whole was troubled by a vague rumour that freight rates were to be advanced. In the two years since the Oil War the region, as a whole, had adjusted itself to the tariff schedule of March 25, 1872, and was doing very well though working on a very much smaller margin of profits than ever before. The margin was sufficient, however, to keep the refineries in the valley running most of the time, and several of the large ones were increasing their plants. Detailed accounts of the condition of the works are to be had in the newspapers of the day. Thus, in the summer of 1874 an editor of the Oil City Derrick made a tour of the creek refineries and reported all of the larger ones in Titusville and Oil City as prosperous and growing, and the small ones in the little towns between these two points as "jogging along pleasantly." The keen competition between the different refining points made it necessary to do business with economy, and a rumour of a raise of freight rates naturally was looked on with dread. It was not until September 12, however, that the new arrangements were made known, and this was some time earlier than was intended. The slip came about in this way. The general freight agent of the New York Central road, James H. Rutter, sent out on September 9 a private circular announcing the new arrangement,* an advance of fifty cents a barrel on refined oil shipped to the seaboard, no corresponding advance for Cleveland and Pittsburg, a rebate of the cost of getting oil to the refineries and a rebate of twenty-two cents to those who patronised certain pipe-lines. And to this new schedule was appended this consoling paragraph: "You will observe that under this system the rate is even and fair to all parties, preventing one locality taking advantage of its neighbour by reason of some alleged or real facility it may possess. Oil refiners and shippers have asked the roads from time to time to make all rates even and they would be satisfied. This scheme does it and we trust will work satisfactorily to all."

Among the refiners to whom the circular went was M. N. Allen of Titusville. Now Mr. Allen was the editor of an aggressive and lively newspaper—the Courier. He had fought rings and deals from the beginning of his career as a refiner and as an editor. He had been one of the strong opponents of the South Improvement Company and of the Refiners' Association which followed, and he saw at once the cloven foot in the Rutter circular and hastened to denounce it in a strong editorial:

If by an agreement of the New York Central, the Erie, and the Pennsylvania Railway Companies, crude oil—delivered from the Titusville pipe—should be hauled from Titusville to Chicago, and there refined, and the refined product then hauled to New York, all at two dollars a barrel, for the refined thus carried, it would be placing, by the railway companies, Chicago refiners upon the same level with the Titusville refiners who, on and after October 1, shall ship to New York refined made from

* See Appendix, Number 23. The Rutter circular.

[141]

crude oil taken from the Titusville pipe. The new freight arrangement does not make such provision for refiners at Chicago. But a Cleveland refiner may come to Titusville and buy oil for delivery from the Titusville, the Pennsylvania, the Church Run, or the Octave pipes, at this point, take it to Cleveland, and, after refining, carry the product to the seaboard at the same expense of freight, all told, that a refiner here, taking his crude oil directly from the above pipes, would have in placing his refined oil at the seaboard. This is stating the matter exactly, and we see no necessity for comment hereupon.

Again, 1,000 barrels of crude oil are to be carried to the seaboard for the same amount of money that will be required for carrying there 715 barrels of refined, notwithstanding that crude oil is a much more hazardous article of freight, from fire, than refined. If this is not a very large discrimination in favour of seaboard refiners, for which there is no compensation given to refiners in the Oil Region, our perceptions are utterly weak.

Now, before putting into effect this new freight arrangement, it may be well for the railway officials having the matter in charge to take into consideration a certain little article of agreement, which the people of Pennsylvania, on the 16th day of December last, entered into among themselves, respecting railroads in this state. In Article 17, Section 7, of our new constitution is the following decree of the sovereign people of this commonwealth: "No discrimination in charges or facilities for transportation shall be made between transportation companies and individuals, or in favour of either, by abatement, drawback or otherwise."

Petroleum is a product of this state, and transportation companies in taking it away must respect the fundamental law of the state. And, while we ask for no favours, always supporting free trade from principle, speaking in behalf of the refining interests of the Oil Region, we do not propose quietly to submit to any discrimination by transportation companies, doing business in the state, against our interests. If by reason of our position we possess advantages for refining oil here, over refiners outside, we have strong objections against the action of the railway companies in taking from us such advantages, by requiring us to pay for hauling a given quantity of oil as much as they require of Cleveland refiners for hauling the same amount of oil 300 miles greater distance; or for requiring us to pay as much for hauling 715 barrels of refined oil as they require for hauling 1,000 barrels of crude oil the same distance. If the railroad companies will make all expenses of refining oil equal to all points, we shall be satisfied. If they will make the price of sulphuric acid 1½ cents a pound, the same as it is in New York, instead of 2½ cents; if they will deliver caustic soda here free of freight from New York; if they will put paints and glues here at the same prices as those articles sell for in New York; if they will put staves and heading and hoops for barrels here at the same figures those articles cost in Cleveland, whether they do all these by giving us rebates sufficient to cover all differences now against us, or in any other way that will bring the same results, we will accept the new arrangement without complaint. Until this shall be done we shall ask the railway companies in hauling oil to confine themselves to legitimate business, and to obey the new constitution, in letter and spirit. It will behoove our citizens to see that their new constitution is carefully respected.

We are opposed to the new arrangement for the large advance in the price of freight upon oil. If the railroad companies have lost money in carrying oil for the Cleveland refineries during several years past, let not the whole petroleum interest, in its depressed condition, be required to sustain the penalty. We submit to the railway managers whether it is not right to charge for hauling goods in proportion to the distance hauled, allowing a small discount, perhaps, upon the rate per mile for the greater distance.

Our remarks upon this subject may have the colour of assurance, but, from the large majority given last winter in favour of the new constitution of this state, we have great confidence that the people will not part with their sovereign rights, nor allow themselves to be ruled by King Pool.

At first the Oil Region was puzzled by the Rutter circular. It certainly was plausible. Was it not true that every man shared equally under it? As the days passed, the dazed mental condition into which it had thrown the oil men cleared up. Mr. Allen's editorials began to take effect. The pipe-lines left out of the pool began to ask how it could be legal that the railroads should enter into an arrangement which obviously would drive them out of business. The creek refiners began to ask by what right the advantage of geographical position at the wells should be taken from them, and Cleveland be allowed to retain the advantages of her proximity to the Western market; Pittsburg her position on the Ohio River and the market it commanded; all of the cities the advantage of their proximity to great local markets and to such necessary supplies as barrels and acids. Besides, was it constitutional for the railroads thus to regulate interstate commerce? Was not the arrangement, as far as the Pennsylvania was concerned, plainly prohibited by the new constitution of the state of Pennsylvania? The producers slowly began to realise, too, that the Rutter circular, like the South Improvement charter and contracts, did not recognise them as a body. The contract of March 25, 1872, provided that the rates fixed should not be "liable to any change either for increase or decrease without first giving to William Hasson, president of the Producers' Union, at Oil City, at least ninety days' notice in writing of such contemplated change." This agreement was totally ignored. It was an "insolent equalisation," the oil men concluded, and the sum total of their dissatisfaction finally found expression at a mass-meeting at Parker's Landing, on October 2. Directly after this meeting a committee appointed sent to Messrs. Scott, Vanderbilt and Jewett, the new president of the Erie, letters calling their attention to the Rutter circular, and stating the objections of the producers to it. These letters sent on October 6 received no attention from any of the railroad presidents addressed for over three weeks, when the following was received from the Pennsylvania:

Gentlemen:—Your communication of the 6th inst., to Thomas A. Scott, president, was received, and has been referred to me.

In establishing the recent rates and arrangements for the transportation of oil, the object which was at all times kept in view was to place all interests on an equality, giving to no one an undue advantage over any other.

We believe that this object has been accomplished, and that by adhering to our present rates the interests both of the producers, refiners and transporters will be promoted.

Very truly yours,

A. J. CASSATT.

"Brief, tardy and unsatisfactory," was the Derrick's characterisation of Mr. Cassatt's letter. It was evidence to the oil men that if anything was to be done to break the new tariff it would have to be done in court, for the railroads meant to stand by their creation.

In this discussion of the Rutter circular Mr. Rockefeller's name scarcely appeared. It was known that he had been admitted to the conferences at which the tariff was arranged. This was taken as a matter of course. There was nothing which concerned the oil business which John Rockefeller was not on the inside of. Mr. Blanchard later stated that the "crude equivalent" scheme was suggested by certain Western refiners. The tremendous advantage Cleveland secured by the new arrangement, practically 300 miles of free transportation, seemed to prove, too, that Mr. Rockefeller had not been inactive during the conference. Whether he had or had not suggested the points in the "Rutter circular" so advantageous to his interests, he used them now to aid him in accomplishing one of the shrewdest and most far-reaching moves of his life —the move which was to lead at last to the realisation of his Great Purpose—the concentration of the oil business in his own hands. For Mr. Rockefeller, quiet as he had been since the breaking up of the Refiners' Association in the summer of 1873, had by no means given up the idea of doing for the refining interest of the whole country what he had done for that of Cleveland through the South Improvement Company.

Mr. Rockefeller has shown repeatedly in his conquering business career remarkable ability to learn from experience. The breaking up of the Refiners' Association *may* have seemed a disaster to him. He did not allow it to be a profitless disaster. He extracted useful lessons from the experience, and, armed with this new wisdom, bent his whole mind to working out a third plan of campaign. He now knew that he could not hope to make again so rich a haul as he had made through the defunct South Improvement scheme. The experience of the past year with the refiners convinced him that it would take time to educate them to his idea of combination; but he had learned who of them were capable of this education. As for the producers, the alliance attempted with them was enough to demonstrate that they would never endure long the restraints of any association. Besides, the bulk of them still held the, to him, unpractical belief that rebates were *wrong*. Mr. Rockefeller had also re-learned in these eighteen months

[145]

what he knew pretty well before, that the promise to give or take away a heavy freight traffic was enough to persuade any railroad king of the day to break the most solemn compact.

With all these reflections fresh in mind, Mr. Rockefeller again bent over a map of the refining interests of the United States. Here was the world he sighed to conquer. If we may suppose him to have begun his campaign as a great general with whom he has many traits in common—the First Napoleon—used to begin his, by studding a map with red-headed pegs marking the points he must capture, Mr. Rockefeller's chart would have shown in and around Boston perhaps three pegs, representing a crude capacity of 3,500 barrels; in and around New York fifteen pegs, a capacity of 9,790 barrels; in and around Philadelphia twelve pegs, a capacity of 2,061 barrels; in Pittsburg twenty-two pegs, a capacity of 6,090 barrels; on the creek twenty-seven pegs, a capacity of 9,231 barrels.* His work was to get control of this multitude of red pegs and to fly above them the flag of what the irreverent call the "holy blue barrel." †

Some time in the summer of 1874, after it had become certain that Colonel Potts's plan for an equalisation of oil freights would be carried out, Mr. Rockefeller wrote to his former colleague in the South Improvement Company, W. G. Warden, of Philadelphia, telling him he wanted to talk over the condition of the oil business with him, and inviting him to bring Charles Lockhart, of Pittsburg, to that Mecca of American schemers, Saratoga, for a conference with him and Mr. Flagler. Mr. Warden hesitated. He had been much abused for his relation with the South Improvement Company. He had seen the National Refiners' Association fail. He had begun to feel a distaste for combination. Besides, he

* These figures are from Henry's "Early and Later History of Petroleum," published in 1873.

† The barrels of the Standard Oil Company are painted blue.

GEORGE H. BISSELL

Founder of the first oil company in the United States.

JONATHAN WATSON

One of the owners of the land on which the first successful well was drilled for oil.

SAMUEL KIER

The first petroleum refined and sold for lighting purpose was made by Mr. Kier in the '50s in Pittsburg.

JOSHUA MERRILL

The chemist and refiner to whom many of the most important processes now in use in making illuminating and lubricating oils are due.

was doing very well in Philadelphia. However, after some hesitation, he and Mr. Lockhart went to Saratoga. The four gentlemen breakfasted together and later strolled out to a pavilion. Here they discussed again, as they had nearly three years before, when they prepared the South Improvement assault, the condition of the oil business. •

Mr. Rockefeller now had something besides a theory to present to the gentlemen he wished to go into his third scheme. He had the most persuasive of all arguments—an actual achievement. "Three years ago," he could tell them, "I took over the Cleveland refineries. I have managed them so that to-day I pay a profit to nobody. I do my own buying, I make my own acid and barrels, I control the New York terminals of both the Erie and Central roads, and ship such quantities that the railroads give me better rates than they do any other shipper. In 1873 I shipped over 700,000 barrels by the Central, and my profit on my capitalisation, $2,500,000, was over $1,000,000. This is the result of combination in one city. The railroads now have arranged a new tariff, by which they mean to put us all on an equal footing. They say they will give no rebates to anyone, but if we can join with Cleveland the strongest forces in other great shipping points, and apply to them the same tactics I have employed, we shall become the largest shipper, and can demand a rebate in return for an equal division of our freight. We proved in 1872–1873 that we could not do anything by an open association. Let us who see what a combination strictly carried out will effect unite secretly to accomplish it. Let us become the nucleus of a *private* company which gradually shall acquire control of all refineries everywhere, become the only shippers, and consequently the master of the railroads in the matter of freight rates." It was six hours before the gentlemen in conference left the pavilion, and when they came out Mr. Warden and Mr. Lockhart had agreed to transfer their refineries in Philadelphia and Pittsburg to the Standard Oil Company, of Cleveland, taking stock in exchange. They had also agreed to absorb, as rapidly as persuasion or other means could bring it about, the refineries in their neighbourhood. Their union with the Standard was to remain an absolute secret—the concerns operating under their respective names.*

On October 15, 1874, Mr. Rockefeller consummated another purchase of as great importance. He bought the works of Charles Pratt and Company, of New York city. As before, the purchase was secret. The strategic importance of these purchases for one holding Mr. Rockefeller's vast ambition was enormous. It gave him as allies men who were among the most successful refiners, without doubt, in each of the three greatest refining centres of the country outside of Cleveland, where he ruled, and of the creek, where he had learned that neither he nor any member of the South Improvement Company could do business with facility. To meet these purchases the stock of the Standard Oil Company was increased, on March 10, 1875, to $3,500,000.† The value of the concern as a money-earner at this early date, 1874, is shown by the fact that Pratt and Company paid not less than 265 for the Standard stock they received in exchange for their works.‡

The first intimation that the Oil Region had that Mr. Rockefeller was pushing another combination was in March of 1875, when it was announced that an organisation of refiners, called the Central Association, of which he was president, had been formed. Its main points were that if a refiner would lease to the association his plant for a term of months he would

---

* This account of the meeting at Saratoga was given to the writer by Charles Lockhart, of Pittsburg.

† See Appendix, Number 24. Standard Oil Company's application for increase of capital stock to $3,500,000 in 1875.

‡ See Appendix, Number 25. Henry M. Flagler's testimony on the union of the Standard Oil Company with outside refiners in 1874.

be allowed to subscribe for stock of the new company. The lease allowed the owner to do his own manufacturing, but gave Mr. Rockefeller's company "irrevocable authority" to make all purchases of crude oil and sales of refined, to decide how much each refinery should manufacture, and *to negotiate for all freight and pipe-line expenses.* The Central Association was a most clever device. It furnished the secret partners of Mr. Rockefeller a plausible proposition with which to approach the firms of which they wished to obtain control.

Little as the Oil Regions knew of the real meaning of the Central Association, the news of its organisation raised a cry of monopoly, and the advocates of the new scheme felt called upon to defend it. The defense took the line that the conditions of the trade made such a combination of refineries necessary. Altogether the ablest explanation was that of H. H. Rogers, of Charles Pratt and Company, to a reporter of the New York Tribune:

"There are five refining points in the country," said Mr. Rogers, "Pittsburg, Philadelphia, Cleveland, the Oil Regions and New York city. Each of these has certain local advantages which may be briefly stated as follows: Pittsburg, cheap oil; Philadelphia, the seaboard; Cleveland, cheap barrels, and canal as well as railroad transportation; the Oil Regions, crude oil at the lowest figure; and all the products of petroleum have the best market in New York city. The supply of oil is three or four times greater than the demand.* If the oil refineries were run to their full capacity, the market would be overstocked. The business is not regular, but spasmodic. When the market is brisk and oil is in demand, all the oil interests are busy and enjoy a fair share of prosperity. At other times, the whole trade is affected by the dullness. It has been estimated that not less than twenty millions of dollars are invested in the oil business. It is therefore to the interest of every man who has put a dollar in it to have the trade protected and established on a permanent footing. Speculators have ruined the market. The brokers heretofore have been speculating upon the market with disastrous effects upon the trade, and this new order of things will force them to pursue

* Mr. Rogers is mistaken here. The production in 1874 was 10,926,945 barrels, the shipments 8,821,500, the stocks at the end of the year 3,705,639. In 1875, the year in which he is speaking, more oil was consumed than produced.

their legitimate calling, and realise their profits from their industry and perseverance. Two years ago an attempt was made to organise an oil refiners' association, but it was subsequently abandoned. There was no cohesion of interests, and agreements were not kept. The movement at the present time is a revival of the former idea, and, it is believed, has already secured fully nine-tenths of the oil refiners in the country in its favour. I do not believe there is any intention among the oil men to 'bull' the market. The endeavour is to equalise all around and protect the capital invested. If by common consent, in good faith, the refiners agree to reduce the quantities to an allotment for each, made in view of the supply and demand, and the capacity for production, the market can be regulated with a reasonable profit for all. The price of oil to-day is fifteen cents per gallon. The proposed allotment of business would probably advance the price to twenty cents. To make an artificial increase, with immense profits, would be recognised as speculative instead of legitimate, and the oil interests would suffer accordingly. Temporary capital would compete with permanent investment and ruin everything. The oil producers to-day are bankrupt. There have been more failures during the last five months than in five years previously. An organisation to protect the oil capital is imperatively needed. Oil to yield a fair profit should be sold for twenty-five cents per gallon. That price would protect every interest and cover every outlay for getting out the crude petroleum, transporting by railroad, refining and the incidental charges of handling, etc. The foreign markets will regulate the price to a great extent, because they are the greatest consumers. The people of China, Germany, and other foreign countries cannot afford to pay high prices. Kerosene oil is a luxury to them, and they do not receive sufficient compensation for their labour to enable them to use this oil at an extravagant price. The price, therefore, must be kept within reasonable limits."

The Oil Regions refused flatly to accept this view of the situation. The world would not buy refined at twenty-five cents, they argued. "You injured the foreign market in 1872 by putting up the price. Our only hope is in increasing consumption. The world is buying more oil to-day than ever before, because it is cheap. We must learn to accept small profits, as other industries do." "The formation of the Refiners' Association has thrust upon the trade an element of uncertainty that has unsettled all sound views as to the general outlook," said the Derrick. "The scope of the Association," wrote a Pittsburg critic, "is an attempt to control the refining of oil, with the ultimate purpose of advancing its price and reaping a rich harvest in profits. This can only be done by reducing the production of refined oil, and this will in turn act on crude oil, making the stock so far in excess of the demand as to send it down to a lower figure than it has yet touched."

"The most important feature of this contract," said a "veteran refiner," "is perhaps that part which provides that the Executive Committee of the Central Association are to have the exclusive power to arrange with the railroads for the carrying of the crude and refined oil. It is intended by this provision to enable the Executive Committee to speak for the whole trade in securing special rates of freight, whereby independent shippers of crude oil, and such refiners as refuse to join the combination, and any new refining interest that may be started, may be driven out of the trade. The whole general purpose of the combination is to reap a large margin by depressing crude and raising the price of refined oil, and the chief means employed is the system of discrimination in railroad freights to the seaboard."

"The veteran refiner" was right in his supposition that Mr. Rockefeller intended to use the enormous power his combination gave him to get a special rate. As a matter of fact he had seen to that before the "veteran refiner" expressed his mind. It will be remembered that in April, 1874, Mr. Rockefeller had made a contract with the Erie by which he was to ship fifty per cent. of his refined oil over that road at a rate as low as any competing line gave any shipper and he was to have a lease of the Weehawken oil terminal. Now this contract remained in force until the first of March, 1875, when a new one was made with the Erie guaranteeing the road the same percentage of freight and giving the Standard a ten-per-cent. rebate on whatever open tariff should be fixed. This rebate Mr. Blanchard says was quite independent of what the Central might be giving the Standard. He says that one reason the

Standard was given the rebate was that it was suspected the Pennsylvania was allowing the Empire Transportation Company an even larger one. If true, this would not affect any refiner necessarily as the Empire was not a refiner in March, 1875. The real reason, of course, was what Mr. Blanchard gives later—that by this rebate they kept the Standard trade, now greatly increased by the purchase of the outside works already mentioned, although it should be noticed the Erie officials knew nothing of the Standard having control of any other refinery than that of Charles Pratt and Company.

The announcement of the Central Association put an altogether new feature on oil transportation. If this organisation succeeded, and the refiners in it claimed nine-tenths of the capacity of the country—it gave Mr. Rockefeller "irrevocable authority" to negotiate freights. The Pennsylvania road immediately felt the pressure. The oil they had carried for big firms like those of Charles Lockhart in Pittsburg and of Warden, Frew and Company in Philadelphia was in the hands of the Standard Oil Company, and Mr. Rockefeller asked a rebate of ten per cent. on open rates. The road demurred. Colonel Potts objected strenuously. Three years later in a paper discussing this rebate and its consequences he said:

"The rebate was a modest one, as was its recipient. Yet the railway Cassandras prophesied from it a multitude of evils—a gradual destruction of all other refiners and a gradual absorption of their property by the favourite, who, with this additional armament, would rapidly progress towards a control of all cars, all pipes, all production, and finally of the roads themselves. Their prophecies met but little faith or consideration. The Standard leaders themselves were especially active in discouraging any such radical purpose. Their little rebate was enough for them. Everybody else should prosper, as would be shortly seen. They needed no more refineries; they had already more than they could employ—why should they hunger after greater burdens? It was the railroads they chiefly cared for, and next in their affections stood the 100 rival refineries. Such beneficent longings as still remained (and their bosoms overflowed with them) spread out their steady waves toward the poor producers whom, not to be impious, they had always been ready to gather under their wings, yet they would not.

"This unselfish language soothed all alarm into quiet slumbering. It resembles the gentle fanning of the vampire's wings, and it had the same end in view—the undisturbed abstraction of the victim's blood."

Colonel Potts's argument against the rebate—doubtless clothed in much less picturesque language in 1875 than his feelings stirred him to in 1878, for a good enough reason, too, as we shall see—failed to convince the Pennsylvania officials. They decided to yield to the Standard. Mr. Cassatt, then third vice-president of the road, in charge of transportation, said in 1879 that the rebate was given because they found the Standard was getting very strong, that they had the backing of the other roads, and that if the Pennsylvania wanted to retain its full share of business and at fair rates they must make arrangements to protect themselves.

No one of the roads knew certainly what the others were doing for the Standard until October 1, 1875. The freight agents then met to discuss again the freight pool they had formed in 1874. It had not been working with perfect satisfaction. The clause granting the rebate of twenty-two cents to the pipe-lines which sustained an agreed rate of pipage had been abandoned after about five months' experiment. It was thought to stimulate new pipes. The roads in making a new adjustment made no effort to regulate pipe-line tariffs. The "crude rebate" as it was called—carrying oil to a refinery for nothing—was left in force. At this meeting Mr. Blanchard found that both of the Erie's big rivals were granting the Standard a ten per cent. rebate. He also found that he was not getting fifty per cent. of the Standard's business as the contract called for—that the Standard controlled not only the Cleveland and New York works of which he knew, but large works in Pittsburg and Philadelphia.*

* See Appendix, Number 26. George R. Blanchard's testimony on the breaking up of the Pipe Pool of 1874.

Mr. Rockefeller was certainly now in an excellent condition to work out his plan of bringing under his own control all the refineries of the country. The Standard Oil Company owned in each of the great refining centres, New York, Pittsburg and Philadelphia, a large and aggressive plant run by the men who had built it up. These works were, so far as the public knew, still independent and their only relation that of the "Central Association." As a matter of fact they were the "Central Association." Not only had Mr. Rockefeller brought these powerful interests into his concern; he had secured for them a rebate of ten per cent. on a rate which should always be as low as any one of the roads gave any of his competitors. He had done away with middlemen, that is, he was "paying nobody a profit." He had undeniably a force wonderfully constructed for what he wanted to do and one made practically impregnable as things were in the oil business then, by virtue of its special transportation rate.

As soon as his new line was complete the work of acquiring all outside refineries began at each of the oil centres. Unquestionably the acquisitions were made through persuasion when this was possible. If the party approached refused to lease or sell, he was told firmly what Mr. Rockefeller had told the Cleveland refiners when he went to them in 1872 with the South Improvement contracts, that there was no hope for him; that a combination was in progress which was bound to work; and that those who stayed out would inevitably go to the wall. Naturally the first fruits to fall into the hands of the new alliance were those refineries which were embarrassed or discouraged by the conditions which Mr. Rogers explains above. Take as an example the case of the Citizens' Oil Refining Company of Pittsburg, as it was explained in 1888 to the House Committee on Manufactures in its trust investigation. A. H. Tack, a partner in the company, told the story:*

* Condensed from Mr. Tack's testimony.

"We began in 1869 with a capacity of 1,000 barrels a day. At the start everything was *couleur de rose*, so much so that we put our works in splendid shape. We manufactured all the products. We even got it down to making wax, and using the very last residuum in the boilers. We got the works in magnificent order and used up everything. We began to feel the squeeze in 1872. We did not know what was the matter. Of course we were all affected the same way in Pennsylvania, and of course we commenced shifting about, and meeting together, and forming delegations, and going down to Philadelphia to see the Pennsylvania Railroad, meeting after meeting and delegation after delegation. We suspected there was something wrong, and told those men there was something wrong somewhere; that we felt, so far as position was concerned, we had the cheapest barrels, the cheapest labour, and the cheapest coal, and the route from the crude district was altogether in our favour. We had a railroad and a river to bring us our raw material. We had made our investment based on the seaboard routes, and we wanted the Pennsylvania Railroad to protect us. But none of our meetings or delegations ever amounted to anything. They were always repulsed in some way, put off, and we never got any satisfaction. The consequence was that in two or three years there was no margin or profit. In order to overcome that we commenced speculating, in the hope that there would be a change some time or other for the better. We did not like the idea of giving up the ship. Now, during these times the Standard Oil Company increased so perceptibly and so strong that we at once recognised it as the element. Instead of looking to the railroad I always looked to the Standard Oil Company. In 1874 I went to see Rockefeller to find if we could make arrangements with him by which we could run a portion of our works. It was a very brief interview. He said there was no hope for us at all. He remarked this—I cannot give the exact quotation —'There is no hope for us,' and probably he said, 'There is no hope for any of us'; but he says, 'The weakest must go first.' And we went."

All over the country the refineries in the same condition as Mr. Tack's firm sold or leased. Those who felt the hard times and had any hope of weathering them resisted at first. With many of them the resistance was due simply to their love for their business and their unwillingness to share its control with outsiders. The thing which a man has begun, cared for, led to a healthy life, from which he has begun to gather fruit, which he knows he can make greater and richer, he loves as he does his life. It is one of the fruits of his life. He is jealous of it—wishes the honour of it, will not divide it with another. He can suffer heavily his own mistakes, learn from them, correct them. He can fight opposition, bear all—so long as the work is his. There were refiners in 1875 who loved their business in this way. Why one should love an oil refinery the outsider may not see; but to the man who had begun with one still and had seen it grow by his own energy and intelligence to ten, who now sold 500 barrels a day where he once sold five, the refinery was the dearest spot on earth save his home. He walked with pride among its evil-smelling places, watched the processes with eagerness, experimented with joy and recounted triumphantly every improvement. To ask such a man to give up his refinery was to ask him to give up the thing which, after his family, meant most in life to him.

To Mr. Rockefeller this feeling was a weak sentiment. To place love of independent work above love of profits was as incomprehensible to him as a refusal to accept a rebate because it was *wrong!* Where persuasion failed then, it was necessary, in his judgment, that pressure be applied—simply a pressure sufficient to demonstrate to these blind or recalcitrant individuals the impossibility of their long being able to do business independently. It was a pressure varied according to locality. Usually it took the form of cutting their market. The system of "predatory competition" was no invention of the Standard Oil Company. It had prevailed in the oil business from the start. Indeed, it was one of the evils Mr. Rockefeller claimed his combination would cure, but until now it had been used spasmodically. Mr. Rockefeller never did anything spasmodically. He applied underselling for destroying his rivals' market with the same deliberation and persistency that characterised all his efforts, and in the long run he always won. There were other forms of pressure. Sometimes the independents found it impossible to get oil; again, they were obliged to wait days for cars to ship in; there seemed to be no end to the ways of making it hard for men to do business, of discouraging them until they would sell or lease, and always at the psychological moment a purchaser was at their side. Take as an example the case of the Harkness refinery in Philadelphia, a story told to the same committee as that of Mr. Tack:

"I was the originator of the enterprise," said William W. Harkness, "believing that there was no better place than Philadelphia to refine oil, particularly for export. We commenced then, as near as I can now recollect, about 1870, and we made money up to probably 1874. We managed our business very close and did not speculate in oil. We bought and we sold, and we paid a great deal of attention to the statistical part of our business so as to save waste, and we did a nice business. But we found in some years that probably five months out of a year we could not sell our oil unless it would be at a positive loss, and then we stopped. Then when we could sell our oil, we found a difficulty about getting cars. My brother would complain of it, but I believed that the time would come when that would be equalised. I had no idea of the iniquity that was going on; I could not conceive it. I went on in good faith until about 1874, and then the trouble commenced. We could not get our oil and were compelled to sell at a loss. Then Warden, Frew and Company formed some kind of running arrangement where they supplied the crude, and we seemed to get along a little better. After a while the business got complicated, and I got tired and handed it over to my brother; I backed out. That was about 1875. I was dissatisfied and wanted to do an independent business, or else I wanted to give it up. In 1876—I recollect that very well, because it was the year of the Centennial Exposition—we were at the Centennial Exposition. I was sitting in front of the great Corliss engine, admiring it, and he told me there was a good opportunity to get out. Warden, Frew and Company, he said, were prepared to buy us out, and I asked him whether he considered that as the best thing to do; whether we had not better hold on and fight it through, for I believed that these difficulties would not continue; that we would get our oil. I knew he was a competent refiner, and I wanted to continue business, but he said he thought he had better make this arrangement, and I consented, and we sold out; we got our investment back." *

Here we have a refiner discouraged by the conditions which Mr. Rockefeller claims his aggregation will cure. Under the Rutter circular and the discrimination in freight to the Standard which followed, his difficulty in getting oil increases, and he consents to a running arrangement with Mr. Rockefeller's partner in Philadelphia, but he wants to do an "independent

* Condensed from Mr. Harkness's testimony.

business." Impossible. As he sits watching the smooth and terrible power of that famous Corliss engine of 1876, an engine which showed to thousands for the first time what great power properly directed means, he realised that something very like it was at work in the oil business—something resistless, silent, perfect in its might—and he sold out to that something. Everywhere men did the same. The history of oil refining on Oil Creek from 1875 to 1879 is almost uncanny. There were at the beginning of that period twenty-seven plants in the region, most of which were in a fair condition, considering the difficulties in the business. During 1873 the demand for refined oil had greatly increased, the exports nearly doubling over those of 1872. The average profit on refined that year in a well-managed refinery was not less than three cents a gallon. During the first half of 1874 the oil business had been depressed, but the oil refiners were looking for better times when the Rutter circular completely demoralised them by putting fifty cents extra freight charges on their shipments without an equivalent raise on competitive points. It was not only this extra charge, enough to cut off their profits, as business then stood, but it was that the same set of men who had thrown their business into confusion in 1872 was again at work. The announcement of the Central Association with Mr. Rockefeller's name at its head confirmed their fears. Nevertheless at first none of the small refiners would listen to the proposition to sell or lease made them in the spring of 1875 by the representative first sent out by the Central Association. They would have nothing to do, they said bluntly, with any combination engineered by John D. Rockefeller. The representative withdrew and the case was considered. In the mean time conditions on the creek grew harder. All sorts of difficulties began to be strewn in their way—cars were hard to get, the markets they had built up were cut under them—a demoralising conviction was abroad in the trade that this new and mysterious combination was going to succeed; that it was doing rapidly what its members were reported to be saying daily: "We mean to secure the entire refining business of the world." Such was the state of things on the creek when in the early fall of 1875 an energetic young refiner and oil buyer well known in the Oil Regions, J. D. Archbold, appeared in Titusville as the representative of a new company, the Acme Oil Company, a concern which everybody believed to be an offshoot of the Standard Oil Company of Cleveland, though nobody could prove it. As a matter of fact the Acme was capitalised and controlled entirely by Standard men, its stockholders being, in addition to Mr. Archbold, William Rockefeller, William G. Warden, Frank Q. Barstow, and Charles Pratt. It was evident at once that the Acme Oil Company had come into the Oil Regions for the purpose of absorbing the independent interests as Mr. Rockefeller and his colleagues were absorbing them elsewhere. The work was done with a promptness and despatch which do great credit to the energy and resourcefulness of the engineer of the enterprise. In three years, by 1878, all but two of the refineries of Titusville had "retired from the business gloriously," as Mr. Archbold, flushed with victory, told the counsel of the Commonwealth of Pennsylvania in 1879, when the state authorities were trying to find what was at work in the oil interests to cause such a general collapse. Most of the concerns were bought outright, the owners being convinced that it was impossible for them to do an independent business, and being unwilling to try combination. All down the creek the little refineries which for years had faced every difficulty with stout hearts collapsed. "Sold out," "dismantled," "shut down," is the melancholy record of the industry during these four years. At the end practically nothing was left in the Oil Regions but the Acme of Titusville and the Imperial of Oil City, both of them now under Standard management. To the oil men this sudden 'wiping out of the score of plants with which they had been familiar for years seemed a crime which nothing could justify. Their bitterness of heart was only intensified by the sight of the idle refiners thrown out of business by the sale of their factories. These men had, many of them, handsome sums to invest, but what were they to put them in? They were refiners, and they carried a pledge in their pockets not to go into that business for a period of ten years. Some of them tried the discouraged oil man's fatal resource, the market, and as a rule left their money there. One refiner who had, according to popular report, received $200,000 for his business, speculated the entire sum away in less than a year. Others tried new enterprises, but men of forty learn new trades with difficulty, and failure followed many of them. The scars left in the Oil Regions by the Standard Combination of 1875–1879 are too deep and ugly for men and women of this generation to forget them.

In Pittsburg the same thing was happening. At the beginning of the work of absorption—1874—there were between twenty-two and thirty refineries in the town.* As we have seen, Lockhart and Frew sold to the Standard Oil Company of Cleveland some time in 1874. In the fall of that year a new company was formed in Pittsburg, called the Standard Oil Company of Pittsburg. Its president was Charles Lockhart; its directors William Frew, David Bushnell, H. M. Flagler, and W. G. Warden—all members of the Standard Oil Company and four of them stockholders in the South Improvement Company. This company at once began to lease or buy refineries. Many of the Pittsburg refiners made a valiant fight to get rates on their oil which would enable them to run

* J. T. Henry, in his "Early and Later History of Petroleum," gives twenty-two; E. G. Patterson, in a list presented in court in 1880, gives the number at the beginning of this combination as thirty.

independently. To save expense they tried to bring oil from the oil fields by barge; the pipe-lines in the pool refused to run oil to barges, the railroad to accept oil brought down by barge. An independent pipe-line attempted to bring it to Pittsburg, but to reach the works the pipe-line must run under a branch of the Pennsylvania railroad. It refused to permit this, and for months the oil from the line was hauled in wagons from the point where it had been held up, over the railroad track, and there repiped and carried to Pittsburg. At every point they met interference until finally one by one they gave in. According to Mr. Frew, who in 1879 was examined as to the condition of things in Pittsburg, the company began to "acquire refiners" in 1875. In 1877 they bought their last one; and at the time Mr. Frew was under examination he could not remember but *one* refinery in operation in Pittsburg not controlled by his company.

Nor was it refiners only who sold out. All departments of the trade began to yield to the pressure. There was in the oil business a class of men known as shippers. They bought crude oil, sent it East, and sold it to refineries there. Among the largest of these was Adnah Neyhart, whose active representative was W. T. Scheide. Now to Mr. Rockefeller the independent shipper was an incubus; he did a business which, in his judgment, a firm ought to do for itself, and reaped a profit which might go direct into the business. Besides, so long as there were shippers to supply crude to the Eastern refineries at living prices, so long these concerns might resist offers to sell or lease.

Some time in the fall of 1872 Mr. Scheide began to lose his customers in New York. He found that they were making some kind of a working arrangement with the Standard Oil Company, just what he did not know. But at all events they no longer bought from him but from the Standard buyer, J. A. Bostwick and Company. At the same time he became convinced that Mr. Rockefeller was after his business. "I knew that they were making some strenuous efforts to get our business," he told the Hepburn Commission in 1879, "because I used to meet Mr. Rockefeller in the Erie office." At the same time that he was facing the loss of customers and the demoralising conviction that the Standard Oil Company wanted his business, he was experiencing more or less disgust over business conditions in New York. "I did not like the character of my customers there," Mr. Scheide told the committee. "I did not think they were treating us fairly and squarely. There was a strong competition in handling oil. The competition had got to be so strong that 'outside refiners,' as they called themselves then, used to go around bidding up the price of their works on the Standard Oil Company, and they were using me to sell their refineries to the Standard. They would say to refiners: 'Neyhart will do so and so, and we are going to continue running.' And they would say to us that the Standard was offering lower prices. I recollect one instance in which they, after having made a contract to buy oil from me if I would bring it over the Erie Railway, broke that contract for the 1-128th part of a cent a gallon. I sold out the next week." When Mr. Scheide went to the freight agent of the Erie road, Mr. Blanchard, and told him of his decision to sell, Mr. Blanchard tried to dissuade him. During the conversation he let out a fact which must have convinced Mr. Scheide more fully than ever that he had been wise in determining to give up his business. Mr. Blanchard told him as a reason for his staying and trusting to the Erie road to keep its contracts with him that the Standard Oil Company had been offering him five cents more a barrel than Mr. Scheide was paying them, and would take all their cars, and load them all regularly if they would throw him over and give them the business. It is interesting to note that when Mr. Scheide sold in the spring of 1875, it was, as he supposed, to Charles

Pratt and Company. Well informed as he was in all the intricacies of the business—and there were few abler or more energetic men in trade at the time—he did not know that Charles Pratt and Company had been part and parcel of the Standard Oil Company since October, 1874.

Of course securing a large crude shipping business like Mr. Neyhart's was a valuable point for the Standard. It threw all of the refiners whom he had supplied out of crude oil and forced several of them to come to the Standard buyer—a first step, of course, toward a lease or sale. At every point, indeed, making it difficult for the refiner to get his raw product was one of the favourite manœuvres of the combination. It was not only to crude oil it was applied. Factories which worked up the residuum or tar into lubricating oil and depended on Standard plants for their supply were cut off. There was one such in Cleveland—the firm of Morehouse and Freeman. Mr. Morehouse had begun to experiment with lubricating oils in 1861, and in 1871 the report of the Cleveland Board of Trade devoted several of its pages to a description of his business. According to this account he was then making oils adapted to lubricating all kinds of machinery—he held patents for several brands and trade marks, and had produced that year over 25,000 barrels of different lubricants besides 120,000 boxes of axle grease. At this time he was buying his stock or residuum from one or another of the twenty-five Cleveland refiners. Then came the South Improvement Company and the concentration of the town's refining interest in Mr. Rockefeller's hands. Mr. Morehouse, according to the testimony he gave the Hepburn Commission in 1879, went to Mr. Rockefeller, after the consolidation, to arrange for supplies. He was welcomed—the Standard Oil Company had not at that time begun to deal in lubricating oils—and encouraged to build a new plant. This was done at a cost of $41,000, and a contract was made with the Standard Oil Company for a daily supply of eighty-five barrels of residuum. Some time in 1874 this supply was cut down to twelve barrels. The price was put up too, and contracts for several months were demanded so that Mr. Morehouse got no advantage from the variation in crude prices. Then the freights went up on the railroads. He paid $1.50 and two dollars for what he says he felt sure his big neighbour was paying but seventy or seventy-five cents (there is no evidence of any such low rate to the Standard from Cleveland to New York by rail). Now it was impossible for Mr. Morehouse to supply his trade on twelve barrels of stock. He begged Mr. Rockefeller for more. It was there in the Standard Oil works. Why could he not have it? He could pay for it. He and his partner offered to buy 5,000 barrels and store it, but Mr. Rockefeller was firm. All he could give Mr. Morehouse was twelve barrels a day. "I saw readily what that meant," said Mr. Morehouse, "that meant squeeze you out—buy your works. They have got the works and are running them; I am without anything. They paid about $15,000 for what cost me $41,000. He said that he had facilities for freighting and that the coal-oil business belonged to them; and any concern that would start in that business, they had sufficient money to lay aside a fund to wipe them out—these are the words." *

At every refining centre in the country this process of consolidation through persuasion, intimidation, or force, went on. As fast as a refinery was brought in line its work was assigned to it. If it was an old and poorly equipped plant it was usually dismantled or shut down. If it was badly placed, that is, if it was not economically placed in regard to a pipe-line and railroad, it was dismantled even though in excellent condition. If it was a large and well-equipped plant advantageously located it was assigned a certain quota to manufacture, and it did nothing but manufacture. The buying of crude, the mak-

* Condensed from testimony of Mr. Morehouse before the special committee on railroads, New York Assembly, 1879.

ing of freight rates, the selling of the output remained with Mr. Rockefeller. The contracts under which all the refineries brought into line were run were of the most detailed and rigid description, and they were executed as a rule with a secrecy which baffles description. Take, for example, a running arrangement made by Rockefeller in 1876, with a Cleveland refinery, that of Scofield, Shurmer and Teagle. The members of this concern had all been in the refining business in Cleveland in 1872 and had all handed over their works to Mr. Rockefeller, when he notified them of the South Improvement Company's contracts. Mr. Shurmer declared once in an affidavit that he alone lost $20,000 by that manœuvre. The members of the firm had not stayed out of business, however. Recovering from the panic caused by the South Improvement Company, they had united in 1875, building a refinery worth $65,000, with a yearly capacity of 180,000 barrels of crude. On the first year's business they made $40,000. Although this was doing well, they were convinced they might do better if they could get as good freight rates as the Standard Oil Company, and in the spring of 1876 they brought suit against the Lake Shore and Michigan Southern and the New York Central and Hudson River Railroads for "unlawful and unjust discrimination, partialities and preferences made and practised . . . in favour of the Standard Oil Company, enabling the said Standard Oil Company to obtain to a great extent the monopoly of the oil and naphtha trade of Cleveland." The suit was not carried through at the time. Mr. Rockefeller seems to have suggested a surer way to the firm of getting the rates they wanted. This was to make a running arrangement with him. He seems to have demonstrated to them that they could make more money under his plan than outside, and they signed a contract for a remarkable "joint adventure." According to this document Scofield, Shurmer and Teagle put into the business a plant worth at that time about $73,000 and their entire time. Mr. Rockefeller put in $10,000 and his rebates! That is, he secured for the firm the same preferential rates on their shipments that the Standard Oil Company enjoyed. The firm bound itself not to refine over 85,000 barrels a year and neither jointly nor separately to engage in any other form of oil business for ten years—the life of the contract. Scofield, Shurmer and Teagle were guaranteed a profit of $35,000 a year. Profits over $35,000 went to Mr. Rockefeller up to $70,000; any further profits were divided.

The making of this contract and its execution were attended by all the secret rites peculiar to Mr. Rockefeller's business ventures. According to the testimony of one of the firm given a few years later on the witness stand in Cleveland the contract was signed at night at Mr. Rockefeller's house on Euclid Avenue in Cleveland, where he told the gentlemen that they must not tell even their wives about the new arrangement, that if they made money they must conceal it—they were not to drive fast horses, "put on style," or do anything to let people suspect there were unusual profits in oil refining. That would invite competition. They were told that all accounts were to be kept secret. Fictitious names were to be used in corresponding, and a special box at the post-office was employed for these fictitious characters. In fact, smugglers and house-breakers never surrounded their operations with more mystery.

But make his operations as thickly as he might in secrecy, the effect of Mr. Rockefeller's steady and united attack on the refining business was daily becoming more apparent. Before the end of 1876 the alarm among oil producers, the few independent refineries still in business, and even in certain railroad circles was serious. On all sides talk of a united effort to meet the consolidation was heard.

CHAPTER SIX

STRENGTHENING THE FOUNDATIONS

FIRST INTERSTATE COMMERCE BILL—THE BILL PIGEON-HOLED THROUGH
EFFORTS OF STANDARD'S FRIENDS—INDEPENDENTS SEEK RELIEF BY PRO-
POSED CONSTRUCTION OF PIPE-LINES—PLANS FOR THE FIRST SEABOARD
PIPE-LINE—SCHEME FAILS ON ACCOUNT OF MISMANAGEMENT AND STAND-
ARD AND RAILROAD OPPOSITION—DEVELOPMENT OF THE EMPIRE TRANS-
PORTATION COMPANY AND ITS PROPOSED CONNECTION WITH THE REFINING
BUSINESS—STANDARD, ERIE AND CENTRAL FIGHT THE EMPIRE TRANSPOR-
TATION COMPANY AND ITS BACKER, THE PENNSYLVANIA RAILROAD—THE
PENNSYLVANIA FINALLY QUITS AFTER A BITTER AND COSTLY WAR—EMPIRE
LINE SOLD TO THE STANDARD—ENTIRE PIPE-LINE SYSTEM OF OIL REGIONS
NOW IN ROCKEFELLER'S HANDS—NEW RAILROAD POOL BETWEEN FOUR
ROADS—ROCKEFELLER PUTS INTO OPERATION SYSTEM OF DRAWBACKS
ON OTHER PEOPLE'S SHIPMENTS—HE PROCEEDS RAPIDLY WITH THE WORK
OF ABSORBING RIVALS.

FROM the time the Central Association announced
itself, independent refiners and the producers as a
body watched developments with suspicion. They
had little to go on. They had no means of proving
what was actually the fact that the Central Association
was the Standard Oil Company working secretly to bring
its competitors under control or drive them out of business.
They had no way of knowing what was actually the fact
that the Standard had contracts with the Central, Erie
and the Pennsylvania which gave them rebates on the lowest tariff which others paid. That this must be the case,
however, they were convinced, and they determined early in
1876 to call on Congress for another investigation. A hearing

was practically insured, for Congress since 1872 had given serious attention to the transportation troubles. The Windom Committee of 1874 had made a report, the sweeping recommendations of which gave much encouragement to those who suffered from the practices of the railroads. Among other things this committee recommended that all rates, drawbacks, etc., be published at every point and no changes allowed in them without proper notification. It recommended the Bureau of Commerce which, in 1902, twenty-eight years later, was created. So serious did the Windom Committee consider the situation in 1874, that it made the following radical recommendations:

The only means of securing and maintaining reliable and effective competition between railways is through national or state ownership, or control of one or more lines which, being unable to enter into combinations, will serve as a regulation of other lines.

One or more double-track freight-railways honestly and thoroughly constructed, owned or controlled by the government, and operated at a low rate of speed, would doubtless be able to carry at a much less cost than can be done under the present system of operating fast and slow trains on the same road; and, being incapable of entering into combinations, would no doubt serve as a very valuable regulator of existing railroads within the range of their influence.

With Congress in such a temper the oil men felt that there might be some hope of securing the regulation of interstate commerce they had asked for in 1872. The agitation resulted in the presentation in the House of Representatives, in April, of the first Interstate Commerce Bill which promised to be effective. The bill was presented by James H. Hopkins of Pittsburg. Mr. Hopkins had before his eyes the uncanny fate of the independent oil interests of Pittsburg, some twenty-five factories in that town having been reduced to two or three in three and one-half years. He had seen the oil-refining business of the state steadily reduced, and he thought it high time that something was done. In aid of his bill a House investigation was asked. It was soon evident that the Standard was an enemy of this investigation. Through the efforts of a good friend of the organisation—Congressman H. B. Payne, of Cleveland—the matter was referred to the Committee on Commerce, where a member of the house, J. N. Camden, whose refinery, the Camden Consolidated Oil Company, if it had not already gone, soon after went into the Standard Oil Alliance, appeared as adviser of the chairman! Now what Mr. Hopkins wanted was to compel the railroads to present their contracts with the Standard Oil Company. The Committee summoned the proper railroad officers, Messrs. Cassatt, Devereux and Rutter, and O. H. Payne, treasurer of the Standard Oil Company. Of the railroad men, only Mr. Cassatt appeared, and he refused to answer the questions asked or to furnish the documents demanded. Mr. Payne refused also to furnish the committee with information. The two principal witnesses of the oil men were E. G. Patterson of Titusville, to whose energy the investigation was largely due, and Frank Rockefeller of Cleveland, a brother of John D. Rockefeller. Mr. Patterson sketched the history of the oil business since the South Improvement Company identified the Standard Oil Company with that organisation, and framed the specific complaint of the oil men, as follows: "The railroad companies have combined with an organisation of individuals known as the Standard Ring; they give to that party the sole and entire control of all the petroleum refining interest and petroleum shipping interest in the United States, and consequently place the whole producing interest entirely at their mercy. If they succeed they place the price of refined oil as high as they please. It is simply optional with them how much to give us for what we produce."

Frank Rockefeller gave a pretty complete story of the trials of an independent refiner in Cleveland during the preceding four years. His testimony in regard to the South

Improvement Company has already been quoted. He declared that at the moment, his concern, the Pioneer Oil Company, was unable to get the same rates as the Standard; the freight agent frankly told him that unless he could give the road the same amount of oil to transport that the Standard did he could not give the rate the Standard enjoyed. Mr. Rockefeller said that in his belief there was a pooling arrangement between the railroads and the Standard and that the rebate given was "divided up between the Standard Oil Company and the railroad officials." He repeatedly declared to the committee that he did not know this to be a positive fact, that he had no proof, but that he believed such was the truth. Among the railroad officials whom he mentioned as in his opinion enjoying spoils were W. H. Vanderbilt, Thomas Scott and General Devereux. Of course the newspapers had it that he had sworn that such was the fact. Colonel Scott promptly wired the following denial:

" The papers of this morning publish that a man named Rockefeller stated before your committee that myself and other officers of this company were participants in rebates made to the Standard Oil Company. So far as the statement relates to myself and the officers of this company it is unqualifiedly false, and I have to ask that you will summon the officers of the Standard Oil Company, or any other parties that may have any knowledge of that subject, in order that such villainous and unwarranted statements may be corrected."

General Devereux published in the Cleveland press an equally emphatic denial. Although Mr. Rockefeller promptly declared that he had stated to the committee that he had no personal knowledge that there was such a pool as he had intimated between the railroad men and the Standard, that he had only given his suspicions, there were plenty of people to overlook his explanation and assert that he had given proof of such a division of spoils. The belief spread and is met even to-day in oil circles. Now the only basis for any such assertion was the fact that W. H. Vanderbilt, Peter H. Watson and Amasa Stone were at that time, 1876, stockholders in the Standard Oil Company. There is no evidence of which the writer knows that General Devereux or Colonel Scott ever held any stock in the concern. Indeed, in 1879, when A. J. Cassatt was under examination as to the relations of the Pennsylvania Railroad and the Standard Oil Company, his own lawyer took pains to question him on this point—an effort, no doubt, to silence the accusation which at that date was constantly repeated.

"Mr. Cassatt," Mr. MacVeagh said, "I want to direct your attention to a personal matter which was asked you to a certain extent. You were asked whether you had any knowledge that Mr. Vanderbilt, representing the New York Central, or Mr. Jewett, representing the Erie, had any interest whatever in the Standard Oil Company or any of its affiliated companies. I wish to extend that question to the other trunk lines. I wish you would state whether or not to your knowledge Mr. Garrett, or anybody representing the Baltimore and Ohio, had any such interest?"

"They have not to my knowledge."

.   .   .   .

"Then I wish you would state whether Mr. Scott or yourself, or any other officers of the Pennsylvania Railroad Company, had any such interest?"

"Never to my knowledge. I speak of absolute knowledge as to myself, but as to Mr. Scott to the best of my knowledge and belief."

Of course after this controversy the railroads were more obdurate than ever. Mr. Payne and Mr. Camden were active, too, in securing the suppression of the investigations and they soon succeeded not only in doing that but in pigeon-holing for the time Mr. Hopkins's Interstate Commerce Bill.

But the oil men had not been trusting entirely to Congressional relief. From the time that they became convinced that the railroads meant to stand by the terms of the "Rutter Circular" they began to seek an independent outlet to the sea. The first project to attract attention was the Columbia Conduit Pipe Line. This line was begun by one of the picturesque characters of Western Pennsylvania, "Dr." David Hostetter, the maker of the famous Hostetter's Bitters. Dr. Hostetter's Bitters' headquarters were in Pittsburg. He had become interested in oil there, and had made investments in Butler County. In 1874 he found himself hampered in disposing of his oil and conceived the idea of piping it to Pittsburg, where he could make a connection with the Baltimore and Ohio road, which up to this time had refused to go into the oil pool. Now at that time the right of eminent domain for pipes had been granted in but eight counties of Western Pennsylvania. Allegheny County, in which Pittsburg is located, was not included in the eight, a restriction which the oil men attributed rightly, no doubt, to the influence of the Pennsylvania Railroad in the State Legislature. That road could hardly have been expected to allow the pipes to go to Pittsburg and connect with a rival road if it could help it. Dr. Hostetter succeeded in buying a right of way through the county, however, and laid his pipes within a few miles of the city to a point where he had to pass under a branch of the Pennsylvania Railroad. The spot chosen was the bed of a stream over which the railroad passed by a bridge. Dr. Hostetter claimed he had bought the bed of the run and that the railroad owned simply the right to span the run. He put down his pipes, and the railroad sent a force of armed men to the spot, tore up the pipes, fortified their position and prepared to hold the fort. The oil men came down in a body, and, seizing an opportune moment, got possession of the disputed point. The railroad had thirty of them arrested for riot, but was not able to get them committed; it did succeed, however, in preventing the relaying of the pipes and a long litigation over Dr. Hostetter's right to pass under the road ensued. Disgusted with this turn of affairs Dr. Hostetter leased the line to three young independent oil men of whom we are to hear more later. They were B. D. Benson, David McKelvy and Major

Robert E. Hopkins, all of Titusville. Resourceful and determined they built tank wagons into which the oil from the pipe was run and was carted across the tracks on the public highway, turned into storage tanks and again repiped and pumped to Pittsburg. They were soon doing a good business. The fight to get the Columbia Conduit Line into Pittsburg aroused again the agitation in favour of a free pipe-line bill, and early in 1875 bills were presented in both the Senate and House of the state and bitter and long fights over them followed. It was charged that the bills were in the interest of Dr. Hostetter. He wants to transport his blood bitters cheaply, sneered one opponent! Many petitions for the bill were circulated, but there were even stronger remonstrances and the source of some of them was suspicious enough; for instance, that of the "Pittsburg refiners representing about one-third of the refining capacity of the Pennsylvania district and nearly one-third of the entire capacity now in business." As the Pittsburg refiners were nearly all either owned or leased by the Standard concern, and the few independents had no hope save in a free pipe-line, there seems to be no doubt about the origin of that remonstrance. Although the bills were strongly supported, they were defeated, and the Columbia Conduit Line continued to "break bulk" and cart its oil over the railroad track.

Another route was arranged which for a time promised success. This was to bring crude oil by barges to Pittsburg, then to carry the refined down the Ohio River to Huntington and thence by the Richmond and Chesapeake road to Richmond. This scheme, started in February, was well under way by May, and "On to Richmond!" was the cry of the independents. Everything possible was done to make this attempt fail. An effort was even made to prevent the barges which came down the Allegheny River from unloading, and this actually succeeded for some time. There seemed to be always some hitch in each one of the channels which the independents tried, some point at which they could be so harassed that the chance of a living freight rate which they had seen was destroyed.

Some time in April, 1876, the most ambitious project of all was announced. This was a seaboard pipe-line to be run from the Oil Regions to Baltimore. Up to this time the pipe-lines had been used merely to gather the oil from the wells and carry it to the railroads. The longest single line in operation was the Columbia Conduit, and it was built thirty miles long. The idea of pumping oil over the mountains to the sea was regarded generally as chimerical. To a trained civil engineer it did not, however, present any insuperable obstacles, and in the winter of 1875 and 1876 Henry Harley, whose connection with the Pennsylvania Transportation Company has already been noted, went to his old chief in the Hoosac Tunnel, General Herman Haupt, and laid the scheme before him. If it was a feasible idea would General Haupt take charge of the engineering for the Pennsylvania Transportation Company? At the same time Mr. Harley employed General Benjamin Butler to look after the legal side of such an undertaking. Both General Haupt and General Butler were enthusiastic over the idea and took hold of the work with a will. It was not long before the scheme began to attract serious attention. The Eastern papers in particular took it up. The references to it were, as a whole, favourable. It was regarded everywhere as a remarkable undertaking: "Worthy," the New York Graphic said, "to be coupled with the Brooklyn Bridge, the blowing up of Hell Gate, and the tunnelling of the Hudson River." As General Haupt's plans show, it was a tremendous undertaking, for the line would be, when finished, at least 500 miles long, and it would be worked by thirty or more tremendous pumps. On July 25 a meeting was held at Parker's Landing, presenting publicly the reports of General Haupt and General Butler. The authority and seriousness of the scheme as set forth at this meeting alarmed the railroads. If this seaboard line went through it was farewell to the railroad-Standard combination. Oil could be shipped to the seaboard by it at a cost of 16 2-3 cents a barrel, General Haupt estimated. All of the interests, little and big, which believed that they would be injured by the success of the line, began an attack.

Curiously enough one of the first points of hostility was General Haupt himself. An effort was made to discredit his estimate in order to scare people from taking stock. They recalled the Hoosac Tunnel scandal and the fact that the General once built a bridge which had tumbled down, ridiculed his estimate of the cost, etc., etc. The "card" in which General Haupt answered his chief critic, one who signed himself "Vidi," was admirable:

A CARD FROM GENERAL HAUPT

What are the charges that I am requested to "smash"?

They are, as I understand them from others, for some I have not seen:

1. That I once built a bridge that tumbled down.

2. That I was connected with the Hoosac Tunnel that cost seventeen millions of dollars.

3. That my estimates of cost of transportation are ridiculously low and unreliable.

1. I did design a bridge some twenty years ago, and constructed a span near Greenfield, in Massachusetts, which gave way, owing to a defective casting, while being tested. The bridge was not finished; had not been opened to the public; had not been accepted from the contractor, who repaired the damage in such a manner that a recurrence of a break would have been impossible. I have built spans of bridges and tested them until they broke, to ascertain their ultimate strength, but I supposed that this was a matter that concerned myself and not the public. If the bridge had been thrown open for public use, and an accident had then occurred from defective design or material, the engineer might have been censurable, but not otherwise. In an experience of nearly forty years I have never had a bridge to fail, after being opened for travel, or a piece of masonry to give way. No accident occurred even upon the temporary military bridges constructed during the war, which President Lincoln used to say were built of bean poles and corn stalks.

2. How about the Hoosac Tunnel?

In 1856 I undertook to build the Hoosac Tunnel, at that time ridiculed as visionary and utterly impracticable. I carried it on until 1862, when its practicability was so fully demonstrated that it was considered some discredit to Massachusetts to allow the work to proceed under engineers from another state, and honourable members of the Legislature declared that Massachusetts had engineers as competent as any that could be found in Pennsylvania. The work in my hands, as was proved by reports of investigating committees, was costing less than $2,000,000, and the trouble then was that the margin was considered too large, and that I was making too much money on the $2,000,000, which the state had agreed to advance. In 1862 the state took the work out of my hands and put it under control of state commissioners and engineers. The result was that instead of getting the Hoosac Tunnel completed for $2,000,000, which was amply sufficient in the hands of H. Haupt and Company, it has now cost, *under state management*, nearly $17,000,000.

I hope this explanation will be considered sufficient to "smash" Number 2.

3. As to Number 3, the insufficiency of my estimate.

The items which enter into such an estimate are pure and simple. There has been but one omission, and that is malicious mischief or deviltry, and this item is so uncertain that, without a more intimate acquaintance with "Vidi" and his supporters, I could not undertake to estimate it.

I have put coal at five dollars per ton or eighteen cents per bushel, now worth five cents at Brady's and eight at Pittsburg. Is not this enough? I have allowed fifty per cent. greater consumption at each station than has been estimated by others. I have allowed $1,000 a year for each of two engine men at each station. Will anyone say this is not sufficient? And I have, to be safe, estimated the work down below the results given by any of the ordinary hydraulic formula. It would be absurd to tell experienced pipe men that oil cannot be pumped fifteen miles under 900 pounds pressure through a four-inch pipe with a discharge of 5,000 barrels per day, which is all that the estimate is based upon, and it allows sixty-five days' stoppage besides.

Please, gentlemen, let me alone. I have had enough of newspaper controversy in former years. I am sick of it.

H. HAUPT.

At the same time that General Haupt was attacked the Pennsylvania Transportation Company was criticised for bad management. A long letter to the Derrick August 14, 1876, claimed that the company in the past had been mismanaged; that the credit it asked could not be given safely; that its management had been such that it had scarcely any business left. Indeed this critic claimed that the last pipe-line organised, a small line known as the Keystone, had during the last six months done almost double the business of the Pennsylvania. Under the direction of the Pennsylvania Railroad, it was believed, the Philadelphia papers began to attack the plan. Their claim was that the charters under which the Pennsylvania Transportation Company expected to operate would not allow them to lay such a pipe-line. The opposition became such that the New York papers began to take notice of it. The Derrick on September 16, 1876, copies an article from the New York Bulletin in which it is said that the railroads and the Standard Oil Company, "now stand in gladiatorial array, with shields poised and sword ready to deal the cut." An opposition began to arise, too, from farmers through whose property an attempt was being made to obtain right of way. In Indiana and Armstrong counties the farmers complained to the secretary of internal affairs, saying that the company had no business to take their property for a pipe-line. One of the common complaints of the farmers' newspapers was that leakage from the pipes would spoil the springs of water, curdle milk, and burn down barns. The matter assumed such proportions that the secretary referred it to the attorney-general for a hearing. In the meantime the Pennsylvania Transportation Company made the most strenuous efforts to secure the right of way. A large number of men were sent out to talk over the farmers into signing the leases. Hand bills were distributed with an appeal to be generous and to free the oil business from a monopoly that was crushing it. These same circulars told the farmers that a monopoly had hired agents all along the route misrepresenting the facts about their intentions. Mr. Harley, under the excitement of the enterprise and the opposition it aroused, became a public figure, and in October the New York Graphic gave a long interview with him. In this interview Mr. Harley claimed that the pipe-line scheme was gotten up to escape the Standard Oil monopoly. Litigation, he declared, was all his scheme had to fear. "John D. Rockefeller, president of the Standard monopoly," he said, "is working against us in the country newspapers, prejudicing the farmers and raising issues in the courts, and seeking also to embroil us with other carrying lines."

It was not long, however, before something more serious than the farmers and their complaints got in the way of the Pennsylvania Transportation Company. This was a rumour that the company was financially embarrassed. Their certificates were refused on the market, and in November a receiver was appointed. Different members of the company were arrested for fraud, among them two or three of the best known men in the Oil Regions. The rumours proved only too true. The company had been grossly mismanaged, and the verification of the charges against it put an end to this first scheme for a seaboard pipe-line.

While all these efforts doomed to failure or to but temporary success were making, a larger attempt to meet Mr. Rockefeller's consolidation was quietly under way. Among those interested in the oil business who had watched the growing power of the Standard with most concern was the head of the Empire Transportation Company, Colonel Joseph D. Potts. In connection with the Pennsylvania Railroad Colonel Potts had built up this concern, founded in 1865, until it was the most perfectly developed oil transporter in the country. It operated 500 miles of pipe, owned a thousand oil-tank cars, controlled large oil yards at Communipaw, New Jersey, was in every respect indeed a model business organisation, and it had the satisfaction of knowing that what it was it had made itself from raw material, that its methods were its own, and that the practices it had developed were those followed by other pipe-line companies. While the Empire

had far outstripped all its early competitors, there had grown
up in the last year a rival concern which Colonel Potts must
have watched with anxiety. This concern, known as the United
Pipe Line, was really a Standard organisation, for Mr. Rockefeller, in carrying out his plan of controlling all the oil refineries of the country, had been forced gradually into the pipe-
line business.

His first venture seems to have been in 1873. In that year the
oil shipping firm of J. A. Bostwick and Company laid a short
pipe in the Lower Field, as the oil country along the Allegheny
River was called. Now J. A. Bostwick was one of the charter
members of the South Improvement Company, and when
Mr. Rockefeller enlarged his business in 1872 because of the
power that enterprise gave him, he took Mr. Bostwick into
the Standard. This alliance, like all the operations of that venture, was secret. The bitterness of the Oil Regions against
the members of the South Improvement Company was so great
for many months after the Oil War that Mr. Bostwick and
Mr. Rockefeller seem to have concluded in 1873 that it would
be a wise precautionary measure for them to lay a pipe-line
upon which they could rely for a supply of oil in case the oil
men attempted again to cut them off from crude, as they had
succeeded in doing in 1872. Accordingly, a line was built and
put in the charge of a man who has since become known as one
of the "strong men" of the Standard Oil Company. This
man, Daniel O'Day, was a young Irishman who had first
appeared in the oil country in 1867, and had at once made so
good a record for himself as transporting agent, that in 1869,
when the oil shipping firm of J. A. Bostwick needed a man
to look after its shipments, he was employed. The record
he made in the next two years was such that it reached the
ear of Jay Gould himself, the president of the Erie, over
which Mr. Bostwick was doing most of his shipping. Now the
Erie at this time was making a hard fight to meet the growth

of the Empire Transportation Company. So important did Jay Gould think this struggle that in 1871 he himself came to the Oil Regions to look after it. One of the first men summoned to his private car as it lay in Titusville was the young Irishman, O'Day. He came as he was, begrimed with the oil of the yards, but Mr. Gould was looking for men who could do things, and was big enough to see through the grime. When the interview was concluded, Daniel O'Day had convinced Jay Gould that he was the man to divert the oil traffic from the Pennsylvania to the Erie road, and he walked out with an order in his pocket which lifted him over the head of everybody on the road so far as that particular freight was concerned, for it gave him the right to seize cars wherever he found them. For weeks after this he practically lived on the road, turning from the Pennsylvania in this time a large volume of freight, and making it certain that it would have to look to its laurels as it never had before.

The next year after this episode came the Oil War. The anger of the oil men was poured out on everyone connected in any way with the stockholders of the South Improvement Company, and among others on Mr. O'Day. He knew no more of the South Improvement Company at the start than the rest of the region, but he did know that it was his business to take care of certain property entrusted to him. Resolutions calling on him to resign were passed by oil exchanges and producers' unions. Mobs threatened his cars, his stations, his person, but with the grit of his race he hung to his post. There was, perhaps, but one other man in the employ of members of the South Improvement Company who showed the same courage, and that was Joseph Seep of Titusville. Almost every other employee fled, the principals in the miserable business took care to stay out of the country, but Mr. O'Day and Mr. Seep polished their shillalahs and stood over their property night and day until the war was over. Their courage did not go unrewarded. They were made the chief executive representatives, in the region, of the consolidated Standard interests which followed the war, though neither of them knew at the time that they were in the Standard employ. They supposed that the shipper Bostwick was an independent concern. It was a man of grit and force and energy then who took hold of the Standard's pipe-line in 1873. Rapid growth went on. The little line with which they started became the American Transfer Company, gradually extending its pipes to seventy or eighty miles in Clarion County, and in 1875 building lines in the Bradford Field.

The American Transfer Company was soon working in harmony with the United Pipe Lines, of which Captain J. J. Vandergrift was the president. This system had its nucleus, like all the others of the country, in a short private line, built in 1869 by Captain Vandergrift. It had grown until in 1874 it handled thirty per cent. of the oil of the region. Now in 1872, after the Oil War, Captain Vandergrift had become a convert to Mr. Rockefeller's theory of the "good of the oil business," and as we have seen, had gone into the National Refiners' Association as vice-president. Later he became a director in the Standard Oil Company. In 1874 he sold a one-third interest of his great pipe-line system to Standard men, and the line was reorganised in the interests of that company. That is, the Standard Oil Combination in 1876 was a large transporter of oil, for the directors and leading stockholders owned and operated fully forty per cent. of the pipe-lines of the Oil Regions, owned all but a very few of the tank cars on both the Central and Erie roads, and controlled under leases two great oil terminals, those of the Erie and Central roads. It was little wonder that Colonel Potts watched this rapid concentration of transportation and refining interests with dread. It was more dangerous than the single shipper, and he had always fought that idea on the ground of policy. "In the first place, it concentrates great power in the hands of one party over the trade of the road," he told an investigating committee of Congress in 1888. "They can remove it at pleasure. In the second place I think a large number of parties engaged in the same trade are very apt to divide themselves into two different classes as to the way of viewing markets; one class will be hopeful, and the other the reverse. The result will be there will be always one or the other class engaged in shipping some of the traffic. . . . The whole question seems to me to resolve itself into determining what policy will bring the largest volume in the most regular way to the carrier; and it is my opinion, based upon such experience as I have had, that a hundred shippers of a carload a day would be sure to give to a carrier a more regular volume of business, and I think, probably, a larger total volume of business in a year's time than one shipper of a hundred cars a day." *

Holding this theory, Colonel Potts had opposed the rebate to the Standard granted by the Pennsylvania in 1875. Three years later he described in a communication, published anonymously, the effect of the rebates granted at that time:

" The final agreement with the railways was scarcely blotter-dried ere stealthy movements toward the whole line of outside refiners were evident, although rather felt than seen. As long as practicable, they were denied as mere rumours, but as they gradually became accomplished victories, as one refiner after another, through terror, through lack of skill in ventures, through financial weakness, fell shivering with dislike into the embrace of this commercial octopus, a sense of dread grew rapidly among those independent interests which yet lived, and notably among a portion of the railroad transporters."

The chief "railroad transporter" who shared with the independents the sense of dread which Mr. Rockefeller's absorption of refineries awakened was Mr. Potts himself. As he saw

* Proceedings in Relation to Trusts, House of Representatives, 1888. Report Number 3112.

the independents of Pittsburg, Philadelphia, New York and the creek, shutting down, selling out, going into bankruptcy, while the Standard and its allies grew bigger day by day, as he saw the Standard interest developing a system of transportation greater than his own, he concluded to prevent, if possible, the one shipper in the oil business. "We reached the conclusion," said Colonel Potts in 1888, "that there were three great divisions in the petroleum business—the production, the carriage of it, and the preparation of it for market. If any one party controlled absolutely any one of those three divisions, it practically would have a very fair show of controlling the others. We were particularly solicitous about the transportation, and we were a little afraid that the refiners might combine in a single institution, and some of them expressed a strong desire to associate themselves permanently with us. We therefore suggested to the Pennsylvania road that we should do what we did not wish to do—associate ourselves. That is, our business was transportation and nothing else; but, in order that we might reserve a nucleus of refining capacity to our lines, we suggested we should become interested in one or more refineries, and we became interested in two, one in Philadelphia and one in New York. It was incidental merely to our transportation. The extreme limit was 4,000 barrels a day only."

It was in the spring of 1876 that the Empire began to interest itself in refineries. No sooner did Mr. Rockefeller discover this than he sought Mr. Scott and Mr. Cassatt, then the third vice-president of the Pennsylvania, in charge of transportation. It was not *fair!* Mr. Rockefeller urged. The Empire was a transportation company. If it went into the refining business it was not to be expected that it would deal as generously with rivals as with its own factories; besides, it would disturb the one shipper who, they all had agreed, was such a benefit to the railroads. Mr. Scott and Mr. Cassatt might have reminded Mr. Rockefeller that he was as truly a transporter as the Empire, but if they did they were met with a prompt denial of this now well-known fact. He was an oil refiner—only that and nothing more. "They tell us that they do not control the United Pipe Lines," Mr. Cassatt said in his testimony in 1879. Besides, urged Mr. Rockefeller, if they have refineries of course they will give them better terms than they do us. Mr. Flagler told the Congressional Committee of 1888 that the Standard was unable to obtain rates through the Empire Transportation Company over the Pennsylvania Railroad for the Pittsburg or Philadelphia refineries as low as were given by competing roads, and, added he, "from the fact that the business during those years *was so very close as to leave scarcely any margin of profit* under the most advantageous circumstances. And we, finding ourselves undersold in the markets by competitors whom we knew had not the same facilities in the way of mechanical appliances for doing the business, knew that there was but one conclusion to be reached, and that was that the Empire Transportation Company favoured certain other shippers, I would say favoured its own refineries to our injury."

As the Standard Oil Company paid a dividend of about fourteen per cent. in both 1875 and 1876, besides spending large sums in increasing its plants and facilities, the margin of profit cannot have been so low as it seemed to Mr. Flagler in 1888 to have been; naturally enough, for he saw dividends of from fifty to nearly 100 per cent. later.

Mr. Vanderbilt and Mr. Jewett soon joined their protests to Mr. Rockefeller's. "The steps it (the Empire) was then taking," said Mr. Jewett, "unless checked would result in a diversion largely of the transportation of oil from our roads; the New York Central road and our own determined that we ought not to stand by and permit those improvements and arrangements to be made which, when completed, would be

A. J. CASSATT IN 1877

Third vice-president of the Pennsylvania Railroad in charge of transportation when first contract was made by that road with the Standard Oil Company.

GENERAL GEORGE B. MC CLELLAN

President of the Atlantic and Great Western Railroad at the time of the South Improvement Company. General McClellan did not sign the contract.

GENERAL JAMES H. DEVEREUX

Who in 1868 as vice-president of the Lake Shore and Michigan Southern Railroad first granted rebates to Mr. Rockefeller's firm.

JOSEPH D. POTTS

President of the Empire Transportation Company. Leader in the struggle between the Pennsylvania Railroad and the Standard Oil Company in 1877.

beyond our control."* These protests increased in vehemence, until finally the Pennsylvania officials remonstrated with Mr. Potts. "We endeavoured," says Mr. Cassatt, "to try to get those difficulties harmonised, talked of getting the Empire Transportation Company to lease its refineries to the Standard Oil Company, or put them into other hands, but we did not succeed in doing that." "Rather than do that," Colonel Potts told Mr. Cassatt, when he proposed that the Empire sell its refineries, "we had rather you would buy us out and close our contract with you."

When the Standard Oil Company and its allies, the Erie and Central, found that the Pennsylvania would not or could not drive the Empire from its position, they determined on war. Mr. Jewett, the Erie president, in his testimony of 1879 before the Hepburn Commission, takes the burden of starting the fight. "Whether the Standard Oil Company was afraid of the Empire Line as a refiner," he said, "I have no means of knowing. I never propounded the question. We were opposed to permitting the Empire Line, a creature of the Pennsylvania Railroad, to be building refineries, to become the owners of pipe-lines leading into the oil field and leading to the coast, without a contest, and we made it without regard to the Standard Oil Company or anybody else; but when we did determine to make it, I have no doubt we demanded of the Standard Oil Company during the contest to withdraw its shipments from the Pennsylvania." Mr. Flagler gave the following version of the affair to the Congressional Committee of 1888 :—

We made an agreement with the Empire Transportation Company for shipments over the Pennsylvania Railroad on behalf of the Pennsylvania interests, which were then owned by the Standard Oil Company, simply because there was no alternative. It was the only vehicle by which these Pittsburg refineries and the Philadelphia refineries carried their crude oil over the Pennsylvania Railroad. There was no other

* Report of the Special Committee on Railroads, New York Assembly, 1879.

[185]

medium by which business could be done over the Pennsylvania Railroad, except through the Empire Transportation Company, a subsidiary company of the Pennsylvania Railroad Company. The Empire Transportation Company was not only the owner of pipe-lines in the Oil Regions, and tank-cars on the Pennsylvania Railroad, but also of refineries at Philadelphia and New York, and to that extent were our competitors. We, *having no interest whatever in transportation*,* naturally felt jealous of the Empire Transportation Company, and drew the attention of the northern lines. By that I mean the New York Central and the Erie railroads. With the peculiar position of the oil business on the Pennsylvania Railroad, their attention was called to this very soon after the Empire Transportation Company began the business of refining. The position taken by the two Northern trunk lines in their intercourse with the Pennsylvania Railroad, as was admitted by Mr. Cassatt in his testimony, and stated to me by the representatives of the two Northern roads, Mr. Vanderbilt and Mr. Jewett, was that it was unfair to them that the Pennsylvania Railroad did not divest itself of the manufacturing business.

Backed by the Erie and Central, Mr. Rockefeller, in the spring of 1877, finally told Mr. Cassatt that he would no longer send any of his freight over the Pennsylvania unless the Empire gave up its refineries. The Pennsylvania refused to compel the Empire to this course. According to Mr. Potts's own story, the road was partially goaded to its decision by a demand for more rebates, which came from Mr. Rockefeller at about the time he pronounced his ultimatum on the Empire. "They swooped upon the railways," says Colonel Potts, "with a demand for a vast increase in their rebate. They threatened, they pleaded, it has been said they purchased— however that may be, they conquered. Minor officials intrusted with the vast power of according secret rates conceded all they were asked to do, even to concealing from their superiors for months the real nature of their illegal agreements." Probably it was at this time that there took place the little scene between Mr. Vanderbilt and Mr. Rockefeller and his colleagues, of which the former told the Hepburn Commis-

* The Standard Oil Company were extensive oil transporters at that time, as has been shown.

sion in 1879. The Standard people were after more rebates. They affirmed other roads were giving larger rebates than Mr. Vanderbilt, and that their contract with him obliged him to give as much as anybody else did.

"Gentlemen," he told them, "you cannot walk into this office and say we are bound by any contract to do business with you at any price that any other road does that is in competition with us; it is only on a fair competitive basis, a fair competition for business at a price that I consider will pay the company to do it."

Soon after this interview, so rumour says, Mr. Vanderbilt sold the Standard stock he had acquired as a result of the deals made through the South Improvement Company. "I think they are smarter fellows than I am, a good deal," he told the commission, somewhat ruefully. "And if you come in contact with them I guess you will come to the same conclusion."

Spurred on then by resentment at the demands for new rebates, as well as by the injustice of Mr. Rockefeller's demand that the Empire give up its refineries, the Pennsylvania accepted the Standard's challenge, resolved to stand by the Empire, and henceforth to treat all its shippers alike. No sooner was its resolution announced in March, 1877, than all the freight of the Standard, amounting to fully sixty-five per cent. of the road's oil traffic, was taken away. An exciting situation, one of out-and-out war, developed, for the Empire at once entered on an energetic campaign to make good its loss by developing its own refineries, and by forming a loyal support among the independent oil men. Day and night the officers worked on their problem, and with growing success. When Mr. Rockefeller saw this he summoned his backers to action. The Erie and Central began to cut rates to entice away the independents. It is a sad reflection on both the honour and the foresight of the body of oil men who had been crying so loudly for help, that as soon as the rates were cut on the Standard lines many of them began to attempt to force the Pennsylvania to follow. "They found the opportunity for immediate profits by playing one belligerent against the other too tempting to resist," says Colonel Potts. "We paid them large rebates," said Mr. Cassatt; "in fact, we took anything we could get for transporting their oil. In some cases we paid out in rebates more than the whole freight. I recollect one instance where we carried oil to New York for Mr. Ohlen, or someone he represented, I think at eight cents less than nothing. I do not say any large quantities, but oil was carried at that rate."

While the railroads were waging this costly war the Standard was carrying the fight into the refined market. The Empire had gone systematically to work to develop markets for the output of its own and of the independent refineries. Mr. Rockefeller's business was to prevent any such development. He was well equipped for the task by his system of "predatory competition," for in spite of the fact that Mr. Rockefeller claimed that underselling to drive a rival from a market was one of the evils he was called to cure, he did not hesitate to employ it himself. Indeed, he had long used his freedom to sell at any price he wished for the sake of driving a competitor out of the market with calculation and infinite patience. Other refiners burst into the market and undersold for a day; but when Mr. Rockefeller began to undersell, he kept it up day in and day out, week in and week out, month in and month out, until there was literally nothing left of his competitor. A former official of the Empire Transportation Company, who in 1877 took an active part in the war his company was waging against the Standard, once told the writer that in every town, North or South, East or West, in which they already had a market for their refined oil, or attempted to make one, they found a Standard agent on hand ready to undersell. The Empire was not slow in underselling. It is very probable that in many cases it began it, for, as Mr. Cassatt says, "They endeavoured to injure us and our shippers all they could in that fight, and we did the same thing."

In spite of the growing bitterness and cost of the contest, the Empire had no thought of yielding. Mr. Potts's hope was in a firm alliance with the independent oil men, many of the strongest of whom were rallying to his side. At the beginning of the fight he had very shrewdly enlisted in his plan one of the largest independent producers of the day, B. B. Campbell, of Butler. "Being a pleasure and a duty to me," says Mr. Campbell, "I entered into the service with all the zeal and power that I have. I made a contract with the Empire Line wherein I bound myself to give all my business to this line." At the same time Mr. Potts sought the help of the man who was generally accepted as the coolest, most intelligent, and trustworthy adviser in matters of transportation the Oil Regions had, E. G. Patterson, of Titusville. Mr. Patterson was a practical railroad man, and an able and logical opponent of the rebate and "one shipper" systems. He had been prominent in the fight against the South Improvement Company, and since that time he had persistently urged the independents to wage war only on the practice of rebates—to refuse them themselves and to hold the railroads strictly to their duty in the matter. Several conferences were held, and finally, in the early summer, Mr. Potts read the two gentlemen a paper he had drawn up as a contract between the producers and the Empire. It speaks well for the fair-mindedness of Mr. Potts that when he read this document to Mr. Campbell and Mr. Patterson, both of whom were skilled in the ways of the transporter, they "accepted it in a moment."

"It was made the duty of Mr. Patterson and myself to get

signatures of producers to this agreement," says Mr. Campbell, "in a sufficient amount to warrant the Pennsylvania road entering into a permanent agreement. The contract, I think, was for three years." The attempt to enlist a solid body of oil men in the scheme was at once set on foot, but hardly was it under way before troubles of most serious import came upon the Pennsylvania road. A great and general strike on all its branches tied up its traffic for weeks. In Pittsburg hundreds of thousands of dollars' worth of property were destroyed by a mob of railroad employees. It is not too much to say that in these troubles the Pennsylvania lost millions of dollars; it is certain that as a result of them the company that fall and the coming spring had to pass its dividends for the first time since it commenced paying them, and that its stock fell to twenty-seven dollars a share (par being fifty dollars). Overwhelmed by the disasters, Mr. Scott and Mr. Cassatt felt that they could not afford any longer to sustain the Empire in its fight for the right to refine as well as transport oil.

While the coffers of the Pennsylvania were empty, those of the Standard were literally bursting with profits; for the Standard, the winter before this fight came on, had carried to completion for the first time the work which it had been organised to accomplish, that is, it had put up the price of refined oil, in defiance of all laws of supply and demand, and held it up for nearly six months. The story of this dramatic commercial hold-up is told in the next chapter; it is enough for present purposes to say that in the winter of 1876–1877 millions of gallons of oil were sold by Mr. Rockefeller and his partners at a profit of from fifteen to twenty-five cents a gallon. The curious can compute the profits; they certainly ran into the multi-millions. A dividend of fifty per cent. was paid for the year following the scoop, and "there was plenty of money made to throw that dividend out twice over and make a profit," Samuel Andrews, one of the Standard's leading men, told an Ohio investigating committee in 1879. The Standard then had a war budget big enough for any opposition, and it is not to be wondered at that the Pennsylvania, knowing this and finding its own treasury depleted, was ready to quit.

It was August when Mr. Scott and Mr. Cassatt decided to give up the fight. Peace negotiations were at once instituted, Mr. Cassatt going to Cleveland to see Messrs. Rockefeller and Flagler, and Mr. Warden, who was visiting them there. Later, the same gentlemen met Mr. Scott and Mr. Cassatt at the St. George Hotel, in Philadelphia. "The subject of discussion at these meetings," said Mr. Cassatt in 1879, when under examination, "was whether we could not make some contract or agreement with the Standard Oil Company by which this contest would cease. They insisted that the first condition of their coming back on our line to ship over our road must be that the Empire Transportation Company, which company represented us in the oil business, must cease the refining of oil in competition with them. The Empire Transportation Company objected to going out of the refining business. The result of this objection Colonel Potts stated in 1888: "Our contract with the Pennsylvania road gave to them the option, at any time they saw proper, upon reasonable notice, of buying our entire plant; they exercised that option." "Was that at your request or desire?" the chairman asked the Colonel. "No, sir. It was at the request of the Pennsylvania road through their officials." The question then came up as to who should buy the plant of the Empire Transportation Company. "The Standard wanted us to do so," says Mr. Cassatt. "They wanted us to buy the pipe-lines and cars; we objected to buying the pipe-lines, and it resulted in their buying them and the refining plants. The negotiations were carried on in Philadelphia, Mr. Rockefeller and Mr. Flagler mainly representing the Standard. A substantial agreement was reached about the last of October. The agreement would have been probably perfected about that time except that the counsel for the Empire Line thought it was necessary that they should advertise the fact that they were going to sell their property, and have a meeting of their stockholders, and get their assent to the sale before the papers were finally signed."

This meeting of which Mr. Cassatt speaks was held on October 17. Colonel Potts made a statement to the stockholders, which he began by a brief review of the growth of the company from the point when twelve years before it had started as a new route charged with the duty of meeting formidable competitors. He pointed out that at the close of the twelfth year the company was the owner of a large fleet of lake vessels, of elevators and docks at the City of Erie, of improved piers in New York City, of nearly 5,000 cars, of over 500 miles of pipe-lines, of valuable interests in refineries, of all the appliances of a great business. In these twelve years, Colonel Potts told his stockholders, the organisation had collected more than one hundred million dollars, and in the last year their cars had moved over 30,000 miles of railway. He explained to the stockholders the condition of the oil business which had made it necessary, in his judgment, for the Empire Transportation Company to go into the refining business. It was done with the greatest reluctance, Colonel Potts declared, but it was done because he and his colleagues believed that there was no other way for them to save to the Pennsylvania road permanently the proportion of the oil traffic which they had acquired in the twelve years in which they had been in business. He reviewed, dispassionately, the circumstances which had led the Pennsylvania road to ask the company to give up its refineries. He stated his reasons for deciding that it was wiser for the Empire to resign its contracts with the Pennsylvania and go into liquidation than to submit to the demands of the Standard interests. Colonel Potts followed his statement by an abstract of the agreements which had been made between the Standard people and the Empire. By these agreements the Standard Oil Company bought of the Empire Transportation Company their pipe-line interest for the sum of $1,094,805.56, their refining interests in New York and Philadelphia for the sum of $501,-652.78, $900,000 worth of Oil Tank Car Trust, and they also settled with outside refiners and paid for personal property to the extent of $900,000 more, making a total cash payment of $3,400,000. Two millions and a half of this money, Colonel Potts told the stockholders, would be paid that evening by certified checks if the agreements were ratified. "Not knowing what your action might be at this meeting," he concluded, "we are still in active business. We could not venture to do anything that would check our trade, that would repel customers, that would drive any of them away from us. We must be prepared if you said no to go right along with our full machinery under our contract, or under such modification of that as we could fight through. We could not stop moving a barrel of oil. We must be ready to take any offered to us; we must supply parties taking oil. There was nothing we could do but what was done; nothing was stopped, nothing is stopped, everything is going on just as vigorously at this moment through as wide an extent of country as ever it did, and it will continue to do so until after you take action, until after we get these securities or the money. That, we suppose, will be about six o'clock to-day, if you act favourably, and at that time we shall, if everything goes through, telegraph to every man in our service, and to the heads of departments what has been done, and at twelve o'clock to-night we shall cease to operate anything in the Empire Transportation Company."

The stockholders accepted the proposition, and that night

at Colonel Potts's office on Girard Street, Philadelphia, Mr. Scott and Mr. Cassatt, of the Pennsylvania Railroad, Colonel Potts and two of his colleagues in the Empire, and two of the refiners with whom he was affiliated, met William Rockefeller, Mr. Flagler, Mr. Warden, Mr. Lockhart, Charles Pratt, Jabez A. Bostwick, Daniel O'Day, and J. J. Vandergrift, and their counsel, and the papers and checks were were signed and passed, wiping out of existence a great business to which a body of the best transportation men the state of Pennsylvania has produced had given twelve years of their lives. After the meeting was over, there were sent out from Philadelphia to scores of employees of the Empire Transportation Company scattered throughout the state, telegrams stating that at twelve o'clock that night the company would cease to exist. For twelve years the organisation had been doing a growing business. On the date of this telegram its operations were more extensive, its opportunities more promising, under fair play, than they had ever been before in its history. The band of men who had built it up to such healthy success were not giving it up because they had lost faith in it, or because they believed there were larger opportunities for them in some other business; they were giving it up because they were compelled to, and probably men never went out of business in this country with a deeper feeling of injustice than that of the officials of the Empire Transportation Company on October 17, 1877, when they sent out the telegrams which put their great creation into liquidation.

The pipe-lines thus acquired were at once consolidated with the other Standard lines. Only a few independent lines, and only one of these of importance—the Columbia Conduit— now remained in the Oil Regions. This company had been doing business, since 1875, under the difficulties already described. Dr. Hostetter, the chief stockholder, had become heartily sick of the oil business and wanted to sell. He had

approached the Empire Line, and there had been some negotiations. Then came the fall of the Empire and Dr. Hostetter
sought the United Pipe Line. Intent on stopping every outlet of oil not under their control the Standard people bought
the Columbia Conduit. By the end of the year the entire pipe-
line system of the Oil Regions was in Mr. Rockefeller's
hands. He was the only oil gatherer. Practically not a barrel
of oil could get to a railroad without his consent. He had
set out to be simply the only oil refiner in the country, but
to achieve that purpose he had been obliged to make himself
an oil transporter. In such unforseen paths do great ambi-
tions lead men!

The first effect of the downfall of the Empire was a new
railroad pool. Indeed when it became evident that the Pennsylvania would yield, the Erie, Central and the Standard had
begun preparing a new adjustment, and the papers for
this were ready to be signed on October 17, with those trans-
ferring the pipe-line property. Never had there been an
arrangement which gathered up so completely the oil outlets,
for now the Baltimore and Ohio road came into a pool for the
first time. Mr. Garrett had always refused the advances of
the other roads, but when he saw that the Columbia Conduit Line, his chief feeder, was sure to fall into Standard
hands; when he began to suspect the Baltimore refiners were
going into the combination, he realised that if he expected
to keep an oil traffic he must join the other roads. The new
pool, therefore, was between four roads. Sixty-three per cent.
of the oil traffic was conceded to New York, and of the sixty-
three per cent. going there the Pennsylvania road was to have
twenty-one per cent. Thirty-seven per cent. of the traffic was
to go to Philadelphia and Baltimore, and of this thirty-seven
per cent. the Pennsylvania had twenty-six per cent. The Standard guaranteed the road not less than 2,000,000 barrels a year,
and if it failed to send that much over the road it was to pay

it a sum equal to the profits it would have realised upon the quantity in deficit. In return for this guarantee of quantity the Standard was to pay such rates as might be fixed from time to time by the four trunk lines (which rates it was understood should be so fixed by the trunk lines as to place them on a parity as to cost of transportation by competing lines), and it was to receive weekly a commission of ten per cent. on its shipments it controlled.* No commission was to be allowed any other shipper unless he should guarantee and furnish such a quantity of oil that after deducting any commission allowed, the road realised from it the same amount of profits as it did from the Standard trade. The points in the agreement were embodied in a letter from William Rockefeller to Mr. Scott. This letter and the answer declaring the arrangement to be satisfactory to the company are both dated October 17.†

Four months later Mr. Rockefeller was able to take another step of great advantage. He was able to put into operation the system of drawbacks on other people's shipments which the South Improvement Company contracts had provided for, and which up to this point he seems not to have been securely enough placed to demand. There were no bones about the request now. Mr. O'Day, the general manager of the American Transfer Company, a pipe-line principally in Clarion County, Pennsylvania, which, including its branches, was from eighty to 100 miles in length, a company now one of the constituents of the United Pipe Line, wrote to Mr. Cassatt:

"I here repeat what I once stated to you, and which I wish you to receive and treat as strictly confidential, that we have been for many months receiving from the New

* See Appendix, Number 27. Mr. Flagler's explanation of the commission of ten per cent. allowed the Standard Oil Company in 1877.

† See Appendix, Number 28. Correspondence between William Rockefeller and Mr. Scott in October, 1877.

York Central and Erie Railroads certain sums of money, in no instance less than twenty cents per barrel on *every barrel of crude oil carried by each of these roads.*" Continuing, Mr. O'Day says: "Co-operating as we are doing with the Standard Oil Company and the trunk lines in every effort to secure for the railroads paying rates of freight on the oil they carry, I am constrained to say to you that in justice to the interests I represent we should receive from your company at least twenty cents on each barrel of crude oil you transport. . . . In submitting this proposition I find that I should ask you to let this date from November 1, 1877, but I am willing to accept as a compromise (which is to be regarded as strictly a private one between your company and ours) the payment by you of twenty cents per barrel on all crude oil shipments commencing with February 1, 1878." *

Mr. Cassatt complied with Mr. O'Day's request. In a letter to the comptroller of the road he said that he had agreed to allow this commission after having seen the receipted bills, showing that the New York Central allowed them a commission of thirty-five cents a barrel, and the Erie Railroad a commission of twenty cents a barrel on Bradford oil and thirty cents on all other oils. Thus the Standard Oil Company, through the American Transfer Company, received, in addition to rebates on its own shipments, from twenty to thirty-five cents drawback a barrel on all crude oil which was sent over the trunk lines by other people as well as by itself.†

The effect of this new concentration of power was immediate in all the refining centres of the country. Most of the Baltimore refiners, some eight in number, which up to this time had remained independent, seeing themselves in danger of losing their oil supply, were united at the end of 1877 into the Baltimore United Oil Company, with J. N. Camden at their head. Mr. Camden was president of the Camden Consolidated Company of Parkersburg, West Virginia, a concern already in the Standard alliance, and he and his partners held the majority stock in the Baltimore concern. The method

* See Appendix, Number 29. Correspondence between Mr. O'Day and Mr. Cassatt.

† See Appendix, Number 30. Henry M. Flagler's testimony on the rebate paid to American Transfer Company.

of reaching the Baltimore independents who looked with dislike or fear on the Standard was a familiar one: An officer of one of the concerns owned by the Standard Oil Company would approach the outsider who was feeling the pressure and propose a sale or a lease to himself personally. It was an escape, and it usually ended in the complete absorption of the plant by the Standard. A few of the Baltimore interests refused to go into the Baltimore United Oil Company. Among them was a woman, a widow, Mrs. Sylvia C. Hunt, who had conducted a successful refinery there for several years, and whose business ability and energy had been the admiration of all those with whom she had come in contact. Her interests had been particularly cherished by the Empire Line, "Mrs. Hunt's cars" being given precedence many a time by agents at Titusville or other shipping points who knew her story. In the summer of 1877 her works burned out. With a courage which was generally commented on at the time Mrs. Hunt at once rebuilt and in less than six months had her plant in running order. Then came the fall of the Empire Transportation Company, the sale of the Columbia Conduit Company, and the entrance of the Baltimore and Ohio into the Oil Pool. Every refiner in Baltimore knew what that meant, and the wise sold when Mr. Camden proposed it. Mrs. Hunt, however, did not want to sell. She distrusted the new company. Finally with many misgivings she leased for five years at $5,000 a year. It was less than half she had been making, so she claimed, and among her old friends there was much indignation. Colonel Potts, indeed, in telling her story in his "Brief History of the Standard Oil Company," said: "It could fairly have been expected that something of chivalrous feeling would be inspired by the sight of this indomitable spirit who had wrought so noble a work against such great odds. But though fine sentiments and generous words find frequent exodus from the lips of the Standard managers, they are never seconded by generous deeds. They crushed her business and her spirit as remorselessly as they would have killed a dog." These are bitter words written when Colonel Potts was still smarting from his defeat. They were written, too, without reflection that Mrs. Hunt, if allowed to have all the oil she wanted, allowed equal rates, allowed to use her ability and experience, allowed freedom to sell in the markets she had built up, would undoubtedly have increased her business. She would have profited by the high prices of refined oil which Mr. Rockefeller was taking all this trouble to secure. She might have grown a formidable competitor even, and disturbed the steadiness of the working of the great machine. Colonel Potts forgot that if the Great Purpose was realised nobody must do business except under Mr. Rockefeller's control.

In New York City the new tariff and pooling arrangements caused the greatest uneasiness, for here was the largest group of prosperous independent refiners. They had all allied themselves with the Empire Transportation Company in the spring of 1877 when its fight with the Standard had begun, but they had been dropped immediately when peace negotiations were begun, and a letter of remonstrance they sent Mr. Scott at the time was never answered.* The experiences of several of these independents have been recorded in court testimony. One or two will suffice here. For instance, among the Eastern refiners was the firm of Denslow and Bush; their works were located in South Brooklyn. They had begun in a very small way in 1870, and by 1879 were doing a business of nearly 1,000 barrels of crude a day. They had transported nearly all their oil by the Empire Line. After that line went out of business in October, 1877, the contract with Denslow and Bush was transferred to the Pennsylvania Railroad Company. This contract terminated on the first day of

* See Appendix, Number 31. Letter to President Scott of the Pennsylvania Railroad from B. B. Campbell and E. G. Patterson.

May, 1878. Some time in March they received formal notice of its expiration, and solicited an interview with the officers of the Pennsylvania Railroad in order to make some arrangements for the further transportation of their oil. Mr. Cassatt named New York. The meeting was held at Mr. Denslow's office, 123 Pearl Street. Besides Mr. Bush, there were present to meet Mr. Cassatt, Messrs. Lombard, Gregory, King, H. C. Ohlen, and C. C. Burke, all independents. When Mr. Bush was under examination in the suit against the Pennsylvania Railroad in 1879 he gave an account of what happened at this interview:

"We asked Mr. Cassatt what rate of freight we should have after the expiration of these contracts, whether we should have as low a rate of freight as the Standard Oil Company or any other shipper? He said, 'No.' We asked why. 'Well, in the first place, you can't ship as much oil as the Standard Oil Company.' 'Well, if we could ship as much oil'—I think Mr. Lombard put this question—'would we then have the same rate?' He said, 'No.' 'Why?' 'Why, you could not keep the road satisfied; it would make trouble.' And he remarked in connection with that, that the Standard Oil Company was the only party that could keep the roads harmonised or satisfied. He intimated, I believe, that each road had a certain percentage of the oil business, and they could divide that up and give each road its proportion, and in that way keep harmony, which we could not do. Right after that he made the remark that he thought that we ought to fix it up with the Standard; we ought to do something so as to all go on and make some money, and I think we gave him very distinctly to understand that we didn't propose to enter into any 'fix up' where we would lose our identity, or sell out, or be under anybody else's thumb. I believe that he went so far as to say that he would see the Standard, and do everything he could to bring that thing about. We told him very clearly that we didn't want any interference in that direction, and if there was anything to be done, we thought we were quite capable of doing it. The interview perhaps lasted an hour. There was a great deal of talk of one kind and another, but this is, I think, the substance. This interview was in March, 1878, I think.

"Another interview at which I was present was either in June or July. Mr. Scott was present. This interview was brought about because we had been deprived, as we believed, of getting a sufficient number of cars we were entitled to. We had telegraphed or written to Mr. Cassatt—at least, Mr. Ohlen, our agent, had, on several occasions, and tried to get an interview, and finally this one was appointed, at which Mr. Scott would be present. When we arrived there we found Mr. Brundred, from Oil City; and Mr. Scott went on to state that he thought that we were receiving our fair proportion of cars. They tried to make us believe and feel, I suppose, that we were getting our due proportion, when for some considerable time previous to this we had not been able to do any business in advance; we could only do business from hand to mouth. We could not sell any refined oil unless we absolutely had the crude oil in our possession in New York, and Mr. Lombard, one of our number, had sold a cargo of crude oil, I think, of 9,000 barrels, and Denslow and Bush absolutely stopped their refinery for three weeks consequently, in order to let their oil go to Ayres and Lombard to finish their vessel, because they would only get three or four cars a day; and we stopped our place for three weeks to give them our crude oil, all we could give—our proportion— in order to lift them out and get their vessel cleared. After trying to impress upon us that we were getting our proportion of cars, we asked Mr. Scott substantially the same question we asked Mr. Cassatt in New York, whether we could have, if there was any means by which we could have, the same rate of freight as other shippers got, and he said flatly, 'No'; and we asked him then if we shipped the same amount of oil as the Standard, and he said, 'No,' and gave the same reasons Mr. Cassatt had in New York, that the Standard Oil Company were the only parties that could keep peace among the roads. We stated to Mr. Scott that we would like to know to what extent we would be discriminated against, because we wanted to know what disadvantage we would have to work under. And we went away very much dissatisfied. All the information we got on that point was from Mr. Cassatt in New York, when he stated that the discrimination would be larger on a high rate of freight than on a low rate of freight, which led us to infer that it was a percentage discrimination. That is all the point that I recollect we ever got as to the amount of the commission. We told Mr. Scott that if they hadn't sufficient cars on their road we would like to put some on, and he told us flatly that they had just bought out one line and they would not allow another one to be put on; that if they hadn't cars enough they would build them. He seemed to show considerable feeling that afternoon, and he said: 'Well, you have cost us in fighting for you now a million dollars' (or a million and a half, something like that—a very large sum), 'and we don't propose to go into another fight.' " *

Strange as it may seem there were not only men in the refining business who were willing to fight under these conditions, there were men among the very ones who had succumbed at the opening of the Standard's onslaught who were ready to try the business again. Among these was William Hark-

* Commonwealth of Pennsylvania *vs.* Pennsylvania Railroad, United Pipe Lines, etc.

ness, whose experience up to 1876 was related in the preceding chapter. Mr. Harkness's next experience in the oil business was related to the same committee as that already mentioned:

"When I was compelled to succumb," he said, "I thought it was only temporarily; that the time would come when I could go into the business I was devoted to. We systematised all our accounts and knew where the weak points were. I was in love with the business. I selected a site near three railroads and the river. I took a run across the water—I was tired and discouraged and used up in 1876, and was gone three or four months. I came back refreshed and ready for work, and had the plans and specifications and estimates made for a refinery that would handle 10,000 barrels of oil a day, right on this hundred acres of land. I believed the time had arrived when the Pennsylvania Railroad would see their true interest as common carriers, and the interest of their stockholders and the business interest of the city of Philadelphia, and I took those plans, specifications, and estimates, and I called on Mr. Roberts, president of the Pennsylvania Railroad Company. I had consulted one or two other gentlemen, whose advice was worth having, whether it would be worth my while to go to see President Roberts. I went there and laid the plans before him, and told him I wanted to build a refinery of 10,000 barrels capacity a day. I was almost on my knees begging him to allow me to do that. He said; 'What is it you want?' I said; 'I simply ask to be put upon an equality with everybody else, and especially the Standard Oil Company.' I said; 'I want you to agree with me that you will give me transportation of crude oil as low as you give it to the Standard Oil Company or anybody else for ten years, and then I will give you a written assurance that I will do this refining of 10,000 barrels of oil a day for ten years.' I asked him if that was not an honest position for us to be in; I, as a manufacturer, and he, the president of a railroad. Mr. Roberts said there was a great deal of force in what I said, but he could not go into any written assurance. He said he would not go into any such agreement, and I saw Mr. Cassatt. He said in his frank way; 'That is not practicable, and you know the reason why.'"

As this work of absorption went on steadily, persistently, the superstitious fear of resistance to proposals to lease or sell which came from parties known or suspected to be working in harmony with the Standard Oil Company, which had been strong in 1875, grew almost insuperable. In Cleveland this was particularly true. A proposal from Mr. Rockefeller was certainly regarded popularly as little better than a command to "stand and deliver." "The coal oil business belongs to us," Mr. Rockefeller had told Mr. Morehouse. "We have facilities; we must have it. Any concern that starts in business we have sufficient money laid aside to wipe out"*—and people believed him! The feeling is admirably shown in a remarkable case still quoted in Cleveland—and which belongs to the same period as the foregoing cases, 1878—a case which took the deeper hold on the public sympathy because the contestant was a woman, the widow of one of the first refiners of the town, a Mr. B——, who had begun refining in Cleveland in 1860. Mr. B——'s principal business was the manufacture of lubricating oil. Now at the start the Standard Oil Company handled only illuminating oil, and accordingly a contract was made between the two parties that Mr. B—— should sell to Mr. Rockefeller his refined oil, and that the Standard Oil Company should let the lubricating business in Cleveland alone. This was the status when in 1874 Mr. B—— died. What happened afterwards has been told in full in affidavits made in 1880,† and they shall tell the story; the only change made in the documents being to transfer them for the sake of clarity from the legal third person to the first, and to condense them on account of space.

Mrs. B——'s story as told in her affidavit is as follows:

"My husband having contracted a debt not long prior to his death for the first time in his life, I, for the interest of my fatherless children, as well as myself, thought it my duty to endeavour to continue the business, and accordingly took $92,000 of the stock of the B—— Oil Company and afterwards reduced it to $72,000 or $75,000, the whole stock of the company being $100,000, and continued business from that time until November, 1878, making handsome profits out of the business during perhaps the hardest years of the time since Mr. B—— had commenced. Some time in November, 1878, the Standard Oil Company sent a man to me by the name of Peter S. Jennings, who had been engaged in the refining business and had sold out

* Testimony of Charles T. Morehouse before the Special Committee on Railroads, New York Assembly, 1879.

† In the case of the Standard Oil Company *vs.* William C. Scofield, *et al.*, in the Court of Common Pleas, Cuyahoga County, Ohio.

to the Standard Oil Company. I told Mr. Jennings that I would carry on no negotiations with him whatever, but that if the Standard Oil Company desired to buy my stock I must transact the business with its principal officer, Mr. Rockefeller. Mr. Jennings, as representing the Standard Oil Company, told me that the president of the company, Mr. Rockefeller, said that said company would control the refining business, and that he hoped it could be done in one or two years; but if not, it would be done, anyway, if it took ten years to do it.

"After two or three days' delay Mr. Rockefeller called upon me at my residence to talk over the negotiation with regard to the purchase of my stock. I told Mr. Rockefeller that I realised the fact that the B—— Oil Company was entirely in the power of the Standard Oil Company, and that all I could do would be to appeal to his honour as a gentleman and to his sympathy to do with me the best that he could; and I begged of him to consider his wife in my position—that I had been left with this business and with my fatherless children, and with a large indebtedness that Mr. B—— had just contracted for the first time in his life; that I felt that I could not do without the income arising from this business, and that I had taken it up and gone on and been successful, and I was left with it in the hardest years since my husband commenced the business. He said he was aware of what I had done, and that his wife could never have accomplished so much. I called his attention to the contract that my husband had made with him in relation to carbon oil, whereby the Standard Oil Company agreed not to touch the lubricating branch of the trade carried on by my husband, and reminded him that I had held to that contract rigidly, at a great loss to the B—— Oil Company, but did so because I regarded it a matter of honour to live up to it. I told him that I had become alarmed because the Standard Oil Company was getting control of all the refineries in the country, and that I feared that the said Standard Oil Company would go into the lubricating trade, and reminded him that he had sent me word that the Standard Oil Company would not interfere with that branch of the trade. He promised, with tears in his eyes, that he would stand by me in this transaction, and that I should not be wronged; and he told me that, in case the sale was made, I might retain whatever amount of the stock of the B—— Oil Company I desired, his object appearing to be only to get the controlling stock of the company. He said that while the negotiations were pending he would come and see me, and I thought that his feelings were such on the subject that I could trust him and that he would deal honourably by me.

"Seeing that I was compelled to sell out, I wanted the Standard Oil Company to make me a proposition, and endeavoured to get them to do so, but they would not make a proposition. I then made a proposition that the whole stock of the B—— Oil Company with accrued dividends should be sold to said Standard Oil Company for $200,000, which was, in fact, much below what the stock ought to have been sold for; but they ridiculed the amount, and at last offered me only $79,000, not including accounts, and required that each stockholder in the B—— Oil Company should enter into a bond that within the period of ten years he or she would not directly or indirectly engage in or in any way be concerned in the refining, manufacturing, producing, piping, or dealing in petroleum or in any of its products within the county of Cuyahoga and state of Ohio, nor at any other place whatever.

"Seeing that the property had to go, I asked that I might, according to the understanding with the president of the company, retain $15,000 of my stock, but the reply to this request was; 'No outsiders can have any interest in this concern; the Standard Oil Company has "dallied" as long as it will over this matter; it must be settled up to-day or go,' and they insisted upon my signing the bond above referred to.

"The promises made by Mr. Rockefeller, president of the Standard Oil Company, were none of them fulfilled; he neither allowed me to retain any portion of my stock, nor did he in any way assist me in my negotiations for the sale of my stock; but, on the contrary, was largely instrumental in my being obliged to sell the property much below its true value, and requiring me to enter into the oppressive bond above referred to.

"After the arrangements for the sale of the refinery and of my stock were fully completed and the property had been sold by myself and the other stockholders, and after I had made arrangements for the disposition of my money, I received a note from Mr. Rockefeller, in reply to one that I had written to him threatening to make the transaction public, saying that he would give me back the business as it stood, or that I might retain stock if I wished to, but this was after the entire transaction was closed, and such arrangements had been made for my money that I could not then conveniently enter into it; and I was so indignant over the offer being made at that late day, after my request for the stock having been made at the proper time, that I threw the letter into the fire and paid no further attention to it."*

The letter which Mrs. B—— destroyed was included in the affidavit in which Mr. Rockefeller answered Mrs. B——'s statement. It reads:

"November 13, 1878. DEAR MADAM: I have held your note of 11th inst., received yesterday, until to-day, as I wished to thoroughly review every point connected with the negotiations for the purchase of the stock of the B—— Oil Company, to satisfy myself as to whether I had unwittingly done anything whereby you could have any

* Coupled with Mrs. B——'s affidavit was one of the company's bookkeeper's testifying that the business had been paying an annual net income of $30,000 to $40,000 when the sale to the Standard was made for $79,000, and another from the cashier, who had been present at most of the interviews between Mrs. B—— and the Standard agents, and who corroborates her statements in every particular.

right to feel injured. It is true that in the interview I had with you I suggested that if you desired to do so, you could retain an interest in the business of the B—— Oil Company, by keeping some number of its shares, and then I understood you to say that if you sold out you wished to go entirely out of the business. That being my understanding, our arrangements were made in case you concluded to make the sale that precluded any other interests being represented, and therefore, when you did make the inquiry as to your taking some of the stock, our answer was given in accordance with the facts noted above, but not at all in the spirit in which you refer to the refusal in your note. In regard to the reference that you make as to my permitting the business of the B—— Oil Company to *be taken* from you, I say that in this, as all else that you have written in your letter of 11th inst., you do me most grievous wrong. It was of but little moment to the interests represented by me whether the business of the B—— Oil Company was purchased or not. I believe that it was for your interest to make the sale, and am entirely candid in this statement, and beg to call your attention to the time, some two years ago, when you consulted Mr. Flagler and myself as to selling out your interests to Mr. Rose, at which time you were desirous of selling at *considerably less price*, and upon time, than you have now received in cash, and which sale you would have been glad to have closed if you could have obtained satisfactory security for the deferred payments. As to the price paid for the property, it is certainly three times greater than the cost at which we could construct equal or better facilities; but wishing to take a liberal view of it, I urged the proposal of paying the $60,000, which was thought much too high by some of our parties. I believe that if you would reconsider what you have written in your letter, to which this is a reply, you must admit having done me great injustice, and I am satisfied to await upon innate sense of right for such admission. However, in view of what seems your present feelings, I now offer to restore to you the purchase made by us, you simply returning the amount of money which we have invested and leaving us as though no purchase had been made. Should you not desire to accept this proposal, I offer to you one hundred, two hundred, or three hundred shares of the stock at the same price that we paid for the same, with this addition, that we keep the property we are under engagement to pay into the treasury of the B—— Oil Company, an amount which, added to the amount already paid, would make a total of $100,000, and thereby make the shares $100 each.

"That you may not be compelled to hastily come to conclusion, I will leave open for three days these propositions for your acceptance or declination, and in the meantime believe me,   Yours very truly,

"John D. Rockefeller."

Mr. Rockefeller says further in the affidavit from which this letter is drawn: "It is not true that I made any promises that I did not keep in the letter and spirit, and it is not true that I was instrumental to any degree in her being obliged to sell the property much below its true value, and I aver that she was not obliged to sell out, and that such was a voluntary one upon her part and for a sum far in excess of its value; and that the construction which was purchased of her could be replaced for a sum not exceeding $20,000." *

It is probably true, as Mr. Rockefeller states, that he could have reproduced Mrs. B——'s plant for $20,000; but the plant was but a small part of her assets. She owned one of the oldest lubricating oil refineries in the country, one with an enviable reputation for good work and fair dealing, and with a trade that had been paying an annual net income of from $30,000 to $40,000. It was this income for which Mr. Rockefeller paid $79,000; this income with the old and honourable name of the B—— Oil Company, with not a few stills and tanks and agitators.

It is undoubtedly true, as Mr. Rockefeller avers, that Mrs. B—— was not obliged to sell out, but the fate of those who in this period of absorption refused to sell was before her eyes. She had seen the twenty Cleveland refineries fall into Mr. Rockefeller's hands in 1872. She had watched the steady collapse of the independents in all the refining centres. She had seen every effort to preserve an individual business thwarted. Rightly or wrongly she had come to believe that a refusal to sell meant a fight with Mr. Rockefeller, that a fight meant ultimately defeat, and she gave up her business to avoid ruin.

* Mr. Rockefeller's statements are supported by affidavits from several members of the firm.

CHAPTER SEVEN

THE CRISIS OF 1878

A RISE IN OIL—A BLOCKADE IN EXPORTS—PRODUCERS DO NOT GET THEIR
SHARE OF THE PROFITS—THEY SECRETLY ORGANISE THE PETROLEUM PRO-
DUCERS' UNION AND PROMISE TO SUPPORT PROPOSED INDEPENDENT PIPE-
LINES—ANOTHER INTERSTATE COMMERCE BILL DEFEATED AT WASHINGTON
—"IMMEDIATE SHIPMENT"—INDEPENDENTS HAVE TROUBLE GETTING
CARS—RIOTS THREATENED—APPEAL TO GOVERNOR HARTRANFT—SUITS
BROUGHT AGAINST UNITED PIPE-LINES, PENNSYLVANIA RAILROAD AND
OTHERS—INVESTIGATIONS PRECIPITATED IN OTHER STATES—THE HEP-
BURN COMMISSION AND THE OHIO INVESTIGATION—EVIDENCE THAT THE
STANDARD IS A CONTINUATION OF THE SOUTH IMPROVEMENT COMPANY—
PRODUCERS FINALLY DECIDE TO PROCEED AGAINST STANDARD OFFICIALS—
ROCKEFELLER AND EIGHT OF HIS ASSOCIATES INDICTED FOR CONSPIRACY.

IT was clear enough by the opening of 1878 that Mr. Rockefeller need no longer fear any serious trouble from the refining element. To be sure there were scattered concerns still
holding out and some of them doing very well; but his latest
move had put him in a position to cut off or at least seriously
to interfere with the very raw material in which they worked.
It was hardly to be expected after the defeat of the Pennsylvania that any railroad would be rash enough to combine
with even a strong group of refiners. As for independent pipe-
lines, there were so many ways of "discouraging" their building that it did not seem probable that any one would ever go
far. It was only a matter of time, then, when all remaining
outside refiners must come into his fold or die. Mr. Rockefeller's path would now have been smooth had it not been
for the oil producers. But the oil producers, naturally his

enemy, he being the buyer and they the seller, had come in the six years before Mr. Rockefeller had made himself the only gatherer of their oil, irreconcilable opponents of whatever he might do. The South Improvement Company they regarded rightly enough as devised to control the price of their product, and that scheme they wrongfully laid entirely at Mr. Rockefeller's door. Mr. Rockefeller had been only one of the originators of the South Improvement Company, but the fact that he had become later practically its only supporter, that he was the only one who had profited by it, and that he had turned his Cleveland plant into a machine for carrying out its provisions, had caused the oil country to fix on him the entire responsibility. Then the oil men's experience with Mr. Rockefeller in 1873 had been unfortunate. They charged the failure of their alliance to his duplicity. There is no doubt that Mr. Rockefeller played a shrewd and false game with the oil men in 1873, but the failure of their alliance was their own fault. They did not hold together—they failed to limit their production as they agreed, they suspected one another, and at a moment, when, if they had been as patient and wise as their great opponent they would have had the game in their own hands, and him at their feet, as he had been in 1872, for the sake of immediate returns, they abandoned some of the best features of their organisation, and allied themselves with a man they distrusted. When that alliance failed they threw on Mr. Rockefeller's shoulders a blame which they should have taken on their own.

Another very real cause for their anxiety and dislike was that as the refiners' alliance progressed the refiners made a much larger share of the profits than the producers thought fair. The abandoning of their alliance in 1873 had of course put an end to their measures for limiting production and for holding over-production until it could be sold at the prices they thought profitable. The drill had gone on merrily through 1873, 1874, and 1875, regardless of consumption or prices. By the end of 1874 there were over three and a half million barrels of oil in stock, more than twice what there had ever been before. Production was well to a million barrels a month and prices that year averaged but $1.15 a barrel. For men who considered three dollars a starvation price this was indeed hard luck. Things looked better by the end of 1875, for production was falling off. By March, 1876, stocks had been so reduced that there was strong confidence that the price of crude oil must advance. By June the Oil City Derrick began to prophesy "three-dollar oil" and to advise oil men to hold crude for that price. In August three dollars was reached in the Oil City exchange. It had been nearly four years since that price had been paid for oil, and the day the point was reached (August 25) the brokers fairly went mad. They jumped on their chairs, threw up their hats, beat one another on the back, while the spectators in the crowded galleries, most of them speculators, yelled in sympathy. Before six o'clock that day oil reached $3.11¼. Nobody thought of stopping because it was supper time. The exchange was open until nearly midnight, prices booming on to $3.17½. It seemed like old times in the Oil Region—the good old flush times when people made a fortune one day and threw it away the next!

Of course refined oil went up steadily with crude. Refined reached 21⅜ cents in New York the day of this boom at Oil City. The day following the rise was one of the most exciting the oil exchange had ever seen. "Never before," declared the Derrick in its report, "was so much business done. From early in the morning until ten o'clock at night the exchange was crowded by frantic speculators. Their awful excitement was clear from their blanched faces and wild voices. Fully 800,000 barrels of oil exchanged hands that day, the advance

between the time the exchange opened and its close was over
fifty-five cents. Refined in New York advanced in accordance
with the market on the creek, closing at twenty-four cents.
This went on for several days, when a new element in the
situation began to force itself on the oil men's attention. One
of the chief reasons on which they based their confidence in
high prices for crude oil was the fact that the foreigners were
short of refined oil. It was the custom then, as now, for exporters to buy their oil for the winter European trade in the late
summer and early fall. When the boom began the harbour at
New York was beginning to fill up with ships for cargoes.
But to the consternation of the oil men intent on keeping up
the boom, the exporters were refusing to buy. They were
declaring the price to which refined had risen to be out of
proportion to the price of crude. More, they declared the
latter a speculative price—only once, they argued, had it
touched four dollars, and the refiners were not buying at
that price for manufacture. They were holding refined too
high. It was early in September when the realisation came
upon the Oil Regions that a new element was in the problem
—a veritable blockade in exports. As the days went on they
saw that this was no temporary affair. They saw that Mr.
Rockefeller's combination was at last carrying out just what
it had been organised to do—forcing the price it wanted for
refined. Day after day refined was held at twenty-six cents.
Day after day the exporters refused to buy. It was not until
the end of September, in fact, that they began to yield—as it
was inevitable they should do, for the game was certainly
in the hands of the refiners, and Europe had to have its light.
The exporters began to see too that if they held off longer they
might have to pay higher prices, for it was rumoured that
the Standard Combination was shutting down its factories,
literally making refined scarce, while crude oil was piling
up in Pennsylvania!

With the yielding of the exporter exactly what they feared occurred, the price was raised! The exporters balked again. The matter began to attract public attention. The New York Herald was particularly active in airing the situation and did not hesitate to denounce it as a "Petroleum Plot." The leaders were interviewed, among them Mr. Rockefeller. Mr. Rockefeller still held to his theory that to make oil dear was worthy of public approval. They had aimed to control the price of oil in a perfectly legitimate way, he told the Herald reporter, and the exporters would have to yield to their prices. By the end of October New York harbour was full of vessels —a mute protest against the corner—and it was not until November that the exporters fully gave in and began to take all the oil they could get at prices asked, which ranged from twenty-six to thirty-five cents. And these prices were held all through the winter of 1876–77, up to February 22. They were held regardless of the price of crude, for, do their utmost, the producers could not keep their oil up to the corresponding price of refined. According to the scale of relative prices then accepted, twenty-six cents a gallon for refined meant five dollars a barrel for crude, yet there was not a month in the entire period of this hold-up that crude averaged that price. In December, when the average price of refined was $29\frac{3}{8}$ cents, crude was but $3.78\frac{1}{8} a barrel. The producers held meetings and passed resolutions, cursed the refiners and talked of building independent refineries, filled the columns of the Derrick with open letters advocating a shut-down, an alliance of their own, restrictive legislation, an oil men's railway, and what was more to the point some of them supported, with more or less fidelity, the efforts to build up counter movements noted in the last chapter: the Columbia Conduit Line, the seaboard pipe-line, and especially the alliance with the Empire Transportation Company, attempted in the spring of 1877. There seemed more hope in this last

WOODEN CAR TANKS

BOILER TANK CARS

WOODEN TANKS FOR STORING OIL

RAILROAD TERMINAL OF AN EARLY PIPE LINE

combination than in any other movement, for they had faith in Colonel Potts, and besides they were accustomed to seeing the Pennsylvania Railroad get what it wanted. The defeat of the Pennsylvania was therefore the heavier blow. Indeed, the news of the sale of the Empire pipe-lines to the Standard was like the sounding of the tocsin in the angry and baffled Oil Regions. It revived the spirit of 1872. But it was the spirit of 1872 with new dignity and a discretion such as had never been before seen in the blatant region. In every town from McKean County southwest to Butler the oil towns hastened to organise themselves into a secret society. Little by little it came out that a Producers' Union had been organised. From all that could be learned it looked very much as if the Petroleum Producers' Union had come into existence to do business. On November 21, 1877, the first meeting of the new organisation was held, "the Petroleum Parliament" or "Congress" it was called. This Congress, which met in Titusville, was composed of 172 delegates. It was claimed that it represented at least 2,000 oil producers, and not less than seventy-five millions in money. It is certain it included the representative men of the Oil Regions, those to whose daring, hard work, and energy the discovery and development of the oil fields, as they were known at that time, were entirely due.

For four days the Congress was in session, and it is a remarkable comment on the seriousness with which it had undertaken its work that, although reporters from all parts of the country interested in oil were present, nothing leaked out. In December a second session of four days was held in Titusville, but no announcement of what was doing was made to the press. Indeed, it was only as lines of action developed that the public became familiar with what the producers had resolved on in the days of secret session which they had held.

Their resolutions had been eminently wise and they undertook their support vigorously and intelligently. First and foremost they resolved to stand by all efforts to secure an outlet to the seaboard independent of the Standard and the allied railroads. Two enterprises were put before them at once. The first was what was known as the Equitable Petroleum Company, an organisation started by one of the most resourceful and active independent men in the oil country, one of whom we are to hear more, Lewis Emery, Jr. This company, in which some 200 oil producers in the Bradford field had taken stock, proposed to lay a pipe-line to Buffalo and to ship their oil thence by the Erie Canal. They had acquired a right of way to Buffalo and had capital pledged to carry out the project. The second enterprise to come before the newly formed union was much more ambitious. It was nothing less than a revival of Mr. Harley's enterprise which had attracted so much attention in 1876. It was revived now by the three men who had been operating the Columbia Conduit Line under a lease—Messrs. Benson, McKelvy and Hopkins, who had been set free by the sale of that property to the Standard. Their experience with the pipe-line business had convinced them it was one of the most lucrative departments of the oil industry. They believed too that oil could be pumped over the mountains, and no sooner were they free than they took up Mr. Harley's old idea and engaged the same engineer he had brought into the enterprise, General Herman Haupt, to survey a route from Brady's Bend on the Allegheny River to Baltimore, Maryland—a distance of 235 miles. To both of these projects the General Council of the Union gave promise of support.

The demand for interstate commerce legislation was renewed at once by the Union, and in December E. G. Patterson, the head of the committee having the matter in hand, prepared the first draft of an act which was put in formal shape by George B. Hibbard, of Buffalo, counsel employed by the Union for this purpose. Mr. Hibbard also prepared a memo-

randum of the law on the subject. The bill prepared by Mr.
Patterson and Mr. Hibbard was introduced into the House
of Representatives in May, 1878, by Lewis F. Watson, whose
home was in Warren County, Pennsylvania. It was called
into committee and came out as the Regan bill and as such
was passed at the end of the year by the House, but only to
be smothered later in the Senate. At the same time that the
effort was going in Washington for relief the Legislature of
Pennsylvania was being besieged again for a free pipe-line
bill and an anti-discrimination bill. Both of these projects
failed, and the committee having them in charge said bitterly
in its report to the Union: "How well we have succeeded
at Harrisburg you all know. It would be in vain for your
committee to describe the efforts of the Council in this direction. It has been simply a history of failure and disgrace. If
it has taught us anything, it is that our present law-makers,
as a body, are ignorant, corrupt and unprincipled; that the
majority of them are, directly or indirectly, under the control
of the very monopolies against whose acts we have been seeking relief. . . . There has been invented by the Standard Oil
Company no argument or assertion, however false or ridicu-
lous, which has not found a man in the Pennsylvania Legislature mean enough to become its champion."

On every side indeed the producers hastened to protect
themselves against the Lord of the Oil Regions, as Mr. Rockefeller, not inaptly, was called, on the completion of his pipe-
line monopoly. That they were not merely alarmists in think-
ing that they must do something to protect their interests was
demonstrated sooner than was anticipated. The demonstration was hurried by an unforeseen and difficult situation—a
great outpouring of oil in a new field—the Bradford or
Northern Field in McKean County, Pennsylvania. About the
time that Mr. Rockefeller's lordship was realised it became
certain that a deposit of oil had been discovered which was

going to lead soon to a production vastly in excess of the consumption, as well as in excess of the then existing facilities for gathering and storing oil. If Mr. Rockefeller wished to keep his monopoly he must, it was evident, enter upon a campaign of expansion calling for an immense expenditure of energy and money. He must lay pipes in a hundred directions to get the output of new wells; he must build tanks holding thousands of barrels to receive the oil. And all of this must be done quickly if rivals were to be kept out of the way. There was no hesitation on the part of the United Pipe Lines. One of the greatest construction feats the country has ever seen was put through in the years 1878, 1879 and 1880 in the Bradford oil field by the Standard interests. It was a wonderful illustration of the surpassing intelligence, energy and courage with which the Standard Oil Company attacks its problems. But while it was putting through this feat it instituted a policy toward the producers which was regarded by them as tyrannical and unjustifiable. The first manœuvre in this new policy hit the producer in a very tender spot, for it concerned the price he was to receive for oil.

The method which prevailed at the time in handling and buying and selling oil was this: At the request of the well owner connected with a pipe-line his oil was run and credited to him in the pipe-line office. Here he could hold it as long as he wished by paying a storage charge. If he wished to sell his "credit balance," as oil to his account was called, he simply gave the buyer an order on the line for the oil, and it was tranferred to the account of the new buyer. The pipe-lines frequently had hundreds of thousands of barrels of oil in hand, and they traded with this oil as banks do with their deposits—that is, they issued certificates for each 1,000 barrels of oil on hand, and these certificates were negotiable like any other paper. Now the United Pipe Lines acknowledged itself a common carrier, and so was obliged to discharge the duty of collecting oil on demand, or at least within a reasonable time after the demand of its patrons.

But in December, 1877, after the monopoly was completed, they refused to discharge their obligations in the customary way. On the plea that they had not sufficient tankage to carry oil in the Bradford field, they issued an order that no oil would be run in that district for any one unless it was sold for "immediate shipment"—that is, no oil would be taken to hold for storage; it would be taken for shipping only. At the same time the Standard buyer, J. A. Bostwick, decreed that henceforth no Bradford oil would be bought for immediate shipment unless it was offered at *less* than the market price. No fixed discount was set. The seller was asked what he would take; his offer was, of course, according to his necessities. Even then an answer was not always immediately given. The seller was told to come back in five or ten days and he would be told if his oil would be taken. A feature of the new order, particularly galling to the oil men, was the manner in which it was enforced. Formerly the buyer and seller had met freely in the oil exchanges and their business offices, and transactions had been carried on as among equals. Now the producers were obliged to form in line before the United Pipe Lines' offices and to enter one at a time to consult the buyer. A line of a hundred men or more often stood during the hours set before the office, waiting their turn to dispose of their oil. It should be said in justice to Mr. Bostwick that he was not the first buyer to take oil at a discount. The producers themselves frequently offered oil at less than the market price when in need of money, but Mr. Bostwick was the first buyer in a situation to force them to make the discount regularly. When these orders came, few of the producers had sufficient private tankage to take care of any amount of oil. Here was the situation then: to keep oil from running on the ground the producer must sell it; but if he sold it he must take a price from two to twenty-five cents or more below the market.

The immediate shipment order was not an invention of the United Pipe Lines. It had been enforced more than once for brief periods by various lines when they found their capacity overcrowded by some unexpected situation. In 1872 epizootic among the horses so upset things in the Oil Regions that for a short time an immediate shipment order was enforced. In 1874, when the pipe-lines were overtaxed by a great outpouring of oil in the Lower Field, immediate shipment had been attempted, but at that time there were still so many independent pipes struggling for business that the movement met no success. Now, however, the United Pipe Lines had things its own way. That they were not ready to meet the growing Bradford production is plain from a study of the figures. There were in the Oil Regions at the close of 1877, according to the Oil City Derrick, 4,000,000 barrels of tankage. There was on hand at this time 3,127,837 barrels of oil, but the empty tankage was in the wrong place. In the Bradford field, where the daily production had suddenly increased from 2,000 barrels in January to 8,451 barrels in December, there was only a little over 200,000 barrels of tankage.* In order to take care of the oil the pipe-lines began to make nearly all their shipments from that field, and oil piled up in the Lower Region to the great dissatisfaction of the producers there.

As soon as the situation of the Bradford field was realised both the United Pipes and the producers began a furious campaign of tank building. By the beginning of April, 1878, the tankage there had been increased to 1,152,028 barrels.† Between April 1 and November 1 seventy tanks of from 10,000 to 25,000 barrels capacity were built in McKean County. The greater number of these belonged to the producers. According to the United Pipe Lines' statement, there was under their con-

* Oil City Derrick, January 5, 1878.   † Derrick Handbook, Vol. II.

trol in the entire Oil Regions in October 5,200,000 barrels of tankage, two-thirds of which belonged to producers, but was held by them under a lease.* But oil poured from the ground faster than tanks could be built. In six months—that is, by July, 1878,—the daily output of Bradford had become over 18,000 barrels, an increase of 10,000 barrels a day over that of the previous December. That it was a most difficult situation for everybody is evident. There was but one way to prevent loss— shut down the wells and stop the drill; but this the producers refused to consider. Of course the price of oil went down rapidly, so far did the production exceed consumption. But why, cried the producer, when oil is already so low, take advantage of our necessity and force us into competition with each other; why enforce this immediate shipment? They answered their question themselves, and began then to make a charge against the Standard, which they continue to make to-day; that is, that it habitually meets the extraordinary expenses to which it is put by depressing the price of crude oil —"taking it out of the producer." The Bradford region demanded great investments, therefore immediate shipment. "The producer pays." The writer has no documentary proof that this is Mr. Rockefeller's policy, but there is no question that the Oil Region believes it is, and this belief must be taken into account if one attempts to explain the long warfare of the oil country on him and his company. It is a common enough thing to-day, indeed, to hear oil producers in Northwestern Pennsylvania remark facetiously when a new endowment to Chicago University is reported: "Yes, I contributed so much on such a day. Don't you remember how the market slumped without a cause? The university needed the money, and so Mr. Rockefeller called on us to stand and deliver."

* The stocks on hand at the end of this month were 4,221,769 barrels. On November 25, 1878, the Derrick published tables showing 4,576,500 barrels of tankage up and building in the Bradford field. Connected with the United Lines were 1,774,500 barrels already in use and 1,347,000 building.

A few months after "immediate shipment" was begun a new cause for dissatisfaction arose. More or less private tankage leased to the lines had always been in existence. It enabled a producer to carry his oil without paying storage, and, of course, it was the business of the company to empty this storage within a reasonable time after the owner demanded it. But in the spring the lines, under the same plea of under capacity, refused to carry out this duty to the tank owner; that is, they refused to give him his tankage, although he had sold his oil. Thus A owns 5,000 barrels of tankage. It is full. He sells a portion of it to Mr. Bostwick and asks the United Pipe Lines to run the oil accumulated at his wells. But the United Pipe Lines refuses on the ground that the line is full. The loss to producers incident upon these orders was terrible. All over the Bradford field men saw their oil running on the ground, though they offered to sell it at ruinous prices, and though they might have thousands of barrels of tankage leased to the United Lines. Yet they did not riot; conscious that their own reckless drilling had brought on the trouble, they cursed the Standard, and put down more wells!

But in the spring of 1878 Mr. Rockefeller and his colleagues instituted a series of manœuvres which shattered the last remnant of confidence the oil men had in the sincerity of their claim that they were doing their utmost to relieve the distressed Oil Regions, and that their measures were necessary to hold the producers in check. The pipe-lines began to refuse to load cars for the shippers who supplied the few independent refiners with oil. The experiences of many of these independent oil men have been told before the courts. For instance, W. H. Nicholson, the representative of Mr. Ohlen, of New York, a shipper of petroleum, testified * that in May, 1878, he began to have difficulty in getting cars. At

* Investigation ordered by the secretary of internal affairs of the Commonwealth of Pennsylvania, 1878.

Olean, one day, Mr. Ohlen telegraphed to the officials of the Erie road to know if he could get 100 cars to run East. The reply came back Yes. About noon, Mr. Nicholson says, he saw Mr. O'Day, the manager of the United Pipe Lines, in which his oil was stored, and told him that he was waiting to have his cars loaded. Mr. O'Day at once said he could not load the cars. "But I have an order from the Erie officials, giving me the cars," Mr. Nicholson objected. "That makes no difference," O'Day replied; "I cannot load cars except upon an order from Pratt." Nor would he do it. The cars were not loaded for Mr. Nicholson, although at that time he had ten thousand barrels of oil in the United Pipe Lines, and an order for 100 cars from the officials of the Erie road in his hand.

B. B. Campbell, at that time president of the Producers' Union, gave his experience at this time in the suit of the Commonwealth against the Pennsylvania Railroad:

"I never heard of a scarcity of cars until the early part of June, 1878; I came to Parker about five o'clock in the evening, and found the citizens in a state of terrible excitement; the Pipe-Lines would not run oil unless it was sold; the only shippers we had in Parker of any amount, viz., the agents of the Standard Oil Company, would not buy oil, stating that they could not get cars; hundreds of wells were stopped to their great injury; thousands more, whose owners were afraid to stop them for fear of damage by salt-water, were pumping the oil on the ground. I used all the influence I had to prevent an outbreak and destruction of railroad and pipe-lines; I at once went over to the Allegheny Valley Railroad office and telegraphed to John Scott, president of the Allegheny Valley Railroad Company:

"'The refusal of the United to run oil unless sold upon immediate shipment, and of the railroad to furnish cars, has created such a degree of excitement here that the more conservative part of the citizens will not be able to control the peace, and I fear that the scenes of last July will be repeated on an aggravated scale.' That message I left in the office about seven o'clock in the evening. I got up the next morning before seven and received an answer:

"'What do you advise should be done? John Scott.' I answered: 'Will meet you to-morrow morning,' which would be Saturday.

"On Saturday morning I came in on an early train and met at the depot Mr. Shinn, then, I believe, vice-president of the Allegheny Valley Railroad Company, David A. Stewart, one of the directors of the road, and Thomas M. King, assistant superintendent. I spoke very plainly to Mr. Shinn, telling him that the idea of a scarcity of cars on daily shipments of less than 30,000 barrels a day was such an absurd, barefaced pretence that he could not expect men of ordinary intelligence to accept it, as the preceding fall, when business required, the railroads could carry day after day from 50,000 to 60,000 barrels of oil. Mr. Shinn stated clearly that I knew that the Allegheny Valley Railroad Company did not control the oil business over its line, but was governed entirely and exclusively by orders received from the Pennsylvania Railroad Company. I then requested him to be the vehicle of communicating to the Pennsylvania Railroad officials my views on the subject, telling him that I was convinced that unless immediate relief was furnished and cars afforded there would be an outbreak in the Oil Regions. After further conversation we parted. My interview with them was not as officials of the Allegheny Valley Railroad Company, but as representatives of the oil traffic carried and controlled by the Pennsylvania road. On the next Monday I returned to Parker. After passing Redbank, where the low grade road, the connecting link between the Valley Road and the Philadelphia and Erie Road, meets the Valley Road—between that point and Parker—the express train was delayed for over half an hour in passing through *hundreds of empty oil cars.*"*

In June another exasperating episode occurred, growing out of the attempts of the oil men to secure independent routes to the seaboard. As we have seen, two enterprises had been launched late in 1877 under the patronage of the Petroleum Producers' Union. As soon as the Equitable had acquired its right of way to Buffalo, Mr. Emery, the head of the company, his papers in hand, sought an interview with representatives of the Buffalo and McKean road, and told them if they did not consent that the Equitable lay a pipe-line to their road, and did not contract to carry the oil from that connection to Buffalo, the pipe-line to Buffalo would be laid. After considerable negotiation a contract was made with the railroad, and by June the new company was ready with pipeline, cars and barges to carry oil to New York. But no sooner did they attempt to begin operations than the railroad, under pressure from the Pennsylvania Railroad it was claimed, re-

* Abridged from Mr. Campbell's testimony.

fused to carry out its contracts. The cars the Equitable ordered sent to the loading track were refused, a side track it had laid was torn up, the frog torn out; everything, indeed, was done to prevent the Equitable doing business, though finally a vigorous appeal to the law brought the road to terms, and in July oil began to flow Eastward by this indirect route. No sooner did the Standard find that the Equitable people were really doing business than they appealed to the railroads. A meeting of the representatives of the trunk lines was held at Saratoga in July, and the rates on crude Eastward were dropped to eighty cents to meet the new competition.

While this fight was going on against the Equitable all sorts of interference were being put in the way of the seaboard line between Brady's Bend and Baltimore. It was ridiculed as chimerical to attempt to pump oil over the mountains, and General Haupt was declared to be a visionary engineer with a record of failures. All the old stories retailed in 1876 were dragged out again. The farmers were told that the leakage from the pipe-line would ruin their fields and endanger their buildings, and an active campaign to excite prejudice was carried on again in the farmers' papers. Philadelphia and Pittsburg both fought the plan, the press and chambers of commerce opposing the free pipe bill at that time before the Legislature, and the project generally. In Pittsburg the opposition created almost a riot, for the oil producers of the Lower Field, who had long bought their supplies there, now threatened to boycott the city if the pipe-line was fought. So strong was the opposition that capital took fright and the company found it most difficult to secure funds. This opposition to the pipe-line was, of course, charged against the Standard and the Pennsylvania Railroad.

Now, while the railroads were refusing cars to independent shippers,—or if they gave an order for them, the United Pipe Lines were refusing to load them,—while the Standard and the railroads were doing their utmost to prevent the Equitable Line doing business, and were discouraging in every way the seaboard pipe-line—new routes which would take care of a proportion, at least, of the oil which they claimed they could not handle—thousands of barrels of oil were running on the ground in Bradford, and two of the independent refineries of New York shut down entirely in order that a third of their number might get oil enough to fill an order.

This interference with the outside interests, thus preventing the small degree of relief which they would have afforded, and a growing conviction that the Standard meant to keep up the "immediate shipment" order, at least until it had built the pipes and tanks needed in the Bradford field, finally aroused the region to a point where riot was imminent. The long line of producers who filed into the United Pipe Lines' office day after day to sell their oil at whatever prices they could get for it, and who, having put in an offer which varied according to their necessities, were usually told to come back in ten days, and the buyer would see whether he wanted it or not—this long line of men began to talk of revolution. Crowds gathered about the offices of the Standard threatening and jeering. Mysterious things, cross-bones and death-heads, were found plentifully sprinkled on the buildings owned by the Standard interests. More than once the slumber of the oil towns was disturbed by marching bodies of men. It was certain that a species of Kuklux had hold of the Bradford region, and that a very little spark was needed to touch off the United Pipe Lines. In the meantime things were scarcely less exciting in the Lower Fields. The "immediate shipment" order was looked upon there as particularly outrageous, because there was no lack of lines or tanks in that field, and when, in the summer of 1878, there was added to this cause an unjustifiable scarcity of cars, excitement rose to fever heat.

The only thing which prevented a riot at this time and

great destruction of property, if not of life, was the strong hand the Petroleum Producers' Union had on the country. Fearing that if violence did occur the different movements they had under way would be prejudiced, they sent a committee of twenty-five men to Harrisburg to see Governor Hartranft. They laid before him and the attorney-general of the state the grievance of the oil producers in an "appeal" reviewing the history of the industry.* They demanded that the United Pipe Lines be made to perform its duty as a public carrier, and the railroads be made to cease their discrimination against shippers both in the matter of rebates and in furnishing cars. They called the Governor's attention to the fact that there were already existing laws touching these matters which, in their judgment, met the case, and if the existing laws did not give them relief, that it was the plain duty of the executive to call a meeting of the Legislature and pass such acts as would do so. Governor Hartranft was much stirred by the story of the producers. He went himself to the Oil Regions to see the situation, and in August directed the producers to put their demands into the form of an appeal. This was done, and it was decided to bring proceedings by writ of *quo warranto* against the United Pipe Lines, and by separate bills in equity against the Pennsylvania Railroad and the other lines doing business in the state. It was September before the state authorities began their investigation of the United Pipe Lines, the hearings being held in Titusville. Many witnesses summoned failed to appear, but enough testimony was brought out in this investigation to show that the railroads had refused to furnish cars for independents when they had them empty, and that the United Pipe Lines had clearly violated its duty as a common carrier. In his report on this investigation the secretary of internal affairs, William McCandless, rendered

* See Appendix, Number 32. Producers' Appeal of 1878 to Governor John F. Hartranft of Pennsylvania.

a verdict that the charges of the oil producers had not been substantiated in any way that demanded action.

The indignation which followed this report was intense. It found a vent in the hanging in effigy of McCandless, who was universally known in the state as "Buck." In the oil exchange at Parker, on the morning of October 19, the figure of a man was found hanged by the neck to a gallows, and the producers left it hanging there all day, so that they might jeer and curse it. Across the forehead of the effigy in large blood-red letters were the words:

PENNSYLVANIA RAILROAD

Pinned to the gallows there was a card bearing a quotation from Secretary McCandless's report:

The charges of the oil producers have not been substantiated in any way that demands action.

In Bradford a huge effigy hung in the streets all day, and in the village of Tarport, near by, another swayed on the gallows. They pulled down the effigy at Bradford, and drew from a pocket what purported to be a check signed by John D. Rockefeller, president of the Standard Oil Company, in favour of "Buck" McCandless, for $20,000, and endorsed by the Pennsylvania Railroad Company. That represented the price, they said, that McCandless got for signing the report. Throughout the oil country there was hardly an oil producer to be found not associated with the Standard Oil Company who did not believe that McCandless had sold himself and his office to the Standard Oil Combination for $20,000, and used the money to help in his Congressional canvass.

The excitement in the Oil Regions spread all over the

country. Something of the importance the press attached to it may be judged from the way the New York Sun handled the question. For six weeks it kept one of the ablest members of its staff in the Oil Regions. Six columns of the first page of the issue for November 13 was taken up with the story of the excitement, coupled with the full account of the South Improvement Company, and the development of the Standard Oil Company out of that concern. On November 23 the first page contained four columns more under blazing headings.

Early in 1879 the hearing in the suits in equity brought by the commonwealth against the various transportation companies of which the producers had been complaining were begun. The witnesses subpœnaed failed at first to appear, and when on the stand they frequently refused to reply; but it soon became apparent to them that the state authorities were in earnest, and that they must "answer or go to Europe." By March, 1879, an important array of testimony had been brought out. Among the Standard men who had appeared had been John D. Archbold, William Frew, Charles Lockhart and J. J. Vandergrift. A score or more of producers also appeared. The most important witness from the railroad circles, and, indeed, the most important witness who appeared, was A. J. Cassatt. Mr. Cassatt's testimony was startling in its candour and its completeness, and substantiated in every particular what the oil men had been claiming: that the Pennsylvania Railroad had become the creature of the Standard Oil Company; that it was not only giving that company rates much lower than to any other organisation, but that it was using its facilities with a direct view of preventing any outside refiner or dealer in oil from carrying on an independent business.*

* The story of the Empire Transportation Company, told in the last chapter. was brought out in this testimony of Mr. Cassatt's.

The same or similar conditions, not only in oil, but in other products, which led to these suits, led to investigations in other states. Toward the end of 1878 the Chamber of Commerce of New York City demanded from the Legislature of the state an investigation of the New York railroads. This investigation was carried on from the beginning of 1879. The revelations were amazing. Before the Hepburn Commission, as it was called from the name of the chairman, was through with its work there had appeared before it to give testimony in regard to the conduct of the Standard Oil Company and of the relation of the Erie and the Central roads to it, H. H. Rogers, J. D. Archbold, Jabez A. Bostwick and W. T. Sheide. A large number of independent oil men had also appeared. William H. Vanderbilt had been examined, and G. H. Blanchard, the freight agent of the Erie road, had given a full account of the relation of the Erie to the Standard, perhaps the most useful piece of testimony, after that of Mr. Cassatt, belonging to this period of the Standard's history.*

At the same time that the Pennsylvania suits were going on, and the Hepburn Commission was doing its work, the Legislature of Ohio instituted an investigation. It was commonly charged that this investigation was smothered, but it was not smothered until H. M. Flagler had appeared before it and given some most interesting facts concerning rebates. A number of gentlemen who were finding it hard to do oil business also appeared before the Ohio committee and told their stories.† By April, 1879, there had been brought out in these

---

* The testimony taken before the Hepburn Committee has never been printed in the series of Assembly documents. An edition of 100 copies was printed during the session for the use of the committee. It is usually bound in five volumes, and is, of course, very rare.

† 300 copies of the report of the testimony taken were printed. No copy is to be found in any library of the state of Ohio. The writer has never seen but one copy of this report.

various investigations a mass of testimony sufficient in the judgment of certain of the producers to establish the truth of a charge which they had long been making, and that was that the Standard was simply a revival of the South Improvement Company. Now the verdict of the Congressional Committee had been that the South Improvement Company was a conspiracy. Therefore, said the producers, the Standard Oil Company is a conspiracy. Their hope had been, from the first, to obtain proof to establish this charge. Having this they believed they could obtain judgment from the courts against the officials of the company, and either break it up or put its members in the penitentiary. The more hotheaded of the producers believed that they now had this evidence.

If one will examine the testimony which had been given thus far in the course of the various examinations one will see that there was reason for their belief. In the first place, it had been established that all the stockholders of the South Improvement Company, excepting four, were now members of the Standard Oil Combination. Indeed, the only persons holding high positions in the new combination at this date who were not South Improvement Company men were, Charles Pratt, J. J. Vandergrift, H. H. Rogers and John D. Archbold.

The South Improvement Company had been a secret organisation. So was the new Standard alliance; that is, the most strenuous efforts had been made to keep it secret; for instance, the sale of the works of Lockhart, Warden and Pratt to the Standard was kept from the public. Indeed, it was a year after these sales before even the Erie Railroad knew that Mr. Rockefeller had any affiliations besides those with Pratt and Company, and it made its contracts with him on this assumption. When purchases of refineries were made it was the custom to continue the business under the name of the original concern; thus, when Mrs. B., of Cleveland, sold in 1878, as recounted in the last chapter, the persons selling were obliged to keep the sale secret even from the employees of the concern. "The understanding was with regard to the sale of the property to the Standard Oil Company," said the shipping clerk in his affidavit, "that it should not be known outside of their own parties, that it was to be kept a profound secret, and that the business was to be carried on as if the B——— Oil Company was still a competitor." The secret rites with which the contract was made in 1876 between Mr. Rockefeller and Scofield, Shurmer and Teagle have already been described.

To keep the relations of the various Standard concerns secret Mr. Rockefeller went so far, in 1880, as to make an affidavit like the following: "It is not true, as stated by Mr. Teagle in his affidavit, that the Standard Oil Company, directly or indirectly through its officers or agents, owns or controls the works of Warden, Frew and Company, Lockhart, Frew and Company, J. A. Bostwick and Company, C. Pratt and Company, Acme Refining Company, Imperial Refining Company, Camden Consolidated Company, and the Devoe Manufacturing Company; nor is it true that the Standard Oil Company, directly or indirectly through its officers or agents, owns or controls the refinery at Hunter's Point, New York. It is not true that the Standard Oil Company, directly or indirectly through its officers or agents, purchased or acquired the Empire Transportation Company, or furnished the money therefor; nor is it true that the Standard Oil Company inaugurated or began or induced any other person or corporation to inaugurate or begin a war upon the Pennsylvania Railroad Company or the Empire Transportation Company, as stated in the affidavit of Mr. Teagle." *

There may be a technical explanation of this affidavit,

* In the case of the Standard Oil Company vs. William C. Scofield et al., in the Court of Common Pleas, Cuyahoga County, Ohio, 1880.

although the writer knows of none. There is certainly abundant testimony in existence that the works of Messrs. Pratt, Lockhart and Warden, at least, had been bought long before this affidavit was made, and paid for in Standard Oil Company stock, and that they were working in alliance with that company. It was shown in the last chapter that on October 17, 1877, the Standard Oil Company paid $2,500,000 in certified checks on the purchasing price of the plant of the Empire Transportation Company.

While none of the other members of the Standard Oil Company examined in 1879 was quite so sweeping in his denials, all of them evaded direct answers. The reason they gave for this evasion was that the investigations were an interference with their rights as private citizens, and that the government had no business to inquire into their methods. Consequently when asked questions they refused to answer "by advice of counsel." Ultimately the gentlemen did answer a great many questions. But taking the testimony all in all through these years it certainly is a mild characterisation to say that it totally lacks in frankness. The testimony of the Standard officials before the Hepburn Commission was so evasive that the committee in making its report spoke bitterly of the company as "a mysterious organisation whose business and transactions are of such a character that its members decline giving a history or description of it lest this testimony be used to convict them of a crime." The producers certainly were right in claiming that secrecy was a characteristic of the Standard as it had been of the South Improvement Company.

The new Standard Combination, like the South Improvement Company, aimed at controlling the entire refining interest. "The coal oil business belongs to us," Mr. Rockefeller once told a recalcitrant refiner. His associates were saying the same on all sides; "the object of the Standard Oil Company is to secure the entire refining business of the world," a member of the concern told B. F. Nye, an Ohio producer.*

The method the Standard depended upon to secure this control was the same as the method of the South Improvement Company—special privileges in transportation. We have seen how intelligently and persistently Mr. Rockefeller worked to secure these special privileges until, in 1877, he had made with all the trunk lines contracts which in every particular paralleled the contracts which in January, 1872, Messrs. Scott, Gould, Vanderbilt and McClellan made with the South Improvement Company. He now had a rebate on every barrel of oil he shipped, and this was given with the understanding that the railroad should allow no rebate to any other shipper unless that shipper could guarantee and furnish a quantity of oil for shipment which would, after deduction of his commission, realise to the road the same amount of profit realised from the Standard trade. He also had a drawback on every barrel his rivals shipped. No clause in the South Improvement Company's contract with railroads had given more offence to the oil world than that which called for a drawback to the company on the oil shipped by outsiders. It will be remembered that the beneficiaries of this contract were to receive drawbacks of $1.06 a barrel on all crude oil that outside parties shipped from the Oil Regions to New York, and a proportionate drawback on that shipped from other points. The rebate system was considered illegal and unjust, but men were more or less accustomed to it. The drawback on other people's shipment was a new device, and it threw the Oil Region into a frenzy of rage. It did not seem possible that the Standard would attempt to revive this practice again, and yet when it had got its hand strongly on the four trunk lines it made a demand for the drawback. It has already been recounted how, on February 15, 1878, four

* Ohio State Investigation of freight discrimination, 1879.

months after the Pennsylvania succumbed to the Standard's demand, Mr. O'Day wrote to Mr. Cassatt: "I here repeat what I once stated to you, and which I wish you to receive and treat as strictly confidential, that we have been for many months receiving from the New York Central and Erie Railroads certain sums of money, in no instance less than twenty cents per barrel on *every barrel of crude oil carried by each of these roads.* . . . Co-operating as we are doing with the Standard Oil Company and the trunk lines in every effort to secure for the railroads paying rates of freight on the oil they carry, I am constrained to say to you that in justice to the interests I represent we should receive from your company at least twenty cents on each barrel of crude oil you transport." And Mr. Cassatt after seeing the freight bills showing that both the Central and Erie allowed a drawback gave orders that the Pennsylvania pay one of 22½ cents. When Mr. Cassatt was under examination in 1874 the examiner remarked:

"I understand, Mr. Cassatt, that this 22½ cents paid to the American Transfer Company is not restricted to all oil that passed through their lines."

"No, sir; it is paid on all oil received and transferred by us."

Among the interesting documents presented at this inquiry was a statement of the crude oil shipments over the Pennsylvania road for February and March, 1878.* They footed up to a total of 343,767½ barrels. On this amount a discount of twenty cents a barrel was allowed to the Standard Oil Company through its agent, the American Transfer Company. Among other independents who shipped this oil was H. C. Ohlen. In all, Mr. Ohlen shipped 29,876 barrels, and on this

* See Appendix, Number 33. Statement of crude oil shipments by Green Line during the months of February and March, 1878, to New York, Philadelphia and Baltimore: showing drawbacks allowed to American Transfer Company.

the Standard Oil Company received twenty cents a barrel! That is, after Mr. Ohlen had paid for his oil, paid for having it carried by the pipe-line to the railroad, and paid the railroad the full rate of freight without the commission the Standard received, the Pennsylvania was obliged to turn over to the Standard Oil Company twenty cents of the amount he had paid on each barrel!

The examiner tried very hard to find out if there was a legitimate reason why such an allowance should have been made to the American Transfer Company on oil it did not handle. "We pay that," Mr. Cassatt said, "as a commission to them to aid in securing us our share of trade." "We pay it," said the comptroller, "for procuring oil to go over the lines in which the Pennsylvania Railroad Company is interested as against the New York lines and the New York Central."

"Do you understand," the examiner questioned of one of the auditors, "that the American Transfer Company secured to the Pennsylvania road the traffic of the outside refiners of New York (mentioned in the statement quoted above)?" "I never raised a question of that kind in my mind," answered the adroit auditor.

But the answer was evident. The American Transfer Company had nothing whatever to do with the oil shipped by Mr. Ohlen or Ayres, Lombard and Company or J. Rousseaux or any one of the other independents mentioned in the statement; unless perchance that oil had come originally from the lines of the American Transfer Company. In that case the shipper had paid the line for the service rendered, at the time he bought the oil—the custom then and now. The tax was paid by the Pennsylvania solely because the Standard Oil Company had the power to demand it. The demand was made in the name of the American Transfer Company as a blind. Naturally the proof that the Standard had revived the most obnoxious feature of the South Improvement Company aroused intense bitterness and disgust among the oil men.

Another offensive clause of the 1872 contracts was that pledging the railroads to lower or raise the gross rates of transportation for such times and to such extent as might be necessary to overcome competition. Now, the new contracts of the Standard provided the same arrangement; that is, they stipulated that the rates were to be lowered if necessary so as to place the Standard on a parity with shippers by competing lines. The workings of the clause were illustrated when the producers got the Equitable Line through in 1878, the railroads dropping their charge to eighty cents a barrel, and in some cases even less. The producers certainly had evidence enough for their claim that the contracts of the South Improvement Company and the Standard Oil Company with the railroads were similar in every particular as far as principles were concerned—that they differed alone in the amounts of the rebates and drawbacks.

There was plenty of evidence brought out, also, to show that the object of the Standard operations was like that of the South Improvement Company—keeping up the price of refined oil. Both combinations were formed to keep the refined article scarce on the market by controlling all the refineries and by refusing to sell under competition. The officials of the South Improvement Company stated under oath that they hoped to raise the price fifty per cent. The Central Organisation hoped to put up the price of refined from fifteen to twenty-five cents. As a matter of fact that organisation when it finally got control of the market put up the price considerably more. The spectacular demonstration in the winter of 1876 and 1877 of what could be done in keeping up the price of refined was still rankling in the minds of the oil men. They saw that it was by that coup that the Standard had gotten the ready money to pay for the plant of the Empire Transportation Company—the money to buy in whatever it wanted —the money to pay the fifty per cent. dividend to which one of its members testified in the Ohio Investigation. They remembered that while the refiners had been selling refined around thirty cents a gallon they had sold crude at less than four dollars a barrel. Little wonder then that they felt they had evidence that the Standard had actually done what they had always claimed it would do if it got hold of the refining interests as it planned. Even in the case where certain large producers had entered into a partnership with the Standard on condition that they pay them prices for crude commensurate with the price of refined, these producers claimed the agreement had not been kept. One of these cases came to light in a suit instituted in 1878. It seems that some time in December, 1874, the large oil company of H. L. Taylor and Company sold one-half interest in its property to the Standard Oil Company. The reason for the sale the plaintiffs stated in their complaint to be as follows:

The extent of their (the Standard's) business and control over pipe-lines and refineries had enabled them to procure, and they had procured from the railways, more favourable terms for transportation than others could obtain. These advantages and facilities placed it within their power to obtain, and they did obtain, far better and more uniform prices for petroleum than could be obtained by the plaintiffs. The said organisation and firms, by virtue of their monopoly of the business of refining and transportation of oil, had been at times almost the only buyers in the market, and at such times had been enabled to dictate and establish a price for crude oil far below its actual value, as determined by prices of refined oil at same dates, and they thus obtained a large share of the profits which should have fallen to the plaintiffs and other purchasers. The sale was made, and in consideration of the foregoing premises, and upon the promise and agreement on the part of the defendants that the partnership thus formed should have the benefit of the advantage and facilities of the said defendants, and the organisations and firms managed and controlled by defendants, in marketing its oil; that the firm should have to the extent of its production the advantage of the sales of refined by the defendants or said Standard Oil Company, either for present or future delivery, so that there should be at no time any margin or difference between the ruling price of refined oil, and the price which defendants would pay the partnership for the crude by it produced, beyond the necessary cost of refining. This thing formed the inducement and the larger part of the consideration for the sale of said property to defendants. The amount actually received for said interest was far beneath its actual value, and without the agreement on the part of the defendants to pay to the partnership for its product prices at all times commensurate with the prices of refined oil, they would not have sold the said interest nor entered into said partnership.

.   .   .   .

The defendants, although requested to do so, have not only failed, neglected, and refused to comply with this agreement, but have, by false and erroneous statements, misled the plaintiffs, and induced them to consent to the sale to them and to the Standard Oil Company of large quantities of crude petroleum, produced by the partnership at prices far below its actual value, to the great loss and damage of the orators. That on or about December 16, 1876, refined was selling at a price equivalent to seven dollars for crude oil, at which time plaintiffs called upon defendants for a compliance with their agreement, and asked that they take or purchase 210,000 barrels of the production of the partnership at a price commensurate with the price of refined at the time. This, defendants neglected and refused to do, and the partnership was forced to sell the same at prices varying from three to four dollars, making a loss to the partnership upon this one transaction of from $600,000 to $1,000,000, for which said defendants neglect and refuse to account.

.   .   .   .

That the said defendants for themselves, and for the said Standard Oil Company, and other organisations and firms aforesaid, have since the formation of the partnership received from the railways a rebate or drawback in the shape of wheelage, or otherwise, at times as high as one dollar per barrel upon all oil shipped by them to the seaboard. That instead of using these advantages which they possess for the benefit and profit of the partnership, as they covenanted to do, they have used them against its interest by restraining trade, preventing competition, and forcing plaintiffs to accept any price which defendants, the said Standard Oil Company, or the other organisations aforesaid, might offer for their production. That the amount of oil produced and sold by the partnership for the three years beginning with the date of its formation, and ending December 1, 1877, was 2,657,830 barrels. That the profits of defendants upon oil refined by them during said period, taking into consideration the rebates and drawbacks received from the railways, have averaged at least one dollar per barrel over and above the cost of refining, and at times as high as four and five dollars. That these profits, under the partnership agreement that no margin should exist between crude and refined prices, should to the extent of the production of the partnership have been paid by defendants to the partnership. That the amount lost by the partnership and realised by the defendants, by reason of the failure and refusal of said defendants to comply with their agreement, is not less than $2,500,000, for one-half of which defendants should account to your orators, but which they neglect and refuse to do.

Naturally enough the producers now pointed out that the case of the H. L. Taylor Company was a demonstration of what they had claimed in 1872, when the South Improvement Company, alarmed at the uprising, offered them a contract, and what they had always claimed since when the Standard offered contracts for oil on a sliding scale, viz., that such contracts were never meant to be kept; that they were a blind to enable the Standard to make scoops such as they had made in the winter of 1876 and 1877.

Taking all these points into consideration—

First—That the Standard Oil Company, like the South Improvement Company, was a secret organisation;

Second—That both companies were composed in the main of the same parties;

Third—That it aimed, like its predecessors, at getting entire control of the refining interest;

Fourth—That it used the power the combination gave it to get rebates on its own oil shipments and drawbacks on the shipments of other people;

Fifth—That it arranged contracts which compelled the railroads to run out all competition by lowering their rates.

Sixth—That it aimed to put up the price of refined without allowing the producer a share of the profits—

Taking all these points into consideration, many of the producers, including the president of the Petroleum Producers' Union, B. B. Campbell, and certain members of his Council, came to the conclusion that as they had sufficient evidence against the members of the Standard Combination to insure conviction for criminal conspiracy, they should proceed against them. Strenuous opposition to the proceedings, as hasty and ill-advised, developed in the Council and the Legal

Committee, but the majority decided that the prosecution should be instituted. Mr. Scott and Mr. Cassatt were omitted from the proposed indictment on the ground that they were already weary of the Standard, and would cease their illegal practices gladly if they could.

On the 29th day of April, 1879, the Grand Jury of the County of Clarion found an indictment against John D. Rockefeller, William Rockefeller, Jabez A. Bostwick, Daniel O'Day, William G. Warden, Charles Lockhart, Henry M. Flagler, Jacob J. Vandergrift and George W. Girty. (Girty was the cashier of the Standard Oil Company.) There were eight counts in the indictment, and charged, in brief, a conspiracy for the purpose of securing a monopoly of the business of buying and selling crude petroleum, and to prevent others than themselves from buying and selling and making a legitimate profit thereby; a combination to oppress and injure those engaged in producing petroleum; a conspiracy to prevent others than themselves from engaging in the business of refining petroleum, and to secure a monopoly of that business for themselves; a combination to injure the carrying trade of the Allegheny Valley and Pennsylvania Railroad Companies by perventing them from receiving the natural petroleum traffic; to divert the traffic naturally belonging to the Pennsylvania carriers to those of other states by unlawful means; and to extort from railroad companies unreasonable rebates and commissions, and by fraudulent means and devices to control the market prices of crude and refined petroleum and acquire unlawful gains thereby.*

Four of the persons mentioned in the indictment—Messrs. O'Day, Warden, Lockhart and Vandergrift—all citizens of Pennsylvania, gave bail, and early in June application was made to Governor Hoyt of Pennsylvania to issue a requisition

* See Appendix, Number 34. Bill of particulars of evidence to be offered by the commonwealth.

before the Governor of New York for the extradition of the other five gentlemen.

With damaging testimony piling up day by day in three states, and with an indictment for conspiracy hanging over the heads of himself and eight of his associates, matters looked gloomy for John D. Rockefeller in the spring of 1879. "The good of the oil business" certainly seemed in danger.

CHAPTER EIGHT

THE COMPROMISE OF 1880

THE PRODUCERS' SUIT AGAINST ROCKEFELLER AND HIS ASSOCIATES USED
BY THE STANDARD TO PROTECT ITSELF—SUITS AGAINST THE TRANSPOR-
TATION COMPANIES ARE DELAYED—TRIAL OF ROCKEFELLER AND HIS
ASSOCIATES FOR CONSPIRACY POSTPONED—ALL OF THE SUITS WITH-
DRAWN IN RETURN FOR AGREEMENTS OF THE STANDARD AND THE
PENNSYLVANIA TO CEASE THEIR PRACTICES AGAINST THE PRODUCERS—
WITH THIS COMPROMISE THE SECOND PETROLEUM PRODUCERS' UNION
COMES TO AN END—PRODUCERS THEMSELVES TO BLAME FOR NOT STAND-
ING BEHIND THEIR LEADERS—STANDARD AGAIN ENFORCES ORDERS OBJEC-
TIONABLE TO PRODUCERS—MORE OUTBREAKS IN THE OIL REGIONS—
ROCKEFELLER HAVING SILENCED ORGANISED OPPOSITION PROCEEDS TO
SILENCE INDIVIDUAL COMPLAINT.

NO doubt the indictment of Mr. Rockefeller in
the spring of 1879 seemed to him the work of
malice and spite. By seven years of persistent effort
he had worked out a well-conceived plan for controlling the oil business of the United States. Another year
and he had reason to believe that the remnant of refiners
who still rebelled against his intentions would either be convinced or dead and he could rule unimpeded. But here at the
very threshold of empire a certain group of people—"people
with a private grievance," "mossbacks naturally left in the
lurch by the progress of this rapidly developing trade," his colleagues described them to the Hepburn Commission—stood
in his way. "You have taken deliberate advantage of the
iniquitous practices of the railroads to build up a monopoly,"
they told him. "We combined to overthrow those practices so

far as the oil business was concerned. You not only refused
to support us in this contention, you persuaded or forced
the railroads to make you the only recipient of their illegal
favours; more than that, you developed the unjust practices,
forcing them into forms unheard of before. Not only have
you secured rebates of extraordinary value on all your own
shipments, you have persuaded the railroads to give you
a commission on the oil that other people ship. You are
guilty of plotting against the prosperity of an industry."
And they indicted him with eight of his colleagues for conspiracy.

The evidence on which the oil men based this serious
charge has already been analysed. At the moment they brought
their suit for conspiracy what was their situation? They had
several months before driven the commonwealth of Pennsylvania to bring suits against four railroads operating within
its borders and against the Standard pipe-lines for infringing
their duties as common carriers. Partial testimony had been
taken in the case against the Pennsylvania road and in that
against the United Pipe Lines. These suits, though far from
finished, had given the Producers' Union the bulk of the
proof on which they had secured the indictment of the Standard officials for conspiracy. Now, since the railroads and
the pipe-lines were the guilty ones—that is, as it was they
who had granted the illegal favours, and as they were the
only ones that could surely be convicted, it seems clear that
the only wise course for the producers would have been to
prosecute energetically and exclusively these first suits. But
evident as the necessity for such persistency was, and just after
Mr. Cassatt had startled the public and given the Union
material with which it certainly in time could have compelled
the commonwealth to a complete investigation, the producers
interrupted their work by bringing their spectacular suit for
conspiracy—a suit which perhaps might have been properly

instituted after the others had been completed, but which, introduced now, completely changed the situation, for it gave the witnesses from whom they were most anxious to hear a loophole for escape.

For instance, the officials of the Standard pipe-lines had been instructed to appear on the 14th of May, 1879, to answer questions which earlier in the trial they had refused to answer "on advice of counsel." Now the president of the United Pipe Lines, J. J. Vandergrift, and the general manager, Daniel O'Day, were both included in the indictment for conspiracy. The evening before the interrogatory the producers' counsel received a telegram from the attorney-general of the state, announcing that the pipe-line people were complaining that the testimony which they would be called on to give on the morrow would be used against them in the conspiracy trial—as it undoubtedly would have been— and that he thought it only fair that their hearing be postponed until after that suit. And so the defendants gained time —the chief desideratum of defendants who do not wish to fight.

Soon after, the conspiracy case was again used to excellent advantage by the Standard people in the investigation which was being conducted in New York before the Hepburn Commission. Mr. Bostwick, the Standard Oil buyer, whose order to buy immediate shipment oil only at a discount had been one of the oil men's chief grievances for a year and a half, was summoned as a witness; but Mr. Bostwick too was under indictment for conspiracy, and when the examiners began to put questions to him which the producers were eager to have answered, he asked: "How can I, a man soon to be tried for conspiracy, be expected to answer these questions? I shall incriminate myself." He was sustained in his plea, and about all the Hepburn Commission got out of him was, "I refuse to answer, lest I incriminate myself." This, then, was the first fruit of the producers' hasty and vindictive suit. It had shut the mouths of the important Standard witnesses.

Discouraging as this discovery was, however, there was no reason why the suits against the railroads should not have been pushed through, and the testimony the officials unquestionably could be made to give, now that Mr. Cassatt had set the pace, have been obtained. But the Producers' Union had lost sight for the moment of the fact that the fundamental difficulty in the trouble was the illegal discrimination of the common carriers. The Union was so much more eager to punish Mr. Rockefeller than it was to punish the railroads, that in bringing the suit for conspiracy it was even guilty of leniency toward the officials of the Pennsylvania. Certainly, if there was to be an indictment for conspiracy, all the supposed conspirators should have been included. It was by discriminations clearly contrary to the constitution of the state that the Pennsylvania Railroad had made it possible for Mr. Rockefeller to achieve his monopoly in Pennsylvania. The Union had proof of these rebates, but they let off Mr. Scott and Mr. Cassatt because "they professed the greatest desire to get rid of Standard domination, and were loudly asserting that they had been victimised and compelled at times to carry oil freights at less than cost." * Evidently the fate of the settlement the oil men had made seven years before with Mr. Scott and the presidents of the other oil-bearing roads had been forgotten. Naturally enough the railroads took advantage of these signs of leniency on the part of the producers, and brought all their enormous influence to bear on the state authorities to delay hearings and bring about a settlement. The Pennsylvania secured delays up to December, 1879, and then the Governor ordered the attorney-general to stop proceedings against the road until the testimony had been taken

* "A History of the Organisation, Purposes and Transactions of the General Council of the Petroleum Producers' Unions," 1880.

in the other four cases; that is, in the cases against (1) the United Pipe Lines; (2) the Lake Shore and Michigan Southern; (3) the Dunkirk, Allegheny and Pittsburg, and (4) the Atlantic and Great Western. It was a heavy blow to the Union, for at the moment its hands were tied by the conspiracy case, as far as the United Pipe Lines were concerned, and the three railroads were foreign corporations, only having branches in Pennsylvania, and accordingly very difficult to reach. The testimony could have been obtained, however, if the Union had been undivided in its interests. It would have been done, of course, if the state authorities had been willing to do what was their obvious duty. But the state authorities really asked nothing better than to escape further prosecution of the railroads. The administration was Republican, the Governor being Henry M. Hoyt. Mr. Hoyt had been elected in the fall of 1878 and so had inherited the suits from Governor Hartranft. He was pledged, however, to see them through, for before the election the Producers' Union had sent him the following letter:

"TITUSVILLE, October 23, 1878.
" HENRY M. HOYT:

Sir—During the past few months, the Association of Producers of Petroleum, long oppressed in their immediate business and kindred industries by the persistent disregard of law by certain great corporations exercising their powers within the state of Pennsylvania, and daily subjected to incalculable loss by a powerful and corrupt combination of these corporations and individuals, have appealed to the executive, legislative and judiciary branches of the government for relief and protection.

The questions which they raise for the consideration of the authorities and the people affect not only themselves but the whole public, not only the particular calling in which they are engaged, but nearly all kinds of business in the commonwealth and the nation.

The Legislature has not responded to the demands made that the provisions of the constitution shall be speedily enforced by appropriate legislation.

The present executive has caused proceedings to be instituted in the courts looking to relief, if it can be had by process of law, and these are still pending, while others may be begun.

In view of the grave duties which will devolve upon you, should you be chosen to the high office to which you aspire, in behalf of the Petroleum Producers' Association I ask from you a definite expression of your views upon the following subjects:

First—Will you, if elected, recommend to the Legislature the passage of laws to carry into effect the third and twelfth sections of the sixteenth, and the third, seventh and twelfth sections of the seventeenth articles of the constitution of Pennsylvania?

Second—If such laws should be passed as referred to in the preceding question, will you, as Governor, approve them, if constitutional?

Third—Will you, as Governor, recommend and approve such other remedial legislation as may be required to cure the evils set forth in a memorial to Governor Hartranft of August 15, 1878?

Fourth—In the selection of the law officer of the state, will you, if elected, secure the services of one who will prosecute with vigour all proceedings already commenced or that may be instituted, having in view the subjection of corporations to the laws of the land?   Very respectfully,

A. N. PERRIN,
Chairman Committee."

Governor Hoyt's answers were eminently satisfactory:

"There were provisions in the constitution," he wrote, "intended to compel the railroads and canal companies of the state to the performance of their duties as common carriers with fairness and equality, without discrimination, to all persons doing business over their lines. This policy is just and right.

"If called to a position requiring official action, I would recommend and approve any legislation necessary and appropriate to carry into effect the sections of the constitution referred to.

"It would be my duty, if elected, to see that no citizen, or class of citizens even, were subjected to hardship or injustice in their business, by illegal acts of corporations or others, where relief lay within executive control. Any proper measures or legislation which would effectually remedy the grievances set forth in the memorial addressed to Governor Hartranft would receive my recommendation and approval.

"It would be my duty, if elected, to select only such officers as would enforce obedience to the constitution and laws, both by corporations and individuals, without fear or favour, and all such officers would be held by me to strict accountability for the full and prompt discharge of all their official duties."

Governor Hoyt had indeed begun the suits, all of the testimony in regard to the Pennsylvania having been taken in his administration. This testimony must have proved to him that the transgressions of the road had been far more flagrant than anyone dreamed of—that they had amounted simply to driving certain men out of business in order to build up the business of certain other men. His evident duty, as his letter to the producers shows clearly enough that he realised, was to push the suits against the railroads even if the oil men entirely withdrew, but instead of that it became evident in the spring that he was using every opportunity to delay. Indeed, one reason the producers gave for bringing the conspiracy suit was that it would give the state authorities a scapegoat; that they would gladly act vigorously against the Standard if they were let off from prosecuting the Pennsylvania. Governor Hoyt now availed himself fully of the vacillation of the Union toward the railroads, using it as an excuse for not prosecuting the railroad cases.

But if the producers were half-hearted toward the railroads they were whole-hearted enough toward the Standard. In spite of the fact that they had gotten in their own way, so to speak, by bringing their conspiracy suit, they felt convinced that they had material enough to win it on, and they sought the extradition of the non-residents who had been indicted.

Early in June Governor Hoyt was called upon to issue a requisition for the extradition of John D. Rockefeller, William Rockefeller, H. M. Flagler, J. A. Bostwick, Daniel O'Day, Charles Pratt and G. W. Girty. A full agreement was made before the state officials, but a decision was deferred repeatedly. Finally, worn out with waiting, Mr. Campbell, in a telegram to the Governor on July 29, threatened, if there was longer delay, to make his request for extradition through the public press. The answer from Harrisburg was that the attorney-general was sick and could not attend to the matter. Mr. Campbell wired back that he was tired of "addition, division, and silence," and he sent out the following letter:

"FAIRFIELD, July 31, 1879.

"To HIS EXCELLENCY HENRY M. HOYT,
    Governor of the Commonwealth of Pennsylvania.

Sir—On behalf of the producers of oil, whom I represent as president of their General Council, I most respectfully ask a decision at your hands, of the requisition on the Governor of the state of New York, for the surrender of the officers of the Standard Oil Company, indicted by the Grand Jury of Clarion County, and now believed to be within the limits of the state of New York.

The case was exhaustively argued before you, more than four weeks ago, and the great oil interest which I have the honour to represent has a right to a prompt decision on this vital question. If these parties—who for their own profit and its ruin control Pennsylvania's most valuable product, and compel its greatest carrier to undertake their warfare and to do their bidding at the sacrifice of its innocent stockholders—can, under the plea of being 'aliens,' defy the law of Pennsylvania and laugh at our impotent attempts to reach them, the sooner it is known the better. It is possible that if we are denied protection within the limits of our commonwealth, we may obtain justice by appealing to the courts of a sister state, where at least the defendants will be obliged to admit that they are residents.

Your obedient servant,

B. B. CAMPBELL,
President of Producers' Council."

The Governor remained obdurate, nor was the request ever granted. In a message sent out in January, 1881, Governor Hoyt gave a review of the case—as he was compelled to do, so great was the popular criticism of his course in not pushing the suits and in refusing the request for extradition—in which he attributed his refusal to the negotiations begun between the railroads and the Producers' Union.

"The details of these negotiations, of course, need not, and did not, reach the office of the executive department," he said. "As a part of them, however, requests were presented in the interest of the petitioners (the Producers' Union) to the Governor, not to issue the requisition, followed again by requests that they be allowed to go out. Finding that the highest process of the commonwealth was being used simply as leverage for and against the parties to these negotiations between contending litigants, and that, however entire and perfect might have been the good faith in which the criminal proceedings in Clarion County had been commenced, they were being regarded and treated as a mere make-weight in the stages of private diplomacy, I deemed it my duty, in the exercise of a sound discretion, to suspend action on the requisitions."

E. G. PATTERSON

From 1872 to 1880 the chief advocate in the Oil Region of an interstate commerce law. Assisted in drafting the bills of 1876 and 1880. Abandoned the independent interests at the time of the compromise of 1880.

ROGER SHERMAN

Chief counsel of the Petroleum Producers' Union from 1878 to 1880. From 1880 to 1885 counsel for the Standard Oil Company. From 1885 to his death in 1893 counsel of the allied independents.

BENJ. B. CAMPBELL

President of the Petroleum Producers' Union from 1878 to 1880. Independent refiner and operator until his death.

JOSIAH LOMBARD

Prominent independent refiner of N. Y. City, whose firm was the only one to keep its contract with the Tidewater Pipe Line Company in 1880.

The writer has examined all the private correspondence which passed at this time between the litigants, but finds no proof of Governor Hoyt's statement that the Union at one time ceased its demands for Mr. Rockefeller's extradition.

The conspiracy suit had been set for the August session of the Clarion County court. When August came the Standard sought a continuance, and it was granted. The delay did not in any way discourage the producers, and when Mr. Rockefeller became convinced of this he tried conciliation. "Come, let us reason together," has always been a favourite proposition of Mr. Rockefeller. He would rather persuade than coerce, rather silence than fight. He had been making peace overtures ever since the suits began. The first had been in the fall of 1878, soon after they were instituted, when he sent the following letter to Captain Vandergrift:

" CAPTAIN J. J. VANDERGRIFT:

My dear Sir—We are now prepared to enter into a contract to refine all the petroleum that can be sold in the markets of the world at a low price for refining. Prices of refined oil to be made by a joint committee of producers and refiners, and the profits to be determined by these; profits to be divided equitably between both parties. This joint interest to have the lowest net rates obtainable from railroads. If your judgment approves, you may consult some of the producers upon this question. This would probably require the United Pipe Lines to make contracts and act as a clearing-house for both parties.

Very respectfully yours,

J. D. ROCKEFELLER."

Captain Vandergrift handed the letter to the executive committee of the Producers' Union. It was returned to him without a reply. The producers had tried an arrangement of this kind with Mr. Rockefeller's National Refiners' Association in the winter of 1872 and 1873, and it had failed. The refiners had thrown up their contract when they found they could get all the oil they wanted at a lower price than they had contracted to pay the Producers' Union, from men who

[249]

had not gone into that organisation. The oil country was familiar, too, with the case of the H. L. Taylor Company, whose complaint against the Standard was referred to in the last chapter. Contracts of that sort were never meant to be kept, they declared. They were meant as "sops, opiates." In November, 1878, after the testimony which had been brought out by the suit against the United Pipe Lines had been pretty well aired in the New York Sun and other papers, and one or two private suits against the railroads were creating a good deal of public discussion, an effort to secure a conference between the representatives of the Union and the Standard officials was made. The Union refused to go into it officially. A meeting was held, however, in New York on November 29, at which several well-known oil men were present. It was announced to the press in advance that it was to be an important but secret meeting between the oil producers, refiners and Standard men; that its object was to settle all grievances, and to secure a withdrawal of the impending suits. As soon as the news of this proposed meeting reached the Oil Regions, the officials of the Union promptly denied their connection with it.

Although these early efforts to get a wedge into the Producers' Union and thus secure a staying of the suits had no results, the Standard was not discouraged—it never is: there is no evidence in its history that it knows what the word means. Not being able to handle the Union as a whole, the Standard began working on individuals. By March, 1879, the idea of a compromise had become particularly strong in Oil City. Indeed, one of the several reasons advanced for bringing the conspiracy suits was that such a proceeding would defeat the efforts the Oil City branch were making to bring about a settlement with Mr. Rockefeller. Accordingly, when it became apparent to Mr. Rockefeller in the fall of 1879 that the producers meant to fight through the conspiracy suit, though they might dally over the others, he notified Roger Sherman, counsel for the Union, that he wished to lay before him a proposition looking to a settlement. The president, Mr. Campbell, was in favour of receiving the proposition. "I have no idea they will present anything we can accept," he wrote Mr. Sherman. "Still it will furnish a first-rate gauge to test how badly they are scared." And the Standard was told that the Union would consider what they had to offer. "But it is a serious question—this of settlement," replied Mr. Rockefeller. "Our trial is set for October 28. We cannot get ready for that and prepare a proposition too. Why not postpone the trial?" This was done—December 15 being set. But no proposition was made to the producers for over six weeks—then they were asked to meet the Standard men on November 29 in New York City. Piqued at the delay, the producers informed the Standard that they could no longer consider their proposition and that the trial would be pushed.

But again the Standard secured delay—this time by petitioning that the case be argued before the Supreme Court of the state. They declared that such was the state of public feeling in Clarion County that they could not obtain justice there. They charged the judges with bias and prejudice, declared secret societies were working against them, and called attention to the civil suits which were still hanging fire. Over this petition serious trouble arose in court—there was a wrangle between the judge and the Standard's counsel. The newspapers took it up—the whole state divided itself into camps, and the case was again postponed, this time until the first of the year. Postponement obtained, compromise was again proposed upon the basis of abandonment of all those methods of doing business which the producers claimed injured them, and as a mark of their sincerity the United Pipe Lines on December 24, 1879, issued an order announcing the abandonment of immediate shipment throughout the region.

A meeting between the legal advisers of the two parties to discuss the proposed terms was arranged for January 7, 1880, at the Fifth Avenue Hotel in New York City—the very time to which the trial of the case for conspiracy had been postponed. It was hardly to be expected that when such negotiations were going on in New York the trial in Clarion County would be pushed very briskly. It was not. There was a hitch again, and for the fourth time proceedings were stayed. The conferences, however, went on.

These negotiations with the Standard continued for a month, and then, early in February, Mr. Campbell, the president of the Union, called a meeting of the Grand Council for February 19, 1880, in Titusville, Pennsylvania. For several weeks the Oil Regions had known that President Campbell and Roger Sherman, the leading lawyer of the Union, were in conference with the Standard officials. It was rumoured that they were arranging a compromise, and it was suspected that the meeting now called was to consider the terms. Naturally the proposition to be made was looked for with suspicion and curiosity. The meeting was the largest the Grand Council had held for many months. It was supposed to be secret, like all gatherings of the Union, but before the first session was over, the word spread over the Oil Regions that Mr. Campbell had brought to the meeting contracts with both Mr. Rockefeller and Mr. Scott, and that they were receiving harsh criticism from the Grand Council. The very meagre accounts which exist of this gathering, historic in oil annals, show that it was one of the most exciting which was ever held in the country, and one can well believe this when one considers the bitter pill the council was asked to swallow that day. Mr. Campbell began the session by reporting that all the suits at which they had been labouring for nearly two years had been withdrawn, and that in return for their withdrawal the Standard and the Pennsylvania Railroad officials had signed contracts to cease certain of the practices of which the producers complained.

The Standard contract, which Mr. Campbell then presented, pledged Mr. Rockefeller, and some sixteen associates, whose names were attached to the document, to the following policy:

1. They would hereafter make no opposition to an entire abrogation of the system of rebates, drawbacks and secret rates of freight in the transportation of petroleum on the railroads.

2. They withdrew their opposition to secrecy in rate making—that is, they promised that they would not hereafter receive any rebate or drawback that the railroad company was not at liberty to make known and to give to other shippers of petroleum.

3. They abandoned entirely the policy which they had been pursuing in the management of the United Pipe Lines—that is, they promised that there should be no discrimination whatever hereafter between their patrons; that the rates should be reasonable and not advanced except on thirty days' notice; that they would make no difference between the price of crude in different districts excepting such as might be properly based upon the difference in the quality of the oil; that they would receive, transport, store and deliver all oil tendered to them, up to a production of 65,000 barrels a day. And if the production should exceed that amount they agreed that they would not purchase any so-called "immediate shipment" oil at a discount on the price of certificate oil.

4. They promised hereafter that when certificates had been given for oil taken into the custody of the pipe-lines, the transfer of these certificates should be considered as a delivery of the oil, and the tankage of the seller would be treated as free.*

Mr. Rockefeller also agreed in making this contract to pay

* See Appendix, Number 35. Contract of Petroleum Producers' Union with Standard Combination.

the Producers' Union $40,000 to cover the expense of their litigation. In return for this money and for the abandonment of secret rebates and of the pipe-line policy to which he had held so strenuously, what was he to receive? He was not to be tried for conspiracy. And that day, after the contract had been presented to the Grand Council, Mr. Campbell sent the following telegram:

"TITUSVILLE, February 19, 1880.

" To His EXCELLENCY HENRY M. HOYT,
    Governor of the Commonwealth of Pennsylvania.

Sir—As prosecutor in the case of the Commonwealth *vs.* J. D. Rockefeller, Number 25, April Sessions of Clarion County, I consent to the withdrawal of the requisition asked of you for extradition of J. D. Rockefeller *et al.*, the same having been in your hands undecided since July last and a *nolle prosequi* having been entered by leave of Court of Clarion County in the case, and I will request William L. Hindman, the prosecuting attorney, to forward a formal withdrawal.

Your obedient servant,

B. B. CAMPBELL."

The contract with the Pennsylvania which was signed by Mr. Scott agreed, in consideration of the withdrawal of the suit against the road, to the following policy:

1. That it would make known to all shippers all rates of freight charged upon petroleum. [This was an abolition of secret rates.]

2. If any rates of freight were allowed one shipper as against another, on demand that rate was to be made known.

3. There should be no longer any discrimination in the allotment and distribution of cars to shippers of petroleum.

4. Any rebate allowed to a large shipper was to be reasonable.*

There were both humiliation and bitterness in the Council when the report was read—humiliation and bitterness that

---

* See Appendix, Number 36. Agreement between B. B. Campbell and the Pennsylvania Railroad Company.

after two years of such strenuous fighting all that was achieved was a contract which sacrificed what everybody knew to be the fundamental principle, the principle which up to this point the producers had always insisted must be recognised in any negotiation—that the rebate system was wrong and must not be compromised with. Hard speeches were made, and Mr. Campbell's head was bowed more than once while big tears ran down his cheeks. He had worked long and hard. Probably most of the members of the Grand Council who were present had a consciousness that no one of them had done anywhere near what Mr. Campbell had done toward prosecuting their cause, and though they might object to the compromise, they could not blame him, knowing all the difficulties which had been put in the way. So they accepted the report, thanking him for his fidelity and energy, but not failing to express their disapproval of the reservation in regard to the rebate system. They ended their meeting by a resolution bitterly condemning the courts, the state administration at Harrisburg, and corporations in general:

"We declare that by the inefficiency and weakness of the secretary of internal affairs in the year 1878; by the interposition on more than one occasion of the attorney-general in 1879, by which the taking of testimony was prevented; by the failure of the present government for many months, either to grant or deny the requisition for criminals indicted for crime, within the commonwealth of Pennsylvania, fugitives to other states; and by the interference of some of the judges of the Supreme Court, by an extraordinary and, according to the best legal judgment of the land, unlawful proceeding, by which the trial of an indictment for misdemeanour pending in a local court was delayed and prevented, the alarming and most dangerous influence of powerful corporations has been demonstrated. While we accept the inevitable result forced upon us by these influences, we aver that the contest is not over and our objects not attained, but we all continue to advocate and maintain the subordination of all corporations to the laws, the constitution, and the will of the people, however and whenever expressed; that the system of freight discrimination by common carriers is absolutely wrong in principle, and tends to the fostering of dangerous monopolies; and that it is the duty of the government, by legislation and executive action, to protect the people from their growing and dangerous power."

And with this resolution the second Petroleum Producers' Union formed to fight Mr. Rockefeller came to an end.

By the morning of February 20 the Oil Regions knew of the compromise. The news was received in sullen anger. It was due to the cowardice of the state officials, the corrupting influence of corporations, the oil men said. They blamed everybody but themselves, and yet if they had done their duty the suits would never have been compromised. The simple fact is that the mass of oil men had not stood by their leaders in the hard fight they had been making. These leaders, Mr. Campbell the president, Mr. Sherman the chief counsel, and Mr. Patterson the head of the legislative committee, had given almost their entire time for two years to the work of the Union. The offices of Mr. Campbell and Mr. Patterson were both honorary, and they had both often used their private funds in prosecuting their work. Mr. Sherman gave his services for months at a time without pay. No one outside of the Council of the Union knew the stress that came upon these three men. Up to the decision to institute the conspiracy suit they had worked in harmony. But when that was decided upon Mr. Patterson withdrew. He saw how fatal such a move must be, how completely it interfered with the real work of the Union, forcing common carriers to do their duty. He saw that the substantial steps gained were given up and that the work would all have to be done over again if their suit went on. Mr. Campbell believed in it, however, and Mr. Sherman, whether he believed in it or not, saw no way but to follow his chief. The nine months of disappointment and disillusion which followed were terrible for both men. They soon saw that the forces against them were too strong, that they would never in all probability be able to get the conspiracy suit tried, and that so long as it was on the docket the proper witnesses could not be secured for the suits against the railroads. Finally it came to be a question with them what out of the wreck of their plans and hopes could they save? And they saved what the compromise granted. If the oil producers they represented, a body of some 2,000 men, had stood behind them throughout 1879 as they did in 1878 the results would have been different. Their power, their means, were derived from this body, and this body for many months had been giving them feeble support. Scattered as they were over a great stretch of country, interested in nothing but their own oil farms, the producers could only be brought into an alliance by hope of overturning disastrous business conditions. They all felt that the monopoly the Standard had achieved was a menace to their interests, and they went willingly into the Union at the start, and supported it generously, but they were an impatient people, demanding quick results, and when they saw that the relief the Union promised could only come through lawsuits and legislation which it would take perhaps years to finish, they lost interest and refused money. At the first meeting of the Grand Council of the Union in November, 1878, there were nearly 200 delegates present—at the last one in February, 1880, scarcely forty. Many of the local lodges were entirely dead. Not even the revival in the summer of 1879 of the hated immediate shipment order, which had caused so much excitement the year before, but which had not been enforced long because of the uprising, brought them back to the Union. In July the order had been put in operation again in a fashion most offensive to the oil men, it being announced by the United Pipe Lines that thereafter oil would be bought by a system of sealed bids. Blanks were to be furnished the producers, the formula of which ran:

BRADFORD, PENNSYLVANIA, ... 187..

I hereby offer to sell J. A. Bostwick .... barrels crude oil, of forty-two gallons per barrel, at .... cents, at the wells, for shipment from the United Pipe Lines, within the next five (5) days, provided that any portion of the oil not delivered to you within the specified time shall be considered cancelled.

[257]

There was a frightful uproar in consequence. The morning after this announcement several hundred men gathered in front of the United Pipe Line's office in Bradford, and held an open-air meeting. They had a band on the ground which played "Hold the Fort"; and the following resolutions were adopted:

"Resolved, That the oil producers of the Northern District in meeting assembled do maintain and declare that the present shipment order is infamous in principle and disreputable in practice, and we hereby declare that we will not sell one barrel of oil in conformity with the requirements of the said order. And we pledge our lives, our fortunes and our sacred honour to resort to every legal means, to use every influence in our power to prevent any sales under the said order. And we also declare that the United Pipe Lines shall hereafter perform their duty as common carriers under the law."

That night a battalion of some 300 masked men in robes of white marched through the streets of Bradford, groaning those that they suspected of being in sympathy with the Standard methods, and cheering their friends. Again there appeared there, that night, all over the upper oil country, cabalistic signs, which had been seen there often the year before. The feeling was so intense, and the danger of riot so great, that twenty-four hours after the order for sealed bids was given, it was withdrawn. The outbreak aroused Mr. Campbell's hope that it might be possible at this moment to arouse the lodges, and he wrote a prominent oil man of Bradford asking his opinion. In reply he received the following letter. It shows very well what the leaders had to contend against. It shows, too, the point of view of a very frank and intelligent oil producer:

" BRADFORD, PENNSYLVANIA, July 30, 1879.
" B. B. CAMPBELL,
Parnassus, Pennsylvania.
Dear Sir—Your despatch of yesterday from O. C. has only just reached me. As I cannot say what I want to over the wires I reply by mail.

[258]

THE COMPROMISE OF 1880

You ask if the high-sounding wording of the declaration of rights of the producers made at their mass-meeting, held here on Monday, in which they pledged their lives, fortunes and sacred honours, means liberal subscriptions to the Council funds. I reply with sorrow and humiliation—*I fear not.* All this high-flown talk is buncombe of the worst kind. The producers are willing to meet in a mass-meeting held out of doors where it costs nothing even for rent of a hall, and pass any kind of a resolution that is offered. It costs nothing to do this, but when asked to contribute a dollar to the legal prosecution of these plunderers, robbers, and fugitives from justice, whom they are denouncing in their resolution, they either positively refuse, say that the Council is doing nothing, that the suits are interminable and will never end, that there is no justice to be obtained in the courts of Pennsylvania, etc., etc., or else plead poverty and say they have contributed all that they are able to.

True, the producers are poor and the suits and legal proceedings are slow, and there is much to discourage them, but I tell you, my honoured chief, that the true inwardness of this state of affairs is, that the people of the Oil Regions have by slow degrees and easy stages been brought into a condition of bondage and serfdom by the monopoly, until now, when they have been aroused to a realisation of their condition, they have not the courage and manhood left to enable them to strike a blow for liberty. And these are the people for whom you and your few faithful followers in the Council are labouring, spending (I fear wasting) your substance—neglecting your own interest to advance theirs, and all for what good—"*cui bono*"?

I fear you will say that I am discouraged. No, not discouraged, but disgusted with the poor, spiritless, and faint-hearted people whom you are labouring so hard to liberate from bondage. As to the prospects of raising funds for the prosecution of the suits by subscription or assessments on the Unions, I am sorry to say that I fear it is impossible—at least it is impossible for me to make any collections—and right here let me make a suggestion. I often feel that the fault may not be with the people, but with the writer. I would therefore suggest that you select from among the members of the Council any good man whom you think has the power of convincing these people that their only hope of relief lies in sustaining you in the prosecution of the suits, and therefore they must contribute to the fund. If you will do this, I will promise you that he will be hospitably received and favourably introduced by the writer. But as for depending on the unaided efforts of myself to raise funds, I fear it would be useless.

I do not write this, my friend, with a view of throwing any discouragement in your path, which, God knows, is rugged and thorny enough, but I must give vent to my righteous indignation in some way, and ask you are the producers as a class (nothing but a d——d cowardly, disorganised mob as they are) worth the efforts you are putting forth to save them?

As for myself, a single individual (and I can speak for no others), I am determined to stand with you until the end, with my best strength and my last dollar."

Now, what was this loose and easily discouraged organisation opposing? A compact body of a few able, cold-blooded men—men to whom anything was right that they could get, men knowing exactly what they wanted, men who loved the game they played because of the reward at the goal, and, above all, men who knew how to hold their tongues and wait. "To Mr. Rockefeller," they say in the Oil Regions, "a day is as a year and a year as a day. He can wait, but he never gives up." Mr. Rockefeller knew the producers, knew how feeble their staying qualities in anything but the putting down of oil wells, and he may have said confidently, at the beginning of their suits against him, as it was reported he did say, that they would never be finished. They had not been finished from any lack of material. If the suits had been pushed but one result was possible, and that was the conviction of both the Standard and the railroads; they had been left unfinished because of the impatience and instability of the prosecuting body and the compactness, resolution and watchfulness of the defendants.

The withdrawal of the suits was a great victory for Mr. Rockefeller. There was no longer any doubt of his power in defensive operations. Having won a victory, he quickly went to work to make it secure. The Union had surrendered, but the men who had made the Union remained; the evidence against him was piled up in indestructible records. In time the same elements which had united to form the serious opposition just overthrown might come together, and if they should it was possible that they would not a second time make the mistake of vacillation. The press of the Oil Regions was largely independent. It had lost, to be sure, the audacity, the wit, the irrepressible spirit of eight years before when it fought the South Improvement Company. Its discretion had outstripped its courage. but there were still signs of intelligent independence in the newspapers. Mr. Rockefeller now entered on a campaign of reconciliation which aimed to placate, or silence, every opposing force.

Many of the great human tragedies of the Oil Regions lie in the individual compromises which followed the public settlement of 1880; for then it was that man after man, from hopelessness, from disgust, from ambition, from love of money, gave up the fight for principle which he had waged for seven years. "The Union has surrendered," they said; "why fight on?" This man took a position with the Standard and became henceforth active in its business; that man took a salary and dropped out of sight; this one went his independent way, but with closed lips; that one shook the dust of the Oil Regions from his feet and went out to seek "God's country," asking only that he should never again hear the word "oil." The newspapers bowed to the victor. A sudden hush came over the region, the hush of defeat, of cowardice, of hopelessness. Only the "poor producer" grumbled. "You can't satisfy the producer," Mr. Rockefeller often has had occasion to remark benignantly and pitifully. The producer alone was not "convinced." He still rehearsed the series of dramatic attacks and sieges which had wiped out independent effort. He taught his children that the cause had been sold, and he stigmatised the men who had gone over to the Standard as traitors. Scores of boys and girls grew up in the Oil Regions in those days with the same feeling of terrified curiosity toward those who had "sold to the Standard" that they had toward those who had "been in jail." The Oil Regions as a whole was at heart as irreconcilable in 1880 as it had been after the South Improvement Company fight, and now it had added to its sense of outrage the humiliation of defeat. Its only immediate hope now was in the success of one of the transportation enterprises which had come into existence with the uprising of 1878 and to which it had been for two years giving what support it could. This enterprise was the seaboard pipe-line which, as we have seen, Messrs. Benson, McKelvy and Hopkins had undertaken.

APPENDIX

NUMBER 1 (See page 7)

PROFESSOR SILLIMAN'S REPORT ON PETROLEUM

[From "The Early and Later History of Petroleum," by J. T. Henry, pages 38-54.]

MESSRS. EVELETH, BISSELL AND REED.

Gentlemen:—I herewith offer you the results of my somewhat extended researches upon the rock-oil, or petroleum, from Venango County, Pennsylvania, which you have requested me to examine with reference to its value for economical purposes.

Numerous localities, well known in different parts of the world, furnish an oily fluid exuding from the surface of the earth, sometimes alone in "tar springs," as they are called in the Western United States; frequently it is found floating upon the surface of water in a thin film, with rainbow colours, or in dark globules, that may, by mechanical means, be separated from the fluid on which it swims.

In some places wells are sunk for the purpose of accumulating the product in a situation convenient for collection by pumping the water out. The oil exudes on the shores of lakes and lagoons, or rises from springs beneath the beds of rivers. Such are the springs of Baku, in Persia, and the wells of Amiano, in the duchy of Parma, in Italy. The usual geological position of the rocks furnishing this natural product is in the coal measures—but it is by no means confined to this group of rocks, since it has been found in deposits much more recent, and also in those that are older—but in whatever deposits it may occur, it is uniformly regarded as a product of vegetable decomposition. Whether this decomposition has been effected by fermentation only, or by the aid of an elevated temperature, and distilled by heated vapour, is perhaps hardly settled.

It is interesting, however, in this connection to remember that the distillation, at an elevated temperature, of certain black, bituminous shales in England and France has furnished large quantities of an oil having many points of resemblance with naphtha, the name given to this colourless oil, which is the usual product of distilling petroleum. The very high boiling point of most of the products of the distillation of the rock oil from Venango County, Pennsylvania, would seem to indicate that it was a pyrogenic (fire-produced) product.

[265]

Bitumen, asphaltum, mineral pitch, chapapote, etc., etc., are names variously given to the more or less hard, black, resinous substance which is produced usually from the exposure of petroleum to the air, and is found either with or without the fluid naphtha or petroleum. The most remarkable examples of the occurrence of these substances, so intimately connected with the history of rock-oil, are the Lake Asphaltites of the Dead Sea, so memorable in history, the well-known Bitumen Lake of Trinidad, and the deposits of mineral pitch or chapapote in Cuba. In one of the provinces of India, vast quantities of petroleum are annually produced, the chief consumption being local, for fuel and lights, but a portion is also exported to Europe for the production of naphtha. In the United States, many points on the Ohio and its tributaries are noted as producing this oil; nearly all of them within the coal measures. A detailed history of these various localities can be found recorded in books of science, and their repetition here would be out of place.

GENERAL CHARACTER OF THE CRUDE PRODUCT

The crude oil, as it is gathered on your lands, has a dark brown colour, which, by reflected light, is greenish or bluish. It is thick even in warm weather—about as thick as thin molasses. In very cold weather it is somewhat more stiff, but can always be poured from a bottle even at 15° below zero. Its odour is strong and peculiar, and recalls to those who are familiar with it the smell of bitumen and naphtha. Exposed for a long time to the air, it does not thicken or form a skin on its surface, and in no sense can it be called a drying oil. The density of the crude oil is .882, water being 1.000. It boils only at a very high temperature, and yet it begins to give off a vapour at a temperature not greatly above that of boiling water. It takes fire with some difficulty and burns with an abundant smoky flame. It stains paper with the appearance of ordinary fat oils, and feels smooth and greasy between the fingers. It is frequently used in its crude state to lubricate coarse machinery. In chemical characters, it is entirely unlike the fat oils. Most of these characters are common to petroleum from various places. In one important respect, however, the product of your lands differs from that obtained in other situations, that is, it does not, by continued exposure to the air, become hard and resinous like mineral pitch or bitumen. I have been informed by those who have visited the locality, that on the surface of the earth above the springs which furnish your oil there is no crust or deposit of this sort such as I have seen in other situations where petroleum or mineral tar is flowing. This difference will be seen to be of considerable importance, as it is understood and represented that this product exists in great abundance upon your property, that it can be gathered wherever a well is sunk in the soil, over a great number of acres, and that it is unfailing in its yield from year to year. The question naturally arises, Of what value is it in the arts, and for what uses can it be employed? These researches answer these inquiries.

APPENDIX, NUMBER I

EXAMINATION OF THE OIL

To determine what products might be obtained in the oil, a portion of it was submitted to fractional distillation.* The temperature of the fluid was constantly regulated by a thermometer, the heat being applied first by a water bath, and then by a bath of linseed oil. This experiment was founded upon the belief that the crude product contained several distinct oils, having different boiling points. The quantity of material used in this experiment was 304 grammes. The thermometer indicated the degrees of the Centigrade scale, but, for convenience, the corresponding degrees of Fahrenheit's scale are added. The water bath failed to distil any portion of the oil at 100° C. (= 212° F.), only a small quantity of acid water came over. An oil bath, linseed oil, was then substituted, and the temperature was regularly raised by slow degrees until distillation commenced. From that point the heat was successively raised by stages of ten degrees, allowing full time at each stage for complete distillation of all that would rise at that temperature before advancing to the next stage. The results of this tedious process are given in the annexed table—304 grammes of crude oil, submitted to fractional distillation, gave

	TEMPERATURE	QUANTITY
1st Prod. at 100° C. = 213° F. (acid water)......		5 gms.
2nd " " 140° C. to 150° C.=284° to 302° F.		26 "
3rd " " 150° C. " 160° C.=302° " 320° F.		29 "
4th " " 160° C. " 170° C.=320° " 388° F.		38 "
5th " " 170° C. " 180° C.=338° " 367° F.		17 "
6th " " 180° C. " 200° C.=356° " 392° F.		16 "
7th " " 200° C. " 220° C.=392° " 428° F.		17 "
8th " " 220° C. " 270° C.=428° " 518° F.		12 "
Whole quantity distilled by this method............		160 "
Leaving residue in the retort......................		144 "
Original quantity.................................		304 "

Product No. 1, as above remarked, was almost entirely water, with a few drops of colourless oil, having an odour similar to the original fluid, but less intense.

Product No. 2 was an oil perfectly colourless, very thin and limpid, and having an exceedingly persistent odour, similar to the crude oil, but less intense.

Product No. 3 was tinged slightly yellow, perfectly transparent, and apparently as limpid as the second product, with the same odour.

* Fractional distillation is a process intended to separate various products in mixture, and having unlike boiling-points, by keeping the mixture contained in an alembic at regulated successive stages of temperature as long as there is any distillate at a given point, and then raising the heat to another degree, etc.

Product No. 4 was more decidedly yellowish than the last, but was in no other respect distinguishable from it.

Product No. 5 was more highly coloured, thicker in consistence, and had a decided empyreumatic odour.

Product No. 6. This and the two subsequent products were each more highly coloured and denser than the preceding. The last product had the colour and consistency of honey, and the odour was less penetrating than that of the preceding oils. The mass of crude product remaining in the retort (equal 47.4 per cent.) was a dark, thick, resinous-looking varnish, which was so stiff when cold that it could be inverted without spilling. This showed no disposition to harden or skin over by exposure to the air. The distillation was arrested at this point in glass, by our having reached the limit of temperature for a bath of linseed oil. The *density* of the several products of this distillation shows a progressive increase, thus:

	DENSITY			DENSITY
No. 2	733		No. 6	800
No. 3	752		No. 7	848
No. 4	766		No. 8	854
No. 5	776			

To form an idea of the comparative density of these several products, it may be well to state that sulphuric ether, which is one of the lightest fluids known, has a density of .736, and alcohol, when absolutely pure, .800.

The *boiling points* of these several fluids present some anomalies, but are usually progressive, thus, No. 2 gave signs of boiling at $115°$ C. ($=239°$ F.), and boiled vigorously and remained constant at $225°$ C. to $228°$ C. ($=437°$ to $442°$ F.). No. 3 began to boil $120°$ ($=248°$ F.), rose to $270°$ ($=518°$ F.), where it remained constant. No. 4 began to vapourise at $140°$ ($=284°$ F.), rose to $290°$ ($=554°$ F.), where it remained constant. On a second heating the temperature continued to rise, and passed $305°$ ($=581°$ F.). No. 5 gave appearance of boiling at $160°$ ($=320°$ F.), boiling more vigorously as the heat was raised, and was still rising at $308°$ ($=581°$ F.). No. 6 commenced boiling at $135°$ ($=275°$ F.), boiled violently at $160°$ ($=320°$ F.), and continued rising above the range of the mercurial thermometer. No. 7 commenced ebullition at the same temperature as No. 6, and rose to $305°$ ($=581°$ F.), where the ebullition was not very active. Much time was consumed in obtaining these results. We infer from them that the rock-oil is a mixture of numerous compounds, all having essentially the same chemical constitution, but differing in density and boiling points, and capable of separation from each other, by a well-regulated heat.

The uncertainty of the boiling points indicates that the products obtained at the temperatures named above were still mixtures of others, and the question forces itself upon us, whether these several oils are to be regarded as *educts* (i. e., bodies previously existing, and simply separated in the process of distillation), or whether they are not rather produced by the heat and chemical change in the process of distillation. The continued application of an elevated temperature alone is sufficient to effect changes in the constitution of many organic products, evolving new bodies not before existing in the original substance.

PROPERTIES OF THE DISTILLED OILS

Exposed to the severest cold of the past winter, all the oils obtained in this distillation remained fluid. Only the last two or three appeared at all stiffened by a cold of 15° below zero, while the first three or four products of distillation retained a perfect degree of fluidity. Exposed to air, as I have said, they suffer no change. The chemical examination of these oils showed that they were all composed of carbon and hydrogen, and probably have these elements in the same numerical relation. When first distilled they all had an acid reaction, due to the presence of a small quantity of free sulphuric acid, derived from the crude oil. This was entirely removed by a weak alkaline water, and even by boiling on pure water. Clean copper remained untarnished in the oil which had thus been prepared, showing its fitness for lubrication, so far as absence of corrosive quality is concerned. The oils contain no oxygen, as is clearly shown by the fact that clean potassium remains bright in them. Strong *sulphuric acid* decomposes and destroys the oil entirely. *Nitric acid* changes it to a yellow, oily fluid, similar to the changes produced by nitric acid on other oils. *Hydrochloric, chromic,* and *acetic acids* do not affect it. *Litharge* and other metallic oxyds do not change it, or convert it in any degree to a drying oil. *Potassium* remains in it unaffected, even at a high temperature. *Hydrates of potash, soda,* and *lime* are also without action upon it. *Chloride of calcium* and many other salts manifest an equal indifference to it. Distilled with *bleaching powders* (chloride of lime) and water in the manner of producing chloroform, the oil is changed into a product having an odour and taste resembling chloroform. Exposed for many days in an open vessel, at a regulated heat below 212°, the oil gradually rises in vapour, as may be seen by its staining the paper used to cover the vessel from dust, and also by its sensible diminution. Six or eight fluid ounces, exposed in this manner in a metallic vessel for six weeks or more, the heat never exceeding 200°, gradually and slowly diminished, grew yellow, and finally left a small residue of dark brown, lustrous-looking resin, or pitchy substance, which in the cold was hard and brittle. The samples of oil employed were very nearly colourless. This is remarkable when we remember that the temperature of the distillation was above 500° F. The oil is nearly insoluble in pure alcohol, not more than 4 or 5 per cent. being dissolved by this agent. In ether the oil dissolves completely, and on gentle heating is left unchanged by the evaporisation of the ether. India-rubber is dissolved by the distilled oil to a pasty mass, forming a thick, black fluid which,

after a short time, deposits the India-rubber. It dissolved a little amber, but only
sufficient to colour the oil red. It also dissolves a small portion of copal in its natural
state, but after roasting, the copal dissolves in it as it does in other oils.

USE FOR GAS–MAKING

The crude oil was tried as a means of illumination. For this purpose, a weighed
quantity was decomposed, by passing it through a wrought-iron retort filled with
carbon, and ignited to full redness. The products of this decomposition were received
in a suitable apparatus. It produced nearly pure carburetted hydrogen gas, the most
highly illuminating of all the carbon gases. In fact, the oil may be regarded as chemi-
cally identical with illuminating gas in a liquid form. The gas produced equalled
ten cubic feet to the pound of oil. It burned with an intense flame, smoking in the
ordinary gas jet, but furnishing the most perfect flame with the Argand burner.

These experiments were not prosecuted further, because it was assumed that other
products, now known and in use, for gas-making, might be employed at less expense
for this purpose, than your oil. Nevertheless, this branch of inquiry may be worthy
of further attention.

DISTILLATION AT A HIGHER TEMPERATURE

The results of the distillation at a regulated temperature in glass led us to believe
that in a metallic vessel, capable of enduring a high degree of heat, we might obtain
a much larger proportion of valuable products. A copper still, holding five or six
gallons, was therefore provided, and furnished with an opening, through which a
thermometer could be introduced into the interior of the vessel. Fourteen imperial
quarts (or, by weight, 560 ounces) of the crude product were placed in this vessel,
and the heat raised rapidly to about 280° C. (= 536° F.), somewhat higher than the
last temperature reached in the first distillation. At this high temperature the distillation was somewhat rapid, and the product was easily condensed without a worm.
The product of the first stage was 130 ounces (or over 28 per cent.), of a very light-
coloured thin oil, having a density of .792. This product was also acid, and as before,
the acid was easily removed by boiling with fresh water. The temperature was now
raised to somewhat above 300° C. (= 572° F.), and 123 ounces more distilled, of a
more viscid and yellowish oil, having a density of .865. This accounts for over 43
per cent. of the whole quantity taken. The temperature being raised now above the
boiling point of mercury, was continued at that until 170 ounces, or over 31 per cent.,
of a dark brown oil had been distilled, having a strong empyreumatic odor. Upon
standing still for some time, a dark blackish sediment was seen to settle from this

portion, and on boiling it with water the unpleasant odour was in a great degree removed, and the fluid became more light-coloured and perfectly bright. (It was on a sample of this that the photometric experiments were made.) The next portion, distilled at about 700° F., gave but about 17 ounces, and this product was both lighter in colour and more fluid than the last. It now became necessary to employ dry hickory wood as a fuel, to obtain flame and sufficient heat to drive over any further portions of the residue remaining in the alembic.

It will be seen that we have already accounted for over 75 per cent. of the whole quantity taken. There was a loss on the whole process of about 10 per cent., made up, in part, of a coaly residue that remained in the alembic, and partly of the unavoidable loss resulting from the necessity of removing the oil twice from the alembic, during the process of distillation, in order to change the arrangements of the thermometer, and provide means of measuring a heat higher than that originally contemplated.

About 15 per cent. of a very thick, dark oil completed this experiment. This last product, which came off slowly at about 750° F., is thicker and darker than the original oil, and when cold, is filled with a dense mass of pearly crystals. These are paraffine, a peculiar product of the destructive distillation of many bodies in the organic kingdom. This substance may be separated, and obtained as a white body, resembling fine spermaceti, and from it beautiful candles have been made. The oil in which the crystals float is of a very dark colour, and by reflected light is blackish green, like the original crude product. Although it distills at so high a temperature, it boils at a point not very different from the denser products of the first distillation. The paraffine, with which this portion of the oil abounds, does not exist ready-formed in the original crude product; but it is a result of the high temperature employed in the process of distillation, by which the elements are newly arranged.

I am not prepared to say, without further investigation, that it would be desirable for the company to manufacture this product in a pure state, fit for producing candles (a somewhat elaborate chemical process); but I may add that, should it be desirable to do so, the quantity of this substance produced may probably be very largely increased by means which it is now unnecessary to mention.

Paraffine derives its name from the unalterable nature of the substance, under the most powerful chemical agents. It is white, in brilliant scales of a greasy lustre; it melts at about 116°, and boils at over 700° F.; it dissolves in boiling alcohol and ether, and burns in the air with a brilliant flame. Associated with paraffine are portions of a very volatile oil, *eupione*, which boils at a lower temperature, and by its presence renders the boiling point of the mixture difficult to determine. I consider this point worthy of further examination than I have been able at present to give it, i.e., whether the last third, and possibly the last half, of the petroleum, may not be advantageously so treated as to produce from it the largest amount of paraffine which it is able to produce.

The result of this graduated distillation, at a high temperature, is that we have obtained over 90 per cent. of the whole crude product in a series of oils, having valuable properties, although not all equally fitted for illumination and lubrication.

A second distillation of a portion of the product which came over in the later stages of the process (a portion distilled at about 650° F., and having a high colour), gave us a thin oil of density about .750, of light yellow colour and faint odour.

It is safe to add that, by the original distillation, about 50 per cent. of the crude oil is obtained in a state fit for use as an illuminator without further preparation than simple clarification by boiling a short time with water.

DISTILLATION BY HIGH STEAM

Bearing in mind that by aid of high steam, at an elevated temperature, many distillations in the arts are affected which cannot be so well accomplished by dry heat, I thought to apply this method in case of the present research. Instances of this mode of distillation are in the new process for Stearine candles, and in the preparation of rosin oil. I accordingly arranged my retort in such a manner that I could admit a jet of high steam into the boiler, and almost at the bottom of the contained petroleum. I was, however, unable to command a jet of steam above 275° to 290° F., and although this produced abundant distillation, it did not effect a separation of the several products, and the fluid distilled had much the same appearance as the petroleum itself, thick and turbid. As this trial was made late in the investigation, I have been unable to give it a satisfactory issue, chiefly for want of steam of a proper temperature. But I suggest, for the consideration of the company, the propriety of availing themselves of the experience already existing on this subject, and particularly among those who are concerned in the distillation of rosin oil—a product having many analogies with petroleum in respect to its manufacture.

USE OF THE NAPHTHA FOR ILLUMINATION

Many fruitless experiments have been made in the course of this investigation which it is needless to recount. I will, therefore, only state those results which are of value.

1. I have found that the only lamp in which this oil can be successfully burned is the camphene lamp, or one having a button to form the flame, and an external cone to direct the current of air, as is now usual in all lamps designed to burn either camphene, rosin oil, sylvic oil, or any other similar product.

2. As the distilled products of petroleum are nearly or quite insoluble in alcohol, burning fluid (i. e., a solution of the oil in alcohol) cannot be manufactured from it.

3. As a consequence, the oil cannot be burned in a hand lamp, since, with an unprotected wick, it smokes badly. Neither can it be burned in a Carcel's mechanical lamp, because a portion of the oil being more volatile than the rest, rises in vapour on the elevated wick required in that lamp, and so causes it to smoke.

I have found all the products of distillation from the copper still capable of burning well in the camphene lamp, except the last third or fourth part (i.e., that portion which came off at 700° F. and rising, and which was thick with the crystals of paraffine). Freed from acidity by boiling on water, the oils of this distillation burned for twelve hours without injuriously coating the wick, and without smoke. The wick may be elevated considerably above the level required for camphene, without any danger of smoking, and the oil shows no signs of crusting the wick tubes with a coating of rosin, such as happens in the case of camphene, and occasions so much inconvenience. The light from the rectified naphtha is pure and white, without odour. The rate of consumption is less than half that of camphene, or rosin oil. The Imperial pint, of 20 fluid ounces, was the one employed—a gallon contains 160 such ounces. A camphene lamp, with a wick one inch thick, consumed of rectified naphtha in one hour, 1¾ ounces of fluid. A Carcel's mechanical lamp of ⅞-inch wick, consumed of best sperm oil, per hour, 2 ounces. A "Diamond Light" lamp, with "sylvic oil," and a wick 1½-inch diameter, consumed, per hour, 4 ounces.

I have submitted the lamp burning petroleum to the inspection of the most experienced lampists who were accessible to me, and their testimony was, that the lamp burning this fluid gave as much light as any which they had seen, that the oil spent more economically, and the uniformity of the light was greater than in camphene, burning for twelve hours without a sensible diminution, and without smoke. I was, however, anxious to test the amount of light given, more accurately than could be done by a comparison of opinions. With your approbation I proceeded therefore to have constructed a *photometer*, or apparatus for the measurement of light, upon an improved plan. Messrs. Grunow, scientific artists of this city, undertook to construct this apparatus, and have done so to my entire satisfaction. This apparatus I shall describe elsewhere—its results only are interesting here. By its means I have brought the petroleum light into rigid comparison with the most important means of artificial illumination. Let us briefly recapitulate the results of these

PHOTOMETRIC EXPERIMENTS

The *unit* adopted for comparison of intensities of illumination is Judd's Patent Sixes Sperm Candle.

The sperm oil used was from Edward Mott Robinson, of New Bedford—the best winter sperm remaining fluid at 32° F. The colza oil and Carcel's lamps were furnished by Dardonville, lampist, Broadway, New York. The gas used was that of the New Haven Gas Light Co., made from best Newcastle coal, and of fair average quality.

The distance between the standard candle, and the illuminator sought to be determined, was constantly 150 inches—the photometer traversed the graduated bar in such a manner as to read, at any point where equality of illumination was produced, the ratio between the two lights. I quote only single examples of the average results, and with as little detail as possible, but I should state that the operation of the photometer was so satisfactory that we obtained constantly the same figures when operating in the same way, evening after evening, and the sensitiveness of the instrument was such that a difference of one-half inch in its position was immediately detected in the comparative illumination of the two equal discs of light in the dark chamber. This is, I believe, a degree of accuracy not before obtained by a photometer.

TABLE OF ILLUMINATING POWER OF VARIOUS ARTIFICIAL LIGHTS COMPARED WITH JUDD'S PATENT CANDLES AS A UNIT

SOURCE OF LIGHT	RATIO TO CANDLE—1
Gas burning in Scotch fish-tail tips, 4 feet to the hour	1: 5.4
Gas burning in Scotch fish-tail tips, 6 feet to the hour	1: 7.55
Gas burning in Cornelius fish-tail tips, 6 feet to the hour	1: 6.3
Gas burning in English Argand burner, 10 feet to the hour	1:16
Rock-oil, burning in 1-inch wick camphene lamp, consuming 1¾ ounces of fluid to the hour	1: 8.1
Carcel's mechanical lamp, burning best sperm oil, 2 ounces of fluid to the hour, wick ⅝ of an inch	1: 7.5
Carcel's mechanical lamp, burning best sperm oil, 2 ounces of colza oil to the hour, wick ⅞ of an inch	1: 7.5
Camphene lamp (same size as rock-oil above) burning best camphene, 4 fluid ounces per hour	1:11
"Diamond Light" by "sylvic oil," in 1½-inch wick, 4 ounces per hour	1: 8.1

From this table it will be seen that the rock-oil lamp was somewhat superior in illuminating power to Carcel's lamp of the same size, burning the most costly of all oils. It was also equal to the "Diamond Light" from a lamp of one-half greater power, and consequently is superior to it in the same ratio in lamps of equal power. The camphene lamp appears to be about one-fifth superior to it, but, on the other hand, the rock-oil surpasses the camphene by more than one-half in economy of consumption (i.e., it does not consume one-half so much fluid by measure), and it burns more constantly. Compared with the sylvic oil and the sperm, the rock-oil gave on the ground glass diaphragm the whitest disc of illumination, while in turn the camphene was whiter than the rock-oil light. By the use of screens of different coloured glass, all inequalities of *colour* were compensated in the use of the photometer, so that the intensity of light could be more accurately compared. Compared with gas, the rock-oil gave more light than any burner used except the costly Argand consuming ten feet of gas per hour. To compare the *cost* of these several fluids with each other, we know the price of the several articles, and this varies very much in different places. Thus, gas in New Haven costs $4 per 1,000 feet, and in New York $3.50 per 1,000, in Philadelphia $2.00 per 1,000, and in Boston about the same amount.

Such sperm oil as was used costs $2.50 per gallon, the colza about $2, the sylvic oil 50 cents, and the camphene 68 cents ; no price has been fixed upon for the rectified rock-oil.

I cannot refrain from expressing my satisfaction at the results of these photometric experiments, since they have given the oil of your company a much higher value as an illuminator than I had dared to hope.

USE OF THE ROCK-OIL AS A LUBRICATOR FOR MACHINERY

A portion of the rectified oil was sent to Boston to be tested upon a trial apparatus there, but I regret to say that the results have not been communicated to me yet. As this oil does not gum or become acid or rancid by exposure, it possesses in that, as well as in its wonderful resistance to extreme cold, important qualities for a lubricator.

CONCLUSION

In conclusion, gentlemen, it appears to me that there is much ground for encouragement in the belief that your company have in their possession a raw material from which, by simple and not expensive process, they may manufacture very valuable products.

It is worthy of note that my experiments prove that nearly the *whole* of the raw product may be manufactured without waste, and this solely by a well-directed process which is in practice one of the most simple of all chemical processes.

There are suggestions of a practical nature, as to the economy of your manufacture, when you are ready to begin operations, which I shall be happy to make, should the company require it ; meanwhile, I remain, gentlemen,

Your obedient servant,

B. SILLIMAN, JR.,
Professor of Chemistry in Yale College.

NEW HAVEN, April 16, 1855.

NUMBER 2 (See page 44)

FIRST ACT OF INCORPORATION OF THE STANDARD OIL COMPANY

KNOW ALL MEN BY THESE PRESENTS: That we, *John D. Rockefeller, Henry M. Flagler, Samuel Andrews,* and *Stephen V. Harkness,* of *Cleveland, Cuyahoga County, Ohio,* and *William Rockefeller,* of the *City, County,* and *State* of *New York,* have associated ourselves together under the provisions of the Act of the Legislature of the State of Ohio, entitled An Act to provide for the creation and regulation of incorporated companies in the State of Ohio, passed May 1, 1852, and the Acts supplementary thereto passed April 8, 1856, and the Act to amend the last-named Act, passed February 14, 1861, and other laws of the State of Ohio applicable thereto, for the purpose of forming a body corporate for manufacturing petroleum and dealing in petroleum, and its products under the corporate name of *THE STANDARD OIL COMPANY.*

And we do certify that the purpose for which said body corporate is formed is the manufacture of petroleum and to deal in petroleum and its products.

That the capital stock necessary for said company, and the amount agreed on as composing the capital stock, is the sum of *One Million Dollars.*

That the amount of each share of capital stock is *One Hundred Dollars.*

That the name of the place where said manufacturing establishment shall be located for doing business is *Cleveland City, Cuyahoga County, State of Ohio.*

That the name and style by which said manufacturing establishment shall be known is *THE STANDARD OIL COMPANY.*

JOHN D. ROCKEFELLER,
HENRY M. FLAGLER,
SAMUEL ANDREWS,
STEPHEN V. HARKNESS,
WILLIAM ROCKEFELLER.

CLEVELAND, OHIO, January 10, 1870.

NUMBER 3 (See page 47)

AFFIDAVIT OF JAMES H. DEVEREUX

[In the case of the Standard Oil Company *vs*. William C. Scofield *et al*. in the Court of Common Pleas, Cuyahoga County, Ohio.]

J. H. Devereux, being first duly sworn, says that he is forty-eight years of age, and is president of the New York, Pennsylvania and Ohio Railroad ; that in 1868 he became vice-president of the Lake Shore Railroad, and remained in that position as well as president and general manager till 1873. That he has heard read the statements of Robert Hanna and George O. Baslington, in their affidavits filed herein in respect to transportation of oil, and in regard thereto he has to say that his experience with the oil traffic began in 1868 when he went upon the Lake Shore Railroad as vice-president, succeeding Mr. Stone who retired from ill health; that the only written memoranda connected with the business of the company with which he was furnished was a book in which it was stated—probably in Mr. Stone's handwriting—that the representatives of the various oil interests of Cleveland would agree to pay a rate of 1 cent. per gallon on crude oil moved from the regions to Cleveland; that in addition to the inevitable friction arising from the competition of these refiners of Cleveland— probably aggregating twenty-five in number, was the further difficulty of the patent right which the Pennsylvania Railroad claimed to the transportation of oil, and the peculiar differences made by them in the rates given to refiners at Titusville, Pittsburg, and other places all thoroughly in competition with the then very limited refining capacity of Cleveland; that he took up the subject as to whether the Lake Shore Railroad could hope to compete for the transportation of oil, and the end of the matter was that the Jamestown and Franklin Railroad was extended from Franklin to Oil City, the then centre of the producing district, and a sharper contest than ever was produced, growing out of the opposition of the Pennsylvania Railroad in competition ; that such rates and arrangements were made by the Pennsylvania Railroad, that it was publicly proclaimed in the public print in Oil City, Titusville, and other places that Cleveland was to be wiped out as a refining centre as with a sponge, and without exception the oil refiners of Cleveland came to affiant as a representative of transportation, and with a single exception expressed their fears that they would have either to abandon their business here or move to Titusville or other points in the Oil Regions; that the only exception to this decision was that offered by Rockefeller, Andrews

[277]

and Flagler, who on its assurance that the Lake Shore Railroad could and would handle oil as cheaply as the Pennsylvania Company, proposed to stand their ground at Cleveland and fight it out on that line. That later, about 1870, the first move was made to transport refined oil by rail regularly and throughout the entire year from Cleveland to New York. That prior to that time the export business from Cleveland was comparatively limited and was confined to the summer months, most of that portion of the traffic refined at Cleveland in competition with Pittsburg, Titusville, and other places being shipped by lake and canal, and as affiant remembers at a rate of about one dollar per barrel, and with a certainty of its being reduced to ninety cents. That the rail rate was nominally two dollars on refined oil from Cleveland to New York. That Mr. Flagler, at this time representing Rockefeller, Andrews and Flagler, proposed to make regular monthly shipments by rail throughout the year provided a proper rate could be made for the business then offered, this rate to cover transportation of crude from the region to Cleveland, and when refined from Cleveland to New York. Rockefeller, Andrews and Flagler being the only refiners here who proposed to compete for the export business or offered oil for the entire haul from the regions to Cleveland and thence to New York; that Mr. Flagler's proposition was to assure to the Lake Shore Railroad sixty carloads of refined oil per day* from Cleveland to New York at a rate of $1.75 per barrel from the regions to New York, being thirty-five cents per barrel for crude from the regions to Cleveland and $1.30 per barrel for refined from Cleveland to New York; and Rockefeller, Andrews and Flagler were to assume all risk and losses from fire or other accidents. That affiant took this proposition into consideration and made careful computation of the cost of this transportation to the railroad, which cost is the proper basis in fixing the rate to be charged; that affiant found that the then average time for a round trip from Cleveland to New York for a freight car was thirty days; to carry sixty cars per day would require 1,800 cars at an average cost of $500 each, making an investment of $900,000 necessary to do this business, as the ordinary freight business had to be done; but affiant found that if sixty carloads could be assured with absolute regularity each and every day, the time for a round trip from Cleveland to New York and return could be reduced to ten days, by moving these cars in solid trains instead of mixing oil cars in other trains, as would be necessary when transported in small quantities and by moving the oil trains steadily without regard to other cars; that by thus reducing the time to ten days for a round-trip, only six hundred cars would be necessary to do this business with an investment therefore of only $300,000. That the regularity of the traffic would insure promptness in the unloading and return of the cars; that upon these considerations affiant concluded that Mr. Flagler's proposition offered to the railroad company a larger measure of profit than would or could ensue from any business to be carried under the old

---

* This must have been in 1872, not 1870. Up to 1872 the capacity of the Standard was but 1,500 barrels of crude a day.

arrangements, and such proved to be pre-eminently the case; that the proposition of Mr. Flagler was therefore accepted, and in affiant's judgment this was the turning-point which secured to Cleveland a considerable portion of the export traffic. That this arrangement was at all times open to any and all parties who would secure or guarantee a like amount of traffic or an amount sufficient to be treated and handled in the same speedy and economical way, the charges for transportation being always necessarily based upon the actual cost of the service to the railroad, and whenever any shipper or shippers will unite to reduce the cost of transportation to the railroad, to refuse to give them the benefit of such reduction would be to the detriment of the public, the consumers, who in the end pay the transportation charges. Affiant says that this legitimate and necessary advantage of the large shipper over the smaller he explained to Mr. Hanna and Mr. Baslington, and they recognised its propriety, and affiant offered them the same terms if by themselves or with others they would assure him like quantities with like regularity, thus securing like speed and economy in transportation. And further affiant saith not.

J. H. DEVEREUX.

Subscribed in my presence and sworn to before me this thirteenth day of November, 1880.

J. C. CANNON,
Notary Public in and for Said County.

NUMBER 4 (See page 55)

TESTIMONY OF HENRY M. FLAGLER ON THE SOUTH
IMPROVEMENT COMPANY

[Proceedings in Relation to Trusts, House of Representatives, 1888. Report Number 3112, pages 289–290.]

A. . . . Neither of the Messrs. Rockefeller, Colonel Payne, nor myself, nor any one connected with the Standard Oil Company, ever had any confidence in or regard for the scheme known as the South Improvement Company. We did not believe in it, but the view presented by other gentlemen was pressed upon us to such an extent that we acquiesced in it to the extent of subscribing our names to a certain amount of the stock, which was never paid for. The company never did a dollar's worth of business, and never had any existence other than its corporative existence, which it obtained through its charter. Through its president it negotiated certain railroad contracts, which, as I remember now, were signed by the company and by the officers of the railroad. Those contracts were held in escrow a few weeks and were destroyed or cancelled by mutual consent.

Q. Who presented these views to you gentlemen? Who was the person that had charge of this South Improvement Company's scheme?

A. I think Mr. Warden and the Messrs. Logan were the great leaders in the South Improvement Company policy.

NUMBER 5 (See page 62)

CONTRACT BETWEEN THE SOUTH IMPROVEMENT COMPANY
AND THE PENNSYLVANIA RAILROAD COMPANY, DATED
JANUARY 18, 1872

[Proceedings in Relation to Trusts, House of Representatives, 1888. Report Number 3112, pages 357–361.]

AGREEMENT made and entered into this eighteenth day of January, in the year eighteen hundred and seventy-two, by and between the South Improvement Company, a corporation organised and existing under the laws of the State of Pennsylvania, party hereto of the first part, and the Pennsylvania Railroad Company, on its own behalf and on behalf of all other railroad companies, whose roads are controlled, owned, or leased by it, or with which it has sufficient running arrangements, which other roads are herein described as the connections of the said Pennsylvania Railroad Company, party hereto of the second part.

WITNESSETH:

Whereas, the party hereto of the first part has been organized for the purpose, among other things, of increasing, facilitating, and developing the trade in and the conveyance and transportation of petroleum and its products, and for that purpose proposes, among other things, to expend large sums of money in the purchase, erection, and construction of, and maintaining and conducting works for storage, distillation, and refining, warehousing and transportation, and in various other ways, upon the inducement, among other things, of this contract.

And Whereas, the magnitude and extent of the business and operations proposed to be carried on by the party hereto of the first part will greatly promote the interest of the party hereto of the second part, and make it desirable for it, by fixing certain rates of freight, drawbacks, and rebates, and by the other provisions of this *agreement*, to encourage the outlay proposed by the party hereto of the first part, and to facilitate and increase the transportation to be received from it.

And Whereas, it has been agreed by and between the party hereto of the second part, for itself and its connections, the Erie Railroad Company, for itself and its connections, and the New York Central Railroad Company, for itself and its connections, that the business of transporting, by railroad, crude petroleum and its products,

[281]

toward the Atlantic coast, from the points of production and refining, on their lines of road, shall be allotted by the party hereto of the first part, to the said three companies, in the proposition of forty-five (45) per cent. of the whole to the Pennsylvania Railroad Company, for itself and its connections, including the Philadelphia and Erie Railway, the Northern Central Railway, the Alleghany Valley Railroad, Camden and Amboy Railway, the Pennsylvania Company, and all other railroads which are, or may be, controlled, owned, and leased by it, or with which it has, or may have, sufficient running arrangements; twenty-seven and a half (27½) per cent. of the whole to the Erie Railway Company, for itself and its connections, and twenty-seven and a half (27½) per cent. of the whole to the New York Central Railroad Company for itself and its connections, and that the transportation beyond Cleveland and Pittsburg over the railroads of the said companies and their connections, in other directions than toward the Atlantic coast, west from said points of production and refining, shall be allotted by the party hereto of the first part, in the proportion of one-third thereof, to the party hereto of the second part, for itself and its western connections, and the remainder to other railroads.

Now, therefore, this agreement witnesseth: That the parties hereto for themselves and their successors, in consideration of the promises, of the mutual execution hereof, and of the mutual advantages hereby conferred, have covenanted and agreed, and hereby do covenant and agree each with the other, as follows:

ARTICLE FIRST

The party hereto of the first part covenants and agrees:

1. To furnish to the party hereto of the second part for transportation, such a proportion of the crude petroleum and its products, owned or controlled by the party hereto of the first part, as shall give to the party hereto of the second part forty-five (45) per cent. of all the crude petroleum and its products, sent from the points of production and refining toward the Atlantic coast, by the said Pennsylvania, the Erie, and the New York Central railroads and their connections, and thirty-three and one-third (33⅓) per cent. of that which is sent west of Pittsburg and Cleveland by those railroads and their connections.

2. To provide suitable tankage at the points where petroleum is produced, on the railroads of the party hereto of the second part and its connections in which to receive crude petroleum preparatory to shipment, with the necessary pipes, pumps, racks, and other appliances for its convenient transfer in bulk into railroad cars.

3. To deliver to the railroads of the party hereto of the second part, and its connections, at the places of shipment, and to receive from them, at the places of destination, all crude petroleum and its products transported over their roads for the party of the first part.

4. To provide at the places of destination on the seaboard, necessary and suitable

yards, wharves, warehouses, sheds, tanks, pipes, pumps, and motive power, for the reception of petroleum and its products, and loading vessels therewith.

5. To provide, maintain, and operate the works necessary to refine crude petroleum upon the largest scale practicable, and with such skill, and on such a system of organisation and division of labour, as will secure both efficiency and economy; and for that purpose and for the purpose of developing and increasing the petroleum trade of the country, to provide and maintain all suitable and necessary means and facilities.

6. To keep records of the transportation over the railroads of the party hereto of the second part, and its connections, and so far as it can obtain the same, over the Erie and the New York Central railroads and their connections, of all petroleum and its products, showing the number of barrels of forty-five gallons each in bulk, and the number of barrels of forty-seven gallons each in barrels, carried by each road with the points of receiving and delivery, and the amount of freight received by each road for such transportation, which records shall at all reasonable times be open to the inspection of the duly constituted representatives of the party hereto of the second part.

Monthly abstracts of all such records shall be regularly sent to the party of the second part.

7. To pay the party of the second part weekly for all transportation over its roads and its connections, of petroleum and its products, such gross rates and half-rates of freight as are hereinafter specified, less the rebates and drawbacks hereinafter provided to be retained by the party hereto of the first part for its own use.

ARTICLE SECOND

The party hereto of the second part covenants and agrees:

1. That the party hereto of the second part will pay and allow to the party hereto of the first part, for its own use, in all petroleum and its products, transported over the railroads of the party hereto of the second part and its connections, for the party hereto of the first part, rebates, and on all transported for others, drawbacks, at the rates hereinafter provided, except in the case specified in Article Third.

2. To deliver to the party hereto of the first part all petroleum and its products in packages, transportation over the railroads, of the party hereto of the second part, and its connections, by whomsoever shipped, and consigned to the party of the first part, at the warehouses of the party of the first part, at the seaboard, and inland, at the depots of the party of the second part, at the places of destination, and to deliver all petroleum and its products, in bulk, owned by or consigned to the said party of the first part, at any point required on the line of the railroads, of the party of the second part and its connections.

3. To transport and deliver petroleum and its products over the railroads of the

party of the second part and its connections, at gross rates, which shall at no time exceed the following, without the consent of both parties hereto.

From any point on the Oil Creek and Allegheny River Railroad to Oil City, Union, Corry or Irvineton, which are herein designated as *common points*, on each barrel of forty-five gallons in bulk, and on each barrel of forty-seven gallons in barrels, thirty cents.

ON CRUDE PETROLEUM

From any common point to Cleveland, for each barrel of 45 gallons										....	$0.80
"	"	"	"	" Pittsburg,	"	"	"	"	"	....	.80
"	"	"	"	" New York,	"	"	"	"	"	....	2.56
"	"	"	"	" Philadelphia,	"	"	"	"	"	....	2.41
"	"	"	"	" Baltimore,	"	"	"	"	"	....	2.41
"	"	"	"	" Boston,	"	"	"	"	"	....	2.71

All other points, except those on the Oil Creek and Allegheny River Railway, to the places of destination last named, the same rates as from the *common points*.

ON REFINED OIL, BENZINE, AND OTHER PRODUCTS OF THE MANUFACTURE OF PETROLEUM

From Pittsburg to New York, for each barrel					....	$2.00
"	"	" Philadelphia,	"	"	....	1.85
"	"	" Baltimore,	"	"	....	1.85
From Cleveland to Boston,		"	"		....	2.15
"	"	" New York,	"	"	....	2.00
"	"	" Philadelphia,	"	"	....	1.85
"	"	" Baltimore,	"	"	....	1.85
From any common point to New York, for each barrel					....	2.92
"	"	" " " Philadelphia,	"	"		....	2.77
"	"	" " " Baltimore,	"	"		....	2.77
"	"	" " " Boston,	"	"		....	3.07

From and to all points intermediate between the points aforesaid, such reasonable rates as the party of the second part shall from time to time establish, on both crude and refined.

From Pittsburg, Cleveland, and other points, to places west of Pittsburg and Cleveland, such reasonable rates as the party of the second part may deem it expedient from time to time to establish.

4. To pay and allow to the party hereto of the first part, on all petroleum and its products, transportation for it over the railroads of the party of the second part and its connections, the following rebates, and on all transported for other parties, drawbacks of like amounts, as the rebates from the gross rates, the same to be deducted and retained by the party hereto of the first part, for its own use from the amounts of freights, payable to the party of the second part.

ON THE TRANSPORTATION OF CRUDE PETROLEUM

From the gross rate from any common point to Cleveland, a rebate per barrel of . $0.40
" " " " " " " " " Pittsburg, " " " " .40
" " " " " " ", " " New York, " " " " 1.06
" " " " " " " " " Philadelphia, " " " " 1.06
" " " " " " " " " Baltimore, " " " " 1.06
" " " " " " . " " " Boston, " " " " 1.06

From the gross rate from all other points, and the six places of destination last named rebates the same as on the rates from the common points.

ON THE TRANSPORTATION OF REFINED OIL, BENZINE, AND OTHER PRODUCTS OF THE MANUFACTURE OF PETROLEUM

From the gross rates from Pittsburg to New York, a rebate per barrel of $0.50
" " " " " " " Philadelphia, " " " " 50
" " " " " " " " Baltimore, " " " " 50
" " " " " " Cleveland to Boston, " " " " 50
" " " " " " " " New York, " " " " 50
" " " " " " " " Philadelphia, " " " " 50
" " " " " " " " Baltimore, " " " " 50
" " " " " " any common point to New York, a rebate per barrel of . 1.32
" " " " " " " " " Philadelphia, " " " " . 1.32
" " " " " " " " " Baltimore, " " " " . 1.32
" " " " " " " " " Boston, " " " " . 1.32

From the gross rates to and from all points, intermediate between the above points, a rebate or drawback of one-third of the gross rate, shall be paid.

From the gross rates from Pittsburg, Cleveland, and other points, to places west of the meridians of Pittsburg and Cleveland, a rebate or drawback of one-third of the gross rate shall be paid.

5. To charge to all other parties (excepting such as are referred to in Article 3d) for the transportation of petroleum and its products, rates which shall not be less than the gross rates above specified, and should at any time any less rate be charged, directly or indirectly, either by way of rebate, commission, allowances, or upon any pretext whatsoever, the same reduction per barrel shall be made to the party hereto of the first part, from the net rates provided for them, on all transportation for them during the period for which such reduction shall be made to others.

6. To permit the party hereto of the first part, if, in its judgment, the currents of trade should so require, temporarily to increase or diminish the proportion, as herein provided to the party hereto of the second part, for itself and its connections, as the whole business of transporting petroleum and its products, as between the party hereto of the second part, the Erie Railway Company and the New York Central Railroad Company. The party of the second part in such case, to receive from the party hereto

of the first part, in full payment or indemnity, for the excess or deficiency, one-half the net schedule rates on such excess or deficiency; the other half to be paid *pro rata* to the said other companies, whose apportioned quantity of transportation shall thus be varied; but such diversion of business shall not, at any time, exceed one week, nor be repeated without an interval of at least sixty days, unless with the consent of the party hereto of the second part. Also, that whenever from time to time, as aforesaid, a temporary diversion of a part of the apportioned transportation of the party of the second part, to the other railroads aforesaid, or to either of them, shall become necessary, cars of the party of the second part may be loaded by the party of the first part, and sent away over such other railroads, or either of them, but the cars so sent away shall be returned without unnecessary delay, and in as good order as when taken to the railroads of the party of the second part, and mileage at the usual rates paid for their use while absent.

7. To furnish with as much regularity as possible, at all times, good and sufficient cars, and other means suitable and necessary for the safe and prompt transportation of all crude petroleum and its products, either in bulk or in barrels, which the party hereto of the first part shall desire to send from one point to another (and which shall be supplied with as much regularity as possible), on or over the railroads of the party of the second part and its connections.

8. To make manifests or way-bills of all petroleum or its products, transported over any portion of the railroads of the party of the second part or its connections, which manifests shall state the name of the consignor, the place of shipment, the kind and actual quantity of the article shipped, the name of the consignee, and the place of destination, with the rate and gross amount of freight and charges; and to send daily to the principal office of the party of the first part, duplicates of all such manifests or way-bills.

ARTICLE THIRD

And it is hereby further covenanted and agreed by and between the parties hereto, that the rebates hereinbefore provided for the party hereto of the first part, may be made to any other party who shall furnish an equal amount of transportation, and who shall possess and use works, means, and facilities for carrying on and promoting the petroleum trade equal to those possessed and used by the party hereto of the first part.

ARTICLE FOURTH

And it is hereby further covenanted and agreed by and between the parties hereto, that the party hereto of the second part shall at all times co-operate, as far as it legally may, with the party hereto of the first part, to maintain the business of the party hereto of the first part, against loss or injury by competition, to the end that the party hereto of the first part may keep up a remunerative, and so a full and regular business, and

[286]

to that end shall lower or raise the gross rates of transportation over its railroads and connections, as far as it legally may, for such times, and to such extent as may be necessary to overcome such competition. The rebates and drawbacks to the party of the first part to be varied *pari passu* with the gross rates.

ARTICLE FIFTH

It is hereby mutually agreed by and between the parties hereto that for the purpose of meeting such exigencies as may from time to time require change of the rates of transportation herein provided, each party, on ten days' written notice from the other, shall appoint a person on behalf of such party, and the two persons thus appointed, shall have power to change and adjust the rates, which shall go into effect on being approved by the said parties hereto.

ARTICLE SIXTH

It is further mutually agreed by and between the parties hereto that the gross rates of freight to the party hereto of the first part shall at all times be kept as near to the net rates as is consistent with the interests of the party hereto of the first part, and that whenever in the judgment of the party hereto of the first part it is expedient to lower the rebate below the rate above specified, it may do so, and from time to time raise the same again, not, however, above the rate hereinbefore specified. The party hereto of the first part, from time to time shall notify the party of the second part in writing of the change required, whereupon the party hereto of the second part shall forthwith make a corresponding change of such gross rates.

ARTICLE SEVENTH

It is further mutually agreed by and between the parties hereto, that this agreement shall continue and remain in force for the period of not less than five years, and shall not then, nor thereafter terminate, until one of the parties shall have given twelve months' written notice to terminate it.

ARTICLE EIGHTH

It is further mutually agreed by and between the parties hereto, that if any doubt, question, difference, cause, or suit shall at any time or times, hereafter, arise or happen between the said parties to these presents, touching the construction of these presents, or any clause, matter, or thing herein contained, or any other matters, cause, or thing whatsoever, in any wise relating to or concerning this agreement, and such doubt, question, difference, or dispute, shall not be fully settled by the parties to these presents within one calendar month after the same shall arise, then, in every such case, upon the request in writing of either of the said parties hereto, specifying such doubt, question, difference, or dispute, it shall be committed and referred to the hearing and arbitration of three disinterested persons; one of them to be chosen by the party of the first part, another of them to be chosen by the party of the second part, and each party on ten days' notice in writing from the other, shall make such choice, and appoint a disinterested person in behalf of such party, but, if either party on such notice shall within such ten days fail to make an appointment, the person appointed by the other party shall choose the second disinterested person, and the third disinterested person shall be chosen within one calendar month next after such request; and the award, order, or determination of the said three persons, to be chosen as aforesaid, or any two of them, shall be binding and conclusive on the parties hereto, and shall be performed and kept by them, without any further suit or trouble whatsoever; provided such award, order, or determination, be made in writing, under the hands of the said three persons, or of any two of them, within the space of sixty days after all the persons shall be so selected, as aforesaid. And for the further and better enforcing the performance of the award, so to be made, as aforesaid, the reference or submission for or in respect of the same, may, at the option of any of the parties to these presents, from time to time be made as a matter of course, a rule of court in any court of record.

In witness whereof, the said South Improvement Company and Pennsylvania Railroad Company have caused their respective corporate seals to be hereto affixed, and these presents to be subscribed by their respective presidents, the day and year first above written.

[SEAL]

SOUTH IMPROVEMENT COMPANY.
By P. H. WATSON,
President.

[SEAL]

PENNSYLVANIA RAILROAD COMPANY.
By J. EDGAR THOMPSON,
President.

Attest: JOSEPH LESLEY, *Secretary.*

NUMBER 6 (See page 63)

STANDARD OIL COMPANY'S APPLICATION FOR INCREASE OF CAPITAL STOCK TO $2,500,000 IN 1872

To the Secretary of the State of Ohio:

The undersigned, being a majority of the Board of Directors of *THE STANDARD OIL COMPANY OF CLEVELAND, OHIO,* do hereby certify that on the first day of January, A.D. 1872, at the annual meeting of the stockholders of said company held at its office in Cleveland, Cuyahoga County, Ohio, by a vote then and there taken, all the stockholders of said company being present and voting therefor, it was resolved and agreed by each and all of them, that the capital stock of said company be increased the sum of *One Million Five Hundred Thousand Dollars,* thereby making the capital stock of said company *Two Millions Five Hundred Thousand Dollars,* which action of the stockholders was as follows, to wit:

Resolved, and it is hereby agreed by each and all of us, that the capital stock of this company, namely, *The Standard Oil Company of Cleveland, Ohio,* be increased to the sum of *Two Millions Five Hundred Thousand Dollars,* and it is also agreed, and the proper officers of the company are hereby instructed to take the requisite steps to so increase said capital stock.

JOHN D. ROCKEFELLER, O. B. JENNINGS, B. BREWSTER, WILLIAM ROCKEFELLER, S. V. HARKNESS, H. M. FLAGLER, T. P. HANDY, S. ANDREWS, A. STONE, JR., S. WITT, *Stockholders.*

Cleveland, O., January 1st, A.D. 1872.
And afterward said meeting was adjourned.   HENRY M. FLAGLER, *Secretary.*

And we further certify that the whole amount of such increase of capital stock has been paid to said company, in money, that no note, bill, bond, or other security has been taken for the same, or any part thereof, and that the credit of the company has not been used directly or indirectly to raise funds to pay the same or any part thereof.

IN WITNESS WHEREOF, We hereunto set our names at *Cleveland, Ohio,* this ninth day of February, A.D. 1872.

JOHN D. ROCKEFELLER, HENRY M. FLAGLER, SAMUEL ANDREWS, STEPHEN V. HARKNESS, *Directors.*

[289]

NUMBER 7 (See page 67)

AFFIDAVITS OF GEORGE O. BASLINGTON

[In the case of the Standard Oil Company *vs.* William C. Scofield, *et al.*, in the Court of Common Pleas, Cuyahoga County, Ohio.]

In the spring of 1869, they (Hanna, Baslington & Company) began the construction of refining works just above the Atlantic depot on the west side of the Cleveland and Columbus Railroad track, and invested in the construction of the works about $67,000, which works were completed so as to commence the refining business about the first of June, 1869, and from that time up to about the first of July, 1870, the works had netted a profit of $40,000 over all expenses of running said works, being about 60 per cent. on the capital invested per annum, and from that time on up to the first of April, 1872, said firm cleared $21,000, being about 30 per cent. per annum on the investment from the time that said firm commenced business.

Some time in February, 1872, the firm received a message from the Standard Oil Company requesting said firm to have an interview as to the disposal of the refining works of said firm; that they were indisposed to enter into any arrangement for the disposition of said works because the investment of capital in said works had proved abundantly profitable to their satisfaction and they had no disposition whatever to part with the works; but upon investigation they were somewhat surprised to find that the Standard Oil Company had already obtained the substantial control of the different refineries in the City of Cleveland; that it had obtained such rates of transportation of crude and refined oil from the different railroads that it was impossible for them to compete with it, and upon an interview which was had by Mr. Hanna and affiant with Mr. Rockefeller who was at the time president of the Standard Oil Company. Mr. Flagler, the secretary of the company, being present, Mr. Rockefeller in substance declared or said that the Standard Oil Company had such control of the refining business already in the City of Cleveland that he thought said firm of Hanna, Baslington & Company could not make any money; that there was no use for them to attempt to do business in competition with the Standard Oil Company.

Affiant further says that after having had an interview both with Mr. Watson, who was the president of a company called "The South Improvement Company," and Mr. Devereux, who was the general manager of the Lake Shore Road, he became satisfied that no arrangement whatever could be effected through which transportation could at least be obtained on the Lake Shore Road that would enable their firm to compete with the Standard Oil Company, the works of said Hanna, Baslington & Company, being so situated that they could only obtain their crude oil through the line of the Lake Shore Road. And finding that the Standard Oil Company had such special rates of transportation that unless the firm of Hanna, Baslington & Company were enabled to bring as much oil as the Standard Oil Company, that it was impossible for said firm of Hanna, Baslington & Company to obtain a fair competing rate with the Standard Oil Company. They at least came to the conclusion that it was better for them to take what they could get from the Standard Oil Company and let their works go.

And affiant further says that under these circumstances they sold their works to the Standard Oil Company, which were on the day of the sale worth at least $100,000, for $45,000 because that was all they could obtain from them, and works too which in cash cost them not less than $76,000, and which with a fair competition would have paid them an income of not less than 30 per cent. per annum on the investment.

Affiant further says that at the interviews which he had with Mr. Rockefeller, Mr. Rockefeller told him that the Standard Oil Company already had control of all the large refineries in the City of Cleveland and there was no use for them to undertake to compete against the Standard Oil Company, for it would only ultimate in their being wiped out, or language to that effect.—(November 1, 1880.)

George O. Baslington being duly sworn (November 12, 1880) says: That the firm of Hanna, Baslington & Company, the first year they were in business, made profit amounting to a little less than $40,000 and from the end of the first year up to the time of the sale to the Standard Oil Company they made no profit at all. At the time of the sale the firm reserved the privilege of running the works to close up and run them up to about April 1, 1872, and during that time they made profit to the amount of about $21,000. At the time my former affidavit was drawn by Mr. Tyler, I stated these facts to him.

In the sale of the works to the Standard Oil Company we were given the option to take cash or to take stock in the Standard Oil Company at par. We decided to and did take cash, and one reason that influenced us to take cash was that we were fearful that refining oil at Cleveland might not be successful, and if so, the cash was better than the stock, and affiant wanted the cash to enable him to embark in other pursuits.

NUMBER 8 (See page 72)

ORGANISATION OF THE PETROLEUM PRODUCERS' UNION OF
1872

[From "A History of the Rise and Fall of the South Improvement Company," pages 8–10.]

1. The territory forming the Pennsylvania petroleum field shall be divided into sixteen districts. . . .

2. The producers in each district shall meet at some convenient place and choose one or more (not to exceed five) men, from their own number, through whose hands they shall pledge themselves to sell all their crude oil.

3. It shall be the duty of these committeemen to sell the crude oil coming into their hands: First, to the local refiners; second, to the agents of the refiners located in distant cities, as may be designated by the executive committee; and third, to such shippers, dealers, and exporters as may be named by the executive committee, and it shall be the further duty of said local committeemen to keep the executive committee fully posted as to what is being done in their respective districts with reference to the sale and removal of all crude oil.

4. There shall be an executive committee composed of members of the Petroleum Producers' Union, to consist of one from each of the sixteen districts, to be chosen by the local committee, whose duty it shall be to meet from time to time, and take all necessary measures to fully carry out this plan in all its details.

5. That for the purpose of paying the expenses of this committee, one cent a barrel on all the crude oil shall be levied, collected, and paid over by the local committeemen to the executive committee, of which the executive committee shall keep an account to be rendered to the producers at a future meeting.

6. It shall be the especial duty of the executive committee to take such measures as they may find necessary to secure uniform mileage rates of freights on all oil and merchandise of every kind, to and from the Oil Region, and employ all lawful measures for the abolition of the railway system of rebates or drawbacks.

PLEDGE

"I do hereby agree to sell all my production of oil through, or with the consent of, the committee of the Petroleum Producers' Union."

First.—That an organisation shall be immediately formed for the exclusive purpose of advancing money to producers upon their depositing proper Tank or Pipe Company receipts therefor with the organisation or its agency.

Second.—That the name of the organisation shall be the "PRODUCERS' PROTECTIVE ASSOCIATION."

Third.—That its capital shall be one million dollars, with power in the directors to increase it to such an amount as in their judgment shall be necessary to accomplish the objects of the organisation.

Fourth.—That its headquarters shall be in Oil City, and its co-operative agencies shall be located at all principal producing points.

Fifth.—That its stock shall be divided into shares of $100 each, which stock shall be transferable only upon the books of the company at its headquarters, with the consent of the board of directors.

Sixth.—That the chairman of the general committee be requested to appoint one person in each of the sixteen producing districts, who shall open books to receive, and every producer, manufacturer, or other party, directly or indirectly interested in our home industries be invited to subscribe to the capital stock of this organisation not exceeding fifty shares, or such part thereof as he shall elect, and no person shall, at any time hold more than said number of shares.

Seventh.—That when the sum of one million dollars shall have been subscribed and ten per cent. thereof paid to five trustees to be appointed by the chairman of the general committee, the said chairman shall give notice of an election of officers, who shall be elected by the votes of the subscribers, each share being entitled to a vote.

Eighth.—That said officers shall consist of a president, vice-president, and such a number of directors as shall give each district a fair presentation.

Ninth.—That the board of directors shall appoint some bank or banker in each district its co-operative agency; or in the absence of a bank or bankers such agencies be established as shall be most convenient for the producer, which bank or agency shall, as necessity requires, by draft or otherwise, obtain its funds from the headquarters of the company, and be held strictly accountable therefor.

Tenth.—That every producer shall be entitled to go to his most convenient agency, and deposit his certificate or receipt for oil, which shall be passed to his credit, and he shall receive such an advance thereof as the board of directors in their discretion shall deem prudent to make.

Eleventh.—That the association shall from time to time sell the oil belonging to it, or held as security for advances overdue in such quantities and at such prices as legitimate demand will justify said prices to be daily telegraphed from headquarters to the several agencies.

Twelfth.—That every producer depositing oil in the hands of the association on which no advance is made, may, if he so elect, have his oil held until such time as he shall direct its sale, and that the appropriation of oils sold from day to day shall be as follows: First, all oils ordered sold by its owner, and the balance *pro rata* on oils on which advances have been made and shall then be overdue.

Thirteenth.—The association shall charge a reasonable rate of interest on all advances made, such interest to be used in defraying the expenses of the association and the surplus, if any, shall be declared as dividends upon the full paid stock. That any surplus stock remaining in the hands of the association shall be the property of the association until taken and paid for by some party entitled thereto under the foregoing provisions, but always at par.

Fourteenth.—When the producers of each district shall have appointed their committees, as provided in the second section of the Producers' Union, and have elected their chairman, he is requested to send to the chairman of the general committee the names thereof.

Fifteenth.—And it shall be the duty of the person appointed by the general committee, as provided in section five, to use due diligence in the circulation thereof, for subscriptions, and within one week from the receipt thereof, he shall collect the ten per cent. of each subscription, as provided by section seventh, and report the same to the chairman of the general committee, together with a list of the subscribers and the amount subscribed.

NUMBER 9 (See page 78)

CHARTER OF THE SOUTH IMPROVEMENT COMPANY

[From "A History of the Rise and Fall of the South Improvement Company," pages 12–14.]

An Act to incorporate the Southern Improvement Company:

SECTION 1. *Be it enacted by the Senate and House of Representatives of the Commonwealth of Pennsylvania in General Assembly met, and it is hereby enacted by the authority of the same,* That S. S. Moon, R. D. Barcley, John A. Fowler, or a majority of them and assigns, be and they are hereby authorised and empowered to form and be a body corporate, to be known as the "Southern Improvement Company," which shall be and is hereby vested with all the powers, privileges, duties, and obligations conferred upon the act to incorporate the Pennsylvania Company by the Act of the Legislature of Pennsylvania, approved the seventh of April, A.D. one thousand eight hundred and seventy, and the supplements thereto.

SEC. 2. That the stockholders of said company, by and with the consent of the holders of not less than two-thirds of the shares of stock, be and they are hereby authorised to change the name of the said company and designate the location of its general office, which changes shall be valid after the filing of a certificate in the office of the secretary of the Commonwealth, signed by the president, and attested by the seal of the said company.

The Act incorporating the Pennsylvania Company, referred to above, is the one that details the powers conferred on the incorporators. We give it entire.

An Act to incorporate the Pennsylvania Company:

SECTION 1. *Be it enacted by the Senate and House of Representatives of the Commonwealth of Pennsylvania in General Assembly met, and it is hereby enacted by the authority of the same,* That Andrew J. Howard, J. S. Swartz, G. B. Edwards, J. D. Welsto, and J. P. Malin, their associates, successors, and assigns, or a majority of them, be and they are hereby authorised to form and be a body corporate, to be known as the Pennsylvania Company, and by that name, style, and title shall have perpetual succession, and all the privileges, franchises and immunities incident to a corporation; may sue and be sued, implead and be impleaded, complain and defend in all courts of law and equity, of record and otherwise; may purchase, receive, hold, and enjoy, to them, their successors, and assigns, all such lands, tenements, leasehold estates and hereditaments, goods and chattels, securities and estates, real, personal and mixed, of what kind and quality soever, as may be necessary to erect depots, engine houses,

[295]

tracks, shops, and other purposes of the said corporation, as hereafter defined by the second section of this act, and the same from time to time may sell, convey, mortgage, encumber, charge, pledge, grant, lease, sub-lease, alien, and dispose of, and also make and have a common seal, and the same to alter and renew at pleasure, and ordain, establish, and put in execution such by-laws or ordinances, rules, and regulations as may be necessary or convenient for the government of the said corporation, not being contrary to the constitution and laws of this commonwealth, and generally may do all and singular the matters and things which to them shall appertain to do for the well-being of the said corporation, and the management and ordering of the affairs and business of the same:

Provided, That nothing herein contained shall be so construed as to give to the said corporation any banking privileges or franchises, or the privilege of issuing their obligations as money.

SEC. 2. That the corporation hereby created shall have power to contract with any person or persons, firms, corporations or any other party, howsoever formed, existing or that may hereafter exist, in any way that said parties or any of them may have authority to do, to build, construct, maintain or manage any work or works, public or private, which may tend or be designed to improve, increase, facilitate, or develop trade, travel, or transportation and conveyance of freight, live stock, passengers, and any other traffic, by land or water, from or to any part of the United States or the territories thereof; and the said company shall also have power and authority to supply or furnish all needful material, labour, implements, instruments, and fixtures of any and every kind whatsoever, on such terms and conditions as may be agreed upon between the parties respectively; also to purchase, erect, construct, maintain, or conduct, in its own name and for its own benefit, or otherwise, any such work, public or private, as they may by law be authorised to do (including also herein lines for telegraphic communication), and to aid, co-operate, and unite with any other company, person or firm in so doing.

SEC. 3. The company hereby created shall also have power to make purchases and sales of or investments in the bonds and securities of other companies, and to make advances of money and of credit to other companies, and to aid in like manner contractors and manufacturers; and to receive and hold, on deposit or as collateral, or otherwise, any estate or property, real or personal, including the notes, obligations, and accounts of individuals and companies, and the same to purchase, collect, adjust, and settle, and also to pledge, sell, and dispose thereof, on such terms as may be agreed on between them and the parties contracting with them; and also to indorse and guarantee the payment of the bonds and the performance of the obligations of other corporations, firms, and individuals, and to assume, become responsible for, execute, and carry out any contracts, leases, or sub-leases made by any company to or with any other company or companies, individuals or firms whatsoever.

[296]

SEC. 4. The company hereby created shall also have power to enter upon and occupy the lands of individuals or of companies, and making payment therefor or giving security according to law, for the purpose of erecting, constructing, maintaining, or managing any public work, such as is provided for or mentioned in the second section of this act, and to construct and erect such works thereon, and also such buildings, improvements, structures, roads, or fixtures as may be necessary or convenient for the purposes of said company, under the powers herein granted; and to purchase, make, use, and maintain any works or improvements connecting or intended to be connected with the works of the said company; and to merge or consolidate, or unite with the said company the improvements, property, and franchises of any other company or companies, on such terms and conditions as the said company may agree upon; and to fix and regulate the tolls or charges to be charged or demanded for any freight, property, or passengers travelling or passing over any improvement erected, managed, or owned by the said company, or on any merchandise or property transported over any road whatever by the said company, and to make, from time to time dividends from the profits made by said company; the several railroads managed by said company shall continue taxable, as heretofore, in proportion to their length within this state respectively; and the said Pennsylvania Company shall be taxable only on the proportion of dividends on its capital stock and upon net earnings or income, only in proportion to the amount actually carried by it within the state of Pennsylvania, and all its earnings or income derived from its business beyond the limits of this Commonwealth shall not be liable for taxation.

SEC. 5. The capital stock of said company shall consist of 2,000 shares, of the value of fifty dollars each, being $100,000, and with the privilege of increasing the same by a vote of the holders of the majority of the stock present at any annual or special meeting, to such an amount as they may from time to time deem needful; and the corporators, or a majority of them, named in the first section of this act, shall have power to open books for subscription at such times and places as they may deem expedient; and when not less than 1,000 shares shall have been subscribed, and twenty per cent. thereon shall have been paid in, the shareholders may elect not less than three nor more than nine directors to serve until the next annual election, or until their successors shall be duly elected and qualified; and the directors so elected may, and they are hereby authorised and empowered to have and to exercise, in the name and in behalf of the company, all the rights and privileges which are intended to be hereby given, subject only to such liabilities as other shareholders are subject to, which liabilities are no more than for the payment to the company of the sums due or to become due on the shares held by them; and should the capital stock at any time be increased, the stockholders, at the time of such increase, shall be entitled to a *pro rata* share of such increase, upon the payment of the instalments thereon called for; and whenever an increase of capital stock is made, a certificate thereof, duly executed under the corporate seal of the company, and signed by·the president and secretary, shall be filed with the auditor-general before the same shall be deemed to be valid.

SEC. 6. The principal office of the said company shall be in the City of Pittsburg, but the directors, under such rules and regulations as they may prescribe, may establish branches or agencies in other parts of the state, or elsewhere; all of the directors of said company shall be citizens of the United States, and reside therein.

SEC. 7. The directors shall be elected annually by the stockholders, on the first Tuesday of June of each year; and they shall elect from their number, at the first meeting of the board after their election, a president, and shall also have power to elect from their number, or otherwise, a vice-president, a treasurer, and secretary, and such other officers, clerks, and agents as the business of the company may require; all elections for directors shall be by ballot, and every stockholder shall be entitled to one vote for each share of stock held by him; but no person shall be eligible as director who is not a stockholder to the amount of ten shares; at the annual or special meetings a quorum shall consist of stockholders owning at least one-half of the capital stock.

SEC. 8. Ten days' notice shall be given, by publication, in two newspapers published in the City of Pittsburg, of the time and place of the annual election; which election shall be conducted by three stockholders, one of whom shall act as judge, and the other two as inspectors.

SEC. 9. The board of directors shall make all by-laws necessary for conducting the business of the company; which by-laws shall be at all times accessible to persons transacting business with them; the said directors shall have power, by a vote of a majority of their number at any meeting of the board, to change the name of the said corporation; and by any new name, thus adopted, upon filing with the secretary of the Commonwealth and the auditor-general a truly certified certificate, the said company shall have, hold, and enjoy all the rights, powers, privileges, and immunities hereby granted; the directors shall have power to require payment of the amount remaining unpaid on the stock of said company, at such time and in such proportions as they shall think proper; the said assessment to be made as the by-laws of said company shall direct.

ELISHA W. DAVIS,
Speaker of the House of Representatives, pro tem.

CHARLES H. STINSON,
Speaker of the Senate.

Approved—The seventh day of April, Anno Domini, one thousand eight hundred and seventy.

JOHN W. GEARY.

NUMBER 10 (See page 80)

DRAFT OF CONTRACT BETWEEN THE SOUTH IMPROVEMENT COMPANY AND PRODUCERS OF PETROLEUM IN THE VALLEY OF THE ALLEGHENY AND ITS TRIBUTARIES. DATED JANUARY, 1872*

[From "A History of the Rise and Fall of the South Improvement Company," pages 121–122.]

AGREEMENT made and entered into this day of January, A.D. 1872, by and between the South Improvement Company, a corporation under the laws of Pennsylvania, and embracing among its stockholders more than two-thirds (reckoned by their refining capacity) of the refineries of petroleum in the United States, parties hereto of the first part; and the Associated Producers of Petroleum, a corporation also organised under the laws of Pennsylvania, and embracing among its stockholders more than two-thirds (reckoned by the actual production of the crude petroleum at their wells) of the producers of petroleum in the Valley of the Allegheny and its tributaries, party hereto of the second part. WITNESSETH.

That whereas, The party of the first part has entered into certain contracts, viz.: The *first* with the Pennsylvania Railroad Company; the *second* with the Erie Railway Company; the *third* with the Atlantic and Great Western Railway Company; and the *fourth* with the New York Central and Hudson River Railroad, and the Lake Shore and Michigan Southern Railway Company, which contracts secure certain advantages in relation to the transportation of petroleum and its products, which it is the purpose of the contracting parties to use for the promotion of the common interests of the producers, refiners, and transporters of petroleum.

To the end that the said object may be more fully attained the said parties hereto have covenanted and agreed, each with the other, as follows, viz.:

I. The party of the first part, that it will appoint five of its members to form, with a like number of the party of the second part, a joint executive committee, who shall choose some competent and discreet person not of their number who shall serve as the chairman and the eleventh member of the joint committee.

* This draft was presented to the committee in lead pencil. It was never presented to the producers. See P. H. Watson's testimony, Appendix, Number 12.

II. The party of the first part, that it will submit all questions, arising under said railroad contracts, which affect the interests of both producers and refiners, to the decision of the joint committee provided for in Article I of the agreement.

III. The party of the second part, that it will appoint five of its members to constitute, with the five members of the party of the first part, the joint executive committee provided for in Article I of this agreement; and will submit to said committee all the questions mentioned in Article II.

IV. The said parties mutually, that the decisions of said joint committee on all questions, affecting the joint interests of producers and refiners, which shall be submitted to them, shall be final and conclusive upon both the parties hereto. That upon the questions which shall at all times be held to affect the joint interests of both producers and refiners are the following, viz.:

1st. The rates of transportation of both crude and refined oil.

2nd. The price of crude oil at the wells and in the market.

3rd. The price of refined oil in the market.

4th. The amount of rebate and drawback which from time to time it may be necessary for the interests of the trade to ask from the railroads.

V. The said parties mutually, that the joint committee shall meet once a month, and at any intermediate time, or times, at which a meeting shall be called by the chairman, or by any four of its members, to consider such questions as shall affect the joint interests of the parties hereto.

VI. The party of the second part that it will agree to increase and lessen the aggregate production of crude petroleum, as the said joint committee shall direct, to adapt as nearly as practicable the supply of the same to the capacity of the markets of the world to absorb at a price remunerative to the producer, the refiner and the transporter.

VII. The parties hereto mutually, that the said joint committee shall, at the beginning of each year, fix the minimum average price at which crude petroleum can be produced and delivered on board railway cars, which price shall be called the minimum cost of production—that at the same periods the said committee shall also fix the minimum average price at which crude oil can be refined, put up in packages and sold, which price shall be called the minimum cost of manufacture.

VIII. The parties hereto mutually, that after paying the minimum cost of production of crude petroleum, the minimum cost of its manufacture, and the cost of transportation and storage, and shipping also, in the case of exported oil, the profits shall be apportioned between the producers and refiners, in the ratio of . . . per cent. to the former, and . . . per cent. to the latter.

IX. The said parties; that in case of a temporary over-production of crude petroleum, the excess shall as far as practicable be taken and withheld from market, and an advance of three-fourths of the minimum cost of production advanced thereon by the party of the first part at eight per cent., intrust the party of the second part keeping the tanked petroleum insured in good and responsible companies to the full amount of the advance, one year's interest added.

X. The said parties mutually, that the party of the first part shall only be bound to pay the prices and make the advances aforesaid, in case the producers shall in good faith obey the instructions of the joint committee, to limit production by stopping the drilling of new wells.

XI. The party of the second part that it will keep a register of the date of the commencement of all new wells, the date at which the same shall be finished, the character of the well and the monthly production, and the date at which it may be abandoned, and that it will make it a condition, precedent to the holding of stock in its company, that the date aforesaid shall be finished by its stockholders.

XII. Both parties, that it is the especial object of this agreement to bring the producers and refiners of petroleum into harmony and co-operation, by reciprocal, fair, and just dealing, for the promotion of their mutual interests, and everything in this agreement is to be construed liberally for the carrying into effect of this object.

NUMBER 11 (See page 82)

EXTRACTS FROM THE TESTIMONY OF W. G. WARDEN

[From "A History of the Rise and Fall of the South Improvement Company,"
pages 30–41.]

WASHINGTON, D. C., March 30, 1872.

William G. Warden affirmed and examined.

By Mr. C. Heydrick (Counsel).

Q. Are you an officer of the South Improvement Company?

A. Yes, sir; or rather, I was.

Q. What office did you hold?

A. I held the office of secretary during all the previous meetings, and was a director of the company.

Q. When was the company organised?

A. Our minutes will show that, if you will allow me to refer to them, and I desire to put them in as evidence. On referring to the minutes I find that the corporators' meeting was held January 2, 1872. As I understand that these minutes are to go in as a part of the evidence, they will furnish you all the information you desire in regard to the organisation and proceedings of the company.

[The chairman stated that the witness could refer to the minutes as memoranda, and that the committee would determine hereafter as to whether they should be received as evidence.]

By Mr. Heydrick.

Q. For what object or business was the company organised?

A. For refining oil.

Q. That meeting was under the charter which has been presented?

A. That was the first meeting held after we got the charter.

Q. The gentlemen who attended that meeting on the second of January were those named in the act of the incorporation?

A. Yes, sir; they met and transferred the company under the charter over to the stockholders.

Q. Did the incorporators named in the act transfer their interest to the stockholders, as you have stated on that occasion?

A. Yes, sir.

Q. What refining capacity does this company possess? State the amount of capital and stock subscribed and put in?

A. At that time 1,100 shares, at $100 per share, was subscribed, and twenty per cent. thereon paid into the treasury.

.   .   .   .

Q. Where did that company intend to refine oil?

A. Their calculation was to get all the refineries in the country into the company.

Q. Was it the design of the stockholders to include all the oil refineries in this country?

A. Yes, sir; every one of them.

.   .   .   .

Q. Can you give us a list of the stockholders?

A. I can give you them from the minutes. They are as follows:

William Frew..............................	10 shares
W. P. Logan................................	10 "
John P. Logan..............................	10 "
Charles Lockhart...........................	10 "
Richard S. Waring..........................	10 "
W. G. Warden..............................	475 "
O. F. Waring...............................	475 "
P. H. Watson...............................	100 "
H. M. Flagler..............................	180 "
O. H. Payne...............................	180 "
William Rockefeller	180 "
J. A. Bostwick.............................	180 "
John D. Rockefeller........................	180 "
	———
	2,000

By Mr. Sheldon.

Q. What was the idea of getting all the refineries of the country into one organisation?

A. The idea when the company started was this: There is a large number of refineries in the country—a great deal larger than is required for the manufacture of the oil produced in the country, or for the want of the consumers in Europe and America; the capacity of the oil refineries in the country is, I think, 45,000 or 50,000 barrels a day; we completed our organisation, and when we met together it was discovered that the parties present represented, in one way or another, a large portion of the refining interest in the country; of course all of us had our friends in the matter, who must be taken care of if any arrangement at all was made; and after discussing the matter at considerable length, it was decided to include within our company every refinery we could possibly get into it. We also had considerable discussion with

[303]

the railroads in regard to the matter of rebate on their charges for freight; they did not want to give us a rebate unless it was with the understanding that all the refineries should be brought into the arrangement and placed upon the same level; there was no difference made as far as we were concerned, in favour of or against any refinery; they were all to come in alike; that was the understanding from the first to the last.

Q. Where are the refineries situated ?

A. Situated in New York, Philadelphia, Baltimore, Boston, on the sea-board, and in the Oil Region, Pittsburg, and Cleveland.

Q. You say you made propositions to railroad companies, which they agreed to accept upon the condition that you could include all the refineries ?

A. No, sir; I did not say that; I said that was the understanding when we discussed this matter with them; it was no proposition on our part; they discussed it not in the form of a proposition that the refineries should be all taken in, but it was the intention and resolution of the company from the first that that should be the result; we never had any other purpose in the matter.

Q. In case you could take the refineries all in, the railroads proposed to give you a rebate upon their freight charges ?

A. No, sir; it was not put in that form; we were to put the refineries all in, upon the same terms; it was the understanding with the railroad companies that we were to have a rebate; there was no rebate given in consideration of our putting the companies all in, but we told them we would do it; the contract with the railroad companies was with us.

Q. But if you did form a company composed of the proprietors of all these refineries, you were to have a rebate upon your freight charges ?

A. No; we were to have the rebate anyhow; but were to give all the refineries the privilege of coming in.

Q. You were to have the rebate whether they came in or not ?

A. Yes, sir.

Q. Were you to have a rebate upon the same freight charges that had been in existence before ?

A. No; the whole object of the railroad authorities was to get better freight prices.

    .   .   .   .

Q. What effect was this arrangement to have upon the producer or upon the refineries that did not go into your combination ?

A. According to our opinion of it that is the way we have got into this trouble; we have been misconstrued and misrepresented as to our purposes all over the country; the whole object was, and our whole talk was, as far as any of my friends came into the matter, or as far as I myself was concerned, that the producers should receive a better price for their oil; we calculated to get five or six dollars a barrel for crude oil;

that was from the beginning of our talk until the end of it; we had not our company organised, or at least the organisation was not completed, nor the contract signed, until all these disturbances commenced to be gotten up; we thought the matter would quiet down and we would get a chance to explain our position and put ourselves right; we asked for the opportunity to do so; we have evidence of that in the telegrams we sent, and I can say, under oath, that they were sent in good faith; there was never an idea in my mind that they were not. . . . I will state further that this matter was discussed with Mr. Scott by myself, personally, and in very great length, and also with Mr. Potts, who never has had any interest and never any part in this contract, and who spoke of this very matter from the start, expressing the opinion that it could not succeed unless the producers were taken care of. That was understood by us all from the start in every discussion we had, and by the railroad people as far as I heard from them. I can only answer for the railroad people from the conversation I had personally with Mr. Scott and Mr. Potts, in which it was perfectly understood that we could not succeed in carrying out these measures for our own benefit and the benefit of the railroads without the co-operation of the producers, and the only point we discussed was whether it should be a combination or co-operation. I took the ground personally against forming a combination inasmuch as the interests of the producers were in one sense antagonistic to ours, one as the seller and the other as the buyer. We held in argument that the producers were abundantly able to take care of their own branch of the business if they took care of the quantity produced. They were only liable to depression from our production, therefore they had in their own hands directly the power of holding the market at six or eight dollars a barrel.

_Q._ You did not take into consideration the good of the consumers of the country, which is by far the larger part of the population of the country?

_A._ Yes, we did.

_Q._ You wanted to put up the price of oil?

_A._ In answer to that I will state that the producers and refiners were both suffering under the depression that existed. The refiners were not getting enough to pay their expenses. All we asked was a fair refiner's profit.

_Q._ What effect were these arrangements to have upon those who did not come into the combination or co-operation, as you have termed it, as to the price to be charged for transporting their oil, both refiners and producers?

_A._ I do not think we ever took that question up.

_Q._ Were the railroad companies to charge the same increase of freights to those who did not come into the combination that they did to you without giving them a rebate?

_A._ Yes, sir.

_Q._ Now in case you could control the oil produced by these people in any combination that you made, were you not to have a rebate upon the oil?

A. We were not to have a rebate, we were to have a drawback.

Q. What is the difference between a rebate and a drawback?

A. There is not much difference in one sense. A rebate is made at the time we pay our freight; a drawback is made afterward.

Q. That is a technical, rather than a real, difference, is it not?

A. I want to state it as you will find it in the contract.

Q. The effect was that those who did not go into the combination could not get their oil as cheaply as you could?

A. No, sir; they could not; I want to explain in what relation that occurred and why this arrangement was made. I may say that it never entered into my head that the refineries would not all be brought in; a fair manufacturer's profit was all we wanted. They were all to be brought in on equal terms, and the object of the drawback was not to cover all the oil to be refined in this country, but only the oil that was to be exported.

Q. If all had gone into the combination, then the result would not have been to injure the producers and refiners, but to injure the consumers of the country?

A. No, sir; the purpose was not to injure them.

Q. Would it not have been to increase the price of oil, if you had increased the cost of freight?

A. Yes, sir.

    •   •   •   •   •   •

Q. You say the railroad companies were going to increase the rate of freight anyhow; they had the right to do that if they were carrying too low, but would that justify them in increasing the rates of freight to such an extent that they could afford to give you a sum of money for it?

A. I will tell you how that was done. The men in our trade are a very hard kind of men to hold. Those of us who deal in oil know that when we have purchased a lot, they would deliver it in New York for less than anybody could afford to deliver it. That has been the fact almost continuously ever since 1869. Oil has been delivered in the East for less money than was apparent from any rates known to the market; less than even we who refined it could deliver it for. The railroads were kept constantly besieged by one or another, and they were continually cutting under other routes for New York or for Cleveland, so that nobody knew what the rates were. They have been paying rebates, more or less, for the last two years.

Q. And you contemplated an increase of rates for the simple purpose of having the railroads divide with you?

A. There was no divide.

Q. A rebate is a divide to a certain extent, is it not? The proposition was that there should be taken out of the producers and consumers of this country a certain percentage of the freight for you?

A. It was done to prevent this cutting of roads one under another, and to prevent speculation.

Q. Was it not done for the purpose of oppressing the producers and consumers of this country?

A. I can only deny that such was the object, or that such would have been the effect.

.   .   .   .

Q. Has it been the practice of both the producer and refiner to make combinations from time to time by storing oils, and by large shipments abroad to affect the general price in the market?

A. The producers have made such combinations on the creek, and a few of the refiners and merchants made two combinations in 1868, which was known as the Deboe combination, and in 1869 and 1870 the Bull Ring, as they called it; but there was no combination that I knew of on the part of the producers, except among themselves; they have several times combined among themselves.

Q. Have there not been combinations of producers, refiners, and merchants to affect the price of oil?

A. There have been all kinds of combinations.

Q. Is there not at this time, if not invalidated by a change of directors of the Erie Railroad Company, a combination between officers of that road and certain parties in New York by which they control the price of coal?

A. If I were allowed to say what I think, I should reply in the affirmative and to say that one great reason why we went into this arrangement was to stop that Erie combination, which was a great source of difficulty; we could not get hold of the matter; we would ship a cargo of oil at a fair price to-day, and would be compelled to sell it to-morrow at a much less price; this arrangement did break up that combination entirely, so that there is no combination of that sort to-day.

By the Chairman.

Q. I understand that your larger combinations swallowed up the Erie combination.

A. It destroyed it at the time.

Q. Yours was somewhat in the direction of the Erie combination, but larger?

A. No, sir; it was not; the Erie was with some merchants, ours embraces the whole refining interest in the country; that was different; I will state that since I came into this Capitol I have been told that the very men engaged in prosecuting this investigation have a combination by which they intend to run up the price of their oil; I hope they will; I do not care what means are used, so that we can carry on our business, and pay just what others have to pay.

.   .   .   .

Q. I understand you to say that under your arrangement the cost of crude oil might be increased \$1.25 a barrel, and that there is produced about 18,000 barrels daily in the Oil Regions of Pennsylvania, but not that on an average; can you state from memory about the amount of annual production?

A. I have a circular here which gives the statement as 5,775,000 barrels.

Q. So that the production in round numbers for last year was 6,000,000 barrels; now, of this $1.25, how much were you to get as your drawback if you had carried out your arrangement?

A. The maximum we would have been entitled to receive is one dollar a barrel.

Q. Then on this production you would have received $6,000,000 a year, and the railroad companies an additional sum of $1,500,000; in other words, under your arrangement the public would have been put to an additional expense of $7,500,000 a year.

A. What public do you refer to? They would have had to pay it in Europe.

By Mr. Negley.

Q. Were there not at the same time combinations upon the part of producers to affect the price of oil in the market?

A. There were not at the time we started this matter; I do not know of any just at that moment; there have been over and over again. I want to state that a large portion of our oil product goes to Europe—of this very crude oil which Mr. Sheldon talks about; I have here a circular to which I call the attention of the committee, which bears out our position in this matter; I desire to put it in evidence because it gives the general opinion of merchants connected with the exportation of crude oil. It has been the impression of everybody in the trade that the oil exported should pay us an additional amount in this country, to be divided between those interested in the handling of it and the producing of it, to the extent of eight or ten millions a year; I have had that figured out three, or four, or five successive years. We have shown over and over again that that amount ought to be retained in this country. I have been engaged for several years in the oil business, and I have yet to sell one barrel to bear the market. I have always been upon the bull side of the market; I believe there ought to be in this country a better price for oil to every one engaged in it. In 1868, 1869, and 1870, there were movements in oil which brought to this country millions of dollars; and if the producers had refrained from sending forward their oil beyond the requirements of the market, the price would have been sustained. That has been the trouble always in making movements for a higher price. There is no man in this country who would not quietly and calmly say that we ought to have a better price for these goods.

By the Chairman.

Q. Do you mean a better price here, or a better price for that exported?

A. You could not get a better price for that exported without having a better price here.

Q. That is what the committee wants to know, whether it is necessary, in order to keep up the price abroad, to keep up the price at home?

NUMBER 12 (See page 82)

EXTRACTS FROM THE TESTIMONY OF PETER H. WATSON

[From "A History of the Rise and Fall of the South Improvement Company,"
pages 76–96.]

WASHINGTON, D. C., April 5, 1872.

By Mr. Townsend.

Q. From such testimony as you have given this morning, am I correct in understanding that this whole arrangement was suspended before its completion and before anything was done under it?

A. Yes, sir.

Q. That no completion of contracts was consummated?

A. No, sir; the conditions of the original understanding about the contracts, on which alone they were to go into effect, had not been complied with.

Q. And a further arrangement was necessary to make it a complete contract?

A. Yes, sir, the South Improvement Company had to enter into a contract, such substantially as I have furnished a draft of here, to give the producers the full benefit of everything connected with the contract before the contract itself could go into effect.

Q. There are three principal interests connected with the oil trade?

A. There are, the producers, refiners and transporters; no injustice could be done to either interest without affecting, injuriously, the others. The object of the railroads in this matter was to promote the interests of the trade in order to promote their own interests.

By the Chairman.

Q. You say there were three interests, producers, refiners and shippers?

A. Yes, sir, connected with the trade.

Q. And that the object of all these arrangements was to protect these three interests?

A. To protect these three interests and incidentally, of course, protecting the general interest in doing that, for this is peculiarly an American traffic.

Q. It was in the direction of increasing to each of these parties, respectively the benefits and profits of the business?

A. Yes, sir, that each might receive a fair profit. The railroad companies had not been receiving cost for transportation, and it was to save them from loss, for they had been transporting at a loss during the whole of the year 1871.

[309]

Q. Well, that is to increase profits, is it not?

A. Yes, to save from loss.

Q. Did it look to increasing in any way the benefits of cheapness to the consumer?

A. Yes, sir.

Q. How?

A. By steadying the trade. You will notice what all those familiar with this trade know, that there are very rapid and excessive fluctuations in the oil market; that when these fluctuations take place the retail dealers are always quick to note a rise in price, but very slow to note a fall. Even if two dollars a barrel had been added to the price of oil, under a steady trade, I think the price of the retail purchaser would not have been increased. That increased price would only amount to one cent a quart, and I think the price would not have been increased to the retail dealer because the fluctuation would have been avoided. That was one object to be accomplished. Moreover, there is only one-sixth of the oil produced here consumed in this country—a very small proportion of the product. In discussing what compensating advantage would arise from an increase of price, the railroad companies considered, in the first place, that there was a very great compensation afforded by a steady trade.

Q. Will you state to the committee how, with your mode of arriving at these conclusions, that cheapness to the consumer is promoted by stability in trade—how that arrangement which gave $1.50 a barrel to the South Improvement Company benefited either the railroad company or the producer?

A. Well, sir, in the agreement you will observe that the maximum rebates and maximum rates are stated. These maximum rebates were exceptions to the rule, which is a cardinal principle in the contract. The actual rates were to be kept as near to net rates as possible. Moreover, this was a contract which, before it was to go into effect, would have been a contract with the producer as well as the refiner.

Q. Does this contract show that?

A. The draft of a contract which I have presented to the committee, and which was to have been entered into with the producers before the contracts with the railroad companies went into operation, shows that.

Q. Does this contract say that anything was to be done in behalf of the producer before it was to go into operation?

A. Not on the face of the contract; it was only a condition on which it was delivered to me.

Q. A written condition so that it would become a part of the contract?

A. It was a part of the contract.

Q. I asked you whether there was anything in writing?

A. I said there was nothing in writing on the face of the contract, but nevertheless it was an essential part of it.

Q. It seems to be essential now that it should be a part of the contract?

A. It was all the time so considered from the beginning.

By Mr. Hambleton.

Q. Was this draft of a contract with the producers drawn prior to the execution of the railroad contracts?

A. Yes, sir, the draft was drawn prior to that.

By the Chairman.

Q. What is the date of that pencilled draft of a contract?

A. I could not give you the date of it; it was written in the office of the Lake Shore Railroad Company.

Q. At what place?

A. New York.

Q. State as near as you can the date?

A. I should say it was probably in December; either late in December or in the beginning of January, probably in December; indeed, I am very confident it was before I went home at Christmas.

Q. Has any copy of this ever been printed?

A. No, sir.

Q. This is all there was of it?

A. Yes, except discussion; we discussed the matter.

Q. I mean all there was committed to writing?

A. Yes, sir, all there was then committed to writing.

Q. Is it all there was as far as making out a contract is concerned?

A. Yes, sir.

Q. Was this submitted to the producers as a body or individually?

A. We were very anxious to submit it to the producers, and I asked them to appoint a committee that we might do it, but they had got up such an excitement at the time that nothing was practicable.

Q. When was that?

A. Before the last of these contracts was signed.

Q. Can you give the dates at all?

A. I cannot give the dates, but the contract with the Lake Shore road had not been signed at the time.

Q. What producers did you ask to call a meeting?

A. Among others I addressed a communication to be delivered to a gentleman who was understood to be the chairman of a meeting about to be held.

Q. What was his name?

A. Foster W. Mitchell, of Franklin.

Q. You addressed a communication to him, of what purport?

A. Asking him to appoint a committee to meet a committee of the South Improvement Company, that they might know what the objects of the South Improvement

Company were. I proposed to submit these contracts with the railroad companies to that committee and also the form of contract which the railroad companies required the South Improvement Company to enter into with the producers, before these contracts went into effect.

Q. Have you a copy of that communication or letter?

A. It was a telegram.

Q. Have you a copy of it here?

A. I have not at present.

Q. Have you it in your possession, anywhere, and can you lay it before the committee?

A. I may have it; am not sure.

Q. Did you receive a reply to that communication?

A. Yes, sir.

Q. Was it stated in your communication that you proposed to lay before the committee the form of contract to be entered into with the producers?

A. No, sir. I proposed to lay that before the committee if it should be appointed.

Q. If you are not able to furnish a copy of that communication I will ask you to state orally its contents.

A. I could not give you the words of it; it was in general terms asking that they appoint a committee to confer with a committee of the South Improvement Company.

Q. To confer in reference to what?

A. I do not know that I should be safe in undertaking to say; I know what my object was in writing it.

Q. That you have stated. If you received a reply from Mr. Mitchell, state whether it was by letter or telegram.

A. I received a reply by telegraph from Mr. Mitchell, stating that the meeting of the producers received the communication with scorn—as of course they would if read to them, as a mass-meeting is always called for a specific object.

Q. That was not in his reply?

A. No, sir, it was not. I replied to him that I had intended the communication to him to be for the purpose of laying it before a few of the principal producers; that to lay the proposition before the meeting was of course to insure its defeat, because the meeting had convened for a predetermined purpose, which was to denounce and treat with scorn the South Improvement Company, because the South Improvement Company had been represented to them as hostile to their interests. This last perhaps was not in the communication.

By Mr. Hambleton.

Q. Have you a copy of that paper which you addressed to Mr. Mitchell?

A. I am not sure whether I have or not. It was a telegram.

Q. Did that substantially close the written communications between you and the producers upon that subject?

[312]

A. No, sir. I had a great many communications with individual producers; I think with more than half the producers, estimating them by the quality of oil produced.

Q. State what occurred.

A. I have corresponded with them and in that correspondence they have expressed their belief that the proposed plan of the South Improvement Company would work greatly for the benefit of the producing interest; that there was something greatly needed for the producing interest, and that it could not thrive without something of this kind, because it could not pay fair, living rates, for transportation to the railroad companies at the price oil was bringing, and that there was no likelihood of oil increasing in price under the existing condition of things; that the railroad could not always, of course, continue carrying at a loss.

.   .   .   .

Q. Will you give the names of the producers who proposed to join the South Improvement Company, or who expressed themselves favourable to the plan of that company, in addition to the name of Mr. Mitchell?

A. I could give you the names of several of them, but I do not think their lives and property would be safe. They requested me not to mention their names because they thought it would be an imprudent thing to do.

Q. You refuse, then, to give the names which you say you could state?

A. I refuse to give the names for the reason I have stated.

Q. Are there any of them you are willing to mention?

A. I will look over the letters and see whether there are any of them not marked confidential. If there are any not so marked, I will give you the names.

Q. Why do you state to this committee that you are not willing to give the names of the parties to whom you refer, when you state that a great many producers were in favour of this plan, and were consulted in regard to it?

A. I stated it because it was a fact.

By Mr. Sheldon.

Q. Did the danger to the lives of these parties arise from the excitement in the Oil Regions in consequence of these proceedings?

A. Yes, sir, one of the presidents of one of the committees representing the producers was in New York, a Mr. Patterson. He stated, as I understood, to one of the railroad officers, that he did not think my life would be safe if I were to go into the Oil Region, although he himself would not take it. I had received a number of threatening letters, but I did not attach any importance to them until Mr. Patterson made that statement.

By the Chairman.

Q. What was the reason given why your life would not be safe?

A. I do not know that the reason given, I think by Mr. Patterson, that there was such an unreasonable excitement among the people as to the nature and object of the

South Improvement Company, which was represented to them to be a measure altogether hostile to them.

Q. Do you know what these misrepresentations were?

A. I only know by what I have seen stated in the papers and what persons have mentioned to me.

Q. Did you make an effort to correct the false impressions?

A. I did; the papers called for the other day by the committee, and which I have here to-day to produce, will show that.

Q. Were your efforts to correct these misrepresentations successful?

A. No, sir, they were not. I will read the despatches which I sent for the purpose of endeavouring to do that, and you will see from them the nature of the efforts I made.

Q. Sent to whom?

A. I sent a despatch to F. W. Mitchell through S. P. McCalmont of Franklin, which I have here.

The Chairman.—We will not stop to read them.

Witness.—It will answer your question in a great deal shorter period than I could answer it verbally.

The Chairman.—We will put the answers themselves in as testimony.

Witness.—Then I will read this as my answer, if you please, because it expresses as fully as I could express the facts you desire to know.

The Chairman.—Very well, you may hand the despatches to the reporter, and they will go in as a part of your testimony, and save the committee the time of reading them.

Witness.—You can hardly comprehend the answer without hearing the despatches. There were three despatches, showing the efforts I made to have the producers understand that the whole arrangement was one which looked as much to their interest as to any other.

The Chairman.—Very well, you may furnish them to the committee; we will not stop to read them now.

Witness.—I then offer you first my despatch to S. P. McCalmont, dated New York, March 4, 1872. I next offer another despatch from myself to F. W. Mitchell, dated New York, March 5, 1872, and also a despatch from myself to the same party, dated New York, March 6, 1872.

The despatches referred to are as follows:

S. P. McCalmont,   New York, March 4, 1872.
    Franklin, Pennsylvania.

Your telegram received. Please deliver the following communication to F. W. Mitchell, or, in his absence, to somebody else who will make its contents known to the principal producers attending the meeting to be held to-morrow at Franklin:

To F. W. Mitchell:

Yesterday I received by mail from you or some other friend in Franklin several newspaper slips, one of which threatened the destruction of my oil at Franklin. At the same time I received an anonymous letter threatening injury to the Jamestown and Franklin Railroad. Disapproval of my connection with the South Improvement Company is alleged as the reason of both threats. This morning the telegraph informs me that the threat to destroy my oil has been executed by tapping the tank and letting it run to waste. While there may be some excuse for working up the present excitement to induce people to subscribe their money to new railroad schemes, there can be nothing but reprobation for the lawless destruction of property. You have sufficient character and influence, and sufficient information of the purposes of the company, to quell this excitement by a word, and I think it your duty to say that word. It seems to me that a great responsibility rests with somebody among you for stimulating the present causeless excitement, and the lawless destruction of property. On meeting you here on your return from the South, I explained to you, very briefly, that the whole plan of the South Improvement Company was founded upon the expectation of co-operation with the oil producers to maintain a good price for crude oil, as the only means of securing a fair remuneration to either the transporter, the refiner, or the merchant.

Unless the producers will co-operate with us, first, by limiting the production or the capacity of the markets of the world to absorb petroleum at a good price; and, secondly, by tanking a large part of the production for the next two or three months, that it may be withheld from the market until the present glut is exhausted and production reduced, it will be impossible, I am convinced from recent advices of the state of supply and demand in the principal markets of the world, to keep the price of crude oil up to $3.50, and of refined oil up to twenty-two cents, during the coming summer.

I stated to you in the strongest terms the desire of the South Improvement Company to enter into an arrangement for a series of years with the producers, whereby good prices for crude oil at the wells and fair and reasonable rates of transportation would at all times be assured. The desire still exists. You expressed to me your concurrence in these views, as others among the leading producers whom I have more recently seen have also done.

I then explained to you certain important business which I had postponed to await the organisation of the South Improvement Company. That business I have been engaged upon for the last ten days. As soon as I get through with it, which I hope will be in a few days, I should like to meet a committee of the principal producers to arrange the details of the plan of co-operation of which we spoke. I therefore request you to have such a committee appointed by the meeting noticed for to-morrow on the newspaper slip sent to me, and if possible have a plan prepared by which, among other things, we could extend to you large facilities of tankage and capital to take care of the surplus oil until the present production can be checked.

P. H. Watson.

To F. W. Mitchell,   New York, March 5, 1872.
      Franklin, Pennsylvania.

Just received another batch of newspaper slips giving proceedings of Oil City meeting.

The meeting acted in ignorance and under a radical misconception of the actual facts, and with far more earnestness and zeal than judgment.

If you will take the trouble to appoint a committee of producers to investigate, we will show that the contracts with the railroads are as favourable to the producing as to any other interests; that the much-denounced rebate will enhance the price of oil at the wells, and that our entire plan in operation and effect will promote every legitimate American interest in the oil trade.

You patiently test a well before deciding upon its merits, like rational men. You examine other subjects before acting upon them. Is not this a subject of sufficient importance to be worthy of rational investigation?

P. H. Watson.

To F. W. Mitchell,   New York, March 6, 1872.
      Franklin, Pennsylvania.

Your telegrams received.

My telegrams were not addressed to the mass-meeting, but to you as a friend, as is also this, to be read at your discretion to some of the principal producers attending the meeting, simply to induce them to investigate the subject about which they are excited before acting upon it.

A mass-meeting is not a deliberative body; it always acts under the feeling of impulse or passions, and meets for predetermined purposes, one of which in this case, as appears in the articles of the newspapers calling the meeting, was to denounce and show its scorn for anything and everything connected with the South Improvement Company. Hence it required no prophet to tell beforehand in what spirit my telegrams to you would be listened to. You ask me to go to Franklin to consult my true friends. I will most gladly meet you and your friends at any place favourable to calm investigation and deliberation, and therefore outside of the atmosphere of excitement by which you are surrounded, say at Albany or New York.

I can well understand that, however, the excited people of your region may misjudge, they have no other purpose than to promote the public interest, and knowing that you deservedly enjoy their confidence, I am strongly convinced that a free and frank interchange of views at the conference suggested would result in satisfying you and the people that there exists no cause for regarding us as enemies. I therefore hope you will name an early day for the meeting.

P. H. WATSON.

Mr. Gilfillan.

I would like to suggest a question that would throw a little light upon this subject, and which I know Mr. Watson will be entirely satisfied to answer. I wish the chairman would ask if the objects of the South Improvement Company, in connection with railroads, were presented to the public through any statement in writing or by telegraph to the public, explaining the objects.

The Chairman.—I am coming to that, but first I want to know of the witness, whether he received any replies to these despatches?

A. Yes, sir, to one of them.

Q. Have you a copy of that?

A. I have not, but I have stated the purport of the answer. To the first I did not receive any answer; there was not time to receive any, and I did not expect it. I sent the second shortly after, and the answer was to the first and second together. To the third I received no telegraphic answer.

Q. You say you have no copy of these answers you received?

A. I have not. I gave the purport of the answer I received at the last meeting.

Q. Were there any other letters or statements published by your authority to the public or to parties in interest among the producers?

A. These were not published by my authority.

Q. Was there any other matter published by your authority, giving explanation to the people?

A. I made similar statements to a great many of the producers.

Q. I mean documentary evidence; was there anything published over your signature?

A. Oh, I did not publish any document at all; I did not publish this.

Q. Did you authorise it?

A. I neither published it nor authorised it, because I considered it useless; the people were so excited that they could not be reasoned with at all. Every one who informed me about it said so.

Q. Did you offer to any of the producers, or any parties in interest to show them these contracts?

A. Yes, I wanted that committee appointed for that purpose; I told them so substantially in my despatch.

Q. Did you make the offer otherwise?

A. I told them that I would, if that can be considered as an offer. I said I would, and I should have done it if they had come to meet us; but they were afraid.

[317]

Q. Would you have published it, do you mean?

A. I should have been perfectly willing to publish the contract; I should have been glad to have published everything in connection with the matter.

Q. If you would have been glad to have published it, why did you not? You had the power.

A. I would have been very glad to have done it, with the assent of these men.

Q. With the assent of what men?

A. The producers. I said to some of the producers that if they would go and examine the whole plan, and after they had examined into it they were not satisfied that it was for their interest, I would be perfectly willing to abandon the whole thing. That was the feeling we had in regard to the matter.

Q. What producers did you say that to?

A. Several of them.

Q. Mention their names.

A. Men with whom I had been in correspondence with on this subject, and whose lives and property I believe would not be safe if I were to mention their names, because they have told me so. I have promised not to expose them, and I feel in honour bound not to give their names.

Q. You have so promised in regard to all of them?

A. Most of those with whom I have had correspondence.

Q. Was there any opportunity offered to explain this matter, to show the contracts and let them know what were the objects of your company? Are there no names you can mention in that connection?

A. I shall have to look over the letters in order to see if there are any not marked confidential. I should like to give you the names if I am at liberty to do so.

Mr. Gilfillan.

I should like to make a suggestion which would throw a little light on this subject. If the chairman will allow me, I will ask the witness if he saw the proceedings of the meeting at Franklin, to which he refers, and if so, whether a resolution was not passed at that meeting asking for the production of these contracts that the public might know what the objects of this company were?

A. I have seen no such resolution; I do not think I have seen the published proceedings of that meeting; I only saw such parts as were sent to me in slips. There was certainly no such resolution as that which came to me. Mr. Mitchell telegraphed to me that my telegrams were received with scorn; that they did not want to know anything about the matter.

Q. Do you remember whether, about the first of March, the railroad companies, with which you made these contracts, or some of them, raised their rates of transportation?

A. I think about that time they did.

.   .   .   .   .   .

Q. Was it for a short time raised to that amount, and a printed schedule published?

A. I never saw the published schedule; I understood that through a mistake between William Vanderbilt, vice-president of the New York Central Railroad Company and freight agent of the Lake Shore road, it was supposed by the freight agent of the Lake Shore road that the rate had been raised by an agreement among the railroads to the maximum rates mentioned in their contracts with the South Improvement Company. A day or two after that mistake, being in Mr. Vanderbilt's office, a telegram came in respect to it, and Mr. Vanderbilt at once directed the correction to be made. Mr. Devereux, the general manager of the Lake Shore Railroad, happened to come in at the time, and he also gave directions to the officers of his road to have the correction promptly made.

Q. Were you present?

A. Yes, sir, I was present. When I said "being in Mr. Vanderbilt's office," I meant that I myself was present.

Q. Was the correction made at your instance, or request, or suggestion?

A. It was not.

By Mr. Hambleton.

Q. Why was it made?

A. Because it was a mistake, a misapprehension, a misunderstanding, as I understood. I had not heard anything of it before that moment, and it was accidental, as I said, that I heard it.

By the Chairman.

Q. Then the rates were raised by the freight agents of the roads to correspond with the rates mentioned in these contracts?

A. I do not know the facts any further than having heard it as I have stated.

Q. And you think they were raised to correspond with these contracts by mistake?

A. I stated I so understood at the time.

Q. You stated the circumstances so minutely as to its being a mistake between Mr. Vanderbilt and the Lake Shore agent, that I inferred you knew the facts?

A. I only know it was so represented at the time.

Q. Did you take any part in that conversation by which the error you speak of was corrected?

A. Only in this sense: Mr. Vanderbilt mentioned the fact to me that a mistake of that kind had been made, that he had just received a despatch in relation to it, and he was about to correct it, and he asked me, I think, if I knew whether Mr. Devereux had given any orders respecting the matter. I told him I did not know anything about it.

[319]

Q. If I understand you, the time had not come for raising the freights under these contracts then?

A. I do not know anything about the time; I did not intend to make any such statement.

By Mr. Hambleton.

Q. At that time, as president of the South Improvement Company, was it not the understanding, and was it not your expectation, that the rates would go up at that time as they did go up to the maximum rates named in these contracts?

A. I do not know that as president I had any knowledge of the matter; and as an individual I took no part in the transaction.

Q. The president is an officer supposed to know more about such details than any of the directors or members of the company; and as president of that company I ask you if it was not the general understanding that the rates would go up about that time?

A. I answer distinctly that it was not, and that as president of that company I had nothing to do with the rates then, because the South Improvement Company's contracts had not gone into operation, and neither the South Improvement Company nor any of its officers had any control of the question in any way.

Q. Had not the contracts at that time been signed?

A. The contracts had been signed, but they were held by me personally in escrow and they had not gone into effect.

Q. They had been signed?

A. Yes, but had not gone into effect.

Q. Were not these contracts so signed and held by you as president of the South Improvement Company, and did you not expect that the rates would advance to the maximum named therein at that time?

A. Certainly I did not; and in regard to the premises stated in the first part of your question I do not want to admit the statements you made. I do not suppose the object was to entrap me into an admission of a statement that is not true.

Mr. Hambleton.—I do not wish to entrap you into anything.

Witness.—I say that when you remark that I hold these contracts as president of the South Improvement Company, you mistake; they were not in my hands as president.

Q. I supposed that as president they passed into your hands?

A. They were passed into my hands as a person, and as such, in execution of the trust, I should hold them as much against the South Improvement Company as against anybody else.

Q. You answer my question then that you did not expect them to raise these rates?

A. Certainly I did not; I had no such idea at all.

Q. State how that mistake, or misunderstanding, or error, happened to occur, and what was the cause of it?

A. I really do not know; it was suggested at the time by Mr. Devereux that Mr. Hills, the freight agent of the Lake Shore Railroad, had a son on his death-bed, that he had to leave the office in charge of subordinates, and that he had not his wits about him as usual, because his mind was so pre-occupied with the sickness of his son, who was a favourite son.

Q. If he had not his wits about him, had he the contracts?

A. I do not wish to use that expression in any offensive sense; I mean he had not the full use of his mind. I do not know whether he had the contracts or not. I think it is probable from the conversation there that all the freight agents had the rates mentioned in these contracts; I have no doubt that the officers of the roads had consulted him; indeed some of them stated that they had been consulted, and that the freight agents knew what rates were provided for in these contracts.

.   .   .   .

Q. I want an answer to my question. By your contracts with the railroad companies you were to purchase all the refineries in the main cities of this country. You had it in your power to furnish more transportation than anybody else?

A. The refineries were not purchased; they have not been purchased.

Q. Was not that contemplated?

A. The company contemplated purchasing if it had gone into operation.

Q. I am getting at the point now; if your scheme had been successful do you suppose anybody in the world could have furnished an equal amount of transportation with your company?

A. If our plan had been carried out it included everybody; there would have been nobody left, and no hostile interest.

Q. You would have had the matter perfectly under your control?

A. Yes, because there would have been nobody left.

Q. Then I am correct in saying that nobody else could have shipped oil under any circumstances, because you were to have an additional rebate in case any rebate was allowed to any other person?

A. But if all interest was drawn into the plan, there would have been no hostile party and no injustice done to anybody.

Q. That is a different matter; now we agree that your advantages of rebate from the leading roads gave you the power of paying larger prices to the oil producers than anybody else?

A. It was expected that these rebates would enable the refiners and producers to maintain a fair price for crude oil at the wells.

Q. Will you answer my question? Could you not have purchased oil and shipped it with these rebates, on terms that nobody else could compete with?

A. If everything had been successful, if the South Improvement Company had

[321]

gone into successful operation, combining all these various interests, of course we could have paid a higher price than anybody else.

Q. Do you not see then that you had the producers of the Oil Regions absolutely in your control?

A. No, sir.

Mr. Sheldon.—I do.

Witness.—I do not, and will tell you why; you asked me a question that is a good deal like attempting to make the Bible prove that it says itself "that there is no God."

The Chairman.—All our time is being expended in this way. Will you answer the direct question put to you?

Witness.—I want to answer it truly. It is an essential part of this contract that the producers should be joined in it; therefore it was not hostile to the producers in any of its intents or purposes; it never would have gone into effect unless the producers had joined.

By Mr. Sheldon.

Q. That may be the fact, but if the producers had refused to join, could you not have forced them into the arrangement on your own terms?

A. No, sir; because the South Improvement Company had no contract.

Q. You have a contract?

A. No, sir; it has no contract.

Q. Did it never have?

A. No, sir; they are placed in escrow with me. It has never had any, that is, there is not to-day and has not at any time been a contract in existence, in activity, or in force between the railroads and the South Improvement Company.

By Mr. Hambleton.

Q. Is not that entirely due to the excitement produced in consequence of the contracts having been entered into?

A. If the purchasers had entered into the contract which was contemplated by the South Improvement Company, it would have been entirely satisfactory to all parties, and both contracts would have gone into operation.

Q. And if a party of the producers had joined, you could have forced the balance to have gone into the arrangement?

A. Two-thirds were required.

Q. You could have forced the balance to have gone in?

A. The majority rules in most kinds of business; unless two-thirds had joined, no arrangement would have been made.

Q. Let us see whether you have not power to force the producers; by your contract with the railroads you had the advantage of forty cents a barrel to Cleveland and Pittsburg, and $1.06 to New York, Philadelphia, Baltimore or Boston on crude petroleum; while on refined petroleum you had the advantage to these cities of fifty cents a barrel, and from any other point to New York, Philadelphia, Baltimore and Boston of thirty-two cents a barrel; it seems to me at that advantage you could have compelled the producers to do exactly what you wanted them to do?

A. The South Improvement Company never could have had that advantage, because the condition on which the main contract with the railroads was to be enforced was that the producers should join with them and participate in the benefits.

Q. Is that embodied in the different contracts?

A. The condition is not embodied upon the face of the contract; it is a condition upon which I held the contracts.

Q. Now Mr. Watson, as a lawyer, if you are such, are verbal conditions made with a third party to change the terms of a written contract executed in all respects?

A. Let me give you an illustration within my experience that is exactly parallel to this: I had a note executed, sealed, and complete in every way, put into my possession to be delivered upon the production of a deed.

The Chairman.—Wait a moment, there must be some kind of order in this proceeding. I wish you to answer the question which has been asked you, whether as a lawyer the conditions stated would change the terms of a written contract. If you are able to give an answer to that legal question you may do so.

Witness.—Let me hear the question and I will endeavour to answer it fully, if you will allow me to answer it in my own way.

By Mr. Sheldon.

Q. The question is, whether a verbal understanding to be performed by other parties not embraced in the written contract can be made effective to modify the terms of that contract as between the parties to it.

A. An agreement between the parties to a contract, whether verbal or written, fixing the terms upon which the contract shall go into effect, is perfectly competent and would be binding.

Q. That is your opinion as a lawyer?

A. That is my opinion.

Q. Now, sir, these contracts contemplated a considerable increase in the freight charges, both upon crude and refined petroleum?

A. They contemplate an increase almost up to the price for coal and lumber, as they are ordinarily carried, amounting to about $1\frac{1}{2}$ cents a pound.

Q. Did it contemplate an increase upon both crude petroleum and refined oil?

A. Certainly; the railroads had been carrying these articles at a loss of nearly a million dollars; they carried for less than cost, and one object of these contracts was to increase the price of freight to the railroads.

The Chairman.—Let me suggest the propriety of first answering the question and then giving your explanation. That is the regular course, and I am sorry to say that during your whole examination there has not been a direct answer given to a question.

Witness.—Well, sir, where a question is such that it would give a false impression unless answered fully and fairly, I do not want to convey that false impression by my testimony.

Mr. Sheldon.

Q. Very well, I am satisfied with your explanation; now could not these railroad companies have raised the price of freight without the intervention of the South Improvement Company?

A. There were a good many difficulties in the way.

Q. Could they not have done it, and had they not the power to do it?

A. The laws of the State of New York forbid the Erie and New York Central Railroads from combining to raise the rates of freight; whether they could have done it I do not know. They tried very hard to agree to raise the freights but did not succeed.

Q. If that is the law of New York, is there an exception to that law so that they could combine with the South Improvement Company?

A. I think it was the opinion of lawyers that this arrangement was perfectly legal and proper; they could not combine, but they could make an independent agreement.

Q. They could raise the rates in your behalf, but they could not in the behalf of anybody else?

A. Not in behalf of anybody, but they could make this transaction. For two or three years they had been cutting under for the purpose of drawing the business away from each other.

Q. What effect would this increase of freight have upon the consumers of oil?

A. I think it would not be to the prejudice of the consumers in this country at all.

Q. Would it not have increased the price?

A. I think it would not have increased the price to the retail consumers in this country. If there had been no countervailing advantage to the retail consumers, of course it would have increased the price.

Q. You mean to say that there was such a margin upon the traffic of oil that to increase the freight charges fifty or 100 per cent. would not affect the retail price?

A. No, sir; I do not mean to say that is the reason.

Q. Is that not the effect of your answer?

A. No, sir, I think not. My explanation of it is this: that the oil trade, unless it is steadied by some artificial process, is subject to violent and rapid fluctuation. The retailers are very quick to note a rise in price, as I explained the other day, but very slow to notice a fall, so that the average price of a retail purchaser is very much above the average wholesale price. Now it was expeetcd that the price under this arrangement would be a steady price, and that with a steady, regular price it would not cause the retailer to raise the price at which he sold at all.

Q. Do you know what profit is made on a barrel of oil sold by retailers to consumers in Northern Ohio?

A. It varies.

Q. Does it ever reach over $1.75 a barrel?

A. I can answer your question with a little calculation. (After computation.) I have known it to be sold at as low a profit as forty cents a barrel. About six or eight cents a gallon is a fair profit.

Q. We gentlemen are supposed to be acting for the public good; will you tell us what public interest you are advancing, or thought you were advancing in making the arrangements that are foreshadowed in these contracts?

A. We were advancing the interests of the railroads, the transporting interest, the interest of the producers, those who mine oil, the interest of the refiners, those who manufacture it, and the interests of the American trade and business generally, for five-sixths of the oil produced is exported, and an increase in the price of crude oil at the mines is essential to the payment of a fair business profit to the refiners; it is essential to the payment of a fair rate of transportation, because without a higher price of transportation more profit to the refiners could not be paid long and allow the producer pay for his labour at the average price of oil last year.

Q. Do you not think the interests of trade in this country are better promoted by leaving everybody to attend to their own matters and protect their own rights rather than by forming a combination as you did?

A. It is essential in many cases beyond individual means to form combinations. Railroads cannot be built without the co-operation of a great many individuals. There are a great many other operations that cannot be managed successfully without co-operation, and this is one of them.

Q. Did the producers ask you to go into this operation?

A. The most intelligent producers did, and to-day, my judgment is, that they are all satisfied that something of that kind is necessary for the protection of American industry.

Q. Did the consumers ask you to go into it?

A. Not any considerable number of consumers; we ourselves are all consumers. The body of them did not.

Q. How much money would the railroad companies have made under these contracts if they had shipped oil at these advanced rates?

A. They would have made about the same profits on that business that they do on coal and lumber, even if the maximum rates had been paid without any rebate; not so much if the net rates only had been charged.

By the Chairman.

Q. State whether in your judgment it was necessary, in order to make provision for these people for the South Improvement Company to receive this million dollars a year for the benefit of American interest, as you have suggested.

A. There was no such provision made, as I understand it.

Q. The testimony is that about six million barrels a year are shipped; the provisions of this contract are that a rebate to that company, supposing the maximum to have been charged, should be over a dollar a barrel.

A. No such thing as charging maximum rates was ever contemplated. The contract on its face says it is a cardinal principle that the gross rates shall be kept as near the net rates as possible.

Q. Suppose it had been kept at the gross rates, your company would then have received over six million?

A. That would be altogether different from the principles on which the contract was based.

Q. If the gross rates which the contract allows had been paid, however, the South Improvement Company would have received a rebate of over six million dollars?

A. Certainly, supposing such an absurdity.

Q. Why did you put such an absurdity in the contract?

A. It is not in the contract, as I stated.

By Mr. Hambleton.

Q. It is the contract as a maximum?

A. But it is also expressly stated that the rates shall be kept as near to net rates as possible.

NUMBER 13 (See page 93)

CONTRACT OF MARCH 25, 1872

[From "A History of the Rise and Fall of the South Improvement Company," pages 27–28.]

I. That all arrangements for the transportation of oil after this date shall be upon a basis of perfect equality to all shippers, producers and refiners, and that no rebates, drawbacks, or other arrangements of any character, shall be made or allowed that will give any party the slightest difference in rates or discrimination of any character whatever.

II. That the present rates from Oil City, Union, Corry, Irvineton, Pittsburg, Cleveland and other competing points, shall be and remain in full force at following rates:

ON REFINED OIL, BENZINE, ETC.

	Per barrel
From Oil City, Union, Corry and Irvineton to Boston	$1.65
From Oil City, Union, Corry and Irvineton to New York	1.50
From Oil City, Union, Corry and Irvineton to Philadelphia	1.35
From Oil City, Union, Corry and Irvineton to Baltimore	1.35
From Cleveland to Boston	1.65
From Cleveland to New York	1.50
From Cleveland to Philadelphia	1.35
From Cleveland to Baltimore	1.35
From Pittsburg to New York	1.50
From Pittsburg to Philadelphia	1.35
From Pittsburg to Baltimore	1.35

ON CRUDE OIL

From Oil City, Union, Corry and Irvineton to Boston	$1.50
From Oil City, Union, Corry and Irvineton to New York	1.35
From Oil City, Union, Corry and Irvineton to Philadelphia	1.20
From Oil City, Union, Corry and Irvineton to Baltimore	1.20
From Oil City, Union, Corry and Irvineton to Cleveland	.50
From Oil City, Union, Corry and Irvineton to Pittsburg	.50

And said rates shall not be liable to any change either for increase or decrease without first giving to William Hasson, president of the Producers' Union at Oil City, at least ninety days' notice in writing of such contemplated change.

III. In the distribution of cars for shipments, it shall be done without discrimination.

IV. On the basis as hereinbefore stated, the parties respectively agree to carry out the arrangements in good faith and work for the mutual interests of each other.

In witness whereof the parties have hereunto affixed their signatures, this twenty-fifth day of March, A.D. 1872:

For the Lake Shore and Michigan Southern Railroad Company: H. F. CLARK, *President*.

For the Erie Railway Company: O. H. P. ARCHER, *Vice-President*.

For the New York Central and Hudson River Railroad Company: WILLIAM H. VANDERBILT, *Vice-President*.

For the Atlantic and Great Western Railroad Company: GEORGE B. McCLELLAN, *President*.

For the Pennsylvania Railroad Company: THOMAS A. SCOTT, *Vice-President*.

On behalf of the Producers and Refiners: G. SHAMBURG, E. G. PATTERSON, WILLIAM HASSON, HENRY BYROM, WILLIAM PARKER, JOHN J. FISHER, *Oil Creek Producers and Refiners*.

J. J. VANDERGRIFT, A. P. BENNETT, WILLIAM M. IRISH, WILLIAM T. SCHEIDE, *Oil City Producers and Refiners*.

HENRY H. ROGERS, F. C. FLEMING, JOSIAH LOMBARD, JR., *New York Refiners*.

B. VAUGHAN, *Boston Refiners*.

NUMBER 14 (See page 100)

TESTIMONY OF HENRY M. FLAGLER

[Before a committee appointed by the Legislature of Ohio, March, 1879.]

Henry M. Flagler; residence, Cleveland, Ohio; occupation, secretary Standard Oil Company; sworn and examined.

By Mr. Norton.

Q. Mr. Flagler, I suppose you understand that this investigation is brought under what is known as House Resolution Number 162?

A. I understand that it is.

Q. How long have you been secretary of the Standard Oil Company?

A. Since its organisation, some time in January, 1870.

Q. Are the articles manufactured or the oil refined by your company shipped over the line of any railroad in the State of Ohio, and if so, state whether or not any rate of freight is contracted for by you or whether your company pays the freight?

A. To the first question, yes, sir; more or less of the product of our refineries is shipped over the railroads of the state. As a rule all of the freight contracts have been made by me.

Q. Please state as near as you can what proportion of your product is shipped out of the state?

A. Well, I should say from sixty-five to seventy per cent.

Q. Now, has your corporation any contracts, written or verbal, with any of the railroads of the State of Ohio for carrying your freight?

A. Yes, sir.

Q. You may state whether these contracts are written or verbal.

A. They are written.

Q. Have you heretofore, prior to this time, any contracts written or verbal?

A. We have.

Q. You may state, Mr. Flagler, whether by virtue of these contracts it has been agreed or allowed by the railroad companies to pay you any drawbacks or rebates on freights.

A. No, sir, it has not.

Q. You may state whether or not you are allowed special rates, or what is known as special privileges.

[329]

A. I can't answer that question from the fact that I do not know what other people get, so I do not know whether they are special rates or general.

Q. I believe, Mr. Flagler, that in your subpœna it was requested of you that if any such contracts were in existence relative to freight matters, you would bring them before the committee. Did you do so?

A. I have never seen the subpœna, so I do not know what the demand was. I have, however, contracts made with our company as far back as the first one ever made.

Q. Can you produce these contracts before this committee?

A. Yes, sir, I can; I am willing to do so, provided they may be used by the committee—if it is proper to ask, to be used in the nature of a confidential communication. None of these contracts provides for any discrimination whatever, but they may contain some business secret of the Standard Oil Company, whose interests I am bound to protect. I do not see how the submission of those contracts as evidence in this case will do other than bear out the statement I have made under oath. I do not see how they will do anything more than sustain the statements I have made. I would be very glad to have our company set right before the public in these matters, but I do not care enough about it, however, to have our business contracts made public. I should be very glad to submit them to you under such circumstances.

Q. Mr. Flagler, do you know anything about the rates of freight from the Southern portions of the state, well, say from Marietta and from Wheeling to the City of Columbus?

A. I do not.

Q. Did you have anything to do, or has the Standard Oil Company anything to do with the making of the rates of freight for the company known as the Camden Consolidated?

A. None whatever.

Q. Have you anything to do with the making of the rate, or the arranging of the freights for the company known as the Marietta Oil Refining Company?

A. None whatever.

Q. Testimony introduced here shows, I think, Mr. Flagler, that about one year ago the rates of freight were raised nearly one-half from the points I have mentioned and from Parkersburg and other places to points in this direction. Had the Standard Oil Company any understanding by and between the railroad companies in regard to this rise in the rates of freight?

A. I should say, to my own knowledge, positively no; I never heard of it before. I do not know what the rates were and I did not know that the raise had been made.

Q. Do you in your capacity, or does the Standard Oil Company through its agents, control the rates of freight or make the rates of any of the oil companies in Cleveland, outside of your own corporation?

A. No, sir.

Q. Mr. Flagler, what is your rate of freight from the seaboard, or to the seaboard from Cleveland?

A. At the present time?

Q. Yes, sir, at the present time.

A. Do you mean per carload or by the barrel?

Q. Well, we'll put it by the barrel, as there is some testimony before the committee relating to that.

A. I do not know that I could answer the question and I do not know but that I would be betraying the business interests of other people. The custom for several years, in fact, for more than five years, has been that the rates of freight on shipments to the seaboard and export oil have been made by what is called trunk lines, the New York Central, the Erie, now New York, Lake Erie and Western, the Pennsylvania, and Baltimore and Ohio. The general freight agents are the officers who make those rates, and their Western connections share in them. I do not know how the freight which is paid for services rendered is divided between their Western connections, having no means of knowing that at all. We do not make any contracts with the Lake Shore for the rates of freight, and the same is equally true of the Atlantic and Great Western. These are the only two roads we ever ship by—I may be wrong; we ship some by way of Pittsburg, over the Cleveland and Pittsburg or over the Baltimore and Ohio.

Q. Do you know what the open rate, the published rate is to the seaboard by the barrel?

A. To Boston and New York, \$1.54½; to Philadelphia and Baltimore, \$1.29½.

Q. Now, Mr. Flagler, you have used your pencil to arrive at that conclusion, why was it necessary to figure out that matter if there is a published rate?

A. Simply because I do not keep that thing in my mind and had to call upon my memory for the way the thing is got at. I got at that by deducting what is called the crude rebate. Nobody pays the crude rebate which is 45½ cents. Whether that form is kept up by the railroad companies I do not know, but my impression is it is not.

Q. It is a fact, isn't it, that you do get a lower rate and pay less freight than the published rate? I believe it is in evidence that the open rate of freight to the seaboard will average about \$1.65.

A. I have never seen the freight tariff, if you mean that which is known as the schedule rate published for the public. I have not seen anything of the kind and do not know anything about it.

Q. What inducement does your company offer to the railroads or what propositions are made by the railroads to your company? Now, I refer to the testimony given by Mr. Hills in regard to the carrying of oils, etc., what inducements do the railroad companies give whereby they lower your rate of freight?

A. They do not give us lower rates of freight for any consideration of that kind.

They pay us for the use of our property, if we furnish them with terminal facilities, cars in which to haul the goods, they pay us a compensation for the use of the property. Perhaps I can give it so you can understand it; we keep a separate account with each refinery and if we spend $50,000, or $100,000 to create what we term terminal facilities, warehouses, loading places, etc., we make an arrangement whereby they pay us a fair compensation for the property that is created by our money. That consideration is credited to that investment and has nothing whatever to do with the freight. The refinery making the oil is charged with the rate of freight just as anybody else pays, and the compensation for the use of tank cars and terminal facilities at the shipping and receiving ends of the line is given for the use of these ends. I will say that in the contracts we have made, the railroad companies have expressly reserved the right to give to other parties the same privileges if they furnish the same conveniences.

Q. Does the Standard Oil Company own and control the Camden Consolidated Company at Parkersburg?

A. Well, I would like to ask a question in reply, and that is, whether that question and answer comes within the scope of this resolution?

Q. I will give you my reason for asking the question. It has been charged here by witnesses that there is a collusion by and between the railroads in the Southern part of the state and the Camden Consolidated Oil Company or the Standard Oil Company, as they term it, for discriminations in the rates of freight. Now, to find out whether or not there is anything for which to blame the Standard Oil Company, I ask this question.

A. Well, it is a business secret of our company, but considering the circumstance, I will answer the question. The Standard Oil Company doesn't own or control the Camden Oil Company, and I would say to every man explicitly and fully that the Standard Oil Company doesn't own a share of stock in the Camden Consolidated Company. I say this so I may be understood and I hope I have done so. I do not own a share in it myself.

Q. Coming back to this question of the contracts, have you any of the written contracts that have been or are now in force, that you can give this committee; contracts between the railroad companies traversing this state and your company?

A. Yes, sir. (Contracts produced.) The price for the shipment of oil per barrel as given in the first contract for the year 1870 was as follows: From the first of February to the first of June, 1870, $1.40; from the first of June to the first of November, 1870, $1.20; this was during the season of navigation. From the first of November until the expiration of the contract, April 1, $1.60.

Q. Is there a line or clause in that contract whereby there is an agreement for rebates or drawbacks?

A. None whatever.

Second contract read: In this contract the rates were as follows: From the first

[332]

of April until the middle of November, 1872, about seven months, $1.25. For the remainder of November, December, January, February and March of 1873, $1.40. These were rates per barrel.

Q. Were there no rebates, drawbacks, or special privileges given outside of what is written in the contract?

A. None whatever. (Third contract introduced.)

Mr. Flagler: I want to say something of this matter and I want to tell the whole truth. Our business was at the time about 4,000 barrels a day and we had contracted this oil for delivery at once, and we had to pay from $50 to $150 gold per day if we kept it an hour longer than the time specified in the contract, so it was very important for us that the railroads put these on board as rapidly as possible.

Q. Mr. Flagler, from the reading of that contract I see that you might, instead of being benefited, sustain damages by the failure on the part of the railroad company to get your oil in there. Did you ever have to pay any demurrage to them?

A. Yes, sir, we had to pay some years as high as $30,000.

Q. Have you ever received any benefits by reason of these contracts that any other shipper might not have received?

A. No, sir. Not in the slightest. All the way through these contracts you will observe that we have undertaken those risks which the law imposes on the common carrier and which no railroad can divest itself of except by written agreement. The handling of these quantities of oil was a very serious matter; there was a constant tendency on the part of the railroad companies to put cars used in this trade to some other purpose, whenever it would pay them better. They used a rack car, such as they could carry cattle in and we have had a great deal of trouble with these roads in the use of those cars, because if they could get cattle to haul from Chicago to St. Louis for something more than they were getting from us they would do it. I want to say what the facts are under the contract just read. You will remember that during seven months of the year we were to give them 4,000 barrels of oil per day or 100,000 barrels a month, and the smallest of the shipments in those months was 108,000. We gave them during the rest of the time more oil and paid them the contract on it when we could have shipped by canal for forty cents less. On the first day of December, a competing line of railway lowered the rate to $1.05 per barrel. I went to Mr. Vanderbilt and told him that the rate should be maintained at the agreed price or else we would not have made the contract with him. I said to Mr. Vanderbilt that if he insisted in the fulfillment of the contract basis and exacted the payment of the contract price, it would result in our being compelled to close our refineries, for we could not afford to pay $1.25, when other people were only paying $1.05. I called his attention to the fact that during the season of canal navigation we had given the maximum shipments of oil, 180,000 barrels a month, and some in excess of it, and paid $1.25. I said, if you will reduce these rates to the rate made by the Pennsylvania Company, in my judgment thirty days will not elapse before they will be willing to restore their rates, and all we ask is to be put on a parity with other shippers. After a moment's hesitation he asked if I thought he ought to stand all of this twenty cents. I told him if he should stand any part of it he should stand it all. I said, it is a transportation fight and not a fight of the manufacturers. When it comes to competition of the manufacturers we would take care of ourselves. I said that we would not have made this contract except on their assurance that the contract price of $1.25 was to be maintained. He said: "I will make your rate $1.05," and this was after we had done more than we had agreed to do under the contract. The next day we sold between 50,000 and 60,000 on the basis of $1.05 per barrel. Mr. Vanderbilt allowed that rate of payment for one month and then said he would exact the contract price, $1.25. I said all right, and we shall ship just the amount of oil we are compelled to ship to fulfill our contract and then we shall stop. We paid him $1.25 for all over the month and then we did not run a barrel of oil from the City of Cleveland more than that until the expiration of this contract for three months. That is the good that the contract worked on us. You might consider it a baby act to plead the equities of the case, but we could not place our oil on the market and compete with other refineries.

(Fourth contract introduced.)

Q. This is the only contract you have now in existence whereby you carry your freight?

A. Yes, sir.

Q. Do you know anything of the suits brought by Teagle and Company against the Lake Shore road for discriminations in freight?

A. Nothing whatever.

Q. Have you had since the organisation of your company any understanding outside of these contracts whereby discriminations are made in favour of your company as against any of the smaller refineries of the state?

A. No, sir.

Q. Has your company or corporation in conjunction with the railroads ever operated so to "squeeze out" as they term it, or injure any other refining company of the state, outside of the Standard Oil Company?

A. No, sir, never. I would like to enlarge upon that question. I suppose it would be fair to the mind of every member of this committee present. A very large business with other mechanical contrivances and an experience which grows up with and comes along with business and always doing a very large business, in the nature and order of things should make its presence felt by the parties doing a comparatively small business. In 1873 and 1874, when we stipulated for those 4,000 per day, if anybody has followed the progress of the Standard Oil Company they would know and I feel justified in saying that we have done a very large business, and aimed to do it with economy and give the purchaser the very best oil manufactured, consistent with a good and safe kind of oil—to manufacture at one point under the eye of one man. With an aggregation of capital and a business experience, and hold upon the channels of trade such as we have, it is idle to say that the small manufacturer can compete with us, and, although it is an offensive term, "squeezing out," yet it has never been done by the conjunction of any railroads with us or by the carrying out of freights.

NUMBER 15 (See page 106)

THE PITTSBURG PLAN

[From the Oil City Derrick, May 17, 1872.]

1. Refiners to lease to the company for five years their superstructure with sufficient real estate to carry on the business of the works.

2. That the rental be eight per cent. per annum on the appraised value of the super-structure, and the company to assume all risks and pay all ordinary taxes.

3. Lessors to pay into the treasury of the company for a working capital one-half of the appraised value of the superstructure in cash or the equivalent in refiner's stock.

4. Said lessors to receive for money paid in as above the bonds of the company, in amount equal to cash paid in, and stocks of the company for an equal amount; said bonds payable in five years or at the option of the company after one year, said bonds to be denominational coupon bonds to bear interest at the rate of eight per cent. per annum, payable semi-annually.

5. The company shall not pay annually more than ten per cent. on the stock as dividends until the said bonds are redeemed.

6. After the bonds are paid, then the company shall have the right and shall be obliged to purchase all said superstructure at the full appraised value first made, and shall give in exchange for the same stock of the company for the full amount.

7. Each district shall appoint a local committee of three persons to make appraisals, and when any appraisements are being made, the chairman of each local committee shall be required to be present to take part in the appraisement.

There shall be a board of appeal which shall be composed of the chairman of each local committee. All presidents of the company shall be presidents ex officio of the board.

The committee shall place a cash valuation on the superstructure and shall be instructed as to the manner in which the valuation shall be obtained.

NUMBER 16 (See page 117)

"THE AGENCY"

[From the Oil City Derrick.]

I. There shall be established, under the auspices of the Council of the Petroleum Producers' Association of Pennsylvania, an organisation under sanction of the laws of Pennsylvania, which shall be known as "THE PETROLEUM PRODUCERS' AGENCY."

II. The capital stock shall be not less than one million dollars, and shall be divided into shares of one hundred dollars each, which shall be subscribed only by members of the Petroleum Producers' Association, or by such other persons as may be approved by the Council.

III. No transfers of the shares of the capital stock shall be made on the books of the Agency, except upon such conditions as the directors may prescribe, subject to the approval of the Council.

IV. The business of the Agency shall be managed by a board of thirteen directors, who shall be elected annually by the stockholders.

V. There shall be an advisory board to consist of one member elected by each local association and approved by the Council. The members of the advisory board shall be admitted to the meetings of the board of directors and shall be entitled to all the privileges of directors, except that of voting. Any member of the advisory board may be removed for any abuse of his trust, or for official misconduct, by a vote of three-fourths of the Council at a regular meeting.

VI. The local associations may appoint committees to solicit and receive subscriptions to the capital stock; they may also appoint responsible trustees to receive payments on account of such subscriptions, to whom the subscribers shall pay at least ten per cent. upon their subscriptions at the time of subscribing. The committees of the local associations shall advise the president of the Council, from day to day, of the amount of subscriptions received by them, and whenever the sum of at least one million dollars shall have been subscribed in good faith, and approved by the Council, and the organisation of the Agency legally completed, subscribers shall be notified to hold an election of directors. The directors shall, as soon as practicable after their election, proceed to elect a president, secretary and treasurer. The trustees, appointed by the local

[337]

associations to receive subscriptions, shall thereupon be required to pay over to the Agency the amounts received by them on account of subscriptions to the capital stock. The Agency shall not be responsible for any subscriptions paid to the trustees appointed by the local associations until the same shall have been paid over to the Agency or its authorised representatives.

Subscriptions to the capital stock may be received, payable in oil at five dollars per barrel, delivered on the cars or in the tanks of the Agency at any sub-agency on the line of the railways; provided, however, that no certificate of stock shall be issued in any case in which payment is made in pipe-line receipts until the oil shall have actually been received upon the order by the Agency or its agents. But a special guaranty of the order shall be required from the subscriber with an agreement that the stock shall be retained as security for the delivery of the oil on demand, and the demand shall be made within thirty days after the order for the oil is received by the Agency.

VII. Members of the Petroleum Producers' Association shall sell their oil only to the Agency. The Agency shall purchase all the oil offered by members of the Association and shall pay therefor at least five dollars per barrel for oil of standard grade, and for the heavy oil of the fifth district. Payment for oil purchased shall be made as follows: If the market will take the entire supply as fast as offered, the full market price shall be paid in cash on delivery; but if the board of directors, or the Council, shall determine that the oil daily offered to the Agency is in excess of the demand, the Agency shall pay three dollars in cash and give the seller a certificate entitling him to the net proceeds of the oil when sold, less the amount advanced thereon.

VIII. The Agency shall sell no oil for a less price than five dollars in cash, on delivery per barrel without the consent of the Council of the Petroleum Producers' Association.

IX. To the redemption of the certificates, on and after the tenth of the month succeeding that in which they were issued, shall be applied the proceeds of all the oil sold and delivered during that month, less the amount advanced and the amount required to tank the surplus oil. For the unpaid balance of the certificate the holder shall, upon the surrender of the same, be entitled to a tank receipt representing his interest in the amount of surplus oil in store and tankage.

X. The Agency shall be entitled to receive for buying and selling the oil such commissions per barrel as the Council may allow, applicable first to the payment of expenses, second to the payment of dividends on the capital stock, which shall be six per cent. semi-annually, free of taxes.

XI. All the net proceeds of surplus oil sold shall be applied specifically to the redemption of the tank receipts at their value, the surrender of which shall be at the option of the holder.

XII. The Agency shall establish sub-agencies at such points within the oil-producing district for the receipt, storage, and shipment of oil as may be necessary to facilitate the convenient and economical transaction of the business of the region, subject to the approval of the Council.

XIII. The Agency shall provide all storage necessary to hold the oil on sale and the surplus oil in store.

XIV. The price on the cars of oil of the standard grade shall be uniform at all the sub-agencies on the line of the railways within the oil-producing district, provided it be practicable to so arrange with the railroads.

XV. A barrel shall be uniformly forty-two gallons.

XVI. Whenever the production of petroleum shall be permanently in excess of the demand the Council of the Petroleum Producers' Association shall determine at what time the production shall be restrained and shall take such measures as may be practicable, necessary, and lawful to prevent the drilling of oil wells, but it shall confine its orders, so far as practicable to preventing the starting of new wells, allowing those already in process of drilling to be completed.

XVII. Whenever in the opinion of the board of directors it may be advisable they may, subject to the approval of the Council, provide such refining capacity as may be required to maintain the highest price for crude petroleum consistent with the consumptive demand.

XVIII. The Agency shall not at any time sell to, or contract with, or make any arrangement whatever, with any individual, organisation, combination, or association, by which they may have a monopoly, inside rate, advantage or preference over, or to the prejudice of, any present or future competitor for the purchase of the crude oil coming into, or passing through its hands; provided, that nothing in this section shall be so construed as to prevent the Agency, with the sanction of the Council, from making such temporary discrimination as may be necessary for the purpose of protecting or promoting the interests of producers by securing higher prices for crude oil, increased consumption of refined oil, or decreased margins between the price of crude and refined oil.

XIX. The Agency, with the approval of the Council, may take such measures as may be expedient to increase the consumption of petroleum by securing its application to new uses.

XX. The Agency shall publish daily a correct statement showing the amount of oil purchased, the oil sold, and oil placed in store during the day; also showing the points at which the same was done and the amounts at the time in store at the various sub-agencies; also the destination of the oil sold.

XXI. The Agency shall publish tri-monthly, full and complete reports of all its transactions and showing its condition at the date of the report; the correctness of the report shall be verified in such manner as may be prescribed by the Council.

XXII. A committee may be appointed by the board of directors, or by the Council of the Petroleum Producers' Association, at any meeting, for the purpose of investigating the condition and management of the affairs of the Agency; and it shall be the right and duty of such committee, duly appointed, to thoroughly investigate everything affecting the interest of the Agency, to examine its books, accounts and vouchers; its safes, vaults and tanks; and to make a true and faithful report of the condition and management of the affairs of the Agency as they may be found, which report shall be published at the expense of the organisation which appointed the committee. It shall be the duty of the Council to see that such committee is appointed and such examination and report made and published at least once in every year.

XXIII. The Agency shall establish a bureau of statistics and information, which shall carefully collect and publish facts, relating to the business of producing, refining, marketing and the consumption of oil. The rooms of the bureau shall at all times be open to the members of the Petroleum Producers' Association, and the Agency shall hold itself open for daily communications by telegraph with local associations.

NUMBER 17 (See page 123)

CONTRACT BETWEEN PETROLEUM PRODUCERS' ASSOCIATION AND PETROLEUM REFINERS' ASSOCIATION

[From the Oil City Derrick.]

The contract between the producers and refiners read as follows:

Whereas, The necessities of trade call for co-operation between the producers and refiners of oil, for purposes of mutual protection:

Therefore, We, the undersigned, representing the Petroleum Producers' Association and the Petroleum Refiners' Association, hereby enter into the following articles of agreement, which stipulate as follows:

First.—Each of the two associations hereby agrees to appoint a representative committee, which committee shall meet together weekly, or as often as may be necessary, and at such places as they may determine.

It shall be the duty of these committees (so far as in their power lies) to see that the provisions of this agreement are executed in good faith, and to discharge such duties as are devolved upon them by this agreement, and in general (within the limitation of their authority) to act for the mutual advantage of the trade, whose interests it is the purpose of this agreement to secure.

Second.—The Producers' Association shall appoint a comptroller, who shall have the right to examine the books of the Refiners' Association, and its daily reports so far as they relate to the purchase, sale, and shipments of crude and refined oil, and who, together with the auditor of the Refiners' Association, shall make joint reports daily to both associations.

The Refiners' Association shall appoint a comptroller, who shall have the right to examine the books of the Producers' Association and its agencies, and their daily reports, so far as they relate to the purchase, sale, and shipments of crude and refined oil, and who, together with the secretary of the Producers' Association, shall make joint reports daily to both associations of all sales and shipments.

Third.—Each association agrees that it will keep accurate books of account, which shall show all purchases, sales, and shipments of crude and refined oil, which shall also be open at all reasonable hours to the inspection and examination of the authorised agents of each association, as hereinbefore provided.

[341]

Fourth.—The Refiners' Association agrees to admit all existing refiners to membership, and to a participation in the future benefits of the association on equal terms with present members, and the Producers' Association agrees to allow all producers to join its association on the same terms with the present members.

Fifth.—The Producers' Association agrees to sell (through its regular appointed agencies) crude oil exclusively to the Refiners' Association and its members, and the Refiners' Association and its members agree to purchase crude oil exclusively of the Producers' Association or its appointed agents.

Sixth.—The Producers' Association agrees that all producers enjoying the benefits of this contract shall be required to bind themselves to sell their oil exclusively through the Producers' Association.

Seventh.—The Refiners' Association and its members agree that they will not until after sixty (60) days from the date of this contract sell any portion of the crude or refined oil now held by them, except so far as they shall have previously purchased the equivalent of crude oil to take the place of the oil so sold.

They further agree to buy from the Producers' Association daily such quantities of crude oil as the markets of the world may take of them, the same to be determined from time to time by the representative committees herein provided for.

Eighth.—The price of crude oil so purchased and sold to be conditionally five dollars per barrel of forty-two gallons each, at "common points," payment to be made as follows:

When refined oil is sold in New York at twenty-six cents per gallon, no additional amount is to be paid; but for every one cent per gallon of advance in the average price of sales of refined oil in New York, twenty-five cents per barrel shall be added to the price of so much crude oil as shall be the equivalent of refined oil sold at such advance until the price reaches five dollars per barrel. A proportionate addition to the average price of crude oil shall be paid for each fraction of one cent per gallon increase in the average price of sales of refined oil at New York, by members of the Refiners' Association.

The price of refined oil in New York and of crude oil at common points to be adjusted by the representative committee herein provided to be appointed.

Ninth.—The representative committees may at any time, when it may be necessary to do so, reduce the prices of crude and refined oils below the minimum or advance them above the maximum prices above named, the increase and reduction in price and the cash payments on crude oil to be determined by said committees.

Tenth.—Settlements to be made to the end of each calendar month and balances to be paid not later than the fifth of the succeeding month.

Eleventh.—The profits on all crude oil sold for export by members of the Refiners' Association shall be credited to the Producers' Association in the next succeeding regular monthly settlement after delivery of said oil.

Twelfth.—Either association may discontinue this agreement at any time by giving to the president of the other association ten (10) days' notice in writing of its purpose to do so.

Thirteenth.—This agreement to remain in full force and effect for and during the term of five years from this date, unless sooner terminated in the manner provided in section twelve (12) of this agreement.

Fourteenth.—Amendments and alterations may be made at any time by the representative committees, subject to the approval of the respective associations.

In testimony whereof, the Petroleum Producers' Association, by its executive committee, and the Petroleum Refiners' Association, by its president and secretary, have hereunto set their hands this nineteenth day of December, A.D. 1872, in the City of New York.

Petroleum Producers' Association, by C. V. CULVER, A. H. BRONSON, SAMUEL Q. BROWN, WILLIAM PARKER, B. B. CAMPBELL, *Executive Committee.*

Petroleum Refiners' Association, by JOHN D. ROCKEFELLER, *President.*

NUMBER 18 (See page 132)

TESTIMONY OF GEORGE R. BLANCHARD ON REBATES GRANTED BY THE ERIE RAILROAD

[Report of the Special Committee on Railroads, New York Assembly, 1879. Volume III, pages 3393–3395.]

October 1, 1872, when I first became general freight agent of the Erie Railroad, no oil was produced in the Bradford District, and all petroleum then transported by the Erie Railway eastward came from the Atlantic and Great Western Railroad. At that time, Adnah Neyhart, of Tidioute, Pennsylvania, represented by W. T. Scheide, afterwards by H. C. Ohlen at New York, shipped small quantities of refined oil, for which he received a rebate of over $7,000 on his shipments for the prior month, to wit, September, 1872. . . . I looked for the reasons, and found the agreement next prior to that time as to shipments and rates was the one already in evidence between producers, shippers, refiners and railroad companies, dated March 25, 1872; I asked why that contract was not observed, and was then convinced in reply that the agreement of March 25 lasted less than two weeks, and that at that early date the Empire Line was receiving a large drawback or commission from the Pennsylvania Railroad, which was either being shared with its shippers or an additional amount was being allowed to them, besides that which the Empire Line itself received from the Pennsylvania system; and as the Empire Line also owned the Union Pipe Line, its shippers had advantages which our company and its shippers did not even jointly possess. At the close of that calendar year (1872), the entire petroleum traffic for the five months of the administration of President Watson, the former president of the South Improvement Company, to January 1, 1873, was but 265,853 barrels, or but about 53,000 barrels per month; while the Pennsylvania Railroad was carrying about six times as much, or 300,000 barrels per month, and the New York Central was carrying the entire refined oil sent from Cleveland to New York. The representations then made to me also convinced the Atlantic and Great Western Company as to what our rivals were doing, and that railway company and our own decided to continue to pay the twenty-four cents per barrel drawback then being paid on the rate of $1.35 provided by this producers' agreement of March 25, 1872.

It is therefore clear that one of the largest of the shippers, who signed that March agreement, did not feel that it bound him to pay the rates he had agreed to pay, and

[344]

he gave convincing reasons to believe that others, signers and parties to that agreement, did not pay them, and possessed equal or greater advantages by way of rival routes. Early in 1873 Mr. Scheide came to our line with Mr. Neyhart's crude business, under the circumstances Mr. Scheide has stated, but being yet without any shippers of refined oil, and believing that the Empire Line would pay a rebate on refined, as I now know from Mr. Scheide's testimony, they had paid Mr. Scheide on crude, I opened negotiations to increase our traffic, which resulted in an agreement, with the concurrence of the Atlantic and Great Western, as follows:

ERIE RAILWAY COMPANY,
OFFICE OF SECOND VICE-PRESIDENT.

NEW YORK, March 29, 1873.

MEMORANDUM

Between John D. Archbold, Mr. Bennett, and Mr. Porter, and Mr. Osborn, and self. Rate for March, 1873, to be 132½ from Union. Rate thereafter to be 125 from same point as the maximum for 1873. If the common point rate is made from Titusville at any time in 1873, on *bona fide* shipments, Erie and Atlantic and Great Western will make same rate from same date. With this rate the refiners agree to give us their entire product to New York for the year, and the preference always at same rate as actual shipment by other lines.

(Signed) JOHN D. ARCHBOLD.
G. R. BLANCHARD.

This Mr. Bennett was also one of the signers to the agreement of March 25, as a refiner, and from these gentlemen I also learned at that time that this producers' agreement was exploded by the action of the Producers' Union before that time.

Notwithstanding this agreement of March 29, 1873, with its reduced rates, its signers left us in November, 1873, and gave the Empire Line their entire shipments; and we were then left with but one small shipper of refined oil, Mr. G. Heye, whose consignments were small, and to retain even this small business, against similar solicitations by our rivals we were compelled to make his rate $1.10 in November, 1873, instead of $1.50, as provided by this producers' agreement.

These facts effectually refute the testimony of Mr. Patterson that the agreement of March 25 continued for two years, or any other period beyond three weeks, at the rates it stipulated, and show that at least two of its signers did not feel bound to pay the rates it named, and that they and others by other lines endeavoured immediately after it was signed to obtain, and did secure reduced rates, as usual before its execution and peddled their oil among different railroads wherever they could secure an advantage, however small, over each other or the railroads.

NUMBER 19 (See page 133)

TESTIMONY OF W. T. SCHEIDE

[Report of the Special Committee on Railroads, New York Assembly, 1879. Volume III, pages 2774–2777.]

Q. Why were you shipping over the Pennsylvania road and not over the Erie?

A. For the reason that the Pennsylvania was most eligibly situated for our purposes.

Q. How did you come, then, to ship over the Erie at all?

A. We came to ship over the Erie because of what we considered very bad treatment on the part of the Pennsylvania Railroad.

Q. What was that bad treatment that you received at the hands of the Pennsylvania road?

A. It consisted, principally, in a discrimination against us in furnishing us with cars.

Q. They refused you transportation?

A. Yes, sir.

Q. Were they refusing you transportation in the interest of the combination?

A. In the interest of a peculiar idea that they had, that all shippers should be placed upon the same basis.

Q. And in consequence of that peculiar idea, they gave to other shippers transportation and did not give it to you?

A. Yes, sir.

Q. And that was the practical way in which that corporation carried out that idea?

A. Yes, sir; you will allow me to explain, please?

Q. Yes; go on.

A. The oil business differs from other business in this, that it is a daily crop; there is a certain amount of oil produced that has to be shipped every day; the consumption, however, is not equal to the daily production of our trade; the consumption varies and the demand varies; the consequence is that there are seasons of the year when a man engaged in shipping oil ships oil really at a loss because there is no demand for it, and there are other seasons when there is a large profit; now the Pennsylvania Railroad always insisted upon having a large number of shippers; this large number of shippers

[346]

would ship only when there was profit, and when there was no profit somebody else had to ship; we had been their shipper for a number of years.

Q. When you speak of their shipper—their leading shipper, do you mean?

A. Yes, sir; we did their business between Philadelphia and Baltimore and New York.

Q. Were you their evener, so to speak?

A. We did not have any eveners in those days.

Q. Did you practically stand in the position of an evener?

A. No, sir; we were simply their shipper of crude oil.

Q. When you speak of their "shipper," in the singular, do you mean that you were their sole shipper, as you subsequently became on the Erie?

A. I mean we had better rates of freight than anybody else could have obtained over the Pennsylvania Railroad at that time.

Q. And therefore monopolised the business; go on?

A. And the consequence is that in consequence of this change in the demand that when there comes a season that there is a little money in it, the Pennsylvania Railroad would encourage these numerous small shippers who would come in and they would pro-rate cars with them; they would only allow us to put in a requisition for a certain number of cars and they would allow anybody else, an entire stranger, a man who never shipped any before, to put in an equal requisition, and they would pro-rate with him, and the consequence was in the paying business we were out and in the unpaying business we were in.

Q. And you left it?

A. Yes, sir.

Q. Because you could not get rates better than other people?

A. No, sir; because we could not stand it; because we were losing money.

Q. On the same basis that other people were?

A. No, sir; other people were not shipping except when there was a profit.

Q. Why did you ship when there was not a profit?

A. Because that was our business; we were shippers of petroleum.

By the Chairman.

Q. I don't understand why you were obliged to ship at a loss?

A. That is the reason why we left the Pennsylvania Railroad.

Q. I don't understand why you were obliged to ship at a loss?

A. We were in the petroleum business and shippers of petroleum, and we had contracts; in order to keep the cars running it was necessary for us to make a contract for one, two, three, five, or six months ahead.

By Mr. Sterne.

Q. Isn't it true that upon the basis of your having better rates than anybody else, you proceeded to make contracts to extend your business?

A. Yes, sir.

Q. With the Pennsylvania road?

A. Yes, sir.

Q. And that the moment that you were placed in the position of having ——

A. No transportation.

Q. No transportation equal to your expectations, with your special rates?

A. I had to buy oil in New York.

Q. That was the real fact?

A. Yes, sir.

Q. The business was based upon the rate of transportation?

By the Chairman.

Q. Why did you have to buy oil in New York?

A. To fill my contract.

Mr. Sterne.—He had made his contract upon the basis of his special rate.

The Witness.—And there was a certain supply of transportation which was given to me.

By Mr. Sterne.

Q. Practically an exclusive supply of transportation you had at one time over the Pennsylvania road, hadn't you?

A. Yes, sir.

Q. And when they changed their policy in that respect and gave other people transportation, you could not fill the orders upon the basis of which you had made your contracts?

A. You will excuse me; this would seem as though this was a sudden arrangement; it was not; it lasted three or four years.

Q. You had reason to suppose that it would last, had you not?

A. This policy of theirs?

Q. This policy.

A. Yes, sir.

Q. That drove you on the Erie?

A. Yes, sir.

NUMBER 20 (See page 133)

STATEMENT OF AMOUNTS PAID FOR OVERCHARGES AND RE-BATES ON OIL DURING THE YEAR 1873 BY THE NEW YORK, LAKE ERIE AND WESTERN RAILROAD

[Report of the Special Committee on Railroads, New York Assembly, 1879. Volume V, page 275 of Exhibits.]

NAME.	ERIE PRO.
A. Neyhart	$188,127.78
Gust. Heye	7,235.31
J. J. Vandergrift	929.11
Durant and Company	145.95
Dutilk and Company	815.95
S. D. Karns	7,089.69
Standard Oil Company	469.11
H. B. Everest	6.66
Lyman and Williams	13.44
J. H. Willever	32.98
L. Van Duzer	3.50
H. Roach and Son	.29
L. Y. Wiggins and Brother	24.11
P. A. Stebbins, Jr	4.53
C. P. Prince and Company	2.69
E. L. Houghton and Company	45.24
McKirgan and Company	2.70
Marks and Bean	45.82
McManagle and Rogers	18.27
Theodore Merritt	4.56
W. F. Smith	3.86
Vacuum Oil Company	8.80
Vandusen Brothers	38.88
Woodbury, Morse and Company	5.40
Ward, Leonard and Company	88.06
Young and Borden	7.97
Total	$205,170.66

NUMBER 21 (See page 135)

AGREEMENT OF 1874 BETWEEN THE ERIE RAILROAD SYSTEM AND THE STANDARD OIL COMPANY

[Report of the Special Committee on Railroads, New York Assembly, 1879. Volume III, pages 3398–3402.]

AGREEMENT concluded this seventeenth day of April, A.D. 1874, by and between the Erie Railway Company and the Atlantic and Great Western Railroad Company, parties of the first part, and the Standard Oil Company, of Cleveland, Ohio, party of the second part, *witnesseth:*

First.—The parties of the first part (Erie Railway Company and the Atlantic and Great Western Railroad Company) agree to furnish a sufficient number of good and suitable cars for the purpose of transporting petroleum and ,its products from the refineries now owned by the party of the second part (Standard Oil Company), at Cleveland, Ohio, and Oil City, Pennsylvania, and any others they may hereafter control or own, to Weehawken Oil Yards, in New Jersey.

Second.—The parties of the first part agree to transport said products of said refineries, and deliver the same in cars (if destined for the New York market) at and upon the side tracks connected with said Weehawken Oil Yards, in good order and condition, except as provided for in Article Four (4), and do all switching of cars at said oil yards necessary to the prompt and rapid discharge and handling of cars employed in said business. They also agree to haul said cars (whenever practicable) in full trains over their respective roads, with promptness and uniformity of movement, and accept compensation therefor as hereinafter provided.

Third.—Rates of freight on all said products to be made from time to time between J. H. Devereux, president of the Atlantic and Great Western Railroad Company, and the Standard Oil Company; the same to be to the satisfaction of the said J. H. Devereux, president; to be, however, no higher than is paid by the competitors of the said Standard Oil Company, from competing Western refineries to New York by all rail lines—each of said railway companies accepting its *pro rata* proportion of the through rate thus made.

Fourth.—The party of the second part agrees not to ship more than fifty (50) per cent. of the product of its said refineries by any other line or lines Eastward, to be

[350]

shown by monthly statements verified by its president and secretary. It also agrees to assume all risks and losses of its property by fire when in the charge or custody of the parties of the first part, whether said property is being moved in trains or stored, or lying at any station between place of shipment and destination (both included). It further agrees to assume all losses from natural leakage or breakage, except the same is caused by collisions or the wrecking of cars by unavoidable accidents. It also agrees, at its own cost, to safely load at places of shipment all of said products, and unload the same when delivered at the said Weehawken Oil Yards, and furnish said products for shipment with as great regularity as possible.

Fifth.—In the event of unavoidable detention, occasioned by the elements, or by strikes of employees of the parties of the first part, or either of them, whereby said first parties are unable (for the time being) to fulfill their covenants under this agreement, then it shall be the duty of said first parties to immediately notify the second party of such casualty or strikes, and such casualty or strike shall be considered good and sufficient cause for delay in the execution (for the time being) of the provisions of this agreement. And said first parties, and each of them, shall be saved from all obligation for the fulfillment of this agreement during the period of such detention, anything in this contract to the contrary notwithstanding. It shall be the duty of said first parties to proceed forthwith to put themselves in position to resume their obligations under this agreement, giving notice at the earliest possible moment to the second party of their ability to resume.

Sixth.—The Erie Railway Company for itself hereby stipulates and agrees to and with the second party, that on or before the first day of May, A.D. 1874, it will give full and complete possession of the property known as the Weehawken Oil Yards, in New Jersey, together with all buildings, erections, docks and appurtenances thereunto, belonging unto the second party to have and to hold, with all revenues derived therefrom, from and after the said first day of May, A.D. 1874, or until the expiration of this agreement, as otherwise herein provided. The Erie Railway Company further agrees, at its own cost, on or before the first day of May, A.D. 1874, to put said buildings, erections and appurtenances in good repair; after which said second party shall maintain the same in like good order, and to do all dredging required to provide and preserve the requisite depth of water.

Seventh.—In consideration of the possession of said Weehawken Oil Yards, the second party hereby agrees to and with the Erie Railway Company as follows: to wit: To pay weekly to said Erie Railway Company the sum of five (5) cents on each and every barrel (of 45 gallons) of crude oil, and the same sum on each and every barrel (not to exceed 46 to 48 gallons) of the products of petroleum passing through or into the aforesaid yards; the rate of five (5) cents to be absolute on all said refined products, but subject to rateable reductions on crude oil, in case the terminal charges on crude oil are reduced, taking present schedule of rates thereon (adopted November, 1872), a copy whereof is hereto annexed, as the standard; the Erie Railway Company retaining the right to reduce said schedule of rates on crude, to meet competition; the second party further agrees to conduct said warehouse business in the name of the Erie Railway Company, at its own cost and expense, to assume such risks on the oil, while in its possession, as the Erie Railway Company, or the Atlantic and Great Western Railroad Company would be responsible for to forwarders, consignees, or owners after its arrival and delivery in cars at yards; to make the charges uniform to all parties who use the yards, or for whom services are performed therein, and always as low as any other oil yard affording proper facilities for the transfer, storage preparation and shipment of the oil at the terminus of any railway, or other line competing with the Erie Railway, at or adjacent to the port of New York, and generally so to manage the premises as to give all patrons of the road fair and equal facilities for their oil business at uniform cost, to retain and pay the present superintendent and other officers and employees of the yard, so long as their duties are satisfactorily performed, and from time to time to appoint such other officers as shall not be objected to by the Erie Railway Company, to maintain the buildings, erections, and mechanical appliances of the premises in as good order as when possession is given, natural wear and unavoidable (by due diligence) damages from the elements excepted, to make no rules or regulations discriminating against any other shipper or shippers, or receivers. It is understood and agreed that the consent of the Erie Railway Company is to be obtained before any refined or crude oil shall be received at the Weehawken Oil Yards, which arrives from the west *via* any transportation line competing with the Erie Railway.

Eighth.—It is further agreed that the second party shall assume the charge and collection of freights and charges—accounts to be rendered and adjusted, and paid weekly—Erie way-bills to govern quantities received, except when the same are shown to be incorrect, or loss in transit (except from natural leakage) has occurred through fault or neglect of said railway companies, or either of them. Any new fixtures which the party of the second part may add to the property shall be and remain its property, and they may remove the same at their cost, at the expiration of this agreement, unless mutually satisfactory terms of purchase and sale can be agreed to.

Ninth.—This agreement to take effect and be binding upon the parties hereto, on the first day of May, A.D. 1874, and to continue until the first day of May, A.D. 1877, provided, however, that either party may terminate the same upon giving notice in writing to the other party six (6) months in advance of its intention so to terminate; and provided further, that within thirty days after the election of a new board of directors, of either the Erie or Atlantic and Great Western Railway Companies, the second party shall have the right to terminate this agreement, by giving notice in writing to the other party one month in advance of its intention so to terminate, and upon the expiration of either of said periods, this agreement shall be then at an end.

Tenth.—In consideration of the premises, the party of the second part agrees to pay to the Erie Railway Company, weekly, the sums which such weekly settlement shall show to be due to the said first parties, as freight on its property delivered at the Weehawken Oil Yards.

Eleventh.—It is hereby expressly understood and agreed that neither of the said parties of the first part shall be liable for the acts or defaults of the other; and that each shall only be liable for its own acts and defaults, on and over its own line and premises.

In Witness Whereof, the parties hereto have affixed their hands, this twentieth day of April, 1874.

(Signed)   THE ERIE RAILWAY COMPANY,
                  By G. R. BLANCHARD, *Second Vice-President.*

(Signed)   THE ATLANTIC AND GREAT WESTERN RAILROAD COMPANY,
                  By J. H. DEVEREUX, *President.*

(Signed)   STANDARD OIL COMPANY,
                  By WILLIAM ROCKEFELLER, *Vice-President.*

NUMBER 22 (See page 139)

AGREEMENT OF 1874 BETWEEN THE RAILROADS AND PIPE-LINES

[Report of the Special Committee on Railroads, New York Assembly, 1879. Volume III, pages 3431–3437.]

Memorandum of agreement entered into this fourth day of September A.D. 1874, by and between the following parties, viz.:

First.—J. J. Vandergrift, G. V. Forman, and John Pitcairn, Jr., partners themselves, and agreeing that they have authority to represent all other partners in the association trading under the name of the United Pipe Lines, and holding themselves individually responsible to the other parties hereto that they have such authority.

Second.—The Union Pipe Company by Charles P. Hatch, manager.

Third.—The Antwerp Pipe Company and the Oil City Pipe Company, each being corporations under the laws of the State of Pennsylvania.

Fourth.—The American Transfer Company, a corporation under the laws of the State of Pennsylvania.

Fifth.—The Grant Pipe Company, a corporation under the laws of the State of Pennsylvania.

Sixth.—The Karns Pipe Line Company, a corporation under the laws of the State of Pennsylvania.

Seventh.—The Relief Pipe Line Company, a corporation under the laws of the State of Pennsylvania.

Eighth.—The Pennsylvania Transportation Company, a corporation under the laws of the State of Pennsylvania.

Ninth.—J. J. Vandergrift, G. V. Forman, and John Pitcairn, Jr., trading under the name of Vandergrift, Forman and Company, and owning and representing the Milton and Sandy Pipe Lines.

Whereas, The pipe lines owned and controlled by the parties hereto have a joint capacity for transportation more than twice as great as the total volume of petroleum produced in the district traversed by said lines; and whereas, the separate and discordant relations now prevailing among the parties hereto, lead to a needless multiplication of extensions, branches, and other matters involving heavy cost, which

[354]

ultimately becomes in some shape a charge upon the business transported, and also leads to the offering of open or secret inducements of an illegitimate nature, such as rebates, special rates, selling oil for less than its cost and full pipage rates, and in other ways hereby to attract an under share of traffic to the respective lines represented herein; and

Whereas, it is believed to be desirable both for the interests of the parties hereto and those of the public whom they serve, that all needless expenditure and all illegitimate inducements should cease; now,

Therefore, for those purposes and for other valuable considerations mutually moving the parties hereto, they do each respectively agree with each other, as follows:

First.—The parties hereto do not by these presents create in any respect a partnership with each other, but each party is to be wholly and solely responsible for all of its own acts in the conduct of its business for its certificates, receipts, and collection of its charges, its expenses, shortages, maintenance, and management of its property, and of its engagements and obligations of every sort.

Second.—The pipe-lines which are covered by this agreement are those which are or may be owned by any of the parties hereto, and which are situated south of Oil City, and which terminate at any of the following points, viz.: points on the Franklin branch of the Atlantic and Great Western Railway, points on the Jamestown and Franklin branch of the Lake Shore and Michigan Southern Railway, points on the Alleghany Valley, between or at Oil City and Pittsburg, points on the Schenango and Alleghany Railroad and points on the Butler branch railroad, excepting two small pipe lines, one owned by F. Prentice and Company, running from Mount Hope to Foster, and one owned by Vandergrift, Forman and Company, called the Franklin Pipe Line, running from the heavy oil district to Franklin, Pennsylvania.

Third.—Each party hereto shall retain eight (8) cents per each forty-two (42) gallons remaining after deduction of allowances for shortage and sediment, on all of the oil it actually pumps; also, all allowances made it on such oil to meet shrinkage and sediment, and also all of its other receipts of every description, except as stated in the next article.

Fourth.—Each party shall account monthly to the executive committee hereinafter provided for, at the rate of twenty-two (22) cents for each forty-two (42) gallons of petroleum (after deducting shrinkage allowances) received by it for transportation during such months; which twenty-two (22) cents shall be considered by said committee as a common fund to be cleared and divided on the basis hereinafter designated.

Fifth.—The executive committee shall consist of one representative from each of the parties hereto.

Each representative to be appointed by the party he represents to be changeable from time to time by such party, at its pleasure; the said committee shall faithfully execute such provisions of this agreement as are by its terms confided to them.

Their action must, in all cases, be unanimous before it shall be binding upon any party hereto.

They shall keep a record of their proceedings, to which each of the members shall have free access, and whenever desired by any, a full transcript, or any part thereof.

The members of said committee shall, until changed, as hereinbefore provided, be as follows: Charles P. Hatch, representing the Union Pipe Company; A. M. Hughes, representing the Antwerp Pipe Company and the Oil City Pipe Company; D. O'Day, representing the American Transfer Company; R. B. Allen, representing the Grant Pipe Company; S. D. Karns, representing the Karns Pipe Line Company; F. Prentice, representing the Relief Pipe Line Company; H. Harley, representing the Pennsylvania Transportation Company; E. Hopkins, representing the United Pipe Lines, Milton Pipe Line, and the Sandy Pipe Lines.

Sixth.—Each party hereto shall furnish to the executive committee, on or before the fifth of each month, a report of its business for the month next preceding, duly verified by the affidavit of its proper officer or agent; and the amounts found due by the executive committee from any of the parties hereto shall be paid by them through the executive committee to the parties to whom they may be due, on or before the tenth of the month in which the report is made.

Seventh.—The committee shall prescribe the form of said return, and shall act as a clearing house thereof. They shall have power to verify the same by inspection of books and records, and shall make to each party hereto, on or before the tenth day of each month, a full exhibit of the results of the returns and clearings for the next preceding month.

Eighth.—The committee shall prescribe and enforce uniform rates and conditions for the reception, storage, and transportation of oil, including substantially uniform wordings of certificates and gaugers' tickets; uniform conditions for the accepting of tanks owned by other parties; uniform conditions as to responsibility for losses through unavoidable causes, such as lightning; and uniform rates of allowances for shrinkages. Until changed by said committee, the rates for transportation shall be as follows:

For each forty-two gallons remaining after deducting allowance for shrinkage and sediment, viz., from all points which, by any pipe-lines represented herein, which terminate at Oil City or on the various railways as hereinbefore described, thirty (30) cents; excepting, *First*, on oil reached by pipes' terminating on the Alleghany Valley Railroad south of Oil City, and north of Parker City. *Second*, on oil from the west side of the Alleghany River, not pumped from north of Bear Creek. *Third*, on oil pumped from Sheakley to Monterey by the United Lines, and from south of Bear Creek, and north of Sheakley district by the Union and Karns lines, all of which shall be twenty-five (25) cents. But the rates on oil covered by the third exception shall be made thirty (30) cents on or before January 1, 1875. The only remaining exceptions to these rates on such private contracts at different figures, as each party may now have, a list of which together with any special conditions appertaining thereto shall be filed with the executive committee on or before September 1, 1874; no new contracts for transportation or storage or tankage shall be made by any party whatever, except at the regular rates as herein fixed, or as shall be, from time to time, fixed by the executive comıittee. All rates less than thirty (30) cents may be at any time advanced to thirty (30) cents by the party subject thereto.

Ninth.—The committee shall adopt all proper and practicable measures to secure the transportation by each line of a share of the total oil pumped each month by all the lines, equal in percentage to the share of the common fund allotted to each herein, having reference to the facilities of each party for doing the work; they shall assign to each party, and as early in each case as possible, such share of the duty of making extensions and connections with wells as most legitimately appertains to it, or as may be required by the well owner, or by the contracts of each party; but constant reference shall be had to maintaining for each party its share as heretofore described of the total oil to be transported, and to distributing the total cost involved as nearly as practicable in the proportion of the common fund assigned to each, and no other party shall make such improvements except by consent of said committee. The committee shall arrange with a chief gauger and the needful assistants (all of whom shall be under oath to act honestly and impartially), to gauge from time to time all tanks with which the lines of the parties hereto are or may be connected, or car tanks which they may load; and may collect the expense thereof from the parties hereto in proportion to their respective shares in the common fund; and may also assess upon the trade such reasonable charge for car gauging, or may wholly waive such charge as they may deem judicious. The committee shall have general power to inaugurate and carry into effect any other features than those especially named herein which will not be inconsistent with and which will in their judgment more effectually accomplish the purposes and spirit of the agreement.

Tenth.—The division of the common fund shall be as follows:

The United Pipe Lines, twenty-nine and one-half (29½) per cent.

The Union Pipe Company, twenty-five and one-half (25½) per cent.

The Antwerp Pipe Company and Oil City Pipe Company, seven (7) per cent.

The American Transfer Company, seven (7) per cent.

The Grant Pipe Company, seven (7) per cent.

The Karns Pipe Line Company, seven (7) per cent.

The Relief Pipe Line Company, seven (7) per cent.

The Pennsylvania Transportation Company, seven (7) per cent.

The Sandy Pipe Line and Milton Pipe Line, three (3) per cent.

Eleventh.—All parties hereto agree to faithfully carry out the spirit and purposes of this agreement, and to do nothing between the date of its execution and the date of its taking effect, inconsistent therewith, and it is mutually agreed that from the date of its taking effect until it is terminated, any violation thereof by any party will work an injury to the whole interest of not less than ten thousand ($10,000) dollars; and if any such violation shall not be fully rectified by the offending party within thirty (30) days after written notice shall have been given to the said offending party by the executive committee, through its secretary, upon a vote of all of said committee except the representative of the offending party, it is agreed that ten thousand ($10,000) dollars shall be the stipulated and liquidated damages for each and every such violation so unrectified, which damages shall be collected by the executive committee, and shall be divided among the other parties hereto in the same relative proportion as the common fund is divided. This contract shall take effect on the first day of October, A.D. 1874, and shall continue for two (2) years, and shall continue after the expiration of said two (2) years until after three (3) months' written notice shall have been given by either of the parties hereto, to the executive committee, through its secretary, of a wish to have it terminate, at the expiration of whch notice it shall cease and determine.

In Witness Whereof, the parties hereto, by their representatives, have affixed their signatures this fourth day of September, A.D. 1874.

The United Pipe Lines: J. J. VANDERGRIFT, GEORGE V. FORMAN, JOHN PITCAIRN, JR., by GEORGE V. FORMAN, *Attorney for themselves and others.*

The Sandy and Milton Lines: J. J. VANDERGRIFT, GEORGE V. FORMAN, JOHN PITCAIRN, JR., by GEORGE V. FORMAN, *Attorney.*

For the Relief Pipe Line Company: F. PRENTICE, *President.*

For the American Transfer Company: DANIEL O'DAY, *Superintendent.*

For the Union Pipe Line Company: CHARLES P. HATCH, *Manager.*

For the Grant Pipe Company: R. B. ALLEN, *President.*

For the Karns Pipe Line Company: S. D. KARNS, *President.*

For the Antwerp Pipe Company and the Oil City Pipe Company: E. C. BRADLEY, *President.*

For the Pennsylvania Transportation Company: HENRY HARLEY, *President.*

NUMBER 23 (See page 141.)

THE RUTTER CIRCULAR

[Proceedings in Relation to Trusts, House of Representatives, 1888. Report Number 3112, page 363.]

THE NEW YORK CENTRAL AND HUDSON RIVER RAILWAY COMPANY,
GENERAL FREIGHT AGENT'S OFFICE, GRAND CENTRAL DEPOT.

NEW YORK, September 9, 1874.

Dear Sir: Commencing October 1, 1874, the following rates on refined and crude oil shall govern all lines:

The rates on refined oil from all refineries at Cleveland, Titusville and elsewhere in and adjacent to the Oil Region shall be as follows:

PER BARREL.

To Boston	$2.10
Philadelphia	1.85
Baltimore	1.85
New York	2.00

Net rate on Albany fifteen per cent. less, from which shall be refunded the amount paid for the transportation of crude oil by rail from the mouth of the pipes to the said refineries, upon the basis of fourteen barrels of crude oil to the refineries for every ten barrels of refined oil forwarded by rail from them (the refineries) to the Eastern points named.

Settlements of this drawback to be made on the refined oil forwarded during each month.

No rebate on these rates will be paid on oil reaching refineries direct by pipes.

On crude oil the rates from all initial points of rail shipments in the Oil Region shall be as follows:

PER BARREL.

To Boston	$1.75
New York	1.50
Philadelphia	1.50
Baltimore	1.50

Net rate on Albany fifteen per cent. less, from which shall be refunded twenty-two cents per barrel only on oil coming from pipes which maintain the agreed rates of pipage.

[359]

A barrel shall in all cases be computed at forty-five gallons.

You will observe that under this system the rate is even and fair to all parties, preventing one locality taking advantage of its neighbour by reason of some alleged or real facility it may possess.

Oil refiners and shippers have asked the roads from time to time to make all rates even, and they would be satisfied. This scheme does it, and we trust will work satisfactorily to all.

Respectfully yours,

J. H. RUTTER,
General Freight Agent.

NUMBER 24 (See page 148)

STANDARD OIL COMPANY'S APPLICATION FOR INCREASE OF CAPITAL STOCK TO $3,500,000 IN 1875

To the Secretary of the State of Ohio:

The undersigned, being a majority of the board of directors of *THE STANDARD OIL COMPANY OF CLEVELAND, OHIO,* do hereby certify that on the tenth day of March, A.D. 1875, at a special meeting of the stockholders of said company held at its office in Cleveland, Cuyahoga County, Ohio, by a vote then and there taken, all the stockholders of said company being present and voting therefor, it was resolved and agreed by each and all of them, that the capital stock of said company be increased the sum of *One Million Dollars,* thereby making the capital stock of said company *Three Million Five Hundred Thousand Dollars,* which action of the stockholders was as follows, to wit:

Resolved, and it is agreed by each and all of us that the capital stock of this company, viz.: *THE STANDARD OIL COMPANY OF CLEVELAND, OHIO,* be increased to the sum of *Three Million Five Hundred Thousand Dollars,* and it is also agreed and the proper officers of this company are hereby instructed to take the requisite steps to so increase said capital stock.

JOHN D. ROCKEFELLER; S. V. HARKNESS; H. M. FLAGLER, *Trustee;* S. ANDREWS; J. D. ROCKEFELLER, *Agent;* J. D. ROCKEFELLER, *Trustee;* O. H. PAYNE; B. BREWSTER, by J. D. ROCKEFELLER, *his Attorney;* T. P. HANDY, by J. D. ROCKEFELLER, *his Attorney;* O. B. JENNINGS, by J. D. ROCKEFELLER, *his Attorney;* WM. ROCKEFELLER, by J. D. ROCKEFELLER, *his Attorney;* JAS. STANLEY, by O. H. PAYNE, *his Attorney;* A. M. McGREGOR, by J. D. ROCKEFELLER, *his Attorney;* W. C. ANDREWS; A. J. POUCH, by J. D. ROCKEFELLER, *his Attorney;* F. A. ARTER, by J. D. ROCKEFELLER, *his Attorney;* P. H. WATSON, by H. M. FLAGLER, *his Attorney;* J. A. BOSTWICK, by J. D. ROCKEFELLER, *his Attorney;* J. HUNTINGTON, by O. H. PAYNE, *his Attorney;* D. M. HARKNESS, by H. M. FLAGLER, *his Attorney;* JOSIAH MACY, by J. D. ROCKEFELLER, *his Attorney;* W. H. MACY, by J. D. ROCKEFELLER, *his Attorney;* W. G. WARDWELL, by H. M. FLAGLER, *his Attorney;* D. P. EELLS, by J. D. ROCKEFELLER, *his Attorney;* S. F. BARGER, by J. D. ROCKEFELLER, *his Attorney;* W. H. VANDERBILT, by J. D. ROCKEFELLER, *his Attorney;* H. W. PAYNE, by O. H. PAYNE, *his Attorney;*

J. J. VANDERGRIFT, by O. H. PAYNE, *his Attorney;* JOHN PITCAIRN, JR., by O. H. PAYNE, *his Attorney;* L. G. HARKNESS, by H. M. FLAGLER, *his Attorney.*

And afterwards said meeting was duly adjourned.

H. M. FLAGLER,

CLEVELAND, March 10, 1875.   *Secretary.*

And we further certify that the whole amount of such increase of capital stock has been paid to said company in money, that no note, bill, bond, or other security has been taken for the same or any part thereof, and that the credit of the company has not been used directly or indirectly to raise funds to pay the same or any part thereof.

In Witness Whereof, we hereunto set our names at Cleveland, this tenth day of March, A.D. 1875.

JOHN D. ROCKEFELLER,
HENRY M. FLAGLER,
SAMUEL ANDREWS,
OLIVER H. PAYNE,
STEPHEN V. HARKNESS.

NUMBER 25 (See page 148)

HENRY M. FLAGLER'S TESTIMONY ON THE UNION OF THE STANDARD OIL COMPANY WITH OUTSIDE REFINERS IN 1874

[Proceedings in Relation to Trusts, House of Representatives, 1888. Report Number 3112, page 291 and page 770.]

A. . . . The original Standard Oil Company was organised in the early part of 1870. The increased capacity and the acquisition of the Cleveland refineries was, as I remember it, in 1872. It remained at that until 1875 or 1876,* according to the best of my recollection. Then was consummated a negotiation which had been pending for some two years, perhaps, with certain parties in Pittsburg, Philadelphia and New York, by which a value was agreed upon, and their refinery property was purchased and the capital of the company was increased a still further sum of a million, and they were paid for these properties, and money which they contributed, in the stock of the Standard Oil Company of Ohio.

By Mr. Gowen.

Q. When did the Standard Oil Company of Ohio first enter into an alliance with other refineries?

A. If you mean, (by) an alliance, Mr. Gowen, I should say never.

Q. I am only endeavouring to aid your friends in getting at what they want. Here, I notice, they propose to prove by you—I will give it in this way—that on account of the disastrous condition of the refining business, the Standard, on October 15, 1874, entered into an alliance with a number of Pittsburg refineries?

A. That is more correctly stated by saying that the Standard Oil Company *purchased* the refineries owned by the parties in Pittsburg.

Q. Who were they?

A. Lockhart, Frew and Company, I think was the company. Wait a moment. It was the Standard Oil Company of Pittsburg, it being a corporation, and Warden, Frew and Company, of Philadelphia, and, I should say, Charles Pratt and Company, of New York.

Q. Any others?

A. That is all.

* It was 1874.

[363]

Q. All those gentlemen, Warden, Frew and Company, and the Standard Oil Company of Pittsburg, Charles Pratt and Company of New York, are now associated with you as parties interested in the present Oil Trust?

A. They are stockholders. The property formerly owned by them was at that time purchased by the Standard Oil Company.

Q. When you speak of purchasing their interest, you do not exclude them from their interest? They united with you and remained as your associates in the business?

A. If it was not from the fact that ours was a corporation, we might call it a co-partnership.

Q. They becoming interested in yours, and you in theirs?

A. Yes, sir.

Q. And you simply used your name to represent the joint ownership, as it was a corporation?

A. Yes, sir.

NUMBER 26 (See page 153)

GEORGE H. BLANCHARD'S TESTIMONY ON THE BREAKING UP OF THE PIPE POOL OF 1874

[Report of the Special Committee on Railroads, New York Assembly, 1879. Volume III, pages 3445–3447 and 3449–3451.]

The contract with the Standard Company of April 17, 1874, as I have said, contained nothing inconsistent with our obligations to the Pennsylvania and New York Central Railroads, and the New York Central, under their later contract, and our company, convinced the Pennsylvania Railroad of that fact during the discussions both as to rates and each and every other detail agreed to, but President Jewett thought it better to rely upon the arrangements between the railway companies alone, and decided to avail himself of the ninth clause of the agreement with the Standard Oil Company of April 17, 1874, which provided that either party might terminate it by six months' written notice, but that notice might be given by the Standard Company within thirty days after the election of a new board of directors of the Erie or Atlantic and Great Western Company. This trunk line oil pool of October 1 being in operation, President Jewett gave notice of the termination of the Standard agreement of April 1, 1874, on October 31, 1874, which would have terminated in six months. It was the thirty-first of the following May, but an election having in the meantime taken place upon the Atlantic and Great Western Railroad, the Standard Oil Company gave the thirty days' notice it had the right to do on January 13, 1875, which, therefore, terminated the agreement upon February 13, 1875, about three months and a half before President Jewett's notice could, under the contract, take effect.

The trunk line agreement of October 1, 1874, continued in force, and pool settlements were made thereunder for but five months, namely, until the close of February, 1875, during which time the Erie Company paid $31,019.05 and received $6,570.55.

Notice of the abandonment of that contract was given by the Erie Company, April 1, 1875, although no statements or moneys were exchanged for March, and dissatisfaction with its operations had been expressed by us prior to that time, the reasons therefor being as follows:

The higher rates of the pipe pool had stimulated new pipe-lines, and the Hunter and Cummings Line and other small pipes had been completed, or did not maintain the agreed rates of pipage. The Columbia Conduit Company had also been completed to Pittsburg, in the interest of the Baltimore and Ohio Company, and either acting upon the then policy or advice of that company, or with a desire to be bought out, declined to charge equal rates of pipage or agree to any fixed rates, a fact which threatened the diversion of oil largely to Baltimore, the Baltimore and Ohio Railroad not being in the trunk line oil pool of October 1, 1874, and publicly and frequently announcing its endeavour to divert the oil trade to Baltimore.

We also believed that large drawbacks or commissions were paid by the Pennsylvania Railroad to the Empire Line in addition to those provided in our joint pool contract; and our belief has since been confirmed by later knowledge of the fact that the Pennsylvania Railroad paid to the Empire Line about 30 per cent., including the use of cars; and the mileage, being about ten (10) per cent. at current rates of car service, left the commission equal to about 20 per cent., an advantage not possessed by any other shipper or company over any of the northern lines.

It was clear that, as the Empire Line added to its already large resources, not only this commission upon the oil business excepting Pittsburg, but the added profits upon its pipe-lines, that its combined operation and profit united to control an increasing share of the entire trade and put it in strong financial shape for a control which it subsequently entered upon to absorb also a large refining interest.

As the northern trunk lines made no similar arrangements, allowances or commissions to any forwarder or receiver, and derived no profit from any pipe-lines, it was clearly unfair to concede them to the Empire Line, and the agreement which gave it these growing advantages was very properly annulled.

We also desired the actual transportation of the oil rather than to receive money from others, as we had done during the pool, as their increased business might finally result in a demand for larger percentages if the pool continued.

I directed careful examination of our records up to date of the abandonment of this oil pool contract; and upon the authority of General Freight Agent Vilas, state that the net rates charged to the Standard Company during this period to through points were uniform with the rates charged by our lines to other shippers, taking into account, as before stated, the transportation of the crude equivalent to their refineries. . . .
The preliminary discussions and general conclusions relating to those (new) contracts were all with President Jewett, although many of their details were subsequently discussed and suggested by me; and the reasons influencing him to make them have been stated by him in his testimony; I was directed to carry them out, and have from time to time attended meetings at which the rates thereunder were advanced or reduced. I believe those contracts were not concluded until the latter part of April or early in May, and were then dated back to the disruption of the trunk line oil pool, in order to secure our guaranteed proportion of oil shipments from that earlier date and without interruption. The transportation contract continued to guarantee us 50 per cent.

of the business of the Standard Oil Company, which 50 per cent. should not be less than the percentage we had received in the year 1874 of the total arrivals at the seaboard; and at this time, for that reason, the Standard Oil Company had no transportation arrangements with the Pennsylvania Railroad, and this fact and guaranty induced us to disregard the question as to whether or not the Standard Company had similar or other contracts with the New York Central or its connections, our only interest in the question being as to whether rates were equal and if we received our guaranteed share of the oil.

There was no understanding or agreement by the Erie Company to my knowledge that the New York Central Company or Pennsylvania Railroad, or either of them, had or had not similar or other contracts with the Standard Oil Company.

They were shipping by the New York Central route, and we assumed from their large business, terminal arrangements, etc., that some defined understanding probably regulated such large interests, but we were not consulted as to the terms or conditions of its contracts with other companies if it had any, because we relied upon their responsible guaranty to give us our proportion of the total arrivals of oil at the seaboard and at rates equal to those of other companies, as ample protection to our interests.

At the time this transportation contract was made by the Erie Company, other considerations than relief from risks and the equalisation of the arrivals at the seaboard bore upon the contracts for an allowance of 10 per cent. It continued to be our belief, since fully confirmed by Mr. Cassatt's testimony, that other shippers *via* the Empire Line over the Pennsylvania Railroad had at least similar rates and arrangements, to which, on the part of the Erie Company, no objection was offered; it also continued to be the fact that the Empire Line continued to receive in addition to its probable pipe profits, the same or about the same, large commission as before, from the Pennsylvania Railroad, and it was believed by the officers of the Erie in making this contract with the Standard Company that the allowance to it of 10 per cent. was not much more than one-half the allowance then being made by the Pennsylvania Railroad to the Empire Line.

In addition thereto, we secured the actual transportation of our full share of the oil, at the agreed rates, without delays or disputes in adjustments, or the preparation or exchange of the pool statements.

It maintained the business to New York and provided against any increase to our rival railways or ports, no matter how the territory of oil production might shift or vary, and while under the trunk line pool we could not influence the various shippers to send them oil over our railway or to this city, unless their varying and dissimilar interests all agreed (as they did not), and no matter how much one company might be in deficit, the Standard Company is compelled to send it over our line. The loading and unloading, and taking the risks, were also important items to us as has before been detailed, and relieved us from a class of claims we had paid prior to that time.

It was also important to us that by this contract we were explicitly released from large losses when the great fire consumed the Weehawken docks in July, 1874.

The ninth section of the contract has also been of much value to us. In the delivery of oil to vessels or exporters, the Standard Company assumes all the risks and expenses of delays to ships, and their demurrage, even if it be the fault of the railway by non-delivery, and I have known of cases where this amounted to a large sum.

In 1877 when the general and extended railway strikes occurred, this clause also released us beyond doubt from large claims that might otherwise have been urged.

The freight rates provided by the railway pool of October 1, 1874, were not changed until October 1, 1875; and my recollection is that it was not until the discussion upon that change that anything was definitely known by any of the trunk lines of the arrangements of the others with the Standard Oil Company. At that meeting the 10 per cent. reduction to be allowed the Standard was distinctly understood as due upon its shipments *via* all the trunk lines in consideration of the facts stated, and it then first came to my knowledge that Warden, Frew and Company, of Philadelphia, represented the Standard Oil Company, as Charles Pratt and Company represented their crude interests at New York *via* our line.

NUMBER 27 (See page 196)

MR. FLAGLER'S EXPLANATION OF THE COMMISSION OF 10 PER CENT. ALLOWED THE STANDARD OIL COMPANY IN 1877

[Proceedings in Relation to Trusts, House of Representatives, 1888. Report Number 3112, pages 774-775.]

I would like the privilege of explaining about that 10 per cent. commission. The railroad companies, as perhaps Mr. Gowen will remember, he at that time having been head of the Reading Railroad, tried and did agree among themselves for divisions of the oil business. I know that they agreed among themselves that a certain percentage of it the New York Central should take; a certain other percentage the Erie should take; a certain other percentage the Pennsylvania Railroad should take; and a certain other percentage the Baltimore and Ohio should take. We were only anxious that uniform rates should be maintained by these roads. All these roads, and each one of the roads, found it impossible to secure the divisions of the business as they had agreed upon. Notwithstanding, we co-operated with them, for we were heartily in favour of its being done and were only seeking for a uniformity of rates by the different roads. But as any gentleman connected with railroad interests well knows there always is that desire to get more than belongs to the line. That desire kept cropping out in the practical shape of cutting under rates for the sake of getting a little more, each road feeling that it was not getting enough to insure it its percentage. The Standard Oil Company at that time owned a very large percentage of the entire oil traffic. It was possible for it to do a service for the roads that the roads were unable to do for themselves. That service, however, involved a good many hardships.

The practical working of it was this, that at the end of each month after the arrangement had been made, each of these railroad companies, they first having agreed how they would divide among themselves and not seek to go beyond that certain percentage —at the end of each month each railroad company sent to us a statement of the number of barrels of oil they had transported during the month. It was incumbent upon us during the succeeding month to ship over the road or roads which had received less than its percentage an amount during that following month sufficient to bring up the deficit of the previous month. Undertaking to do that meant, as I well knew at the time, a responsibility imposed upon us, and an obligation to run refineries at certain localities which perhaps at the time it was unprofitable for us to run. It meant a steady continuance of a large volume of business at periods of time when it might not be profitable to run them; and if the gentlemen of the committee will bear with me just a moment you will see the difficulties. It was not only the three trunk lines—the New York Central, terminating at Buffalo, the Pennsylvania, terminating at Pittsburg, and the Baltimore and Ohio, I don't know where—but there came in their Western connections. I remember well the New York Central had two; the Lake Shore was its connection west of Buffalo to Cleveland, and the Dunkirk and Allegheny Valley was its western division to the Oil Region. It was not an easy matter, for we had not only to regard the percentage delivered at the seaboard, but we had to try to keep the Lake Shore satisfied with its proportion, the New York Central's proportion, and the Dunkirk and Allegheny Valley's proportion. As I say, it was no light task, and realising that, I said to these gentlemen, "we will undertake to do this business for you, to secure to each one of you the percentage which we may have agreed upon, upon condition that we are paid for that service a sum which shall be equal to 10 per cent. of the rate you receive for doing the business." There were, however, to be added to what I have already stated as an inducement for the railroad companies to pay that commission, other agreements, one of which was that we assumed the risk of loss by fire in transportation. That may seem to be to the gentlemen of the committee a cheap thing to do, but Mr. Gowen understands, as well as I do, that a railroad company cannot divest itself of the obligations by the common law imposed upon it as a common carrier without a special agreement to that effect. We took that risk, and did not collect from the railroad companies, any of them, any losses sustained by fire in transit. We furnished terminal facilities at the seaboard free of charge to the railroad companies, and for all this service the Pennsylvania Railroad agreed to pay us a commission of 10 per cent. We carried out our part of the contract faithfully, and secured to the roads such a division of the traffic as kept them in a state of accord and peace, so far as quantity was concerned, and yet the Pennsylvania Railroad paid to other shippers than ourselves a rebate or a drawback, or whatever you choose to call it, on their shipments, which were exactly equal to the 10 per cent. they agreed to pay us. So that in that respect we were not favoured at all

NUMBER 28 (See page 196)

CORRESPONDENCE BETWEEN WILLIAM ROCKEFELLER AND MR. SCOTT IN OCTOBER, 1877

[Commonwealth of Pennsylvania *vs.* Pennsylvania Railroad Company, United Pipe Lines, etc., Testimony. Appendix, pages 734–736.]

PHILADELPHIA, October 17, 1877.

THOMAS A. SCOTT,
> President Pennsylvania Railroad Company.

Dear Sir: In consideration of the covenants by your company to be performed as hereinafter mentioned, we will agree as follows:

First.—It having been agreed by the trunk lines that of all the oil shipped by the trunk lines to the cities of New York, Philadelphia, and Baltimore, 63 per cent. shall be considered as the proportion which would naturally go to the City of New York, and it having been further agreed that of this percentage one-third shall be transported over each of the trunk lines having termini in New York, viz.: The New York Central, Erie, and Pennsylvania, we agree, unless the aforesaid division shall be changed by mutual consent of said trunk lines, to ship such quantities of oil over your lines, from time to time, as will, when added to the quantities shipped by parties other than ourselves, give your line one-third of the shipments to New York by the said trunk lines, or 21 per cent. of the whole amount shipped to the three cities above named by the said trunk lines; it being understood that in stating the number of barrels for the purpose of making this division or for carrying out any of the other stipulations herein contained, the barrel of forty-five gallons of crude shall be the unit, and that each barrel of the usual size of refined oil shall be counted as equal to one and three-tenths barrels of crude.

Second.—It having been agreed, as we are informed, between your company and the Baltimore and Ohio Railroad Company, that of the remaining 37 per cent. of the total shipments aforesaid you should be entitled to transport by lines owned and controlled by your company to Philadelphia and Baltimore, 26 per cent., and the Baltimore and Ohio Railroad Company to Baltimore by its lines 11 per cent., we agree, until these proportions are changed by mutual consent, to ship such quantities to Philadelphia and Baltimore by lines owned and controlled by your company as will,

[371]

when added to shipments of parties other than ourselves, give for transportation by your lines to Philadelphia and Baltimore, 26 per cent. of the total shipments by the four trunk lines to the three seaboard cities above named.

Third.—We further agree that the quantity of oil which we will ourselves ship over your line shall not in any calendar year be less than two million barrels, based upon an average production of not less than thirty thousand barrels per day. If we should fail to give you traffic herein named, we will pay to you a sum equal to the profits which you would have realised upon the quantity in deficit—provided, however, that you will at all times furnish us with transportation, as we may reasonably require it.

Fourth.—We will, of the proportion of oil going to Philadelphia, refine as much as is practicable in Philadelphia, as we understand that you desire to see the refining capacity of Philadelphia fully employed, and, if needful, increased. And in shipping by your lines, whether to Philadelphia, Baltimore, or New York, we will endeavour to deliver the oil to you at points from which you will have short hauls; and to the extent that we can, we will make the proportion of crude shipped as large as possible, as we understand its transportation to be more profitable to you than that of refined oil.

Fifth.—We ask, in consideration of the above named guarantee of business, upon which it is understood we shall pay such rates as may be fixed from time to time by the four trunk lines (which rates it is understood shall be so fixed by the trunk lines as to place us on a parity as to cost of transportation with shippers by competing lines), that you shall furnish us promptly all the transportation we may reasonably require; and that you shall allow to, and pay us, weekly, such commission on our own shipments and the shipments which we may control, as may be agreed to by your company and the other trunk lines from time to time; this commission, it is understood, has for the present been fixed at 10 per cent. upon the rate, and shall not be fixed at a less percentage, except by mutual agreement of your company and ours— provided, that no other shipper of oil by your line shall pay less than the rate fixed for us before such commission is deducted; and no commission shall be allowed any other shipper unless he shall guarantee and furnish you such quantity of oil for shipment as will, after deduction of commission allowed him, realise to you the same amount of profit you realise from our trade; that is, you will not allow any other shipper of oil any part of such commission, unless after such allowance you realise from the total of his business the same total amount of profit you realise from the total of our business, except so far as your company may be compelled to fill certain contracts for transportation made by the Empire Line with refiners and producers, which contracts terminate on or before May 1, 1878, a statement of which shall accompany your reply to this letter—such contracts to be fulfilled. We agree that all the stipulations herein contained shall be carried out by us for the period of five years from the date hereof, unless sooner changed or terminated by mutual consent, provided that you advise us in writing within ten days that your company accept, and will carry out, its part of the arrangement for the like term. In entering into this agreement we desire to put ourselves on record as expressing our wish and intention of making our business relations with your company such that not only your main lines but the connecting lines controlled by you, especially the Allegheny Valley Railroad, shall secure the best possible results from the oil traffic consistent with our existing obligations to other transportation interests. We feel that the location of our refineries—all of which can be reached by your lines—should naturally create a close alliance between your company and ours, and that the best results from this important traffic can only be secured to yourselves and ourselves, and, we might add, to the entire petroleum interests of the country, by the establishment of friendly and mutually satisfactory arrangements between us.

Yours truly,

STANDARD OIL COMPANY,
By WILLIAM ROCKEFELLER,
Vice-President.

OFFICE OF THE PENNSYLVANIA RAILROAD COMPANY,
PHILADELPHIA, October 17, 1877.

WILLIAM ROCKEFELLER,
Vice-President Standard Oil Company.

My Dear Sir: I am in receipt of your letter of this date, reciting the understanding and agreement to exist between the Pennsylvania Railroad Company and your company for a period of five years.

I beg leave to say that the same covers the whole basis of the arrangements, and is satisfactory to this company—the provisions of which will be duly carried out by it. Very respectfully yours,

THOMAS A. SCOTT,
President.

NUMBER 29 (See page 197)

CORRESPONDENCE BETWEEN MR. O'DAY AND MR. CASSATT

[Commonwealth of Pennsylvania *vs.* Pennsylvania Railroad Company, United Pipe Lines, etc., Testimony. Appendix, pages 732–733.]

OFFICE OF THE AMERICAN TRANSFER COMPANY,
OIL CITY, PENNSYLVANIA, February 15, 1878.

A. J. CASSATT,
Third Vice-President, Philadelphia.

Dear Sir: Referring to the conversation I had with you in January, I wish to submit the following facts: That our company has at large expense (involving the payment of several hundred thousand dollars), purchased and created certain pipe-lines to Pittsburg, through which we are able not only to protect the Allegheny Valley road in a paying rate of freight for the oil it carries, but also to secure to that company (by agreement with it) its full proportion of the oil traffic going to Pittsburg.

You are acquainted with the efforts we have put forth in other directions during the last months in which we have acted in thorough accord with the trunk line interests, and I believe I may say without egotism, we have, to the extent of our ability, effectually protected their interests in such action. I here repeat what I once stated to you and which I asked you to receive and treat as strictly confidential, that we have been for many months receiving from the New York Central and Erie Railroads certain sums of money, in no instance less than twenty cents per barrel on every barrel of crude oil carried by each of those roads.

Co-operating, as we are doing, with the Standard Oil Company and the trunk lines in every effort to secure for the railroads paying rates of freight on the oil they carry, I am constrained to say to you that, in justice to the interest I represent, we should receive from your company at least twenty cents on each barrel of crude oil you transport.

The fruit of co-operation referred to has been fully evidenced in the fact that since last fall your company has received fifty to sixty cents per barrel more freight than was obtained by it prior to our co-operation.

In submitting this proposition I feel I should ask you to let this date from the first of November, 1877, but I am willing to accept as a compromise (which is to be re-

[374]

garded as strictly a private one between your company and ours) the payment by you of twenty cents per barrel on all crude oil shipments commencing with February 1, 1878.

I make this proposition with the full expectation that it will be acceptable to your company, but with the understanding on my part that in so doing, I am not asking as much of the Pennsylvania road and its connections as I have been and am receiving from the other trunk lines.

You are doubtless aware that during the last two years a large amount of oil has been shipped to Richmond *via* the Chesapeake and Ohio road, and that since the purchase of the Pittsburg lines by us not one barrel has been permitted to go in that direction.

During the season of 1877, and so long as the Columbia Conduit Company afforded the Baltimore and Ohio road access to the Oil Regions, that company, I understood, refused to accept from the other trunk lines (for its proportion of the oil traffic) less than 20 per cent., but after the purchase by us of the Columbia Conduit you succeeded in arranging with the Baltimore and Ohio for about half as much as they previously claimed.

I may add that the Baltimore and Ohio road are wholly dependent upon us for any oil they may carry. Yours truly,

> (Signed) DANIEL O'DAY,
> *General Manager.*

PHILADELPHIA, May 15, 1878.

R. W. DOWNING, Comptroller.

Dear Sir: I enclose herewith copy of letter from Daniel O'Day, general manager of the American Transfer Company, which refers to a conversation I had with him in January last in reference to allowing the American Transfer Company a commission of twenty cents per barrel on all crude oil transported over this company's lines to New York, Philadelphia and Baltimore.

I agreed to allow this commission from and after February 1, until further notice, after having seen receipted bills showing that the New York Central Railroad allowed them a commission of thirty-five cents per barrel and that the Erie Railway allowed them a commission of twenty cents per barrel on Bradford oil, and thirty cents per barrel on all other oil, and that they had been doing so continuously since the 17th of October last.

Of this, however, you saw the evidence yourself in the bills which I submitted to you last week. Please, therefore, prepare vouchers in favour of the American Transfer Company per Daniel O'Day, for this commission of twenty cents on shipments during February, March and April, and hereafter make settlements with that company monthly. Yours truly,

> (Signed) A. J. CASSATT,
> *Third Vice-President.*

[375]

NUMBER 30 (See page 197)

HENRY M. FLAGLER'S TESTIMONY ON THE REBATE PAID TO THE AMERICAN TRANSFER COMPANY

[Proceedings in Relation to Trusts, House of Representatives, 1888. Report Number 3112, pages 777–778.]

Q. Mr. Cassatt testified and offered in evidence the correspondence which showed that his company agreed to the payment of that 22½ cents to the American Transfer Company on every barrel of crude oil passing over their line in consequence of the fact that the writer of the first letter on behalf of the American Transfer Company had asserted that the New York Central and the New York and Lake Erie roads paid the same amount. You know that to be a fact, do you not?

A. May I explain that now?

Q. You are entitled to make any explanation you wish.

A. The American Transfer Company was built originally for, really, the New York Central road. The New York Central had no means of getting south of Titusville with its cars. The American Transfer Company's lines were built really in the interest of the New York Central road. In those days the pipe-lines purchased the oil and oftentimes sold it at just what they paid for it, and sometimes less. They got more when they could. The New York Central, as I said, paid the American Transfer Company a price, which I presume was the figures named in Mr. Cassatt's testimony, for collecting oil in the lower country and delivering it to the Dunkirk and Allegheny Valley, which is the New York Central's connection. As that pipe-line increased its business the Erie road did the same thing. Later the Pennsylvania Railroad wanted the service of that pipe-line in collecting oil. Mr. O'Day did what I suppose any manager would do. He said to Mr. Cassatt, if you do the same thing for me that the other roads are doing, I have no objection to making the same arrangement with you. The payment made by the Pennsylvania, the Erie, and the New York Central roads constituted the gross income of the American Transfer Company, out of which it paid its expenses of doing its business and its losses, if it made any, in the purchase and sale of oil. It acted as a factor for those northern roads, and, as I said, was originally built in order that oils might be reached by the New York Central.

Q. But in addition to the sum of 22½ cents, or whatever it may have been, which

[376]

these trunk lines paid to the American Transfer Company, that company as a transporter of oil through its own pipe got this pipage charge besides?

A. I never so understood it. As I remember the facts in the case, while there was a nominal pipage—there might have been; I do not say there was; I do not remember.

Q. You do not say there was?

A. I do not remember. But while there might have been a nominal pipage, that nominal pipage might have been absorbed in the crude oil. In other words, it threw away its nominal pipage and relied——

Q. I am speaking now solely of the relations of the American Transfer Company to the railroads. The former received 22½ cents on every barrel of oil passing over the Pennsylvania road and the other roads. But the American Transfer Company was a transporter of oil itself, and to the extent it transported oil through its pipes it made charge for that service also?

A. That is a point where I say I want to correct you. While it may have made a nominal charge, about which my memory fails me, I say it threw away that nominal charge by paying to the owner or the producer of the oil the value of the oil at the wells, plus what that pipage might have been, and that twenty odd cents paid by the Pennsylvania constituted its gross revenue.

NUMBER 31 (See page 199)

LETTER TO PRESIDENT SCOTT OF THE PENNSYLVANIA RAILROAD FROM B. B. CAMPBELL AND E. G. PATTERSON

[Proceedings in Relation to Trusts, House of Representatives, 1888. Report Number 3112, pages 363–365.]

To THE PRESIDENT AND DIRECTORS PENNSYLVANIA RAILROAD COMPANY.

Gentlemen: About July 1 last the undersigned were of a delegation from the Oil Region of our state, asking of your road an assurance that its course during the preceding two months, in giving to all producers and shippers of petroleum equal facilities and impartial rates, might be formally made its permanent policy.

In an interview with your president at that time, that assurance was given, coupled with the requisition that such support should be given it by the producers and shippers as would repay it for the exertion it must make in defending that policy, and guaranteeing that such support should be continuous and permanent.

The people of the Oil Region were only too glad to enter into such an agreement, and steps were immediately taken of a practical nature to carry it out.

It was understood that it could not be *immediately* done.

After the formal abandonment by the trunk lines of the South Improvement Company in 1872, your road for some months faithfully adhered, as we believe, to the pledge then given by all the trunk lines, that no discrimination should thenceforth be permitted. We believe also that it stood alone among the roads in adhering to it, for gradually the persons constituting the South Improvement Company were placed by the roads in as favourable a position as to rates and facilities as had been stipulated in the original contract with that company. At this time the line of your road in Western Pennsylvania, including that under your influence and control, was dotted with refineries capable of producing a large proportion of the refined oil needed by the world. The policy of the Standard Oil Company, the successor in everything but name of the South Improvement Company, has resulted in the dismantling and abandonment of every one of those refineries (as soon as they fell into their possession) which could not be reached by some other and a rival road to yours, and now there are in the Oil Region proper but few refineries and those universally owned by the Standard Oil Company, those in Pittsburg being owned or controlled by that combination or by

[378]

the Conduit or Empire lines. The use and export of crude oil is but a small proportion of the consumption, and time and money were required to re-establish this great product upon its former basis, and these people were glad to furnish all needed means to accomplish this end, as are also capitalists at other points not strictly within the Oil Region, yet upon your lines.

We are met in the midst of this preparation by assertion of agents of the combination, and as accepted news by the press, that such a combination is entered into, or under consideration by your road and the Empire Transportation Company, the Erie, Central, Lake Shore, and Baltimore roads of the one part, and the Standard Oil Company of the other, as would preclude your road from carrying out the policy announced by your president at the interview heretofore referred to.

We believe there is danger that such a result may be reached, and we in behalf of these whom we represent, in making our efforts to prevent its accomplishment, or if accomplished to defeat it, as the first step, address this communication to you, desiring to present its aspect as affecting your road from our standpoint.

So far as we, and the general public are affected, you will not question that the present scheme is but the repetition of the South Improvement scheme, never abandoned by its authors, and seeking the sole and absolute control of all petroleum produced, purchased, refined, and shipped within the states of Pennsylvania, New York, Ohio, or West Virginia.

The overproduction of 1873, 1874, 1875, and the consequent almost entire destruction of petroleum values, gave the Standard Oil Company, with its organisation and capital, almost the desired monopoly. The equalisation of consumption and production of 1876–1877 brought that combination to the same point that they were in 1872—utterly unable by reason of geographical position, if for no other, to monopolise this product without the co-operation of *all* the transportation, and then only under a contract similar to that of the South Improvement Company, and including all of its dangerous and extraordinary features. None other can serve them, and so they stand to-day, and we believe that your road can enter into no compromise, treaty, or arrangement which will serve the ends of the monopoly, under any less stringent stipulations and devoid of the liabilities thereof.

Under such an arrangement it is probable that the Central and Erie have transported its oil, during nearly all of this year. It is now an open secret in the producing region, that no charges follow the shipments over at least one of these roads, and crude oil is delivered in New York, on shipping order, at prices which barely repay the cost of packages and contents, with little or no remainder for transportation charges. This aid to the scheme of the combination is possibly given in view of the high tariff and consequent large revenue promised to be derived hereafter, when the scheme has been made a success, and all opposition in trade and transportation extinguished.

Suppose your opposition to be withdrawn, and you join the alliance, when does your profit come in? We are entitled to impartiality. As we are advised, the law, common and statute, provides for it; it pronounces those participating in such a scheme conspirators against the public weal, and there is no court upon your line but what will enforce by mandamus and injunction the impartiality that we ask. The combination will promise you an immediate increase of revenue. If we are well advised, will you realise upon that promise? Can you make a contract with them that if we do not succeed in destroying, it will be their interest to keep? You will not have a refinery left; and they are now completing pipe-lines from Pittsburg to Oil City, and can deliver the oil received by all their pipe-lines, independent of your road and its branches. In case of a contract with them executed but afterwards broken, from what source will you derive your oil traffic and what court will enforce the broken contract in your favour? We urge that you cannot enter into any arrangement with the monopoly that can be permanently useful to it and to you, and doubt if it can be made temporarily so.

Suppose that you decline to enter into such a treaty, or any such scheme, but announce and adhere to the opposite policy? There is no law, not even that of necessity, to compel you to serve the ends of the Standard Oil Company.

If Messrs. Vanderbilt and Jewett believe that their aid alone is insufficient to the establishment of the monopoly, for how long will they carry its oil as at present for nothing, when they could have full rates, by uniting the railroad interest, and leaving the Standard Oil Company to do its business in common with all others?

If the Pennsylvania Railroad, having the geographical position in its favour, will announce and adhere to the policy of impartial and competitive rates, in three or six months, it can have all the facilities and extent of business which the Standard Oil Company can give the competitive roads, and by men who have all to gain by so doing.

We ask consideration of our views and of our assurance of good results from their favourable consideration.

If you choose to place the matter in the light of an experiment, its trial can cost you nothing but the failure to realise upon the immediate fulfillment of the promises of the common enemy, and that realisation we believe will not be permitted.

Very respectfully,

B. B. CAMPBELL, of Pittsburg,
E. G. PATTERSON, of Titusville.

PHILADELPHIA, September 11, 1877.

NUMBER 32 (See page 225)

PRODUCERS' APPEAL OF 1878 TO GOVERNOR JOHN F. HARTRANFT, OF PENNSYLVANIA

[Proceedings in Relation to Trusts, House of Representatives, 1888. Report Number 3112, pages 351–356.]

Sir: The undersigned, members of a committee appointed by the General Council of the Petroleum Producers' Union for that purpose, address to you, as the official head of the Commonwealth, a plain statement of facts, to a great extent known to be true from personal knowledge, and all material parts of which are susceptible of proof by competent evidence.

We address you, not only as individuals whose personal interests have been affected, whose property has been rendered comparatively valueless, and whose capital and labour are bound against their consent, to increasing the gains of grasping corporations, but as citizens of the great Commonwealth of Pennsylvania, apparently prostrate and powerless to control one of its greatest products, and the immense business that annually flows from it.

The petroleum production of Pennsylvania is confined geographically to the North-western portion of the state, extending from its border upon New York State nearly to Pittsburg, and is the chief interest in the counties of McKean, Warren, Forest, Crawford, Venango, Clarion, Butler and Armstrong.

The amount of money invested in well property, constantly to be renewed and kept good, represents at least twenty millions of dollars, and while the value of the lands upon which the wells are located is not easily determined, it represents many times the value of the well property.

Petroleum should yield at the wells, with its transportation and sale unfettered, twenty-five to thirty-five million dollars annually, while as an article of export, it ranks third among the products of the nation, and as first among its manufactured exports.

For transportation outlets, it has the Pennsylvania Railroad to the seaboard at an average distance therefrom of less than 400 miles. The New York Central and Lake Shore Railroads reach Oil City by way of Cleveland, Ohio, 764 miles from the seaboard, and Titusville, by way of Dunkirk, New York, 571 miles to the sea-

[381]

board, and the New York, Lake Erie and Western, and Atlantic and Great Western Railways reach Oil City by way of Meadville, 550 miles to the seaboard.

CONDITION OF THE TRADE IN 1871

At that time the lines of the Pennsylvania Railroad in the Oil Region were dotted with refineries located at Tidioute, Henry's Bend, Oleopolis, Oil City, Corry, Titusville, Miller Farm, Rouseville, and other points on the Oil Creek Railroad, at various points on the Philadelphia and Erie Railroad, and on the Allegheny Valley Railroad, these roads being tributaries of and controlled by the Pennsylvania Railroad, while upon its main line extensive refineries were located at Pittsburg and Philadelphia. The refineries at Cleveland, Ohio, confined themselves in a measure to the Western domestic trade, and those of Portland, Boston and New York had generally specialties in the trade.

The markets were filled with buyers of crude and refined; information as to stocks, production and consumption was open and obtainable, and values were regulated by the law of supply and demand.

In its relation to this trade, Western Pennsylvania almost exclusively possessing this product, with ample refineries in its midst, with its great state railroad penetrating the producing region, and by it, having the shortest route to the seaboard, with the Allegheny River as an additional means of transportation to Pittsburg, the Western terminus of the Pennsylvania Railroad, and with Philadelphia, its Eastern terminus as an exporting point, Pennsylvania had, and was entitled to, the control of the refining and transportation of its own product.

CONDITION OF THE TRADE IN 1877–1878

Now, this is all changed! The refineries on the lines of the Pennsylvania Railroad have been demolished, excepting where reached by rival railroads, and this business has been transferred to Cleveland and New York, the refineries remaining in this state having passed into the ownership and control of a foreign organisation, as has also the local transportation from the wells, by means of pipe-lines to the lines of the railways.

The transportation of every nature is subject to its dictation; it possesses every avenue of information; it affixes its own value to the crude product when purchasing and the refined products when selling; it establishes its own rates of compensation to be paid the railways, and the laws of commerce which govern values in other products are in this a part of the history of the past. So far as the petroleum trade is concerned an enterprise or investment therein is only a wager as to what step the Standard Oil combination will next take. With the world consuming double the amount of our petroleum that it did in 1871, the thirty millions which should be received from the crude product has dwindled to its half; the fifteen millions which should be the profit of Pennsylvania refineries has been transferred to Ohio and New York, and the twenty millions which should have swelled the earnings of the railways have gone—no one dare say where—but the colossal fortunes acquired since 1872 by every member (so far as its members are known) of this now world-renowned organisation, are proofs of the success attendant upon a scheme, no less unlawful than gigantic, and which has all the outward and visible signs of inward and spiritual corruption. To-day a foreign corporation is the absolute master of the production and its value, of transportation by pipe-lines, transportation by railroad and the compensation therefor, of storage and refining, and the profit thereof, and dictates prices through the world of the first, or among the first, of the products of Pennsylvania, and of the United States, and this to the impoverishment of thousands of citizens, and the destruction of each of these interests within the state. That this has been accomplished through and by means of the co-operation of the Pennsylvania Railroad, its management and influence, is matter of record.

THE FIRST ATTEMPT TO MONOPOLISE THE TRADE

was initiated by the conveyance, by R. D. Barclay, Thomas A. Scott's private secretary, and S. S. Moon, the legislative agent of the Pennsylvania Railroad, to a party composed principally of Cleveland and New York men, headed by an agent of the New York Central and Erie Railways, of a charter granted by the Legislature of Pennsylvania for a different purpose, under which they organised for the seizure of the petroleum trade, retaining the charter title of

"THE SOUTH IMPROVEMENT COMPANY,"

the then managers thereof being the managers of the organisation now known as the Standard Oil Company.

With the South Improvement Company, not a member of which lived in the Oil Region, or was an owner of oil wells or oil lands, the Pennsylvania Railroad hastened to execute a contract (January 18, 1872), giving it the sole and exclusive control of all petroleum shipments thereon, regardless of ownership, and securing this by the payment by the railroad of a rebate or drawback to the South Improvement Company of such a sum as would have inevitably driven all others out of the trade, and lest there might be doubt as to the intent to so do, it was expressly stipulated in the fourth article thereof that that was the result aimed at, and the Pennsylvania Railroad therein bound itself, so far as it legally might, to aid in accomplishing it.

The action of the Legislature and of Congress, and the uprising of the people against this unparalleled iniquity, destroyed the combination for the time being, the railroads having pledged themselves to never attempt a similar outrage.

The local transportation of crude petroleum had been gradually changing from movement by barrels to carriage in

PIPE-LINES

from the wells to tankage located on the lines of railway, the principal of which pipe-lines, at this time known as the Pennsylvania Transportation Company (formerly Allegheny Transportation Company), was under special charters of the Legislature and owned and controlled by Messrs. Scott, of the Pennsylvania, and Fisk and Gould, of the Erie Railways. The Legislature had been petitioned at various times since 1866 to pass a Free Pipe Law, but the various bills introduced for that purpose could never overcome the opposition of the Pennsylvania Railroad in the Legislature. During the excitement attendant upon the rise and fall of the South Improvement Company scheme, the effort was renewed, and the Legislature enacted a law, restricted to the eight oil producing counties, but the Pennsylvania Railroad influence was strong enough to exclude Allegheny County from the operation of the Act, thus shutting out Western Pennsylvania from Pittsburg, the terminus of the Pennsylvania Railroad, the natural outlet of the Oil Region, and the natural refining point of the United States.

The succeeding efforts to pass a Free Pipe Law, either general in its nature or to permit construction of pipe-lines to lines of railway within the state, or to include Allegheny County in the law of 1872, have been defeated invariably by the opposition of the Pennsylvania Railroad, and the law of 1874, known as the Wallace Act, was so framed and enacted as to leave it doubtful whether it had not succeeded in withdrawing from the eight counties referred to all the rights conceded to them by the Act of 1872, a wrong which no subsequent Legislature has been able to redress.

Under the law of 1872, pipe-lines owned by citizens in the Oil Region had been organised and were in operation, giving free access to the railways, but after the passage of the Wallace Act (April 29, 1874), the Standard Combination, which had never really abandoned the South Improvement scheme, systematically undertook their destruction by forcing them into insolvency and then absorbing them. This required railway co-operation, and various means were employed therein, notably among which is the scheme adopted by the ring and promulgated by the railroads October 1, 1874. An explanation is necessary to understand why the railroads should unite: *First*, to carry oil received by them through pipe-lines that had combined to maintain a given rate for pipage twenty-two cents per barrel cheaper than on oil received from pipe-lines not so combining, and *Second*, to further weaken the refineries remaining in Western Pennsylvania by depriving them of their geographical advantage of proximity to the crude product, to the coal used as fuel, and to the exporting ports by *free transportation* of crude petroleum to the ring refineries in other states. Various pipe-lines had already been forced out of existence, had been bought up and united under the name of "The United Pipe Lines," which was owned, one-third by the Standard Oil Company, one-third by the Lake Shore and New York Central Railroads, and one-third by individuals who were members of and directors in the Standard Oil Company. The Pennsylvania Railroad had as its particular feeder a similar organisation, known as the "Empire Pipe Line." This explains the *first* point referred to above. The *second*, so far as the Pennsylvania Railroad is concerned, is inexplicable upon any ordinary hypothesis or under any known theory in railroad politics. The scheme was a success, pipe-lines one after another succumbed, and refiner after refiner was bankrupted and his works absorbed.

This effected, the monopoly, backed by the New York railroads, in one of which it exercised unlimited power, felt strong enough to demand of the railroads that it should be given the future sole conduct of the trade under the old South Improvement plan. Upon this the Pennsylvania Railroad apparently awoke to its danger, resisted the demand, and in July, 1877, President Scott announced as the policy of the Pennsylvania Railroad open and free trade to all shippers of petroleum. It was then conducting its oil traffic through its ally, the Empire Transportation Company, which possessed a system of pipe-lines (before referred to) extending over the Oil Region, controlling a large portion of the production, with ample tankage, with a large rolling stock upon the Pennsylvania Railroad, and owning or controlling a refining capacity nearly equal to one-half the consumption of the world. In the following month (August, 1877), immediately after the riots at Pittsburg, which were in their extent the natural outgrowth of railroad freight discrimination against that city, the monopolists succeeded in convincing the officials of the Pennsylvania Railroad that it was to their or its interests to force the Empire Company, its cars, its pipe-lines, its tankage and its refineries into their hands. The people of Western Pennsylvania protested in a communication to the president and directors of the Pennsylvania Railroad in September, before the extent of the proposed iniquity had become fully known to the public, which communication seems never to have reached the board of directors. The outrage was finally consummated October 17, 1877, and the Pennsylvania Railroad was left without the control of a foot of pipe-line together, a tank to receive, or a still to refine a barrel of petroleum and without the ability to secure the transportation of one except at the will of men who live and whose interests lie in Ohio and New York.

Into those hands had now passed the last refineries of Pennsylvania, the last means of transportation from the wells to the railroads, and the last means of carriage to the markets of this country and of the world. The South Improvement scheme (less its chartered organisation as in 1872) was at last an accomplished fact, and in the successful designing, prosecution, consummation and operation of which it is impossible not to believe that railroad officials were personally interested.

CONGRESSIONAL LEGISLATION

As the conspiracy was evidently gaining strength, the people of Pennsylvania united in an effort to induce Congress to again interfere as in 1872, and in 1876 it directed an investigation, which was conducted in a dilatory manner by a committee, a prominent member of the Standard Oil Company, and not a member of Congress, presiding behind the seat of the chairman. Vice-President Cassatt, of the Pennsylvania Railroad, was the only prominent railway official who appeared in obedience to the subpœnas of the Speaker of the House of Representatives, and he refused to give the committee any information as to the matter under investigation, and the counsel of the Pennsylvania Railroad, ex-Senator Scott, appeared before the committee in justification of his so doing. The financial officer of the Standard Oil Company appeared before the committee, accompanied by a member of Congress—also a member of that Company, and promptly refused to give the committee any information as to the organisation, or the names of its members, or its relations with the railroads. The influence and power of the combination was apparent; the committee never reported, never complained of the contempt of its witnesses, and all the evidence and record of its proceedings effectively disappeared. In 1877–78, a bill was introduced by Representative Watson, of Western Pennsylvania, seeking to prevent discrimination in interstate commerce, which has been reported by a committee, but which can hardly overcome the covert opposition which it meets.

RECENT STATE LEGISLATION

All efforts to obtain a Free Pipe Law in this state having through a series of years proved unavailing, although New York, in its efforts to control the trade in Pennsylvania petroleum, had enacted such a law, a bill was prepared enforcing in this state the Third and Seventh Sections of the Seventeenth Article of its Constitution. This bill, known as

THE ANTI-DISCRIMINATION ACT,

provided that shippers of property by car-load from any point on a railroad within the state to any other point within the state, should be charged equal rates and given equal facilities. Copies of the proposed law were sent to the prominent railroad officials in the state, but its provisions were so fair and protective to every citizen of the state, and to every legitimate railroad interest, that neither before the Judiciary Committee of the Senate, which reported it favourably by an unanimous vote, nor in the Senate, which passed it with but one dissenting voice, nor before the Judiciary Committee of the House, which reported it unanimously, did any railroad stockholder, official, or legislative agent appear to offer an objection to its becoming a law. Yet it was killed in the House by the familiar means employed by legislative agents in disposing of measures objectionable, but not debatable. Had the bill become a law, it would have rebuilt the refineries of the state, with Philadelphia (whose petroleum trade under the monopoly has gradually dwindled to a fraction of its former magnitude) as the exporting point, with the Pennsylvania Railroad as the transporter thereto, and the people of Western Pennsylvania might have arisen from a community of miners, working for the benefit, and under the rule, of a foreign corporation, to their former conditions as citizens of a prosperous mining and manufacturing section of the state.

RESULTS AND EFFECT OF THE SUCCESS OF THE CONSPIRACY

Upon or with the New York railroads no appeal or representation of the people of this section would have any weight or influence. Their managers reside in Cleveland and New York, and are subject to the daily manipulations of the monopoly managers, while in our own state, to all efforts for emancipation or toward the restoration of trade to its natural channels the Pennsylvania Railroad and its power is as a Chinese wall. Its president and vice-president admit the preferences in rates given to the monopoly, and boldly announce their intent to continue in so doing; they claim the legal right to so do, and challenge resistance; they obstruct all efforts of producers, shippers and refiners by delaying or restricting facilities; by threatening other railroads with severance of connections and deprivation of general traffic if they transport petroleum for parties outside the monopoly; they refer applicants for rates and facilities over the Pennsylvania Railroad to the Standard Oil Company, and offering their personal service as negotiators for such rates and facilities, assure all that there is no hope of success in the trade unless by a coalition with the Standard.

We have thus far given not more than an outlined sketch of this enormous monopoly, its plan, its growth, and its results. We have not burdened your Excellency with details of individual oppression and outrage, but we should fail to discharge our duties to ourselves and as citizens if we neglect to recite some of the means by which the most deplorable results are produced to our state and section. Wrong is constantly perpetuated and right driven from us. True it is that in many things the monopoly has been unwittingly aided in its schemes by unwary concessions as to the management of its business, by producers of petroleum themselves, but they had a right, as men pursuing an honest calling, to believe that they were dealing with honest men, and not with a gang of public plunderers, leagued together by no better tie than the sordid desire of gain, to be acquired by methods of corruption and lawlessness.

By the theory of the law, corporations derive their powers from the people of the Commonwealth in General Assembly convened; they have no powers not delegated to them by the people; they take nothing by implication; they are public servants, invested for the public benefit with extraordinary privileges, and their charters may be taken from them when they cease to properly perform the duties of their creation. The railroad and pipe-line companies are common carriers of freight for all persons, are bound to receive it when offered at convenient and usual places, and to transport it for all, for reasonable compensation, without unreasonable discrimination in favour of any. These are but simple statements of well established legal principles, never doubted in any court, but affirmed by every tribunal that has ever considered them. Yet the people who granted these special privileges are now upon the defensive, their rights denied by these corporations, and they are challenged to enter the courts to establish them, while in the meantime they are inoperative to the irreparable injury of their business. They have yielded to the railways that they have created a part of their sovereignty, and given them the right to take private property for public use, but restricting such taking, strictly to such use. Yet where the narrow strip of land used as a railway roadbed runs through valuable oil lands, this combination is strong enough to demand from the railways its transfer to them, that they may and do thereon sink their own oil wells, and thereby drain the oil from the adjoining lands whose owners gave the strip for public use by a railroad.

The owners of lands along the line of the Allegheny Valley Railroad, producing petroleum from those lands, with their own pipe-line running to their own shipping racks by the side tracks of that railroad, are unable to obtain cars in which to load their product for transportation, at any rate of freight, while their tanks overflow. Shippers of petroleum are refused cars, or are promised them, only to find the promises broken, and their contracts rendered impossible of fulfillment, while the monopoly demands and is given all the cars belonging to the railroads, it permitting its own private cars to meantime stand idle, so that the railroads may assert its inability to accommodate all.

Owners of tanks connected with the monopoly pipe-lines, with ample storage therein for their own product, are refused transportation from their own wells upon the ground that "their tanks are full," a barefaced and daily demonstrated falsehood. Other producers of petroleum are refused transportation by the pipe-lines, on the plea of want of capacity to carry, and at the same time are informed that their oil will be carried if they will sell it to the ring, "immediate shipment."

If the applicant's tanks are overflowing, or if he needs money and complies with their terms, he is offered a price from two and a half to twenty-five cents below the market value. If he accepts and sells a fixed amount of his oil, the pipe-line removes all but five or ten barrels, delays for days and weeks to take the remainder, and refuses to pay for any until all is taken. This is known as the "immediate shipment swindle."

By their use of the petroleum of others stored in their tanks and lines; by the overissue of Pipe Line Certificates; by refusal to perform their public duties; by open defiance of the law and impudent evasions of its provisions, the pipe-line and railroad companies leave to the people, whose creatures they are, but two remedies—an appeal for protection, first to the law of the land, next to the higher law of nature!

These corporations have made themselves the interested tools of a monopoly that has become the buyer, the carrier, the manufacturer, and the seller of this product of immense value. It needs no argument or illustration to convince that in such a position this foreign corporation is in direct antagonism to the producer, the labourer and the consumer.

The South Improvement conspiracy embraced in its scheme the ownership of the oil producing territory, wells and machinery. If the present course of its successor cannot be stayed, it is merely a question of time when the ownership of the entire oil production will fall into its hands through the impoverishment of thousands of our citizens and their inability to contend longer.

That monopolies are dangerous to free institutions is a political maxim so old as to have lost its force by irrelevant repetition, but if anything were needed to awaken the public sense to its truth, the immediate effect of this giant combination is before us. Throughout the Oil Region, as wherever it does business, it now has its own acid works, glue factories, hardware stores and barrel works. We have seen that it is master of the railroads, and owns and controls all the refineries, all the pipe-lines. All these enumerated industries controlled by them employ large numbers of labourers dependent for the support of themselves and their families upon the daily labour given or withheld by this powerful conspirator. At the flash of the telegraphic message from Cleveland, Ohio, hundreds of men have been thrown out of employment on a few hours' notice and kept for weeks in a state of semi-starvation and justifiable discontent, deceived meanwhile with delusive promises of work, until the autocrat of a foreign corporation, maintained and upheld by the chief among Pennsylvania corporations, gives leave from within the borders of a foreign state for the Pennsylvania labourer to earn his bread.

Along the valley of Oil Creek and the Allegheny Valley, where a few years since the smoke of busy refineries and their attendant industries darkened the air, piles of rusted iron and heaps of demolished brick work mark the results of the conspiracy; where a few years since busy men crowded to and fro in the pursuit of lawful trade in a great staple, there is now silence and emptiness. The producer, once surrounded with competitive buyers of his product, now goes with crowds of his fellow victims to wait his turn for leave to sell it at a dictated price to a single agent of a single purchaser.

To permit to stand unattacked the foul principles of such an organisation, to permit them to be fastened as lawful or right upon the policy of the Commonwealth or the nation, is to lay the foundation for the exile of capital, endless injury to the public interests, endless oppression of the labourer, riots, tumults, and the decay of the state.

So far as this public wrong is within the scope of Executive interference, we ask that immediate steps be taken to enforce by legislative enactment the wise provisions of our State Constitution, and by such legal processes as are necessary, compel obedience to law and the performance by chartered companies of their public duties.

B. B. CAMPBELL, of Pittsburg,

E. W. CODINGTON, of Bradford, McKean County,

LEWIS EMERY, JR., of Bradford, McKean County,

GEORGE H. GRAHAM, of Petrolia, Butler County,

J. A. VERA, of St. Petersburg, Clarion County,

H. O. ROBBINS, of Turkey City, Clarion County,

L. H. SMITH, Petrolia,

R. B. BROWN, Clarion,

D. S. CRISWELL, Oil City,

A. J. SALISBURY, Karns City,

A. N. PERRIN, Titusville, Crawford County,

W. B. BENEDICT, Enterprise, Warren County,

H. W. BUMPUS, Monroe, Clarion County,

SAMUEL Q. BROWN, Pleasantville, Venango County.

NUMBER 33 (See page 233)

STATEMENT OF CRUDE OIL SHIPMENTS BY GREEN LINE DUR-
ING THE MONTHS OF FEBRUARY AND MARCH, 1878, TO
NEW YORK, PHILADELPHIA, AND BALTIMORE; SHOW-
ING DRAWBACKS ALLOWED TO AMERICAN
TRANSFER COMPANY

[Commonwealth of Pennsylvania *vs.* Pennsylvania Railroad Company, United Pipe Lines, etc. Testimony. Appendix, page 737.]

SHIPPER.	CONSIGNEE.	DESTINA-TION.	No. OF BARRELS. Feb.	March.	TOTAL. BARRELS.
H. C. Ohlen..........H. H. Ohlen............	Com'paw	18,320	11,556	29,876
W. H. Nicholson......	"	....	"	16,983	31,169½	48,152½
E. N. Hallock.........	"	....	"	1,160½	......	1,160½
S. Craig..............	"	....	"	......	2,384½	2,384½
H. L. Taylor & Co....	"	....	"	......	1,439½	1,439½
Ayres, Lombard & Co.	"	....	"	......	2,688½	2,688½
J. Rousseaux.........J. Rousseaux..........	"	6,377½	6,932½	13,310
W. L. Fox...........	"	....	"	......	3,150½	3,150½
W. H. Nicholson......Ayres, Lombard & Co...	"	979½	......	979½
J. A. Bostwick & Co...J. A. Bostwick & Co....	"	43,074	45,915½	88,989½
D. Grimm...........Jno. Ellis & Co.......	"	722½	1,185½	1,908
			87,617	106,422	194,039
J. Bushnell..........Warden, Frew & Co....	Phila.	1,725½	22,105½	23,831
J. A Bostwick & Co..	"	...	"	12,994		12,994
J. Bushnell..........care Atlantic Ref. Co. ...	"	10,137	31,917	42,054
J. Bushnell..........W. L. Elkins & Co......	"	14,684	7,793	22,477
G. M. Robinson.......	"	.....	"	761½	1,382	2,143½
E. N. Hallock. ......Greenwich Refining Co..	"	3,413½	......	3,414½
Mary R. Fox..........	"	..	"	1,308	......	1,308
S. Craig..............	"	..	"	1,241½	......	1,241½
Fox & Fink..........	"	..	"	......	2,541	2,541
Fox Estate...........	"	..	"	......	501	501
M. Lloyd...........M. Lloyd..............	"	3,803	2,690	6,493
S. Craig..............	"	....	"	......	2,426	2,426
W. L. Fox...........	"	....	"	......	1,960½	1,960½
G. M. Robinson.......F. Farnsworth.........	"	362½	80	442½

[391]

SHIPPER.	CONSIGNEE.	DESTINA-TION.	No. OF BARRELS. Feb.	March.	TOTAL. BARRELS.
W. G. Laird, agent.	W. G. Laird, agent	Phila.	302	......	302
Paine, Abbott & Co	Paine, Abbott & Co	"	403	......	403
J. S. Davis	J. S. Davis	"	......	501	501
A. & G. W. R. R.	A. & B. Cooley & Co.	"	......	25	25
			51,135½	73,922	125,057½
J. Bushnell	Balto. United Oil Co.	Balto.	7,435	16,692½	24,127½
G. M. Robinson.	"	"	......	261½	261½
E. J. Waring & Co.	E. J. Waring & Co., care of S. E. Poultney.	"	282	......	282
			7,717	16,954	24,671
Grand Total			146,469½	197,298	343,767½

Total, 343,767½ barrels at 20 cents per barrel, $68,753.50.

This amount, $68,753.50 to be paid to American Transfer Company, per Daniel O'Day, general manager.

Audited May 29, 1878.

G. H. D.

Approved,

A. J. CASSATT,
Third Vice-President.

NUMBER 34 (See page 239)

BILL OF PARTICULARS OF EVIDENCE TO BE OFFERED BY THE COMMONWEALTH

[In the case of Commonwealth of Pennsylvania *vs.* John D. Rockefeller, William Rockefeller, Jabez A. Bostwick, Daniel O'Day, William G. Warden, Charles Lockhart, Henry M. Flagler, Jacob J. Vandergrift, Charles Pratt and George W. Girty, in the Court of Quarter Sessions of the Peace for the County of Clarion, Pennsylvania, 1879.]

First Count. *First.*—That each one of the defendants is associated with each and all others, in business, by means of stock, issued to each, of several corporations, to-wit: The Standard Oil Company of Cleveland, Ohio. The Standard Oil Company of Pittsburg, Pennsylvania. The Acme Oil Company of Titusville, Pennsylvania. The Imperial Refining Company of Oil City, Pennsylvania. The Camden Consolidated Oil Company of West Virginia. The Devoe Manufacturing Company of New York.

Second.—That Charles Pratt is associated in business with others, under the name of Charles Pratt and Company; that William G. Warden and Charles Lockhart are associated in business with others under the firm name of Lockhart and Frew, and Warden, Frew and Company; that J. A. Bostwick is associated with others in business under the name of J. A. Bostwick and Company.

Third.—That the several defendants and others now unknown are associated together by means of the corporate and co-partnership organisations stated in paragraphs one and two for the purpose of carrying on the business of refining crude petroleum and selling the refined product. That each of the said defendants is interested in each of the several corporations and firms in refining and selling refined petroleum, and, in refining and selling, the said defendants, each and all, act in concert and harmony with each other, and as against all other persons not associated with them, and share in the profits of the business.

Fourth.—That the said several defendants, and all of them, and the said several firms and corporations of which they and each of them are members, by stock ownership or otherwise, are engaged in the business of buying crude petroleum, in the county of Clarion, in the state of Pennsylvania, and also in the counties of Armstrong, Butler, Crawford, Forest, McKean, Venango, and Warren, in the state of Pennsylvania, also

[393]

in the counties of Allegheny and Philadelphia in said state, and in the counties of Cattaraugus and New York, in the state of New York, also in the city of Cleveland in the state of Ohio, and in counties in the state of West Virginia.

Fifth.—That in the said several states and counties, and in divers localities in said several states and counties, to-wit: at Pittsburg, Philadelphia, Butler, Carbon Centre, Millerstown, Petrolia, Parker's Landing, Foxburg, Turkey City, Edenburg, Shippensville, Pickwick, Elk City, Monterey, Emlenton, Bullion, Scrubgrass, Forster's Station, Oil City, Franklin, Reno, Rouseville, Titusville, Warren, Tidioute, Hickory, Bradford, Degolia, Derrick City, Gilmore, Forster Brook, and Tarport, in the State of Pennsylvania; Knap Creek, Rock City, Four Mile, Two Mile, Olean, Carrollton, Salamanca, and in the city of New York, in the state of New York, the said defendants, and the several firms and corporations with which they are associated and in which they were interested, carried on the business of buying crude petroleum from producers and owners thereof, and the business of refining said crude petroleum, and selling the refined product, and in so doing acted in concert.

Sixth.—That the said business thereinbefore referred to was so carried on at the several counties, cities, localities, and in the several states aforesaid, by the said defendants in concert, in person, and through agents acting under the instructions of the said defendants, and pursuant to their directions.

Seventh.—That the said defendants were engaged, and are engaged, in the business of transporting crude petroleum through iron pipes, in the counties of Allegheny, Armstrong, Butler, Clarion, Crawford, Forest, McKean, Warren, and Venango, in the state of Pennsylvania; and the county of Cattaraugus, in the state of New York. That they are so engaged by being associated together in the ownership of several pipe-lines, such association being accomplished by the said defendants being owners of shares of stock in incorporated companies, to-wit: the United Pipe Line and American Transfer Company, and interest in capital in limited partnerships, to-wit: the Tidioute and Titusville Pipe Companies, Limited, and others, which said companies, the said defendants, at the time of the conspiracy and combination charged in the indictment, controlled, and thereby controlled the transportation of crude petroleum from wells and points of storage in said several counties and at the said several localities.

Eighth.—That the said defendants, and each of them, and the said several corporations, firms, and limited partnerships, were and are engaged by means of the ownership and control of said several firms, limited partnerships, and corporations, and by means of ownership of stock and interests therein, were and are engaged in the business of storing crude petroleum in the said several localities, cities, counties and states, by means of storage tanks, and said business was carried on in said counties, each and all of them, by themselves, personally, and also through agents acting by their directions.

Ninth.—That each one of the said defendants and all of them in concert were engaged in the several kinds of business hereinbefore referred to, by themselves and their agents in the county of Clarion, and in the other places mentioned hereinbefore, during the whole period of two years prior to the day upon which the indictment was found against them in this case, and during that time by themselves and their agents acting under their directions in the said county of Clarion, combined, confederated and conspired together to cheat and defraud numerous citizens of the county of Clarion, to-wit: J. A. Vera, William L. Fox, and M. L. Lockwood, and divers others, and to cheat and defraud the public by securing to themselves a monopoly of the business and occupation of buying and selling crude petroleum in the county of Clarion, and to prevent all other persons engaged in said business, from making, receiving and obtaining the fair value, profit, price and return from such business, by fraudulent devices, practices and secret contrivances, and among others the following:

A.—Falsely pretending during the times aforesaid and at all times that the storage tanks owned and controlled by them, and of which they had the possession, measurement and accounts, were full of crude petroleum to the extent of the capacity of said tanks, and that the said defendants could not receive and store crude petroleum from and for citizens of Clarion County and the other counties and localities named, when in truth such representations and statements were false, and thereby divers citizens lost oil and were compelled to sell petroleum at less than the value thereof.

B.—By representing to divers citizens of the county of Clarion engaged in the business of producing, buying and selling petroleum, and to divers other persons engaged in said business in the other counties and localities named, that the said defendants were enabled to receive and transport for said well owners, citizens and producers of such petroleum, by reason of lack of capacity and transportation facilities, when in fact said representations were false, and thereby divers producers dealers and well owners were compelled to sell petroleum at less than the value thereof.

C.—That said defendants by themselves and their agents within the county of Clarion, in the state of Pennsylvania, and at the other counties, cities and localities, hereinbefore named, had the control of the entire transportation of crude petroleum from the producing wells and districts, and the control of storing of crude petroleum produced, that they and the several firms and corporations of which they were members, and their agents and the agents of said firms and corporations acting under the direction of the said defendants corruptly and oppressively used the power and control they so as aforesaid held, to compel producers and owners of petroleum to sell the same to them, the said defendants, their agents and the several firms and corporations aforesaid and their agents, and to sell the said crude petroleum at less than its value, and less than the market price thereof.

D.—That the said defendants and each of them, through the several firms and corporations of which they were members, and by their agents acting under their directions and the agents of the said firms and corporations, corruptly and oppressively used the power so acquired by them to enable them to become the sole buyers and refiners of crude petroleum.

E.—That among the means used to obtain control of the business of transporting crude petroleum were the following:

First.—The said defendants and the several firms and corporations of which they were members laid iron pipes in the county of Clarion, and the other counties and states named, under charters and pretended charters from the state of Pennsylvania, pretending that they so did for the purpose of transporting for the public petroleum from the oil wells and producing districts, to the railroads, for shipment to the seaboard, when in fact the said pipe-lines were not laid for that purpose, but for the purpose of transporting oil for the said defendants, and the said several firms and corporations of which they were the members, and not for the public, and to enable the said defendants and the said firms and corporations to dictate the rate of freight to be charged to them by the railroad companies engaged in the business of carrying petroleum as common carriers, and to force the said railroad companies to charge a greater and unreasonably high rate of freight to all others, and that this was for the purpose of preventing citizens of Clarion County and the public from engaging in the business of buying, selling and shipping crude petroleum.

Second.—The said defendants, and their agents acting under their directions, and the several firms and corporations of which they were members also so acting, pretended and represented to the several railroad companies engaged in the transportation of petroleum, and to the agents and officers of said companies, that they, the said defendants and the several firms and corporations of which they were members, and in which they were interested, controlled the shipments of said crude and refined petroleum, by deliveries thereof to the said railroad companies, and that the said defendants were enabled to withhold, and drive said traffic and business from them.

Said representations were false, but by means thereof, they, the said defendants, procured and obtained from said several railroad companies enormous and unjust rebates, commissions and deductions from the rates of freight charged to citizens of Clarion County and the public. The Citizens of Clarion County and the public were thereby prevented from engaging in the business of producing and shipping crude petroleum.

Third.—That on or about the thirtieth day of August, 1877, and again on or about the seventeenth day of October, 1877, the said defendants met together in the city of Philadelphia and then and there agreed together that they would represent to the officers of the Pennsylvania Railroad Company that they, the said defendants, and the several firms and corporations of which they were members, could and would control and guarantee to the said railroad company a certain proportion of the carrying traffic of crude petroleum over said railroad.

And on or about the same dates the said defendants further agreed together and did represent to the officers of the New York, Lake Erie and Western Railroad Company, and to the officers of the Erie Railroad Company, and to Mr. Jewett, receiver of the Erie Railroad Company, and to the officers of the New York Central and Hudson River Railroad Company, and to the officers of the Atlantic and Great Western Railroad Company, and to V. H. Devereux, receiver thereof, and to the officers of the Michigan Southern and Lake Shore Railroad Company, and to the officers of the Baltimore and Ohio Railroad Company, that they the said defendants and the several firms and corporations of which they were members, could and would control and guarantee to each of them a certain proportion of the carrying traffic of the crude petroleum over said railroads respectively. But by reason thereof the said Pennsylvania Railroad Company and the Empire Transportation Company were induced to, and did sell, transfer, mortgage and dispose of, to said defendants and to the several corporations and firms of which they were members, all of the pipe-lines, crude oil cars and transportation equipment of which they had control or ownership in the Oil Regions of Pennsylvania, including the county of Clarion, and all the refineries, for refining crude petroleum, of which they had ownership or control.

Fourth.—The objects and purposes of said representations and said transfer were to enable the said defendants to control the business of buying and selling crude and refined petroleum, and the transportation and storage thereof.

Fifth.—That, as stated in the foregoing paragraphs, during the greater part of the year of 1877, and for some time previously, the Pennsylvania Railroad Company owned or controlled through its shipping agents, the Empire Line, a full and complete system of pipe-lines throughout the counties of Clarion, Armstrong and Butler, known as the Empire Line, numerous and well appointed tank oil cars, the shortest and best route to the seaboard over its own lines and the Allegheny Valley Railroad, and other connecting lines, also controlled large and complete refineries, situated in Pittsburg, Philadelphia and New York, and was by these means a competitor with the defendants and the several corporations owned by them, in the business of piping, transporting, buying and refining crude oil, enabling producers, citizens of Clarion County and elsewhere, without difficulty, to have their oil piped and transported, and to sell the same at enhanced prices, owing to competition. That the defendants, combining and conspiring to monopolise the entire and sole business of buying, selling and refining oil in Clarion County and elsewhere, did demand of the Empire Line and the Pennsylvania Railroad Company that they and each of them should abandon and desist from the said business of buying, selling and refining oil, and that the said railroad company and Empire Line should grant to them exclusively large rebates and low or cheap rates of transportation of oil, and by means of withdrawing and procuring others to withdraw the transportation of crude and refined oil over and along said Pennsylvania Railroad, and by means of the procuring from other railroads exclusive rebates and low rates of freight for transportation below a fair and just compensation for such transportation did compel the said Pennsylvania Railroad Company and the Empire Line to sell to said defendants, or to some of the corporations controlled and owned by them, said pipe-line, tank cars and refineries, to the injury of the producers of oil of Clarion County and elsewhere, by depriving them of the benefit of competition in buying, piping, storing or refining this crude oil.

Sixth.—That the defendants and others combined and confederated with them did conspire to monopolise the entire and exclusive business of refining crude petroleum in Clarion County and elsewhere by means of throwing quantities of refined oil on the market and selling the same at less price than the fair market value of the same in the vicinity of independent refiners in Clarion County and elsewhere, and by means of such sales did compel such refineries to sell out to companies with which defendants were connected, or to abandon or quit the business of refining.

Seventh.—That the said defendants did with others conspire together to purchase all the pipe-lines for the transportation of oil within the producing oil region and all the refineries for the refining of oil, for the purpose of controlling the price of oil and compelling the oil producers of Clarion County and elsewhere to sell their oil to the said defendants at ruinous low rates far below the value thereof and the price that could have been obtained for the same in a competitive market.

Eighth.—Although the said representations were false, the said defendants and the several firms and corporations of which they were members procured the control of the business of producing, buying and selling crude petroleum, and of about ninety per cent. thereof by following acts done in furtherance of the agreements aforesaid:

A.—To buy only petroleum for immediate shipment from the wells of producers. And when so bought they refused to remove it. It was so bought at less than its value and market price, and the producers of petroleum were compelled to sell the same by reason of the false representations as to capacity, storage and transportation hereinbefore fully set forth.

B.—By giving themselves and procuring for themselves exorbitant and unreasonable rebates, commissions and allowances from the railroads and pipe-lines owned and controlled by them, which rebates, commissions and allowance could not be procured by any other than the said defendants and the several firms and corporations of which they were members.

C.—By impeding transportation by railroads, procuring them to refuse and delay cars for shipment of petroleum, procuring the breaking connections with connecting railroad lines, refusing and procuring the refusal of railroad companies and pipe-lines to receive and transport petroleum, by refusals and procuring refusals to store petroleum, by refusing and procuring the refusal of railroad companies to furnish side tracks, cars and transportation facilities to pipe-line companies other than those of the defendants and to individuals, by selling refined petroleum at less than the cost of manufacture, by carrying and storing oil at less than the cost of transportation and storage, by thereby forcing competing lines to sell to them at a loss, by issuing certificates or accepted orders of pipe-line companies in violation of law not representing the petroleum in the custody of said corporations of the said defendants, and placing such certificates upon the market, thereby causing an apparent increase in the quantity of oil in the market for sale and depressing the price of crude petroleum by making false and fictitious reports of stock of petroleum in the custody of the United Pipe Lines, a corporation of which the defendants are the owners and which they control, by violating the laws relative to making reports of business of the said pipe-line company; by neglecting and refusing to make the required oath thereto, by destroying refineries purchased by them at less than their value, of those they had compelled to sell to them by the fraudulent acts aforesaid, by hiring and paying salaries to men to remain out of business for a term of years, and to act as spies for the said defendants and the corporations and firms of which they are members; by selling crude and refined petroleum at less than its cost to them; by increasing the production by entering into agreements relative to the price the said defendants and the corporations and firms of which they were members; by threatening common carriers with destruction of the business of carrying oil, if they carried for others than themselves, and those associated with them, or permitted other pipe-line companies to deliver petroleum to them, or railroads to carry to them; by means of said threats to prevent the building or operation of competing lines of pipe or railroad for transportation of petroleum; by refusing to store petroleum in tanks owned by individuals for them, and by filling such tanks with their own oil, thereby causing a waste and loss both of petroleum and in the price obtained; by refusals to the citizens of Clarion County and elsewhere, at the several localities named, to transport or store crude petroleum.

SECOND COUNT. All of the evidence hereinbefore offered in support of the first count.

THIRD COUNT. All of the evidence hereinbefore stated to be offered in support of the first and second counts, and, in addition thereto, evidence of purchase of refineries under false representations; that refiners were forced to sell by reasons of enormous rebates, fraudulently obtained from railroad companies, as hereinbefore stated, the business being thereby, and not otherwise, rendered unprofitable to such refineries as could not obtain said rebates, commissions and allowances, they being all in the said business, except the said defendants, and the firms and corporations of which they were members.

FOURTH COUNT. All the evidence hereinbefore stated to be offered in support of the first, second and the third counts, and, in addition thereto, that the said defendants and their agents diverted traffic from the Allegheny Valley Railroad Company by threatening the said company and those who were delivering petroleum to it for transportation, with loss and injury to their business, and by shipping themselves over other railroads, unless the said Allegheny Valley Railroad Company would allow them exorbitant rebates, commissions and allowances upon petroleum carried, that other dealers and shippers could not obtain.

FIFTH COUNT. All the evidence hereinbefore stated to be offered in support of the first, second, third and fourth counts, and, in addition thereto, that the traffic was diverted from the Pennsylvania Railroad Company, a common carrier, by the same means, devices and threats as hereinbefore stated.

SIXTH, SEVENTH AND EIGHTH COUNTS. All the evidence hereinbefore stated to be offered as the first, second, third, fourth and fifth counts.

NUMBER 35 (See page 253)

CONTRACT OF PETROLEUM PRODUCERS' UNION WITH STANDARD COMBINATION

[From "A History of the Organisation, Purposes and Transactions of the General Council of the Petroleum Producers' Unions, and of the Suits and Prosecutions instituted by it from 1878 to 1880," pages 41–44.]

Articles of agreement made the 29th day of January, 1880, by and between the Standard Oil Company, a corporation of the state of Ohio; the Standard Oil Company of Pittsburg, a corporation of the state of Pennsylvania; the Imperial Refining Company (limited) of Oil City, Pennsylvania; the Acme Oil Company of New York and Pennsylvania; the Atlantic Refining Company of Philadelphia; the American Transfer Company; the United Pipe Lines, a corporation of Pennsylvania; the Devoe Manufacturing Company of New York; the Eclipse Lubricating Oil Company (limited) of Franklin, Pennsylvania; J. D. Rockefeller, William Rockefeller, H. M. Flagler, William G. Warden, Charles Lockhart, William Frew, Charles Pratt, Henry H. Rogers, Jabez A. Bostwick, Jacob J. Vandergrift, O. H. Payne, John D. Archbold, respectively, buyers, refiners and carriers of petroleum, parties of the first part, each, however, contracting severally for himself, themselves or itself, and not one for the others, and Benjamin B. Campbell, for himself and as president of the General Council of Petroleum Producers' Union, and for the members thereof as shall signify their assent hereto by signing this agreement within sixty days from the date thereof, the parties of the second part, each contracting severally and in the manner aforesaid, Witnesseth,

Whereas, The several parties above named have been and are now engaged in some one or all of the branches of business connected with the petroleum trade, in buying, selling, shipping, storing, refining, transporting and producing petroleum, and controversies have arisen between the said parties of the first and second part hereinbefore named, out of which have grown certain suits hereinafter named, and it is desirable to amicably adjust said controversies and settle said suits and proceedings, therefore, it is hereby agreed between the said parties of the first and second parts:

I. That the said parties of the first part shall and will make no opposition to an entire abrogation of the system of rebates, drawbacks and secret rates of freight in the transportation of petroleum on the railroads.

[401]

II. That said parties of the first part further agree that the railroad companies may make known to the other shippers of petroleum on their several roads all the rates of freight, and that said parties of the first part or any of them will not receive any rebate or drawback that the railroad companies are not at liberty to give to other shippers of petroleum.

III. The said parties of the first part further agree that so far as the said pipe-lines are concerned there shall be no discrimination used or permitted by the said pipe-line companies between or against their patrons; that the rates of pipage and storage shall be reasonable, uniform, and equal to all parties, and shall not be advanced except on thirty days' notice; that to the extent of their influence the United Pipe Lines and the other companies parties hereto do agree that there shall be no difference in the price of crude oil between one district and another, excepting such as may be based upon a difference in quality, to be determined by tests; that the said pipe-lines will make every reasonable effort to receive, transport, store and deliver all oil tendered them, and will receive, transport, store and deliver all oil so tendered so long as the production does not exceed an average of sixty-five thousand barrels per day during fifteen (15) consecutive days, unforeseen emergencies and unavoidable accidents excepted, and if the production shall exceed the amount stated, and also the storage capacity of the pipe-lines, the parties of the first part, buyers of oil, agree that they will not purchase any so-called immediate shipment oil, at a lower price than the price of certificate oil, provided that the owners of immediate shipment oil in the Oil Region do not sell to any other party or parties at a lower price.

IV. And all the parties of the first part further agree that until the production of oil reaches the daily maximum of sixty-five thousand barrels as aforesaid, certificates or other vouchers will be given for all oil taken into the custody of the pipe-lines and the transfer of such certificates or other vouchers in the usual manner shall be considered as a delivery of the oil mentioned therein as between the pipe-lines and the seller, subject to the provisions of such certificate or other vouchers.

In consideration of the agreement hereinbefore set forth, and of the execution thereof by the first parties, the said second parties do hereby agree as follows:

That the Governor and Attorney-General of the Commonwealth of Pennsylvania shall be requested by them within ten days of the execution hereof, to enter a motion to dismiss the bill filed by the Commonwealth of Pennsylvania against the United Pipe Lines and others at Number 309, October and November term, 1878, in the Supreme Court of Pennsylvania, and the proceedings by *quo warranto* Number 12, November term, 1878, in Venango County, and will do all that may be lawfully done to have the same dismissed of record. That upon written motion and agreement the Supreme Court of Pennsylvania may make of record by consent of both parties, an order discharging the rules to show cause in the case of the Commonwealth *vs.* Rockefeller *et al.*, granted by E. M. Paxson on the 11th day of December, 1879, and made returnable January 5, 1880, and annulling the order staying proceedings made by the Supreme Court on the 8th day of January, 1880.

It is further agreed that this agreement shall, upon execution thereof by the parties, be a full release and satisfaction between the parties of all causes of action of any and every kind whatsoever, arising out of the past transactions involved in the said several suits, controversies, or prosecutions, or incident thereto, so far as the parties hereto or any of them are in any manner interested or have any cause or rights of action for or against each other. And it is hereby further agreed that the Court of Quarter Sessions of Clarion County be, and they are hereby respectfully requested to give their consent to the entering of a *nolle prosequi* in the case of the Commonwealth of Pennsylvania *vs.* John D. Rockefeller *et al.*, of April sessions, 1879, Number 25, in which the defendants named in said case are charged with conspiracy, and the district attorney of said county is hereby requested, on receiving the consent of the said court, to enter in said case a *nolle prosequi*, and the same to be entered of record in said court, with the intent that the same be a judgment of said court disposing of and ending all proceedings under indictment hereinbefore referred to, forever.

In Witness Whereof the aforesaid parties to these presents have hereunto set their hands and seals, the said corporations having caused their seals to be affixed this fifth day of February, A.D. 1880.

Standard Oil Company, by
    (Seal)   JOHN D. ROCKEFELLER, *President,*   [L.S.]
             Attest: H. M. FLAGLER,   [L.S.]
                  JOHN D. ROCKEFELLER,   [L.S.]
                  O. H. PAYNE.   [L.S.]

United Pipe Lines, by
    (Seal)   J. J. VANDERGRIFT, *President,*   [L.S.]
             Attest: H. M. HUGHES, *Secretary,*   [L.S.]
                  HENRY M. FLAGLER,   [L.S.]
                  J. J. VANDERGRIFT,   [L.S.]
                  WILLIAM ROCKEFELLER.   [L.S.]

Imperial Refining Company, Limited, by
    (Seal)   J. J. VANDERGRIFT, *Chairman,*   [L.S.]
             Attest: D. McINTOSH, *Secretary.*   [L.S.]

Eclipse Lubricating Oil Company, Limited, by
                  THOMAS BROWN, *Chairman,*   [L.S.]
                  F. Q. BARSTOW, *Secretary.*   [L.S.]

Standard Oil Company, by
    (Seal)   CHARLES LOCKHART, *President,*   [L.S.]
                  A. F. BROOKS, *Secretary,*   [L.S.]

W. G. WARDEN,   [L.S.]

CHARLES LOCKHART.   [L.S.]

The Atlantic Refining Company, by

CHARLES LOCKHART, *President*,   [L.S.]

CHARLES PRATT,   [L.S.]

HENRY H. ROGERS.   [L.S.]

Acme Oil Company, by

JOHN D. ARCHBOLD, *President*,   [L.S.]

Attest: GEORGE F. CHESTER, *Secretary*,   [L.S.]

JOHN D. ARCHBOLD.   [L.S.]

American Transfer Company, by

GEORGE H. VILAS, *President*,   [L.S.]

Attest: GEORGE F. CHESTER, *Secretary*,   [L.S.]

J. A. BOSTWICK,   [L.S.]

B. B. CAMPBELL.   [L.S.]

Witness,   JOHN V. KEEF.

Witness as to signature of B. B. Campbell,

W. BAKEWELL.

NUMBER 36 (See page 254)

AGREEMENT BETWEEN B. B. CAMPBELL AND THE PENNSYL-
VANIA RAILROAD COMPANY

[From "A History of the Organisation, Purposes and Transactions of the General Council of the Petroleum Producers' Unions, and of the Suits and Prosecutions instituted by it from 1878 to 1880," pages 45–46.]

This agreement, made on the twenty-seventh day of April, A.D. 1880, between B. B. Campbell and the Pennsylvania Railroad Company.

Whereas, It having been alleged by persons engaged in the production and shipping of petroleum and the products of petroleum, that discrimination had been practised in the rates of freight and in the distribution of cars by the Pennsylvania Railroad Company, in such manner as to be injurious to the business of such producers, and bills in equity having been filed in the name of the Commonwealth in the Western District of the Supreme Court of the state of Pennsylvania, for the purpose of restraining such discrimination; and

Whereas, In pursuance of an agreement signed on the twelfth of February, 1880, by the said B. B. Campbell, representing the oil producers, at whose instance such bills were filed, and Thomas A. Scott as president of the Pennsylvania Railroad Company, the said bills were withdrawn; and

Whereas, In said agreement the Pennsylvania Railroad Company agreed, upon the withdrawal of said bills, that it would enter into written contracts with the said B. B. Campbell, representing said producers, and all such producers as should within sixty days after the date of said agreement signify their assent to said agreement by signature to the same or duplicate thereof, which contracts should stipulate as therein mentioned, and as hereinafter provided; and

Whereas, On the twenty-fifth of February, 1880, the board of directors of the Pennsylvania Railroad Company approved the action of the president in signing said agreement, and authorised the president or one of the vice-presidents to execute such further and formal agreements as might be deemed necessary to carry out the terms of said agreement,

Now therefore, this agreement witnesseth, That in consideration of the premises, and other good and valuable considerations to them thereunto moving, it is covenanted and agreed between the parties hereto as follows, to wit:

[405]

First, That the Pennsylvania Railroad Company shall and will make known to all shippers of petroleum and its products all the rates of freight intended to be charged to all shippers upon such petroleum and its products.

Second, That the said Pennsylvania Railroad Company shall not and will not pay or allow any shipper of petroleum or its products any rebate, drawback or commission upon the shipments of such petroleum or products different from or greater than that which shall be paid to any other person shipping or offering to ship like quantity; and that any discrimination that may be made in favour of shippers of the large quantities shall be reasonable, and shall, upon demand made, be communicated to all persons shipping, or who are now or may be hereafter engaged in the business and desire to ship petroleum and its products.

Third, That the said Pennsylvania Railroad Company further agrees that upon its own road, and upon any other road or roads upon which it shall furnish cars and engage in the business of a common carrier of petroleum and its products, it will not practise any discrimination in the distribution of its cars, but will make fair apportionment in such distribution among all applicants for cars having actually in their custody and ready for shipment at the time of their application the petroleum or products for the shipment of which they ask facilities.

In Witness Whereof, the individuals parties hereto have hereunto set their hands and seals, and the said Pennsylvania Railroad Company has caused its corporate seal to be hereunto affixed, duly attested, the day and year first above written.

The Pennsylvania Railroad Company, by

THOMAS A. SCOTT,
President.

Attest:

JOHN C. SIMS,
Assistant Secretary.

B. B. CAMPBELL.

(Seal)

COSIMO is a specialty publisher of books and publications that inspire, inform, and engage readers. Our mission is to offer unique books to niche audiences around the world.

COSIMO BOOKS publishes books and publications for innovative authors, nonprofit organizations, and businesses. **COSIMO BOOKS** specializes in bringing books back into print, publishing new books quickly and effectively, and making these publications available to readers around the world.

COSIMO CLASSICS offers a collection of distinctive titles by the great authors and thinkers throughout the ages. At **COSIMO CLASSICS** timeless works find new life as affordable books, covering a variety of subjects including: Business, Economics, History, Personal Development, Philosophy, Religion & Spirituality, and much more!

COSIMO REPORTS publishes public reports that affect your world, from global trends to the economy, and from health to geopolitics.

FOR MORE INFORMATION CONTACT US AT
INFO@COSIMOBOOKS.COM

※ if you are a book lover interested in our current catalog of books

※ if you represent a bookstore, book club, or anyone else interested in special discounts for bulk purchases

※ if you are an author who wants to get published

※ if you represent an organization or business seeking to publish books and other publications for your members, donors, or customers.

**COSIMO BOOKS ARE ALWAYS
AVAILABLE AT ONLINE BOOKSTORES**

VISIT COSIMOBOOKS.COM
BE INSPIRED, BE INFORMED

LaVergne, TN USA
26 August 2010
194853LV00001B/6/P